EDUCATION REFORM IN NEW YORK CITY

AMBITIOUS CHANGE IN THE NATION'S MOST COMPLEX SCHOOL SYSTEM

Edited by Jennifer A. O'Day,
Catherine S. Bitter,
and Louis M. Gomez

Harvard Education Press
Cambridge, Massachusetts

Library of Congress Control Number 2010942137

Paperback ISBN 978-1-934742-83-9

Library Edition ISBN 978-1-934742-84-6

Published by Harvard Education Press,
an imprint of the Harvard Education Publishing Group

Harvard Education Press
8 Story Street
Cambridge, MA 02138

Cover Design: Sarah Henderson

The typefaces used in this book are Adobe Garamond Pro, Akzidenz-Grotesk, and Helvetica Neue.

Contents

Introduction to the Volume
and Children First

Jennifer A. O'Day, Catherine S. Bitter, and Joan E. Talbert

The educational reforms in New York City's public schools under the administration of Mayor Michael Bloomberg and Chancellor Joel Klein from 2003–2010 were among the most ambitious of any large urban system in the country. Directed toward instituting evidence-based practices to produce higher and more equitable outcomes for all students, the Children First initiative evolved over time from an initial focus on establishing coherence, stability, and rigor in the system to one of building on three pillars for system change and improvement: (1) *empowerment*—empowering and supporting local schools, (2) *leadership*—developing instructional leadership capacity of school principals and others in order to more effectively promote student success, and (3) *accountability*—instituting a comprehensive system of school and system accountability based on improved assessment, data use, incentives, and reporting mechanisms.

The sheer scale of the city school system, with its 1.1 million students and over fifteen hundred schools, and the ever-present drama of New York City politics might be reason enough to engender interest in any period, but under Bloomberg and Klein it was the specific collection of reform policies and actions that captured national attention. These included a combination of mayoral control and fundamental restructuring of the system; the introduction of accountability practices, test-based metrics, and human capital models from the business sector; and the implementation of a panoply of reform strategies currently in vogue, such as small secondary schools, public school choice, and the closure of so-called high school dropout factories. Indeed, New York City seems to have drawn together many of the threads of what is emerging as a national education agenda, and is doing so on a massive scale.

The logic and coherence in this fabric of reforms, however, are often obscured by the intensity and polarization of the controversy surrounding them. For example, as proponents point to increasing test scores and graduation rates as proof that the reforms have worked, detractors question the validity of the tests, suspect the accuracy of the data, and criticize what they perceive as a perverse focus on testing. Proponents praise the sweeping changes enabled through mayoral control and the removal of interest-group politicking, while opponents lament the loss of checks and balances and have called for greater public voice and oversight. And so it goes.

Despite all the controversy—or perhaps because of it—and despite the national significance of the NYC education agenda under Joel Klein's leadership, there has been surprisingly little independent documentation of the reforms during this eight-year period. Now, with Joel Klein's resignation as Chancellor taking effect in January 2011, the opportunity for such documentation in real time has effectively closed. Yet the need to learn from this dynamic and bold experiment in system change remains great. Indeed, this turn of events, unexpected at the time that these papers were commissioned and written, only serves to underscore their timeliness and significance. The chapters in this volume derive from a recent foundation-funded project, the purpose of which is to inform improvement efforts as they continue to evolve in the city and as jurisdictions around the country consider lessons from the NYC story. In this introduction, we describe the approach of the New York City Education Reform Retrospective, briefly outline the chronology of reform policies in the city system to which the chapters refer, and introduce the chapters themselves.

The New York City Education Reform Retrospective Project

In early winter 2009, the American Institutes for Research received support from four cooperating foundations to organize the New York City Education Reform Retrospective.[1] The project's purpose was to document key reform policies of NYC's Children First initiative, illuminate the rationales ("theories of action") underlying those policies, explore implementation patterns and challenges, analyze or review results, and identify possible lessons for consideration by local and national stakeholders. The primary vehicle for this work was to be a set of commissioned, evidence-based papers on core topics of interest and an invitational conference to discuss the findings and consider alternative perspectives and implications.

To lead this effort, project director Jennifer O'Day convened a small review panel of national experts in arenas relevant to the NYC initiative. The panel collectively brought a diverse set of disciplinary lenses, experiences in either leading or studying district reform initiatives, and varying levels of prior knowledge and understanding of the NYC education reform context.[2] The panel reviewed hundreds of pages of reports, media articles, and extant research findings to decide on an approach to the project and to identify a set of topics and authors for the commissioned papers.

There are many ways to structure an exploration of a phenomenon as large and complex as the Children First initiative. Based on preliminary dialogue with a broad range of stakeholders and its own review of available material on the reforms, the panel decided to select topics focused on key domains of reform activity such as changes to the governance and leadership of the system, human capital management policies, instructional guidance, school accountability, and high school transformation.

An approach that focuses on discrete reform arenas carries with it inherent trade-offs. First, important elements of reform activity are inevitably left out—particularly when the overall effort is as comprehensive as that in New York City. For example, the volume does not include individual papers on strategies addressing the needs of English language learners, on the New York City Department of Education's (DOE) systematic approach to school closure and start-up, or on partnerships and institutions focused on teacher and school leader development, as well as many other specific topics. However, many of these strategies are incorporated into other papers in the volume. Second, the focus on specific bounded spheres of activity may make it difficult to recognize and capture the interconnections among reform strategies in different but interacting arenas. To address these challenges, the panel organized periodic conference calls with the authors as well as two 2-day meetings of all author groups and panel members to discuss the approaches, content, and cross-cutting themes among the papers. In the first of these meetings, authors presented their outlines and initial findings and shared feedback with one another, while the second meeting in June 2010 brought external peer reviewers and relevant current or former DOE staff to the table to comment on initial full drafts, correct inaccuracies, and consider connections and alternative interpretations.

In selecting authors for the papers, the panel again solicited input from a range of local and national sources. Considerations guiding the selection included not only the expertise of the authors but also their independence and ability to present a balanced perspective on the topic in question. Further, the panel wanted to ensure that the set of authors would reflect a range of disciplinary perspectives and approaches. Finally, because resources for the commissioned papers were limited to small honoraria inadequate to support new research, the panel tried to select authors who already had prior or ongoing research in the city school system that could be readily extended or updated for this purpose. The necessary reliance on existing data and ongoing research projects has implications for the interpretation of the papers. In particular, we stress that none of the papers, nor the retrospective project as a whole, should be construed as an *evaluation* either of components of the reforms or of Children First as a whole. Rather, they are evidence-based descriptions and exploratory analyses of a set of reform arenas and activities under the umbrella of Children First. The chapters are intended to enrich the dialogue locally and nationally about this important experiment in system improvement, and specific conclusions are those of the authors and not of the panel or the funders of this endeavor.

Children First: A Brief Chronology

A brief chronology of key events and policies relevant to the Children First reforms provides initial framing of this volume (see figure I-1 for specific reform events

FIGURE I-1 New York City reform implementation timeline (2001–2010)

Governance and management

	Phase 1: Consolidation begins					Phase 2: Autonomy/ accountability exchange begins			
Bloomberg elected 2001	2002–2003	2003–2004	2004–2005	2005–2006	2006–2007	2007–2008	2008–2009	2009–2010
	• Bloomberg gains mayoral control over the DOE	• Children First Initiative launched	• Autonomy Zone created—29 schools participate	• DOE creates Office of Accountability	• Schools select among 11 School Support Organizations (SSOs)	• Fair Student Funding formula takes effect	• P311 parent hot-line established	• Formation of 6 school clusters with 10 Children First networks (CFNs) in each
	• Joel Klein appointed chancellor	• Authority of 32 community school districts restructured into 10 regions	• NYC Charter School Center established		• Autonomy zone renamed Empowerment Schools—332 schools join	• Site-based autonomy/SSOs scaled up across district	• ARIS Parent Link created and rolled out	• Schools allowed to choose CFN affiliation
	• Public Education Panel (PEP) replaces NYC Board of Education	• Parent coordinators required at all schools			• Office of Family Engagement and Advocacy created	• Schools allowed to choose SSO affiliation		• 100th charter school opens
	• Gates Foundation Intermediary Organizations introduced				• District family advocates assigned	• LIM position created in all SSOs		• Division of Students with Disabilities and English Language Learners created
					• Five Integrated Service Centers (ISCs) created to support SSOs	• SSOs fully implemented		

Teaching and learning

	Phase 1: Consolidation begins				Phase 2: Autonomy/accountability exchange begins			
Bloomberg elected 2001	2002–2003	2003–2004	2004–2005	2005–2006	2006–2007	2007–2008	2008–2009	2009–2010
		• Common math and literacy approaches implemented • The DOE invests in classroom libraries • School math and literacy coaches required • Policies implemented to end social promotion • Reading First grant awarded to the DOE			• School Progress Reports piloted • Children First Intensive (CFI) inquiry team piloted in Empowerment schools • Quality Reviews begin • Senior achievement facilitator (SAF) position created to support schools • Distribution of parent surveys begins	• CFI launched systemwide (at least one team per school) • Data specialist role created to support inquiry teams and other data-focused work in each school • ARIS launched • Periodic assessments required	• CFI expanded to two or more teams per school • Gifted and talented admissions process revised	• Schools asked to involve most teachers in CFI inquiry teams

continued

FIGURE I-1 *continued*

Human capital

	Phase 1: Consolidation begins				Phase 2: Autonomy/ accountability exchange begins			
Bloomberg elected								
2001	2002–2003	2003–2004	2004–2005	2005–2006	2006–2007	2007–2008	2008–2009	2009–2010
		• Leadership Academy launched	• New teacher mentoring program developed with UFT, CSA and local universities • The New School Intensive to support new principals launched	• DOE and UFT agree to "open-market" transfer system, also called the School-Based Option • Housing support program established	• Principal performance review and reward system renegotiated • Lead teacher program begins	• Schoolwide performance bonus program begins • New teacher mentoring devolved to school site		• Statewide comprehensive evaluation system for teachers (policy change) • LEAP becomes the citywide model for the Aspiring Principals Program

High school reform

2001	2002–2003	2003–2004	2004–2005	2005–2006	2006–2007	2007–2008	2008–2009	2009–2010

Bloomberg elected (2001)

Phase 1: Consolidation begins (2002–2003)

Phase 2: Autonomy/accountability exchange begins (2006–2007)

- New Century High Schools Initiative launched (2002–2003)

- New High School Admissions system launched (2003–2004)
- New Visions creates 78 high schools
- Office of New Schools created by the DOE

- State changes requirements for Regents exams (must pass 5 with a score of 55 for local diploma and 65 for regents diploma) (2005–2006)
- Office of Multiple Pathways to Graduation, transfer schools, and Learning to Work Initiative created

- Reform of District 79, Alternative Schools and Programs, announced (2007–2008)

- After remaining flat for 10 years, NYC graduation rate increased 33% since 2002 (2008–2009)
- DOE reaches goal of opening 200 small high schools and closing 20 large comprehensive high schools
- State raises Regents passing score to 65 for all current ninth-graders (takes effect 2012)
- *Mayoral Task Force Report on Career and Technical Education* released

and actions). Additional details relevant to any given topic appear in some of the individual chapters, but this overview should help readers less familiar with the evolution of the NYC reform efforts to put subsequent chapters into a broader context.

A New Era of Governance

When Mayor Michael Bloomberg assumed control of the school system in 2002, one of his earliest initiatives was to change its structure and governance, replacing the NYC Board of Education with the NYC Department of Education (DOE) and a thirteen-member advisory Panel for Educational Policy (PEP). He appointed Joel Klein, an outsider to education with a background in law, as chancellor. For decades, the graduation rate had remained stagnant at 50 percent. Upon taking office, Bloomberg and Klein sought sweeping changes to improve the level of achievement among students citywide—particularly those who traditionally met with failure within the existing system.

Phase 1: Building System Capacity and Coherence

The early initiatives of the Bloomberg/Klein administration focused on building capacity, coherence, and rigor across NYC schools. They began in 2003 by dismantling the thirty-two community school boards that had been in place since 1969 and creating ten administrative regions. Each of the new regions comprised approximately 120 schools, mixed in income and performance level, and led by a regional superintendent who was expected to foster the sharing of best practices within the region. To provide more equitable access to high-quality and rigorous instruction, the DOE then adopted (and required all schools to use) a set of common curricula and instructional approaches in English/language arts (ELA) and mathematics, including balanced literacy and Everyday Mathematics at the elementary level. The institution of a core curricular program marked a major shift in the approach the DOE took to instructional improvement—one in which the city system provided direct guidance to schools regarding what is taught in classrooms. The DOE supported the implementation of these curricula by investing significantly in classroom materials and professional development and by placing coaches and parent coordinators in every school. At the same time, it invested heavily in the development of human capital, significantly increasing teacher salaries and establishing the New York City Leadership Academy to train principals to work in the most struggling schools in the city.

Although the first few years of Children First centered on stabilizing the city's schools and increasing the coherence across and rigor within them, early signs were present of the *autonomy-accountability* exchange that would later become a cornerstone of the reform. In 2004–2005, the DOE established the Autonomy Zone. Starting with only twenty-nine schools but growing rapidly in each subsequent year, the Autonomy Zone demonstrated the emerging DOE belief that empowerment should be granted outright to schools as a *precondition* for improvement and change rather than awarded as an earned privilege to a select few. The DOE granted the principals of these schools greater discretion over the use of funds, hiring processes, instructional programs, and professional development. In turn, school leaders were held accountable for meeting specific performance targets. The creation of the Office of Accountability in 2005–2006 affirmed the DOE's intent to make accountability a core feature of their reform efforts moving forward.

At the same time, the DOE began actively closing down large poor-performing high schools—termed *dropout factories*—and creating new small high schools through initiatives such as the New Century High Schools Initiative. Student access to these small schools was bolstered in 2003–2004 by an expanded citywide high school choice process, in which students are matched to high schools based on the schools' admissions methods and the students' ranking of their own school choices. This shift to smaller, innovative high schools that competed for students through the choice process was yet another precursor to the DOE's more recent efforts to empower principals and hold schools more accountable.

Phase 2: Empowerment, Accountability, and Leadership

The system consolidation and consistency that characterized the early years of the reform laid a foundation for the more recent years of Children First, where school *leadership*, *empowerment*, and *accountability* have been the stated pillars. In 2006–2007, the DOE restructured the school system again, dissolving the regional structure and requiring schools to choose from among eleven (later twelve) School Support Organizations (SSOs) that were charged with assisting principals with goal setting, strategies for improvement, and professional development. Schools were organized into *networks* of approximately twenty-five schools, supported by the SSOs. Schools could choose their SSO and network within it, allowing them to partner with an organizational unit that would best support their instructional goals and approach. With this restructuring, the DOE dismantled the traditional line of authority in the system, placing ultimate authority with principals as "CEOs" for student outcomes and allowing them to choose the support and resources to help them meet their goals.

Additional initiatives granted principals greater discretion in their core work. In 2007–2008 *all* schools received greater autonomy for their instructional program: schools could choose to continue using the core curricula of the city, or adopt other programs customized to their school philosophy and students' needs. By moving the decision making for instruction closer to those who were doing the work, the DOE expected teachers and administrators to be more motivated to work hard and to develop more creative and effective strategies to improve student learning. Earlier, principals had gained greater discretion in hiring through the establishment of an open-market transfer system. No longer would teachers be placed solely on the basis of seniority. Rather, the new hiring system allowed schools to choose teachers whose approach and experience were aligned with the school goals and program.

While granting greater flexibility to schools, the DOE also put in place a comprehensive system to monitor results, provide more information to teachers and principals, and hold schools accountable for the performance of all students. *Progress Reports* present annual summative data on each school's success in improving student outcomes. To provide more formative information at the school level, the DOE implemented Quality Reviews (QRs), in which teams of administrators assess schools annually on a series of leading indicators of school organization and culture. To create more useful information for teachers in making instructional decisions, no-stakes benchmark assessments were developed and required in all schools. In addition, the *inquiry team* initiative called for teachers and administrators to meet in school teams to closely examine student data (including these benchmark assessments), troubleshoot instructional challenges, and focus attention on students most in need of additional support. Finally, a comprehensive data system—the Achievement Reporting and Innovation System (ARIS)—was built to provide student assessment data to teachers in an easily accessible format and to support cross-school sharing of effective practices for boosting student achievement.

The role of principal as CEO requires the development of leaders who are adept at managing all aspects of a school's instructional and operational programs. While empowerment allows principals greater autonomy in their work, it also creates challenges in that school leaders must make important decisions about key functions of their school and face real consequences if they are unable to demonstrate positive results from their decisions. To prepare new leaders for these challenges, the Leadership Academy has shifted the focus of its training to better prepare principals for this new model of leadership. In addition, the resources available to principals to implement strategies to improve outcomes have been bolstered by increased funding over the course of Children First and the institution of the Fair Student Funding process that allocates resources based on student characteristics. Finally, the development of inquiry teams aims to build leadership among all staff in the school by fostering teacher leadership and decision-making within collaborative teams.

With a change in term limits that allowed Mayor Bloomberg to be reelected for a third term, the Children First reform continues to evolve. In 2009–2010, the twelve SSOs were replaced with ten clusters and schools were asked to expand the inquiry team initiative to include nearly all teachers. With three more years to go in the mayor's term, it remains to be seen what ideas and strategies the new chancellor will put in place.

Overview of the Chapters

The chapters in this volume explore many of the specific reform strategies and policies outlined in the chronology above. The chapters are organized into five sections, four of which contain revised and edited versions of the commissioned papers prepared for the NYC Education Reform Retrospective and presented at the Retrospective invitational conference in November 2010—ironically, the day after Chancellor Klein announced his resignation. Below, we introduce the sections and the papers and then suggest a set of cross-cutting themes or challenges to which we return in the reflections section at the end of the book.

Governance and Management

The volume begins with a set of three chapters focused on core issues of system management and governance. Chapter 1, by Paul Hill, opens the set with an examination of the evolution of— and tensions in—the DOE approach to system leadership and governance under mayoral control. Distinguishing theoretically between the concepts of *governance* and *leadership* and using data from interviews with DOE officials and civic and interest group representatives, the chapter describes how the reforms have increased the powers and opportunities of leaders both in the school sites and at the very top of the system, while they have weakened traditional central administration and political oversight bodies. Hill emphasizes the *autonomy-for-accountability bargain* with school leaders, the recruitment of talented leaders from outside education, and Klein's political strategy of engaging new constituencies while winning over or neutralizing others. The paper ends with a discussion of threats to the sustainability of the reforms and argues that overcoming these threats will require a new balance between governance and leadership in the system.

In chapter 2, Jeffrey Henig and his colleagues use stakeholder interview data and document review to provide both a counterpoint to and extension of Hill's discussion of governance and leadership. This chapter explores competing visions of parent and public engagement—one that focuses on involving individual parents in the education of their own children, and an alternative view that emphasizes collective participation in educational decision-making processes. The authors argue that the Bloomberg/Klein administration failed to appreciate the alternative view of active community engagement as a more robust and reliable approach to creating constituencies to sustain reform over time.

Chapter 3 describes a key but often overlooked element in the reforms: financial resources, including the level of available funding, the sources of that funding, and the ways in which resources are spent. Using data from school-based expenditure reports, authors Leanna Stiefel and Amy Schwartz find that per pupil revenues in New York City rose by roughly $5,000 between 2002 and 2008, but they note that this real growth in funding is unlikely to be sustainable—particularly in the current fiscal climate. Meanwhile, private and philanthropic sources may provide more flexible support for innovation but are only a very tiny fraction of the overall education budget.

Teaching and Learning

Part II moves into policies that are more directly focused on improving teaching and learning across the system. In chapter 4, Stacey Childress, Monica Higgins, Ann

Ishimaru, and Sola Takahashi tackle an area that many see as the cornerstone of the Bloomberg/Klein theory of action: results-based school accountability. Like chapter 1, this chapter focuses on the accountability-autonomy exchange, but they do so by describing specific mechanisms and metrics of the accountability system and their potential linkages to organizational learning and improvement. The authors then analyze survey data designed to examine this linkage, based on items inserted into the DOE's 2009 learning environment survey for teachers.

In chapter 5, Jennifer O'Day and Catherine Bitter address an issue that has been noticeably absent from much of the public and media debate: the role of the central office in improving the content and form of instruction in the classroom. The authors observe that over the course of Children First, the DOE's approach shifted from one of centrally managing curriculum and instruction across the system to one of empowering schools to make instructionally relevant decisions while being held accountable for the results. Expanding on the issues raised in chapter 4, this chapter pays particular attention to the accountability-capacity dynamic in the most recent iteration of the reforms, examining this dynamic in light of systems theory and similar accountability-based improvement models in other jurisdictions. The authors identify strengths of the NYC approach while also pointing to design and implementation challenges that could attenuate improvement and sustainability at scale.

Next, in chapter 6, Joan Talbert digs more deeply into a particular strategy for moving the instructional core: *collaborative inquiry*, through which teachers and schools use evidence of student learning gaps to design responses that continuously bring more students into the school's "sphere of success." Although the collaborative inquiry initiative was rolled out systemwide in 2007–2008, Talbert uses evidence from her four-year documentation of inquiry teams in NYC schools working with the New Visions Partnership Support Organization to explore both the potential of the inquiry process for fundamentally shifting teaching practice and the challenges entailed in implementing the model within schools and at scale across the system.

Chapter 7, the final piece in this section, focuses on teachers. Authors Margaret Goertz, Susanna Loeb, and James Wyckoff synthesize their own and others' research on Children First policies in four key human capital arenas: compensation, recruitment, working conditions and teacher retention, and teacher evaluation. The authors discuss the concerted effort during the Bloomberg/Klein administration to improve the quality of the teaching force, and present evidence that efforts to recruit and select more effective teachers have produced positive results. They note that many strategies for improving teacher quality in NYC have either not been examined in detail or are only just emerging in DOE policy.

High School Reform

High schools have traditionally been the most intractable of grade levels in which to improve student outcomes. In chapter 8, Leslie Siskin begins her exploration of NYC's high school transformation approach by placing NYC high schools in a national and historical context. She then describes the key strategies affecting high schools in NYC, including the changes in performance measures, shifts in support systems for schools, large-scale opening of new small schools and closing of large ones, expansion of the portfolio of schools and institution of choice for all students, and the development of multiple pathways to graduation. Siskin notes that with the expansion of the portfolio to almost seven hundred distinct programs and schools, the particular contexts and capacities of schools are tremendously disparate, suggesting that the effects of any given policy may profoundly differ across schools.

Chapter 9, the second high school–focused paper, describes the reformed high school choice system in NYC, which requires all incoming freshmen to rank up to twelve preferred programs and then matches these students' rankings against schools' lists to determine final placements. Authors Sean Corcoran and Henry Levin analyze student-level administrative data from four years of the high school admissions process to answer questions about who applies where, and where they are ultimately placed. Analyses explore how answers to these questions depend on students' race, gender, poverty status, and residential location.

Ronald Ferguson closes the high school section with chapter 10, which is focused on student perceptions of instruction in New York City high schools and classrooms. Using the DOE's own learning environment survey, Ferguson shows how the differences in the quality of teaching that students perceive across schools help predict variation in graduation and Regents diploma rates across schools. Then, using data from the Tripod Project for School Improvement surveys, he demonstrates that there is even greater variation across classrooms than there is between schools. The chapter identifies five types of classroom conditions that correspond to key elements of teaching quality, and argues that schools and teachers need differentiated supports, just as students do, to ensure high-quality instruction and improved student outcomes.

Student Outcomes

Chapter 11, the final commissioned paper in this volume, forms a section of its own, as it is the only one focused on the ultimate goal of the reforms: improved student performance. James Kemple uses rigorous statistical modeling and both school-level and student-level data to explore (1) trends in grade 4 and grade 8 mathematics and ELA test scores, (2) the relationship between individual students' eighth-grade scores and their subsequent graduation from high school, and (3) trends in high school graduation rates. The findings from these analyses provide strong evidence that what was happening educationally in New York City from 2003–2009 had a positive effect on ELA and mathematics proficiency rates in grades 4 and 8 and on graduation rates, over and above any continuing effects of prior reforms or conditions shared by other districts across the state. Kemple also finds that student performance on the state's grade 8 ELA and mathematics assessments is positively associated with the likelihood that students will graduate within four years of entering high school.

Reflections on Children First

As noted earlier, our approach of organizing the review by specific domains of reform activity risks obscuring the interconnections and cross-cutting themes across them. To help make these connections, authors sometimes refer to one another's chapters for more detail or discussion of related policies or phenomena. More directly, the final chapter of the book looks across the Children First reforms to highlight several cross-cutting patterns and themes.

To anticipate these final reflections, readers might want to consider the following six questions while perusing the chapters:

- Do the authors collectively capture the dynamic, multifaceted, and evolutionary nature of Children First? What, if any, coherent Children First strategy emerges across time and across the domains of reform activity?
- In what ways has this systemic improvement effort challenged (or not) the boundaries and definition of the system itself, including who is involved both in the decision-making and in the implementation and support functions of school improvement?
- How has the system addressed the dynamic tension between school autonomy, capacity, and accountability, and how has this changed over time?
- How do activities and results in the various domains reflect the goal of more equitable outcomes for all NYC students?
- What implications do the findings and discussions in these chapters have for sustaining the reforms over time and across changes in city and system leadership?
- In what ways does the unique context of New York City and its public school system shape the direction and results of the reform efforts? Put another way, what lessons and strategies might be transportable to other jurisdictions and under what conditions?

We return to these six questions in chapter 12, considering how themes relevant to each emerge across the chapters and incorporating reflections relevant to these themes from a variety of stakeholders and observers inside and outside New York City. This chapter concludes the book by providing a range of perspectives on the many accomplishments and challenges associated with reforming the largest school system in the nation.

PART I

Governance and Management

1

Leadership and Governance in New York City School Reform

Paul T. Hill

Contrary to media reports, Chancellor Joel Klein and Mayor Michael Bloomberg did not call all the shots in New York City's education reform. But they, particularly Klein and a small number of like-minded people, have an unprecedented degree of influence over NYC schools policy. This paper shows how a small number of people, possibly as few as forty, under Klein's leadership have set the basic terms for profound changes in NYC's public education system.[1]

The core of my analysis is the distinction between leadership and governance. The boundaries between these terms are sometimes blurry, but here I delineate them sharply. By *leadership* I mean the use of discretion by officials to cause change in the organizations they head. In contrast, by *governance* I mean constraints on leadership via established policies and routines, distributed powers, required consultations, and multiple independent approvals of actions. Under these definitions, leadership and governance are yin and yang: governance creates predictability and clarity; it constrains and in some cases crowds out leadership. Leadership can work within governance constraints but it can also try to work around or eliminate them.[2]

Before the Bloomberg/Klein administration, governance in city schools was so strong that it left little room for leadership, at either the citywide or the school level. For example, as the *New York Times* wrote of Chancellor Klein's immediate predecessor as he left the job:

> The job of New York City schools chancellor is a thankless one. In recent years the most a departing chancellor could hope for was to slip out in a barrage of chilly silence. The alternative was to be ridden out of town on a rail. That's one of the reasons that when there's a vacancy, top-flight candidates don't exactly line up at the door . . . The New

York City school system is like a massive old battleship, and all Mr. Levy could do was to nudge it closer to the right direction.[3]

Bloomberg and Klein have reversed this arrangement, greatly strengthening leadership at both the system and school levels, and weakening if not eliminating governance constraints. How did they do this, why, and to what effect? I try to provide answers.

Leadership Over Governance

Shortly after Michael Bloomberg became mayor in 2002, he sought the state legislature's approval to take over the city's schools. After a brief legislative battle, the school board was disbanded and Bloomberg gained the control he sought. In May 2002, he appointed Joel Klein, an antitrust lawyer and communications company executive, as chancellor. To symbolize a break with the past and the close connection between the school system and the city, Klein moved system headquarters from 110 Livingston Street in Brooklyn to the Tweed Courthouse on the City Hall grounds.

Before Mayor Bloomberg took over the city's schools, governance constraints were paramount; for example:

- Meeting the demands of the elected NYC Board of Education and other oversight bodies limited the chancellor's freedom of action and took up a great deal of his time.
- The existence of thirty-two community school districts within the city system, each with its own superintendent, board, and groups of supporters and vendors, buffered schools and educators against systemwide initiatives.
- State requirements governed teacher and principal hiring and school staffing tables.
- Federal and state laws governed allocation of money to schools and work assignments of people who were paid from those funds.
- Union contracts determined how teachers were assigned to schools, how teachers got pay increases, and what work teachers could be assigned.
- Other contracts also governed who could lead a school and limited school leaders' roles. Policies giving janitors control of building keys limited principals' and teachers' access to their own school buildings.[4]

Though the story of school reform under Bloomberg and Klein is mostly a local one, it was made possible by the state's transfer of authority from the school board to the mayor. Though the mayor—and through him, Klein—gained unprecedented freedom of action, many constraints remained in place, including state and federal requirements on uses of grant funds and financial reporting, and laws governing collective bargaining and education of students with disabilities. The mayoral takeover legislation and subsequent actions by Bloomberg and Klein weakened some of these constraints on the chancellor and school leaders and eliminated others, by (for example):

- Replacing the elected school board with a virtually powerless Panel on Education Policy (2002).
- Eliminating the thirty-two community school boards in favor of ten administrative regions (2003).
- Negotiating changes in the teacher contract to allow principals to choose among applicants and base teachers' pay on other factors in addition to seniority (2005).
- Transforming the allocation of funds to schools, basing it on weighted pupil counts, and increasing principals' ability to allocate funds and control their buildings (2006–2007).

The story of how each of these changes was made is worth a paper in itself. For this chapter, however, they only illustrate a broader point, which is that Klein and Bloomberg altered the balance of leadership and governance for a purpose. That purpose, contrary to the claims of critics, was not simply to put themselves in control of everything. In fact, many of their actions were meant to improve instruction throughout the city system by empowering school leaders. This weakened the chancellor's ability to dictate school practices, schedules, and uses of funds. Klein and Bloomberg sought a system of strong schools, each fitted to the needs of its student body and the strengths of its teachers, not a strong bureaucracy that could bend all schools to its will. They strengthened leadership at both the central and the school levels, hoping to profoundly and permanently alter the way the NYC school system operates and the outcomes it achieves.

One close associate of Klein's explained the premises on which the chancellor, his associates, and the mayor agreed: "The [pre-2002] school system does what it was built to do: make stable jobs, accommodate the demands of interest groups and comply with state laws. It can do those things without providing effective schools for all kids. We intended to rebuild the system around a new mission, one that puts children and their learning first."

The collaboration between Klein and Bloomberg is also worth its own paper. In general, Bloomberg operated as a CEO of a conglomerate, overseeing a trusted and competent CEO of one of the conglomerate's businesses: he did not dictate Klein's actions, but wanted to be consulted and informed, not surprised. Bloomberg expected Klein to be effective both as a politician and a manager and backed Klein in political controversies. However, Klein understood the need to avoid political firestorms, share credit when the news was good, and take the blame when it was bad. The two men were bound together—Klein could not have been effective without Bloomberg's support; and major missteps by Klein could threaten Bloomberg's reelection. But both were determined to transform the city's public education system, especially to improve educational outcomes for poor and minority students, and both agreed on the need for bold action.

Leadership and Governance in Theory

At the highest level of generality, the current NYC school reform strategy is one of decentralization as practiced in business. In education. decentralization has often been an effort to encourage initiative at the school level without changing the constraints imposed by central offices and unions.[5] In business, however, decentralization is something else; it often strengthens both the top and the bottom of the organization, but weakens the middle—the central and regional office bureaucrats who stand between the CEO and the people doing the day-to-day work. Top-level leaders do not abdicate responsibility or stop setting goals and allocating resources away from less-productive initiatives toward more promising ones, or rewarding performance and punishing failure. However, top-level leaders cede control over means to the people doing the day-to-day work—plant managers, sales groups, R&D units, and so on. Units that use their freedom to get good results are rewarded, but those with bad results are liable to being restaffed or replaced.

In business decentralization, the governance units—those that that enforce rules, control hiring, routinize human resource management, manage complex consultations and clearances, and impose time and compliance demands on the leaders of productive units—shrink, if they do not disappear entirely. They are seen as blurring the organization's focus on its goals, buffering compliant nonperformers from scrutiny, discouraging initiative, and standardizing functions that should be subject to experimentation and continuous improvement.[6]

The Klein/Bloomberg approach to decentralization evolved and sharpened over time. At this writing, NYC's reform strategy fits the description of business decentralization almost perfectly. The theory of change: strengthen the top and bottom (i.e., schools) against the middle (including unions and central and regional administration); let local productive units (schools) make the consequential decisions that affect their productivity; encourage innovation; centralize accountability via common outcome measures; make all arrangements contingent on performance; and continually search for better people and providers. Also like a business, the schools seek to continuously improve the options available to customers (families).

The NYC reform puts into practice, perhaps unconsciously, a body of work by Columbia Law School political scientist Charles Sabel. Sabel writes about *experimentalist democracy*—governments that create opportunities for differentiation and innovation in services, but monitor results and press for continuous improvement of practice in light of evidence.[7] Sabel argues that experimentalist democracy gives citizens greater opportunities to solve problems and permits greater differentiation of government-sponsored activities in light of diverse needs. Democracies, he contends, do not need to limit themselves to centralized policy making by elected officials and the bureaucrats whom they employ (e.g., by the former NYC school board and bureaucracy). Citizens who are neither elected officials nor bureaucrats can take part in problem solving by designing and operating some services, while government creates performance standards and open databases that support all parties' "learning by monitoring."[8] Sabel's theories intersect with ideas from education. Some senior leaders of Klein's leadership team said they were inspired by Mike Schmoker's papers urging decentralization as a path to evidence-based practice in schools.[9]

Transition to the Current Strategy

Klein's approach to systemwide reform was not clear, at least to observers, in his first few years. Though the mayoral takeover had given him tremendous freedom of action, he did things that conventional superintendents might have done: hired a high-profile instructional leader, mandated citywide use of a reading method, and took some powers away from local community school district superintendents. However, after a year in office, Klein started to strengthen principals' hands and reengineer the system to become a supporter of strong schools, not a source of mandates about instructional method.

Did Klein change direction sometime late in 2004 or intend all along to standardize one part of the system and then decentralize? It seems likely that Klein came in with a vision of a system driven by—in Sabel's terms—democratic experimentalism and learning by monitoring, and that this vision became sharper over his first several years in office as he became more sure that tight central management could not improve the schools very much.

After his first year, Klein reorganized the system several times, incrementally cutting the powers and staffing of the central bureaucracy, expanding school autonomy (via increased school-level control over staffing and spending decisions and choice of professional development providers), and strengthening his immediate leadership team's ability to hold school leaders accountable for performance.

The key action in this process was creating the Autonomy Zone in 2004. That year, twenty-nine schools were selected to gain control over key staffing and spending decisions. Schools in the Autonomy Zone were funded on the basis of enrollment, did not have to accept the most senior teacher who applied for a vacancy, and could select their own sources of instructional assistance and teacher professional development. The school leaders chosen for the Autonomy Zone, including those starting new schools, were those judged the most likely to be able to handle the new demands of financial and human resource management. Klein and his leadership team also hoped that the new principals' academy, the New York City Leadership Academy created in 2003, would offer relevant training and assistance.

After a one-year trial of the Autonomy Zone, Klein expanded it very quickly, to 48 schools the second year, 332 the third year (then named Empowerment Schools), and to most of the schools in the city in 2006–2007.

Expansion of the Autonomy Zone was a critical turning point in the development of the reform. Klein's leadership team was initially split on whether to treat autonomy as a reward for high performance—and thus offer it only to high-performing schools—or to commit to autonomy as a premise for the improvement of all schools. On the "reward" side were educators and businesspeople who did not believe the typical school had the leadership or staff capacity necessary to build an effective improvement strategy. On the "premise" side were educator Eric Nadelstern and noneducators who believed that central office mandates and assistance could make schools mediocre at best; that the only way to get dramatic improvements in performance was to create room for experimentation, build incrementally on successes, and abandon failures. Those arguing for universal autonomy did not expect immediate success in all schools. Instead, they foresaw a continuous improvement process in which they would expand or duplicate schools that were making gains and prune out those in which students were not learning, and local educators and nonprofits would learn how to help schools whose staffs were determined to improve but needed new ideas.

Klein himself probably shifted from one side to another, in part to keep a productive debate going, but ultimately came down on the side of autonomy as a precondition for reform.[10]

Expanding school autonomy systemwide required major changes in policy. Robert Gordon, a member of Klein's core leadership team, designed a new school funding system, which allocated most state and local funds directly to schools, based on enrollment weighted to take account of student risk factors.

In 2005, the city's Department of Education (DOE) and the United Federation of Teachers (UFT) also built a systemwide collective bargaining agreement that allowed a school's principal—in collaboration with the school's teachers—to ignore seniority in all teacher hiring decisions. This amounted to abandonment of a core tenet of teacher unionism. Union leaders explained the agreement as being in teachers' interest. As one said in an interview for this paper, "Any time we can help teachers gain greater control over their working environments, we will do so." This agreement also came at a time of rapidly expanding teacher salaries, as chapter 3 (Stiefel and Schwartz) and 7 (Goertz, Wyckoff, and Loeb) in this book will discuss.

Relations between the UFT and Klein's leadership team have been extremely complex and are impossible to categorize in just one way. Some union actions in support of the reform strategy continued after teacher salaries stopped rising: in 2006 the UFT agreed to operate a charter campus with a middle and elementary school in East New York. Overall, however, the two entities are like nations with many interests in opposition that nonetheless have found ways to cooperate on some matters. While going along with parts of Klein's reform strategy, the UFT has remained a constant source of criticism, and did not support Bloomberg's candidacy for a third term in 2009 or Klein's successful campaign to raise the number of charter schools allowed in New York State.

For his part, Klein let the union bear the brunt of criticism for union protection of teachers in so-called *rubber rooms*—facilities where hundreds of tenured teachers who had been removed from their jobs in schools, or whom no school wanted to hire, drew full pay while waiting, sometimes years, for dismissal hearings. Salaries and benefits for teachers in this status grew to nearly $100 million per year in 2009—a huge liability to both the city and the union. In 2010, owing to a budget crisis and the UFT's embarrassment over a *New Yorker* expose, Klein and the UFT reached a new agreement: Klein would force schools to accept some senior teachers they otherwise did not want and the union would agree to simpler processes to terminate unplace-able teachers.[11]

The devolution strategy had its complement in the central office. Klein took as much business as possible away from established central office bureaus and had key decisions made by members of his small leadership team. He created new talent, accountability, and portfolio-management offices, which subsumed existing human resources and assessment functions, and put members of his immediate leadership team in charge.

The Leadership Team

Klein created a small and very coherent leadership team, initially composed of approximately fifteen New Yorkers with broad experience in business, law, education, government, and nonprofits. Many of them shared Klein's antitrust views. As the government litigator in the Microsoft antitrust case, Klein had acted on the assumption that monopolies stifle innovation, sequester funds that should be available to the rest of the economy, retard economic growth and social progress, and hurt consumers. When Klein took office, the vast NYC schools bureaucracy looked a lot like a business monopoly, and the leadership team wanted to break its grip and set off competition and innovation.

Starting in Klein's first year and increasingly thereafter, the leadership team took charge of key parts of the system, including design of a new data-based school accountability system, the general counsel's office, funds distribution and financial oversight, talent (teacher and principal recruitment, development, and assignment), in-service teacher and principal training, portfolio management (monitoring the overall supply of schools to identify high performers, unmet needs, and schools in trouble), and overall operations management.

The fact that Klein and his key associates were New Yorkers familiar with the community and its politics sets this reform initiative apart. Big-city superintendents and their close associates are usually outsiders—itinerant school administrators who lack local contacts and experience and are not prepared for political leadership.

Klein personally recruited the individuals who filled these positions, and worked intimately with them in an open office environment where all key actors could see all others and communicate spontaneously at any time. The result was that functions that often hamstring a bold reform (e.g., the general counsel's legal interpretations) were tightly coordinated with the rest of the reform. As a key staffer explained, the general counsel is usually a force independent of the superintendent, and works to steer the district away from any actions that might lead to lawsuits. Under Klein, the general counsel was the chancellor's lawyer, whose job it was to develop legal arguments for needed actions. The general counsel is responsible for steering the system away from actions that courts would likely reverse, but Klein and his lawyer were willing to take actions that might lead to litigation if they believed they could prevail in court. As one attorney associated with Klein said, "We will do things some people won't like and we expect to be sued. That's not troubling in itself. Of course we want our actions to be on firm legal grounds, so if we are sued we expect to win."

Klein's leadership team included people who previously controlled major government bureaucracies (e.g., the State Controller's Office) and knew how to work with them and keep them from hamstringing the reform. It also included major corporate lawyers and successful investment bankers, management consultants, and people who had been both business CEOs and government agency heads. The first director of the DOE Office of Accountability was Columbia law professor James Liebman, a world-renowned expert on efforts to avoid errors in death-penalty cases, who was recruited to the team in January 2006.

The leadership group also included career educators, such as lawyer-educator Andrés Alonso and widely admired school principal Eric Nadelstern, who served as communication links between Klein and rank-and-file educators. Nadelstern, Alonso, and others (e.g., Chief Accountability Officer, later named Chief Academic Officer, Shael Polakow-Suransky) were trusted both to constrain Klein's initiatives so they would be tolerable to educators, and to make the case for the reforms to them. Senior counselor Michele Cahill, who had developed small high school strategies nationwide for the Carnegie Corporation of New York, was perhaps the chief "boundary spanner" on the leadership team until mid-2007, when she left to rejoin the Carnegie Corporation.

Membership in Klein's leadership team changed over time as individuals left to return to their core professions or went to other cities to lead reform strategies with at least some of the elements present in NYC (Alonso became CEO of the Baltimore City Public Schools). Assignments with the core leadership also shifted every year or so. Leadership team members say this was meant to ensure that team members did not become highly specialized or captured by the part of the system they oversaw.

In 2009 and 2010 the number of educator members of the team increased, so that educators were doing jobs previously assigned only to people with roots in law and business. The educators brought into the leadership team were generally drawn from teachers and principals who had worked on earlier Klein initiatives such as small schools and the Autonomy Zone.

The central group was strikingly similar to the *commando center* described by Sabel: "a crack team of civil servants at the very center of government who use the powers of the bureaucracy to foster cross-cutting behaviors, and so transcend the structural limits."[12]

Expansion and Evolution

Klein's reliance on a small, evolving leadership group has led some to assume that he started with a fully worked-out game plan, but hid it from the public. I will argue for an alternative interpretation: that Klein and his intimates agreed on the goal of a diverse, innovative system of schools but were constantly learning from experience and adjusting the reform accordingly.

The shift from centralized mandates to a devolution strategy is the first of many examples of their commitment to continuous improvement, even when it meant abandoning earlier initiatives. When Klein and colleagues committed to devolution, school autonomy, and performance-based accountability, they were not sure of all the places the strategy would take them. Without knowing exactly when the decision to take additional actions was reached, it is still possible to identify elaborations of the strategy that Klein and others might not have anticipated. These include:

Organizational structure

- *Revamping the structures for school support.* The authority associated with the thirty-two community school districts that existed in 2002 was (in 2003) replaced by a set of ten administrative regions. Later (2007), the DOE dismantled the regions and established eleven (later twelve) School Support Organizations (SSOs), some run by district staff and others by nonprofit organizations. Each SSO ran at least one (and often several) voluntary school support networks, and schools could choose which SSO and network to join. In 2010, trying to give schools more choices and cut out the layer of staff located in the SSOs, the chancellor dissolved the DOE-run SSOs and replaced them with sixty voluntary school support networks citywide. Some privately run SSOs remained, but as managers of networks. The sixty networks also absorbed previously separate Children First Networks that provided financial and facilities services.

Human capital

- *Developing a citywide talent strategy to address teacher shortages and diversify the teacher and administrator workforce.* Strategies include recruitment of teachers and principals from nontraditional sources (e.g., Teach for America and The

New Teacher Project) and a new partnership with Hunter College for innovative teacher training programs.

- *Giving school leaders more power over hiring decisions.* The 2005 collective bargaining agreement established *mutual consent hiring* and eliminated a practice known as *seniority bumping,* by which teachers were able to transfer schools based solely on their seniority. Principals are now able to interview all prospective teacher candidates and are no longer forced to hire teachers with the greatest seniority. Teachers who are unable to secure a new job after losing their position in a school for budgetary reasons or on account of a school's closing are offered substitute positions within their district. They are not, however, able to displace more-junior teachers.

Portfolio of school options

- *Creating new schools and using charters on a large scale to replace low-performing schools.* Though precedents for creating new small high schools were established under earlier chancellors, Klein accelerated the development of small new high schools in facilities that previously housed just one large comprehensive school. Starting in 2004, he also used chartering as a way to establish many schools' freedom from close bureaucratic and union oversight, urged formation of local charter provider organizations, and invited nationally known charter school providers to work in New York City. He also tried to eliminate one of the toughest barriers to charter schools' success by offering them space in public facilities.
- *Assembling a subportfolio of schools offering multiple pathways to graduation.* Realizing that overall high school graduation rates could not improve dramatically unless something was done to reduce the nearly 50 percent dropout rate among disadvantaged students, Klein's leadership team created a subportfolio of schools designed to rescue students who had dropped out of school or were likely to do so soon.[13] As with chartering, this effort involved partnerships with nonprofit organizations and innovation in uses of school time, staff, and facilities. JoEllen Lynch, who had created community-based education programs for Good Shepherd Center, and Michele Cahill and Leah Hamilton, now of the Carnegie Corporation, supported this effort from both within and outside the city system.
- *Establishing a portfolio-management office to coordinate school openings and closings.* The school accountability system identified schools in need of dramatic improvement, and the new schools development function identified promising new school providers. However, these functions were not well coordinated until Klein combined them in an office of portfolio management. The office was responsible both for allocating promising new school providers to the neighborhoods that need them most, and for developing new schooling options to meet the most severe needs.

Evidence and data

- *Building tools and incentives for evidence-based practice in schools.* Realizing that greater school-level autonomy was a necessary but not sufficient condition for evidence-based practice in schools, Klein and his associates created new tools to assist school-level reflection and problem solving—inquiry teams and the Achievement Reporting and Innovation System (ARIS) data system (both described elsewhere in this volume). They also designed the school accountability system to include on-site Quality Reviews (QRs) that graded schools in part on evidence-based practice. In combination with the data-based accountability system and QRs, the inquiry teams and ARIS system are intended to fuel the continuous improvement of existing schools via what Sabel has called "learning by monitoring."[14]

- *Sharpening the focus of the accountability system on student learning.* When the formal value-added-based school accountability system produced anomalous results in 2009 (implausible improvements in grades given to previously low-performing schools), Klein and Polakow-Suransky adopted a more stable method of measuring rates of student learning, based on Colorado's student growth model.[15]

Continued innovation

- *Investing in new technology-rich school models.* Looking to make more effective use of existing funds, in 2010 the DOE started a new Innovation Zone (iZone) that would experiment with new uses of student and teacher time, schedules, and student grouping. New school models, gathered from European as well as American innovators, would be tested on a small scale before being used broadly in the city, ultimately replacing or redesigning many existing schools.

- Other than the iZone, these initiatives are described in depth in other chapters. A future analysis might find still other initiatives and possibly abandonment or changes in some of these. The point is that they demonstrate learning and adaptation by the leadership team. Contrary to charges that Klein and others thought they knew all the answers and were ideologically committed to privatization, these initiatives demonstrate the leadership team's commitment to experimentation, private-public partnerships in an enterprise of democratic experimentalism, and "learning by monitoring."

Political Leadership

Mayoral control and the absence of a school board mean that the chancellor has a constituency of one. However, that does not exempt the chancellor and his leadership team from paying attention to politics. School system leaders can lose the mayor's confidence, and even contribute to the mayor's downfall, if they cause unnecessary firestorms (as was demonstrated in the defeat of Washington, D.C., mayor Adrian Fenty in September 2010). Moreover, leaders like Klein, who hope to set the school system permanently on a more productive path, need to build lasting support for what they have done.

Klein and his close associates developed a positive political strategy intended not only to limit the strength of opposition, but also to build new sources of support for a permanently reformed city system. Based on numerous interviews with key DOE leaders, I conclude that the strategy had three parts:

1. Build new constituencies in favor of a permanent strategy of devolution to strong, accountable schools.
2. Convert some groups that traditionally support a centralized, bureaucratic school system.
3. Accept that some groups will not support the new model, but limit their influence.

The most important element of this political strategy is the first. DOE leaders hoped to activate some publics that had previously paid little attention to public education and to create new organized groups whose interests were closely tied to the reform. New attentive publics included business and media organizations concerned about the quality of the city's workforce; leaders of higher education institutions, such as Hunter College, that trained teachers and leaders for new roles created by the reform; families that might be drawn back to the city's schools from private and suburban schools; and philanthropic foundations. New organized groups included the nonprofit organizations that schools could hire to provide assistance (curriculum, assessment, and training), teachers and school leaders whose career opportunities the reform created, and families that previously felt trapped in and poorly served by the public schools. Klein also reached out to the pastors and congregations of African American churches, hoping to convince them that the most disadvantaged children would benefit from the reform.

Groups to be converted from support for a more traditional system included incumbent and new public school teachers and administrators (including union members), former central office employees who would now get the opportunity to work more effectively in new nonprofit assistance organizations, and parents and members of the public who had come to accept the old system but might change their minds if the reform made schools much fairer and more effective.

DOE leaders did not automatically relegate anyone to the status of intransigent opposition. Because they were able to win agreement from the UFT to allow schools to discount seniority preference in hiring, they knew that this most important union would cooperate to some degree. However, they assumed the unions would be hard to move on many other issues.

Leaders also knew that families already highly satisfied with their schools might oppose the reforms, especially pupil-based funding, which reallocated money away from schools that traditionally captured disproportionate public funding—usually those in the most stable and highest-income neighborhoods. But Klein and his team hoped those families would be mollified by better overall school performance and better outcomes for disadvantaged students.

At its core, the political strategy depended on key groups' seeing that the reform was both consistent with their interests and good for the city as a whole. That meant the reform had to be put in place as quickly and as thoroughly as possible so its benefits would be evident. As a member of Klein's leadership team said, "We were in a big hurry. We thought we might have only three years and we needed to put things in place so people could see results." Klein and others did not think a major charm offensive would fool anyone who would be naturally opposed to the reform, or convince any group that had learned over time to distrust school reform promises. Thus, though Klein, Cahill, and others met with many groups and held public forums to answer questions, they did not put a great deal of time or money into symbolic politics or courtship of individuals other than African American pastors (including the Reverend Al Sharpton).

Klein and his collaborators also expected, but were surprised at the virulence of, opposition from neighborhood political figures (including some state legislators) who had been able to work as "fixers" under the old system, getting jobs and contracts for supporters and intervening in the schools on behalf of constituent families. Klein closed off opportunities for fixing by eliminating central office employees' ability to make deals with neighborhood figures. As one leadership team member said, "Minor elected officials would call to get someone a job or ask someone in the central office to lean on a principal, and they would be outraged that there was no one able to do what they wanted." As a result, some neighborhood political figures complained that the DOE had moved too fast, consulted too briefly, excluded good people from jobs and opportunities for influence, and failed to negotiate on actions on which individuals had once held veto power.

Klein and his close associates thought they were seeking a deeply democratic purpose—providing good education for the disadvantaged—and would not pay a great price for going about it quickly. In that light, they took a calculated risk in closing down many preexisting forums and channels of influence. Klein and others took pride in saying that there were no places in the bureaucracy where jobs could be bartered or groups paid off.

Thus, Klein's political strategy required that the DOE avoid the "politics of paralysis" by acting fast and avoiding consultations that could only delay action or dilute results. Klein and his team believed that this was the only way to attract new supporters and convert parties that care about results above all else. But the strategy also generated opposition, much of it from groups that took the position, "We want better schools, just not this way."[16] School closings, a complement to Klein's strategy of continuously searching for better school providers and better matches to the needs of groups of children, are always rallying points for opposition. In NYC as elsewhere, the strength of opposition has little to do with the performance of the school up for closure or the quality of alternatives available. Opponents focus on jobs, neighborhood identity, and general suspicion of "downtown" authority.

The current local dispute over whether Klein's methods were democratic or dictatorial is itself evidence that democracy is not dead, or even sleeping, in New York City. Both sides frame choices in ways they believe will help them. Proponents emphasize the positive and try to minimize discussion of the downsides experienced by former employees, school communities that lost money when the city went to pupil-based funding, and supporters of schools that were closed. Opponents like Diane Ravitch oversimplify the reform when they say it is based on privatization and naive overreliance on testing.[17] Other opponents pose an ideological claim—that by making parents into customers, the reform weakens citizenship and detaches low-income people from (presumed more appropriate) neighborhood, class, and ethnic political affiliations.

The "elite" conversation often turns on different assumptions about democracy—whether, for example, all decisions on provision of public services should be subject to public deliberation and controlled directly by elected officials. Sabel's theory of democratic experimentalism, which Klein and his colleagues put into practice even if they did not all know about it, assumes that elected officials can and should delegate some decisions to small groups of citizens, as long as the results are constantly available, shared, and built on. Sabel's theory says that democracies can legitimately prioritize problem solving over what he calls *aggregative* policymaking, where all interests converge on one decision point and one binding decision is hammered out.[18] Some critics of the reform claim that only aggregative policymaking is legitimate, and that when people become customers of government they are no longer truly citizens.

To date, it is not possible to say for sure whether the opposition generated by NYC's reforms is strong enough to outweigh the support from new attentive publics, new groups that owe their existence to the reform, and families whose children have benefited from new educational opportunities. In New York City, as in New Orleans, large numbers of parents appear content with the reforms for now.[19] However, there is enough opposition to keep system leaders under pressure. Democratic processes will, of course, decide the results of the current political struggles, as voters select the next mayor or determine whether the city's schools should once again be controlled by an all-powerful elected school board.

Stabilization and Institutionalization

Bloomberg and Klein will certainly have left the scene long before all the implications of their initiatives are worked out and all opponents co-opted or defeated.

Members of Klein's leadership team say that the reform still has a long way to go to convert all teachers and principals to the idea of working in schools whose existence is contingent on performance and to turn all central office bureaucracies into responsive service providers. Despite Bloomberg's election to a third term, Klein's freedom of action had already been constrained by legislation strengthening the role of the Panel on Education Policy and new procedures for school closing.

The current reform—as defined by school empowerment—faces two threats, one internal and one external. The internal threat is that the DOE's leadership team could lose track of its school empowerment objectives and erode school autonomy via new policies and compliance demands. This is unlikely to happen deliberately, but it is easy for central officials to add just a few new rules and reporting requirements every time a new problem arises. That was one of the processes by which the system bureaucracy grew up in the first place and why, before the Klein reforms, school leaders had so little control over their schools. School and support network leaders complain that data reporting and compliance demands are increasing over time and that the leadership group does not have a good way of screening out such demands or terminating one demand when it is necessary to impose a new one.

The external threat is that opponents will gather enough allies to force abandonment of devolution and accountability and a return to control of schools by politics, labor contracts, and mandates. Though some elements of the current reform initiative are likely to persist (e.g., independent networks to provide help to schools, data systems), it is possible that the NYC schools will revert to a system with a weak chancellor and weak school leaders, and no clear process for continuous improvement.[20]

If the reform is to be stabilized against both threats, the system must find a new balance of leadership and governance. The leadership of a mayor or chancellor is too transitory a basis for sustained reform. If the current initiative is to be continued past the end of Bloomberg's term, something must be put into law or policy to guarantee school leaders' control over budgets, hiring, and choice of assistance providers, and to limit central authorities' powers to performance-based-accountability and portfolio management.

The eventual return of some sort of school board, whether appointed or elected, seems likely. If there are no clear limits to that board's powers—if it can make policy about anything it chooses, intervene in any decision, or once again control hiring and enter contracts that trade away school leaders' authority—it will probably exercise them. A more limited constitutional arrangement, one in which the school board and chancellor have control over only a few decisions like school opening and closing and guaranteeing fair admissions to all schools, could sustain the empowerment aspects of the current reform. The state of Louisiana, which faces similar issues in returning control of New Orleans schools to a local oversight body, has made some progress in this direction.[21]

These issues might be too politically hot to resolve in New York City. Klein and Bloomberg might indeed have more time to pursue their reform strategy today if they do not press to make it permanent. Given the opposition to the reform by some state legislators, they might have difficulty legislating a permanent change in board powers. Alternatively, any clear statement of the rules for the future, even an executive order from the state superintendent, governor, or mayor, would provide some stability.

As other chapters in this book will show, the reform's results are just emerging. The early indications, especially the high school graduation rate among high-risk students and the city's scores on the National Assessment of Educational Progress, are encouraging but not definitive. Several years of increases in the numbers of city students rated "proficient" on New York State exams came to an end in 2010. Though the numbers of questions students answered correctly on those tests continued to rise, higher cut scores meant that fewer students in the city and statewide won the *proficient* label. Critics were quick to seize on this change as evidence that Klein's strategies had not improved student achievement.

At this writing, New York City is probably only about halfway through the implementation of the reforms described here. Another book written nine years from now might tell a very different story. If the current reform or a related successor is still present in NYC, it will be because the city has found a new and sustainable balance between governance and leadership.

2

Parent and Community Engagement in New York City and the Sustainability Challenge for Urban Education Reform

Jeffrey R. Henig, Eva Gold, Marion Orr,
Megan Silander, and Elaine Simon[1]

> Anyone can get up and say parents are important partners
> in the education of their kids. In New York City, look at this:
> we are walking the walk.
>
> —Joel Klein[2]

> Under the current system, while there is plenty of lip service
> regarding the need for parental involvement, parents are shut
> out. This must be reversed.
>
> —Dan Jacoby[3]

P arent and community engagement is a typical mom-and-apple-pie issue. Like national prosperity, quality health care, and safe streets, the goal of promoting community and parent engagement in schools is broadly endorsed. Consensus in this instance depends on keeping definitions of *engagement* vague. Some think of it in individualistic terms (parents getting involved to improve their children's education); others think of it collectively (parents trying to make school- or districtwide changes). Some see it as a collaborative exercise marked by defined roles; others see it as adversarial because parents, teachers, and central administrators have different needs and priorities. And there is often sharp disagreement when it comes to identifying just who represents the authentic and legitimate voice of parents and community—disagreement that carries extra resonance because it often aligns with racial, class, and geographical boundaries.

In New York City, the Bloomberg/Klein administration's approach to parent and community engagement was framed in contradistinction to the community school districts (CSDs) that predated it; CSDs were rooted in a vision of a more collective and aggressive form of engagement in which parents and communities directly set priorities, selected policies, and shaped implementation. The administration considered this preexisting system to be fundamentally flawed in both concept and practice.

In place of engagement at the community level, the administration's approach centers on engagement at the level of families and schools. In place of involvement in setting goals and priorities, it focuses on engagement in implementation of policies. In place of emphasizing political voice as a way for communities to exercise their demands, it puts a strong emphasis on exit—giving families the option to choose a different school if they consider it a better fit for their child than the one to which the child has been assigned. Finally, while the CSDs provided education-specific agenda-setting venues in which parents and teachers were influential actors, the administration's position on mayoral control of schools deliberately shifts authority for agenda setting and policy making to general-purpose politics and mayoral elections, where other issues compete for priority and where most groups do not have a direct stake in public education.

In this chapter, we review these competing visions of engagement as manifested in the formal and informal policies of the Bloomberg/Klein administration and as challenged within the context of conflicts surrounding the 2009 extension of mayoral control of the city's schools. We draw on extensive interviewing, field observations, and document analysis.[4] The mayor and his allies were victorious on key points of contention in the battle over the renewal of mayoral control, but the conflict revealed that allegiance to a more active form of engagement was deeper than they anticipated. Failure to fully credit and understand the motivating force behind the movement for a stronger role for public engagement in setting policies and priorities (instead of simply supporting them) can feed resentments and political backlash that undermine the long-term sustainability of reform initiatives.

Out with the Old: New York City's Legacy of Community School Districts

"To inform the conversation, it is critical to think about mayoral control and accountability in relation to what preceded it," Dennis Walcott, deputy mayor for education and community development, told a public hearing in January 2009. "Under the old system, decisions were shared by several power centers . . . 32 elected school boards across the city hired 32 community superintendents who had 32 different standards, 32 different policies, and sometimes 32 different ways of operating." While decentralization to the community level worked for some, Walcott's overall verdict was decidedly negative: "I remember the inequities inherent in the 32 school systems, some run capably, and some run corruptly."[5]

The belief that the CSDs were a key part of the problem underpinned the administration's earliest reform efforts. Even before a chancellor was appointed, Bloomberg aggressively pursued a strategy of shifting power and authority away from the CSDs. Under the mayoral control law passed by the state legislature in June 2002, the CSDs would remain, but each district's board was eliminated and the chancellor would appoint each community superintendent.[6] In January 2003, the mayor announced a restructuring of the system that would strip the CSDs of almost all of their remaining authority. Calling them "notorious bureaucratic dinosaurs [that] will be extinct," the mayor told the New York Urban League that in their place "will be one, unified, focused, streamlined chain of command."[7]

From Community Control to Community School Districts

Spurred by a push by parents and community leaders for community control of the public schools, the New York state legislature enacted decentralization legislation in 1969. The push for community control was a demand for *strong democracy*, a transformation of the relationship between parents and the NYC schools. Strong democracy calls for robust public engagement and meaningful participation of community members.[8] It is similar to theories and strategies used by community organizers.[9] Community control advocates' theory of action was based on the transfer of authority from education bureaucrats to parents and community leaders. African American and Hispanic parents had long argued that while their voices might be heard, education officials were not responding to them in the same way they responded to white parents.[10] If democracy means having a say in the decisions that affect family and community, it was missing for the parents of Hispanic and African American students in the city's public schools. The idea was to give parents a viable role in the operation of the NYC schools, to shift power downward.

The legislature's decentralization plan, which was in effect until 1996, created the thirty-two CSDs, each with a nine-member school board, elected every three years. The boards were responsible for administering elementary and junior high schools, including hiring the district superintendent, teachers, and supervisory staff. They also managed the districts' budgets of tens of millions of dollars. High schools and certain citywide programs were kept under central office control. The top central administrator, the school chancellor, was to oversee the local districts.

From the start of decentralization, the city's clubhouse politicians captured control of the local school board elections in many parts of the city. Local politicians, activist parent organizations, and leaders of the local teachers union controlled elections in which turnout typically was low. Some CSDs, especially those in the more affluent areas of the city, were able to mobilize and use decentralization as an avenue for educational innovation, but many community school districts had reputations for malfeasance and patronage.[11] Many of these districts were home to the most low-performing, violent schools.

Reforming Decentralization

Prior to Mayor Bloomberg's election, there were major efforts to reform the 1969 decentralization law. For example, in 1996, to rein in corruption, patronage, and mismanagement, the state legislature stripped the local school boards of their power to hire and fire principals and allowed the chancellor to take over a school district.[12] In the late 1990s, under Chancellor Rudy Crew, the state legislature moved more authority to the central office, giving the chancellor authority to fire school superintendents in low-performing districts.

Many observers believe that by the time of Mayor Bloomberg's election in 2001, community school boards "had already been dying a long, slow death."[13] The CSDs and the elected school boards that had governed them for over thirty years had been stripped of much of their influence. However, as a mayoral candidate, Michael Bloomberg used the decentralized CSDs' reputation for corruption, patronage, and low student performance to build support to further recentralize school decision making. Bloomberg's call for more centralization of school authority also implicitly discredited community control and the idea of strong democracy.

In 2002, state leaders acceded to Bloomberg's request to dramatically change the governing structure of NYC public schools. The new system put in place a thirteen-member central school board, the Panel for Educational Policy (PEP): each borough president would appoint one member, and the mayor the remaining eight. In addition, the mayor was given the authority to appoint the chancellor. No longer would the district boards appoint a local superintendent; this role was given to the chancellor. After the mayor appointed Joel Klein as chancellor, and as Klein's administrative and educational vision came into focus, the role of the CSDs was weakened further. Administratively, the key units were a leaner and more restrained central office playing a guiding function for substantially empowered schools. The thirty-two geographically defined districts were seen as too large and complex to focus on the learning environment in individual schools and, at the same time, too small and parochial to represent broad city interests and enforce a coherent plan.

Contrasting Visions of Parent and Community Engagement

The targeting of the CSDs was partly tactical. The administration wanted to move quickly and boldly, and the CSDs were a likely focal point for resistance. But portraying this as a one-dimensional battle between forces of change and resistance obscures nuances on both sides. Also at stake were competing visions of the most appropriate forms of parental and public engagement and differing beliefs about how to reconcile the need for strong and coherent policy making and the need to build coalitions to ensure that reforms are sustained.

Figure 2-1 distinguishes among four conceptions of the proper role for engagement, based on whether the key unit for engagement is individualistic (student and

FIGURE 2-1   Types of parent and community engagement

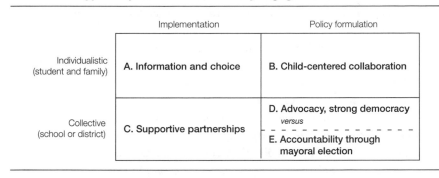

	Implementation	Policy formulation
Individualistic (student and family)	A. Information and choice	B. Child-centered collaboration
Collective (school or district)	C. Supportive partnerships	D. Advocacy, strong democracy *versus* E. Accountability through mayoral election

family) or collective (community or districtwide) and whether engagement focuses on policy formulation (setting priorities and shaping policies) or implementation (collaborating in carrying out policies). Although these things are not mutually exclusive, crafting a policy of engagement in practice demands emphasizing some more than others. Attending to the differences in emphasis can help us illuminate the lines of cleavage that developed between the New York City Department of Education (DOE) and its critics and clarify how such tensions could be so high despite the fact that all involved believe themselves to be promoting parent and community engagement:

- *Cell A: Information and choice:* The emphasis here is on giving parents better information about what their child's school offers and how their child is performing to help them reinforce the school's efforts at home. School and district policies are set by school and district administrators (often working in collaboration with intermediary organizations), with engagement efforts centered around ensuring that parents have established channels for asking questions and registering concerns about their own children and their children's classrooms and schools. If there is a mismatch between their child's need and what the school provides, the DOE policy emphasizes the option for parents to select one of an array of alternative publicly supported schools outside their attendance zone. Formal DOE policy, including some of its most innovative efforts, is best represented by cell A.
- *Cell B: Child-centered collaboration:* Compared with cell A, this conception of engagement envisions parents less as passive consumers of school and district services than as active collaborators in their own children's educational experience. Parents' role is partly as "extenders" of the teacher and school mission: overseeing homework, ensuring attendance, encouraging educational aspirations. But in return they also share with teachers and principals a role in shaping an individualized educational program for their child. DOE efforts to increase individual schools' autonomy provides room to put such practices in place.

- *Cell C: Supportive partnerships:* This vision of parental and community engagement is more collective; it involves organized bodies of parents (e.g., PTAs or School Leadership Teams) and community-based stakeholders in efforts to better enable schools and the district to pursue their policies and programs. Examples include school-based fundraisers, adopt-a-school relationships with local businesses or nonprofits, and collective efforts to lobby on behalf of the district for more resources at the city or state levels. While collective in nature, as with cell A engagement is passive and supportive, keyed to enlisting parents and community to extend the impact of policies and priorities they did not directly participate in establishing.
- *Cells D and E: Strong democracy versus mayoral control:* The notion of strong democracy holds that conflicts among individuals can best be addressed through "a participatory process of ongoing proximate self-legislation and the creation of a political community capable of transforming dependent private individuals into free citizens and partial and private interests into public goods."[14] In democratic theory, strong democracy is sometimes contrasted with representative government, in which citizens choose leaders they expect to govern wisely and then hold them responsible by voting them out of office if their performance does not meet expectations. Much of the mayoral control battle that we discuss below centers on the issue of whether the chance to vote every four years in general elections in which those without a direct stake in the schools also participate provides parents with a sufficient opportunity to influence policies and priorities.

DOE Initiatives for Family Engagement and Parent Leadership

DOE officials approach parent engagement through either family engagement or parent leadership engagement. Family engagement initiatives primarily fall within cell A as represented in figure 2-1, and these are more innovative and arguably more central to the DOE's efforts. Parent leadership initiatives, in contrast, were largely inherited by the administration and maintained under the watchful eye of the state legislature, which mandated key elements. Since 2002, the DOE has implemented multiple parent engagement structures and initiatives; we discuss in this section the components that have been particularly central to DOE's efforts.

Office of Family Engagement and Advocacy

As with other aspects of the administration's reform agenda, the first stage of reforming parent and community engagement efforts involved centralization. Previously, responsibilities were housed in different offices, and were not necessarily connected between district, school, and the central office.[15] "You had parent support officers without any real clear direction or mission," a current official notes. In 2007, the

Office for Family Engagement and Advocacy (OFEA) was established to centrally direct and monitor the district's engagement initiatives. It started the 2008–2009 school year with a budget of approximately $5.4 million and roughly one hundred staff members.[16]

Parent Coordinators

At the same time it was centralizing some key functions, the administration gave attention to a new effort to facilitate engagement with parents at the school level.[17] Parent coordinators were placed in every school as part of the first set of Children First reforms, with the goals of increasing parent involvement with their children's learning and school, and providing information and assistance. Welcoming the roughly twelve hundred new coordinators in August 2003, Klein told them they would be "one of the key levers for change." Funding for these positions totaled approximately $43 million in the first year.[18]

The DOE continues to see parent coordinators as an important—and in some cases, *the* most important—element of parent engagement.[19] The department reports that 95 percent of schools have a functioning parent coordinator, and that almost all of the coordinators in 2009 had been in that position since it was instituted in 2003.[20] By the DOE's count, based on parent coordinator logs, parent coordinators answered 1.6 million phone calls and assisted parents with 7.8 million walk-in visits in 2008–2009.[21]

Nonetheless, some have questioned the quality of the services these coordinators provide. When the program began in 2003, critics saw it as a self-conscious effort by the administration to soothe anger over the dismantling of the CSDs, and regarded it more as symbolic appeasement than a genuine effort to provide parents an active role. They predicted that the parent coordinators would have too little power to resolve parent-principal conflicts, would be too beholden to the principals who hired and could fire them, and might end up being an obstacle blocking parents from reaching the principal. Much of the press coverage focused on the price tag and the uncertain benefits. Some criticized the coordinators' lack of availability. The Public Advocate conducted phone surveys of parent coordinators in 2003, 2004, and 2008, and each time cited the coordinators for lack of response to phone messages.[22]

District Family Advocates

The DOE created the district family advocate (DFA) position in 2007, following the reorganization of the school system and dissolution of the ten regions. The DOE suggests that these positions help parents "get answers and support close to home, rather than at far-away regional offices."[23] DFAs are supposed to step in to assist elementary and middle school families if the local parent coordinator cannot (high school families are served by the deputy borough directors). DFAs assisted 9,418 parents in district offices and received 40,379 phone calls in 2008–2009.[24] However, during the debate about the renewal of mayoral control, which we discuss below, many parents as well as local legislators voiced frustration regarding their inability to find assistance outside of the local school to resolve problems, and one of the changes in the governance legislation in 2009 was to try to address this concern by making the DFAs report to superintendents rather than OFEA.[25]

ARIS Parent Link and P311

Introduced in May 2009, ARIS (Achievement Reporting and Innovation System) Parent Link is an online platform designed to provide parents with information about their child's educational progress and to support relationships between parents and teachers. The Link provides parents with the same data about their child that are available to the teacher, including attendance rates, state test scores, English language learner assessment results, and transcript information. The system is designed to create an online parent network, providing parents opportunities to join online discussions, develop blogs, and post documents. In the year since ARIS Parent Link was introduced, approximately 300,000 accounts (roughly 35 percent of families) have been created and accessed by parents.[26]

In 2009 the DOE introduced P311, an extension of the city's 311 government information and services telephone hotline. P311 was designed to streamline and simplify parent access to information about city schools, such as enrollment and choice, special education, transportation, and ARIS. District administrators reported that they track the P311 calls as well as the DFA's responses, and that these data are compiled for superintendents to review to ensure parents are receiving adequate support and information.[27] Data on parent calls indicate that the majority of inquiries were related to finding a school or school zone (28 percent of calls), or regarding the public school calendar (17 percent of calls).[28]

Parent Survey

A major parent engagement initiative in 2008 was the development of a parent survey "to solicit parent views of what was working and what was not in the system."[29] Parents are asked to rate their satisfaction with their children's school in academic expectations, communication, engagement, and safety and respect. It focuses only on the school; there are no questions about the policies or performance of DOE as whole.[30]

The scale of the survey effort is substantial. In 2009, 381,543 parents completed the survey. Response rates increased from 26 percent of parents in the first year to 45 percent in 2009.[31] The DOE reports results publicly for each school, publishes a citywide report summarizing survey results by question, and provides an online tool with graphs comparing an individual school's responses to the overall city's responses. The DOE also offers feedback sessions with principals, schools, unions, and others to discuss results.

The most prominent use of the survey data is their incorporation into the metric used to grade schools on their performance. Parent survey data are combined with student and teacher survey responses to generate each school's "learning environment" score, which formally counts for 15 percent of the performance score (although schools can get "extra credit" for certain achievements not included in the basic formula, meaning the learning environment may contribute less than 15 percent to the final score). The survey report also informs principal performance reviews, although it carries very small weight.

Choice and Charters

Although not always presented this way, school choice appears to be another avenue for parent engagement. The administration has built on a long-standing tradition of public school choice at the secondary level—for example, its innovative high schoool match system requires eighth graders to choose high schools, allowing them to rank up to twelve from among more than six hundred available programs citywide—but the embrace of charter schools has attracted the most attention. In most of the country, traditional districts have been wary about charters, if not directly hostile, but the mayor and chancellor have embraced them enthusiastically. The administration lobbied aggressively to raise the state's cap on charters and has given charters access to the system's school buildings to a degree perhaps unmatched across the country.[32]

The administration's support for charters is based on several considerations, including its belief that charters introduce beneficial competition and bring in innovative educators with new ideas. National charter school proponents emphasize engagement as another benefit, arguing that empowering parents to select their schools increases commitment. The administration seems to share that view: "We sometimes get hung up on whether we ought to consult parents about how we teach long division, and it strikes me that the choice issue is a much more significant way to engage families."[33] While many of the parent engagement tools discussed above tend to provide information from the administration to parents, school choice provides a potential feedback mechanism in the system. Parents and students vote with their feet, and the DOE reports that it uses their patterns of school choice to inform decisions about school closures and new school sites. For example, declining school enrollment is one indicator used to determine whether to close a school.[34]

Partnerships: Engaging Parents in School Leadership

Under the engagement stream, the DOE has channeled extensive resources into parent engagement in supporting the academic achievement of their own child. Efforts related to what the department calls *leadership* and we call *partnerships* have been more halting and occasionally contentious.

The administration has accepted in principle the role of parents and community in providing feedback to inform its decisions, but it has retained unadulterated authority to act once its decisions are made. Tensions have arisen as the department has implemented a parent engagement approach grounded in information provision, consumer service, and choice while the state legislature has in contrast insisted on retaining some ideas and structures that had evolved out of the more active vision of community-based engagement. In addition, parent and community advocates continue to resist what they see as their disempowerment and have proved over time to be more persistent and to have a broader constituency than the administration initially thought.

School Leadership Teams

School Leadership Teams (SLTs), required by state law, are composed of elected parents and staff. The role of the SLTs in school decision-making has been a point of controversy. Critics of the administration suggest that, following the advent of mayoral control, SLTs have ceased to function in any effective manner. Numbers from 2008 indicate that approximately half of schools have functioning SLTs.[35] A May 2009 report by City Comptroller William C. Thompson Jr. attributes this lack of functioning to ineffective parent and parent-teacher associations (PAs/PTAs) at the school site.[36] Other contributing factors are a perceived lack of power granted to the SLTs, and inadequate parent training provided by OFEA.[37] While acknowledging that it has more to do on this front, DOE officials suggest that this level of engagement is impressive, considering the challenges.[38]

In addition, controversy about the SLTs under this administration involves state law regarding the role they should play in developing the Comprehensive Education Plan (CEP), hiring principals, and establishing the school budget. In 2007, the chancellor strengthened the authority of principals to make the final determination on the budget and CEP. In an appeals process, the state education commissioner ruled in 2008 that the principal cannot have final decision-making authority over the CEP, but instead must work collaboratively with the SLTs to develop the CEP. In response, the chancellor revised SLT guidelines, although critics still condemn the vague language requiring principals to "consult" with the SLT to develop the budget and use "consensus-based decision-making processes."[39]

Community Education Councils

The community education councils (CECs) are required through state law to oversee policy for elementary and middle schools within each of the thirty-two districts. The state instituted CECs in 2003 following the elimination of the community school boards. One stated purpose of the CECs was to focus on parent rather than community participation; CEC members now must be public school parents, while prior to these changes any community member could serve.[40] Responsibilities of CECs also include "approving school zoning lines, holding hearings on the capital plan, evaluating community superintendents, and providing input on other important policy issues."[41]

Reports suggest that two of the thirty-four CECs are not functioning, the number of candidates for the position has decreased over time, and many elections are uncontested.[42] In 2009, the DOE hired Grassroots Initiative to oversee the CEC elections and to encourage more parents to become involved, but the problem remains.[43] "I think they're very aware there's not a lot of authority under the current law," one CEC president told a reporter in attempting to account for the low levels of involvement.[44] Similar to the controversies surrounding SLT powers, the state and DOE continue to grapple over the responsibilities and powers of CECs. We discuss some of these points of contention later in the context of the battle over the extension of mayoral control.

Support Organizations and Networks

Although the specifics have changed over time, a reform strategy since at least 2007 has included encouraging or requiring schools to align with support organizations, which included nonrofts and some universities, to expand their capacity to undertake their new responsibilities.[45] Some support organizations have emphasized parent engagement while others have not. The DOE's stance of devolving responsibilities permits schools to select partners that will take parent engagement seriously, but it does not mandate or systematically encourage them to.[46]

Rival Visions of Democratic Engagement: The Battle Over Mayoral Control

As the previous section illustrated, DOE officials see collective engagement as a potential source of good ideas and feedback on what is and is not working. They mistrust calls for more active forms of engagement (what we call *advocacy* and *strong democracy* in figure 2-1, cell D), suspecting that some activists use such processes to mask a self-interest in resisting change, and that others hold sincere but naive notions that effective policy can be based on consensus. As one DOE official explained, "For the most part, placing consensus at the high end of the value hierarchy often leads to either stagnation or least-common-denominator solutions."[47] This impatience with the prospect of taking the time to build a supportive coalition before acting seems largely due to a sense of urgency, legitimizing an approach of "act now and make corrections later." The rationale for this approach is based at least in part on sincere indignation at the persistent low performance of many NYC schools and an assessment that the system is incapable of reforming itself.

This impatience with discussion and debate that delays active intervention is also linked to and buttressed by a broader and more philosophical vision of governance. The administration accepts the premise that the community broadly has a legitimate role to play in shaping policy, but prefers that this role take the form of what we term in figure 2-1 accountability through mayoral elections. In place of an active and day-to-day role for parents in setting goals and priorities, this view of public engagement has a broader array of voters and groups (including but extending beyond parents and teachers) exercising their agenda-setting power by endorsing or rejecting an administration in mayoral elections. In addition to broadening participation, the model calls for sharpening accountability by reducing checks and balances that diffuse responsibility, empower interest groups, and demand endless bargaining and compromise at the expense of enacting a coherent plan. Candidates compete by presenting clear and distinct platforms, and once elected should be able to put their ideas into place and get them sufficiently developed for voters to have something to evaluate and respond to in the next election. Under this model, mayoral control is the answer to critics' claims that DOE policies fail to provide sufficient opportunity for parents to shape policies.

The battle over whether and in what form to extend mayoral control of NYC schools provides insights into how this conception of school governance clashes with notions of strong democracy as favored by some parent and community-based groups. Failure to understand the depth and breadth of this fundamental clash in perspectives risks fueling a political backlash and may substantially exacerbate the challenge of sustaining reform.

Broad Pressure for Greater Engagement

Despite the initial agreement on the need for dramatic change in school governance to remedy a fragmented system, it was not long before many concluded that Bloomberg was overstepping the spirit of the 2002 law. "Before the ink was dry," as one legislative leader from that era put it, "the mayor began to do things clearly contrary to discussions we had about how to implement."[48]

A sense that centralization had gone too far was crystallized when the mayor arranged the firing and replacement of three Panel on Education Policy (PEP) members who disagreed with him on a decision about social promotion. The chancellor's use of executive power to limit the authority of district superintendents by removing their oversight of principals and reducing their jurisdictional authority by assigning them systemwide responsibilities was another flashpoint. Thinning out the middle layers between the central office and the schools, one legislator suggested, meant "there isn't a structure anymore where there's somebody on the local level who knows the local schools."[49] Furthermore, the parent leadership components of the DOE's parent engagement portfolio—the PTAs, SLTs, and CECs—had been required by state law to provide some means for collective parent input to decision making at different system levels, but over the life of mayoral control had become substantially weakened.

During fall 2008, three groups emerged, representing three distinct positions on mayoral control.[50] Although the administration was ready with the argument that any change to the mayoral control legislation represented a return to a discredited past, these groups—even the one initiated by the mayor's own allies—agreed that there were problems with the current system—especially in the area of parent and community engagement. The groups differed on whether, and what type of, changes should be made to the mayoral control law (see figure 2-2). Taken together, the three groups reveal that there was a broader and more diverse set of interests than the administration was acknowledging. Here we briefly describe the three groups and their relative positions, and the emergence of one group, the Campaign for Better Schools, and its ability to give legitimacy to a counternarrative to that of the mayor and DOE. We will discuss in more detail how the Campaign's platform for improving mayoral control advanced stronger democratic participation in school governance.

The Three Groups

The crux of the mayoral control debate was around the degree of authority granted the mayor, and by extension the degree to which opportunities to shape policy and priorities were limited to the arena of mayoral elections every four years. The core of this struggle, which took place in the media and at public events, was the three groups' differing views on changes to the PEP, which, if enacted, would provide checks and balances to the mayor's control.

Learn NY. Learn NY ("Learn") included institutions with close ties to the mayor and the DOE as well as charter school advocates and operators that could mobilize charter school parents. In recalling the impetus to create Learn, one member of the administration stated that it was to "create a counternarrative" to those who criticized the administration.

Learn pressed for continuation of mayoral control, with no change to the PEP and ultimately to the mayor's authority. Nonetheless, one of its chief spokesmen, Geoffrey Canada, did acknowledge the need for improvement in the area of parent engagement, stating that parents needed more information provided in a more timely way.[51]

Of the three groups, Learn was by far the best funded. There had been rumors that Bloomberg himself had funded Learn, but in August 2009 it was revealed that Bill Gates and Eli Broad personally had provided Learn with a substantial portion of its budget of several million dollars.[52]

A media analysis we conducted indicated that Learn had limited success in portraying itself as an authentic voice of parents.[53] The fact that many of its supporting groups were recipients of city or DOE funds, or even beneficiaries of support from Bloomberg himself, contributed to suspicions they were part of "the strategy the mayor has, for these last eight years, which is. . . to buy off community groups."[54] As one journalist put it, "I don't think the elected officials were fully persuaded that these [Learn NY representatives] were real people . . . "[55] The fact that Learn virtually faded away when the debate went to Albany added to the perception that Learn had no real roots.

Parent Commission on School Governance and Mayoral Control. The Parent Commission on School Governance and Mayoral Control ("Parent Commission") was at the other end of the spectrum from Learn; it was an all-volunteer organization with proposals for legislative changes that came the closest to calling for an outright end to mayoral control and a return to the structures that the administration argued

FIGURE 2-2 **The playing field: The three parent groups**

	Who	When	How
Keep it	**Learn NY** **Proposed that mayoral control be extended** • Coalition of 60–70 community groups, parents, and religious leaders • Some had received funding from the city, the DOE, and possibly Bloomberg • Constituency included many low-income charter school parents	• Emerged in fall 2008 • Dissolved after mayoral control was renewed in August 2009	• Advocated for no change to PEP but greater transparency and participation, and argued this could be done without changing statutes • Gave testimony at Assembly and Senate hearings, citywide forums, CEC meetings, and media interviews • Coalition funded with an estimated $4 million from philanthropists Bill Gates and Eli Broad
Change it	**Campaign for Better Schools** **Proposed that mayoral control be continued with significant changes to the law** • Coalition of 26 advocacy, organizing, research, and policy organizations • Constituency included a spectrum of low-income parents and youth from diverse racial and ethnic groups, including immigrants	• Formed in summer 2008 • Disbanded officially June 30, 2009, but continued activity through August 2009, and groups continue to collaborate informally around issues of mutual interest	• Developed a platform recommending that mayoral control legislation be amended to provide checks and balances at the level of the PEP, as well as greater transparency, and public participation • Organized press events, speak outs, rallies; attended Assembly and Senate hearings, CEC meetings, and Parent Association meetings • Supported by an estimated $445,000, largely from the Donors' Education Collaborative (DEC)
End it	**Parent Commission** **Proposed that mayoral control be allowed to end, with recommendations for reforming NYC school governance** • Group of individuals, including members and leaders of the CECs and Presidents' Councils, and those associated with iCope or Class Size Matters • Many constituents were middle class parents from Manhattan's upper West and upper and lower East sides	• Formed in summer 2008 • Some members wanted to disband after their recommendations were released in spring 2009, but activity continued through August 2009, and groups continue to collaborate around issues of mutual interest	• Developed a "Recommendations" document that proposed legislative changes creating a board of education, restoration of the community school districts and CDECs as the basic units of governance. • Conducted press interviews, met with legislators, and planned rallies, held public forums and attended Assembly and Senate hearings • Did not receive outside funding; staffed solely by volunteers

Position on mayoral control

had been proven failures. The Parent Commission consisted of members of NYC's formal structures for collective parental engagement: PTAs/PAs, CECs, and SLTs. It focused on revamping the formal governance institutions to return to greater parent input. For example, it recommended revitalizing the community school districts together with CECs "to be the basic unit of school governance."[56]

Even though the Parent Commission was an all-volunteer organization of members from all five boroughs, our media analysis indicated that coverage of the Parent Commission, while substantial during the heat of the debate in May, June, and July 2009, was mainly in just a few sources.[57] The Parent Commission was active in Albany during the period of legislative negotiations, but they had little experience there and their impact on the ultimate legislation and amendments was limited.[58]

The Campaign for Better Schools. The Campaign for Better Schools ("the Campaign") was in the middle of the continuum between Learn and the Parent Commission. We had the opportunity to closely follow its activity as part of a two-year study from May 2008 to May 2010 for the Donors Education Collaborative (DEC). We concluded that the depth and breadth of the constituency it represented forced the mayor and his supporters to work harder to defend their position than they might have initially anticipated.

The Campaign consisted of coalitions of constituency-based groups such as the Coalition for Educational Justice (CEJ) and the New York Immigration Coalition (NYIC), along with public school advocacy, policy, and research organizations. Demographically, the Campaign's membership tended to be minority groups in economically struggling neighborhoods and new immigrants citywide.

Among its first tasks, the Campaign conducted research into mayoral control in other cities and learned that NYC represented an extreme version in its concentration of power in the mayor. The Campaign positioned itself as being for continuing mayoral control, but with significant changes to the legislation that would rebalance the mayor's authority. The Campaign's recommendations included making official structures like the SLTs and CECs more representative and increasing their role in policy decisions as well as expanding the processes for public input. Its framework for change—greater checks and balances to the mayor's authority, increased transparency of achievement and financial data, and expanded public participation—resonated with many parents and community-based organizations and a number of legislators.

The Campaign's strategy for building a strong coalition and for mobilizing its constituency had several features that strengthened its claim of—and increased its recognition in the media as—being a fresh voice speaking for parents and community, and not simply wanting to protect a privileged old guard. The groups that made up the Campaign were well-established, often multi-issue, organizations. Many had wide reach across the city and were embedded in local communities and/or constituencies.

Several of the member groups were constituency-based organizations and coalitions that had strong relationships with members who represented new and emerging civic actors in the city, including immigrants, English language learners, low-income African American and Hipanic communities, and youth. The Campaign was able to get large turnouts at its own rallies and press events as well as at other public events. Further, Campaign constituents, because of the extensive process of education about school governance that had accompanied the creation of their platform for improving mayoral control, gave clear and consistent messages at these events. Although some of the groups received city or DOE funding for their core agendas, they agreed to stand by the platform once it had been formed. Finally, in press accounts, quotes from Campaign members were more likely to be attributed to a parent than a staff member—strengthening the Campaign's image as representing parents' perspectives. One media observer noted that, as "opposed to Learn [which] had money, [the Campaign] had the people. . . people who were angry about something. . . "[59]

The Campaign, of the three groups, had the greatest capacity to carry the debate to Albany, where the state legislature would have the ultimate say. Several of its member organizations had previous experience working together in Albany around issues of fiscal equity and public education. These earlier efforts—and successes—had increased the Campaign's visibility and earned its members the reputation of being knowledgeable players in the education arena. In the next section, we will show how the Campaign was able to gain traction for its vision of strong democratic governance embedded in its platform.

Competing Visions of What Counts as Genuine Engagement

With the three groups vying for the attention and support of the public and lawmakers, a wider range of possibilities were being seriously considered in the mayoral control debate than most observers had predicted in early 2008.[60] The Campaign's position offers a clear example of a strong democracy vision of public engagement (cell D in figure 2-1). For the Campaign, as well as the Parent Commission, it was critical for parents and community members to be able to influence policies, even to share in their development, not just every four years, but as they were being formulated.

Having established itself as a "pragmatic" voice in the debate, the Campaign got a full hearing for its platform recommendations. While it did not win its bid to change the balance of power on the PEP, the final legislation and amendments reflected a number of the other changes it had pushed for. The Campaign's critique of parent engagement under Bloomberg, embedded in its platform recommendations, centered around two dimensions: (1) the amount of *power* parents and community members should have in the system and (2) structures that ensure that parents can act *collectively* to have input in policy decisions.

The Campaign's platform included elements designed to increase the power and capacity of parents, students, and community members to participate in decision making. The platform called for giving the SLTs more input at the school level by restoring their contribution and oversight of the principal in aligning the school's comprehensive education plan with the annual school budget. It also called for principals to hold public meetings to provide the necessary information so that the school's community could weigh in on planning and budgeting as a means for increasing the capacity of parents to participate fully and effectively on the SLTs.

While power at the school level is critical, there are some policies and functions that have an impact at the community or neighborhood level, and the DOE's decisions about the role of the district superintendents and the CECs were perceived to have undercut parents' ability to address concerns at this level. The DOE's changes to the authority and role of district superintendents eliminated the administrative level between the central administration and the school, effectively removing the means by which the public could have input to policies with community-wide impact. "I think there is a general consensus . . . that many issues are local and you can't solve everything from the bottom of Manhattan," suggested one of our interviewees, with a front seat to the implementation of the DOE's parent and community engagement strategies.[61] The Campaign's platform called for restoring the geographically bounded jurisdiction of the district superintendents as well as some of their powers, particularly as these related to decision making about school closings.

School closings were a particularly sore spot and represented a significant chasm between the administration and many in the public. For the administration, closing schools that were underenrolled or that had failed to make progress on tests was an integral part of its mission, and it viewed parents as too subjective when it came to their neighborhood schools. "Parents didn't want it closed," a key official observed about one illustrative case, "but if you looked at the feedback, it was about nostalgia. And it was about communication, not feeling as if they had been brought along in the process. . . "[62] The Campaign emphasized that parents and community members should be informed about the rationale for school closings well in advance and that they should have input into the decisions. The Campaign platform called for advance public notice and the completion of an education impact statement that would help parents and community members make informed judgments. The platform also called for the CECs to be able to vote on or appeal these decisions to the PEP. It intended to provide levers for collective action codified in the law that would enable the public to influence policy in a timely way, exemplifying the strong democracy vision that the Campaign was advancing.

To bolster parents' and community members' power, the Campaign recommended provisions that would increase the public's capacity to monitor the progress of reform. For one, the Campaign recommended changes to the Independent Budget Office (IBO) as another way to hold the mayor accountable by assuring the trustworthiness of information on the school district's strategies, academic progress, and spending. One of the recommendations it pushed for was the establishment of an independent center that would train both parents and students as another way to build the capacity of public actors to participate in policy decision-making.[63]

Most of the media attention following the passage of the mayoral control bill was on the mayor's retention of control of the PEP. Less attention was paid initially to the many new provisions in the legislation and amendments that directly reflected those elements of the Campaign platform that strengthened parents' power through various levers for input, action, and capacity building. Those provisions, if parents and the public took full advantage of them, provided opportunities to realize the strong democracy vision that the Campaign forwarded on behalf of a significant share of public school constituents. In the next section, we examine recent events and show how these elements added to the legislation are playing out in the months since it was enacted, and consider the legislation's implications for the future of mayoral control in New York City.

The Extension of Mayoral Control and Its Aftermath

The battle leading up to the mayoral control legislation had many twists and turns, and the final weeks were made even more chaotic by a series of unrelated political and organizational upheavals in Albany, which resulted in NYC briefly reverting back to pre-mayoral-control governance structures during a Senate impasse. Ultimately, the Senate passed the Assembly's bill on August 6, 2009, along with four amendments that the DOE agreed to enact regardless of whether they later passed through the Assembly and became law. The most prominent among these was a provision establishing a parent training center.

Because of efforts by the Campaign, Parent Commission, and others, the mayor and his team had to work harder to defend their interests in Albany and had to accept some changes, despite their original negotiating stance that any changes risked weakening the institutional structures on which their reforms were built. Measured by legislative changes, the score sheet indicated that the mayor had largely achieved his goal of resisting any alteration to his and the chancellor's authority.[64] On the key battles around checks and balances and the composition and autonomy of the PEP, Bloomberg and Klein had held their ground. On issues related to more transparent and independent handling of financial and achievement data, they gave up some ground, but they did so on points they had never aggressively resisted, in part because some key elements within their own constituency thought such changes were a good idea. On greater citizen participation, the concessions initially were barely acknowledged in the media. Aside from establishing the parent training center, which has yet to take form, groups that championed stronger forms of community engagement won what seemed at the time to be largely symbolic victories, including the requirement that school closures require an impact statement, a public hearing, and six months' notice.

Yet the battle appears to have had residual consequences that can prove meaningful. Several factors have produced subtle but important changes in the political landscape, creating room for public challenge of administration policies and seeding elements of what might develop into a vision and organizational foundation for an alternative view of public education reform.

In November 2009, Michael Bloomberg won reelection to his third term, but by a considerably smaller margin (51 percent to 46 percent) than most observers had expected. While the mayor and his Democratic opponent traded charges and countercharges about who would do a better job of running the public schools, exit polls suggested that other issues—most notably the economic collapse and the need for job creation—had eclipsed education as a deciding factor for most voters. Significantly, candidates for other offices featured criticism of the mayor and chancellor in their successful campaigns and offered indications that they would use their new positions to stand up for a different vision of school reform. For example, in campaigning for the position of public advocate, generally considered the second-highest-ranking citywide elected office, Bill de Blasio had supported the general notion of mayoral control but sharply criticized the mayor's governing style. Similarly, John Liu, in his campaign for city comptroller, promised to provide greater transparency and oversight over the DOE, particularly its achievement and accountability data, and proposed to audit the administration's decision-making process around school closures.[65] Perhaps the most dramatic mark of the changing landscape was the January 2010 PEP meeting on nineteen planned school closures, attended by two thousand people. Other schools had been closed in the past—over one hundred in New York City in the past decade, including twelve in 2009 and fifteen in 2008—but this meeting overshadowed previous ones in terms of visibility and sympathetic coverage. Although the provisions for impact statements and public hearings had received little attention when mayoral control was extended, they seem to have played an important role in setting the stage for this massive protest and for ongoing legal challenges to the administration's closure and turnaround policies.

The degree to which the extension law shifted the landscape by opening the field for judicial intervention is illustrated by the March 26, 2010, decision by Justice Joan B. Lobis of the State Supreme Court in Manhattan to block the DOE's planned closure of nineteen schools based on violations of the law's requirement that school closures follow detailed educational impact statements. The UFT, NAACP, and other plaintiffs, including the Alliance for Quality Education—one of the Campaign's key member organizations—had argued that the PEP vote to close the schools was improper because the nominal impact statements were vague and formulaic and failed to address key community concerns. According to the *New York Times*, "Justice Lobis. . . said the new law 'created a public process with meaningful community involvement regarding the chancellor's proposals.'" The entire mayoral control law must be enforced "not merely the portion extending mayoral control of the schools."[66]

In July 2010, the appellate court unanimously reaffirmed this ruling, rejecting the city's claim that it had substantially complied with the state law. Coverage of the legislature's extension of mayoral control had focused more on opponents' failure to shake the mayor's dominance of the PEP, but the Campaign quietly believed that some of the concessions it won would later prove to be important.[67] What is clear is that the change in the law gave opponents of the administration's policies an additional weapon, one that they will likely use, or at least threaten to use, again.

Parental Engagement and the Sustainability of Reform: Implications for New York City and Elsewhere

In broad terms, there are at least three reasons a city or district might encourage parent and community engagement: (1) to engage others as partners to *make the policies and practices it has adopted work better*; (2) to enlist a broader range of ideas to *formulate better policies and practices*; (3) to create a broader and more fully engaged constituency to *create a coalition more likely to sustain the policies and practices over time*. These are not necessarily incompatible goals, but in practice an emphasis on one often comes at the expense of the others.

The ardor and urgency with which the administration launched its reform efforts, combined with suspicion that many of the most mobilized opponents were invested in the status quo and therefore part of the problem, appears to have made DOE leaders wary of calls for extended consultation and debate. While admitting that they did not have all the answers, they had confidence they could learn on the run, and to the extent they needed additional knowledge they were inclined to look to individuals and organizations that brought fresh ideas and were not locked into traditional ways of getting things done. The administration was concerned early on about sustainability, but it believed the first stage of reform required eliminating obstacles and getting new procedures into place. The confidence of the mayor and his team that they were doing the right thing was combined with the belief that a silent majority within the city either supported them from the first or would come to support them once they experienced the benefits of the reforms. In that sense, sustainability would take care of itself. A supportive coalition would follow in the wake of the reforms' successes and be validated first by the mayor's reelection and eventually by the election of a successor who would campaign on a promise to retain the core elements or, even if tempted to do otherwise, would find those elements too entrenched and well defended to dismantle.

In our view, the administration failed to appreciate an alternative view of community engagement as a more robust approach to creating the constituencies needed to sustain reform over time. The demand for a stronger and more clearly defined collective role for parents and community, including the establishment of priorities and the formulation of policies, fueled resentment that was deeper and broader than the administration anticipated. Efforts to characterize protesting groups as professional advocates reflexively protecting a status quo in which they enjoyed special privilege failed to reckon with the fact that many unmobilized parents saw these groups as more legitimate. It is true and important that the mayor won the political battle over extending mayoral control with no change to his authority over the PEP and was elected to a second and third term. The multi-issue nature of mayoral elections, however, makes it problematic to interpret this as an endorsement of his educational policies; the economy, safety, and managerial competence were powerful considerations in the minds of NYC voters in November 2010. Mayor Bloomberg's winning edge seems to have depended not on swaying public school parents but on convincing others that his school reform efforts were on the right track; exit polls suggest the mayor won only 43 percent of the votes of public school parents, compared with 55 percent for his Democratic competitor.[68] This fact—that mayoral elections do not hinge on education even when a mayor makes that a defining issue—helps explain why parent and community groups concerned about public schools remain wary of a governance system that rests primarily on those elections as the mechanism for affirmative engagement in shaping the local educational agenda.

At this point, with the advantage of a third term, it is possible that the administration will nonetheless succeed in implanting many of its initiatives and make it unfeasible for future mayors and chancellors to undo key elements of their reforms. However, pursuing a strategy to get policies and programs in place rapidly, in the expectation that they will create their own sustaining coalition, is very risky. An unusual concentration of formal and informal power made it possible for the mayor and chancellor to move much more quickly and authoritatively in changing policies and practices than could be expected in other places where multiple veto points and powerful rivals make the up-front challenges of winning legislative victories or negotiating compromise the first and foremost issue of concern. The high visibility of NYC on the national stage made it an attractive place for national foundations and philanthropists to invest, and the home-grown wealth of the local financial community provided critical enabling resources as well. For other cities and districts, which are not likely to have the full range of formal and informal resources that the mayor and chancellor could muster, naively attempting to replicate their theory of action could prove to be a huge mistake.

Even in New York City and despite the seeming victory in the mayoral control battle, the backlash is strong and the potential exists that a counter-movement, animated by a different vision of community engagement, will force the administration to back off or rethink some of its initiatives. The persistent unhappiness and potential for it to crystallize into effective opposition was manifested in the strong negative reaction to Mayor Bloomberg's announcement in early November 2010 that Joel Klein would be stepping down and would be replaced by Cathleeen Black, a publishing executive. Interest groups already opposed to the administration vociferously complained about her lack of relevant experience, and public opinion polls revealed widespread dissatisfaction with the choice.[69] In the context of this opposition, and to the surprise of many, the state commissioner for education refused to approve Black unless she named a Chief Academic Officer. The mayor acceded. At the time of writing, it remains to be seen whether the opposition consolidates or whether Black, once in office, finds ways to further institutionalize the city's reforms during Bloomberg's remaining three years in office. Regardless, it seems likely that these competing visions will be an important fulcrum as candidates and supporters form the messages and alliances that will determine the next administration and how it will define and execute its own agenda for school reform.

3

Financing K–12 Education in the Bloomberg Years, 2002–2008

Leanna Stiefel and Amy Ellen Schwartz

Under the leadership of Mayor Michael Bloomberg and Chancellor Joel Klein, the New York City (NYC) school system has undergone a change in curriculum, organization, and, reportedly, outcomes since 2002.[1] Improving schools and school districts is always difficult, however, and some argue that sizeable inflows of resources made the transformation in NYC possible. This chapter analyzes the sources, levels of, and growth in, resources for K–12 education during the first two terms of Bloomberg's mayoral leadership and Klein's leadership of the New York City Department of Education (DOE). More specifically, we examine the amount of resources available for Bloomberg's Children First initiative, the funding sources, and, to some extent, how these resources were used.[2]

To preview the results, total revenues rose from $14.2 billion to $19.5 billion (adjusted for inflation) between 2002 and 2008, representing an increase of roughly $5,800 per pupil.[3] As detailed below, this translated into roughly $5,000 more for each student enrolled in a DOE school.[4] The composition of students shifted significantly, with the portion of special education students increasing over time. Teacher salaries increased about 25 percent, including fringe benefits. In addition, the distribution of resources across elementary and middle schools became more closely aligned with school characteristics and needs. By 2008, a greater share of the variation in resources across elementary and middle schools was explained by characteristics used in the mayor's Fair Student Funding (FSF) allocation formula, although these characteristics explained little of the variation across high schools in any year.

The following section of the paper provides a national and historical context of school finance. We then turn to an analysis of the growth in overall resources from state, local, and federal sources, followed by an examination of how resources are distributed across general and special education programs; across elementary, middle, and high schools; and across schools. We also explore the private/philanthropic support garnered during the first two Bloomberg terms.

U.S. and Historical Context for School Financing

Public K–12 education in the United States is decentralized in its organization and financing, with responsibilities lodged in fifty different state systems. While each state constitution contains some sort of "education clause" broadly defining the state's education responsibilities, the U.S. Constitution is silent on the provision of education services. New York's state constitution's education clause, for example, reads: "The legislature shall provide for the maintenance and support of a system of free common schools, wherein all the children of this state may be educated."[5]

Although there is significant variation in the legal provisions for education across states, all states (except Hawaii) provide education services through a system of sub-state school districts financed through a combination of federal, state, and local revenues.[6] While locally raised revenues (and property taxes in particular) once provided the majority of support for public education across the country, there is now considerable regional variation in the share of revenues provided by federal, state, and local governments. The Northeast, for example, relies less on state and federal sources, but compensates with higher local shares.[7]

In addition to government revenues, support for public schools is also provided through philanthropy—especially for charter schools. Although the revenue share of nonpublic funds is very small, as discussed more fully below, these funds may serve special purposes and thus be valuable in reform efforts.

With regard to New York State, while there has been some variation since the late 1980s, state support currently accounts for less than 45 percent of total per pupil revenues. Further, while total per pupil revenue has steadily increased, the growth in state revenues has been variable, with local (and to a lesser extent federal) revenues filling in. In 2008 New York State's elementary and secondary revenues totaled $52.1 billion: $2.6 billion from federal sources, $23.6 billion from state sources, and $26 billion from local and other sources (see figure 3-1).

Although school finance policy and research has focused largely on school district resources, the allocation of resources from districts to their schools is critical in large districts with many schools and students. (New York City's more than one million students and fifteen hundred schools make it the largest U.S. school district.) Although the allocation process may be fairly straightforward and transparent in small districts, resource distribution in large districts is far from trivial, and understanding equity and efficiency in education requires examining the intradistrict distribution of resources as well as the overall level of federal, state, and local support.

FIGURE 3-1 **New York State total revenue by source, elementary and secondary education**

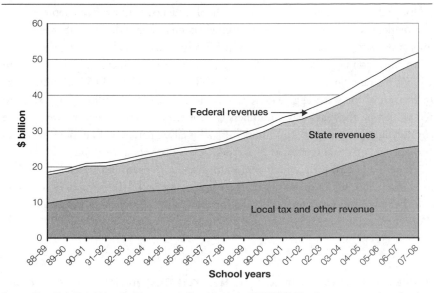

Source: New York State Education Department, Fiscal Analysis, 2006–2007, http://www.oms.nysed.gov/faru/PDFDocuments/2008_Analysis.pdf.

New York City Education Revenue

How much money did the NYC school system have to finance Children First and other initiatives? To gain insight into the available educational resources, we use revenue data from the New York State Education Department (NYSED) to compare the experience of NYC to that of the other districts in New York State and data from the National Center for Education Statistics (NCES) to compare NYC to other large districts in the United States.[8] Our purpose is to document and describe the changes in revenues; determining the causes of particular changes in financing NYC schools is beyond the scope of this paper.

The level and growth in NYC's resources in the 1996–2008 period could have been shaped by a variety of factors.[9] These include a strong economy during the late 1990s, a national recession in 2001–2002, the passage of No Child Left Behind (NCLB) in 2002, an increase in school accountability both from NCLB and the state, changes in the compositions or costs of students or compliance with federal or state laws, and a decision against New York State on state financing of NYC schools in 2001 (*Campaign for Fiscal Equity [CFE] v. State of New York*).[10] This final factor deserves additional explanation, particularly given its long-awaited resolution. Under the ruling, the courts required New York State to provide the city with additional funds to fulfill its constitutional obligation of a "sound basic education" (defined as a "meaningful high school education") for all public school students. While the case represented a landmark victory for the city, it was extremely contentious and, due to the recession's impact on state total revenues, the awarded funding has yet to be fully received.[11]

In the Bloomberg years, New York City's total revenues increased $5.3 billion in 2008 inflation-adjusted dollars, from $14.2 billion in 2002 to $19.5 billion in 2008. In the rest of the state, aggregate revenues increased by $5.1 billion, from $27.5 to $32.6 billion. These aggregate numbers do not tell the whole story, however, since enrollments also changed. To address this, we analyze patterns of per pupil revenues available to NYC and the rest of New York State's districts since 1996.[12]

In per pupil terms, the Bloomberg years saw increases in total revenue of $5,785 in NYC and $3,205 in the rest of the state (see figure 3-2).[13] The growth in total revenue per pupil was faster for NYC than for the rest of the state both before and after Bloomberg assumed office, although the disparity was smaller after 2002.[14] While

FIGURE 3-2 **New York State (without New York City) and New York City, total revenue per pupil, 1996–2008***

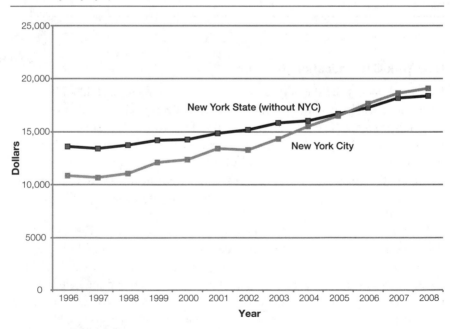

*CPI adjusted with a base year of 2008; total revenue is the sum of state, local, and federal revenue; pupils measured using duplicated combined adjusted average daily membership.

Source: New York State Education Department.

the city began with lower total revenue per pupil than other New York State districts in 2002, three years later it matched the state and by 2008 received $19,075 in total per pupil revenues compared with $18,374 in other New York State districts.

To provide some context for NYC's large per pupil revenues, we compare per pupil expenditures across the twenty-five highest-spending large public school districts in 2007, the latest year available from the National Center for Education Statistics.[15] Only Boston spent more ($21,801) than NYC's $20,162 per pupil, and Washington, D.C., spent approximately the same ($20,029). NYC's spending is high, but not uniquely so.[16]

What are the sources of funds in NYC and New York State? Unsurprisingly, there are different patterns in per pupil revenues across funding sources between the city and the rest of the state's districts. *Federal* revenue, although a small portion of total per pupil revenue, was always higher in NYC, although those revenues grew more slowly before 2002 and more rapidly after 2002, compared with the rest of the state. By 2008, NYC was receiving more than twice the per pupil amount received by the rest of the state in federal dollars ($1,428 compared with $630). The city's revenue from *state* sources, on the other hand, was lower than the rest of the state and grew at about the same rate before 2002. From 2002 forward, NYC grew considerably faster, achieving parity in 2005 and receiving over $600 more per pupil by 2008 ($8,820 versus $8,207). In contrast, NYC's per pupil *local* revenue remained below the rest of the state throughout this period.[17] It grew more rapidly than the state's before 2002 and at the same rate afterward. The city ended the period in 2008 with $8,827 per pupil compared with the rest of the state's $9,537.

In summary, compared with the rest of the state, NYC's per pupil revenues increased more between 2002 and 2008. The rest of the state experienced an increase of just over $3,000 per pupil: 2.1 percent of the increase from federal sources, 31.7 percent from state sources, and 66.3 percent from local sources. New York City, however, received nearly $5,800 additional inflation-adjusted dollars per pupil (on a base of $13,290 in 2002), with federal revenues accounting for 7.2 percent, state revenues 34.5 percent, and local revenues 58.2 percent of that growth. This is a striking increase in revenues available to finance new initiatives and improve the performance of the city's students.

At the same time, this increase could be matched (or even outpaced) by increases in the number or share of high-cost students or, more broadly, increases in the cost of education. The factors usually contributing to higher costs include an increased concentration of poor, special education, and English language learners (ELLs); increased student mobility in and out of the school system or across schools; and increased costs of comparable quality school inputs such as teachers, equipment, or physical plants. In the next section, we present evidence speaking to some of these factors and explore how the expenditures were distributed across broad programs, levels of education, and schools.

Funding Across Schools Within New York City

To date, there has been limited research on the distribution of funding across schools within districts, largely due to data constraints. The recent availability of detailed school-level data in NYC (as well as in Ohio, Florida, and Texas), however, has yielded several studies offering insight on disparities among schools. Perhaps most relevant, Rubenstein et al. use school-level data from NYC, Cleveland, and Columbus to explore how per pupil funding and teacher qualifications vary across schools.[18] They find that higher-poverty schools receive more funding per student—usually a result of smaller class sizes—but lag behind other schools in teacher qualifications. Research on the variation in resources across schools in other districts finds similar results.[19] More recently, Bruce Baker, using school level data from Texas and Ohio, finds that resources vary in predictable ways within districts (often according to student need), but that even well-funded schools in poor districts are under-funded relative to neighboring schools in more advantaged districts.[20]

Although there is relatively little research examining the intradisrict distribution of financial resources across schools, the related literature examining the distribution of teachers finds (almost uniformly) that schools with lower shares of students who are poor, minority, or low performing have more experienced and more qualified teachers.[21] There are many possible reasons for this distribution of teachers. Although sorting through these is outside the scope of this paper, one explanation is that a uniform salary schedule—which prevents variation in salaries across schools—combined with teacher transfer privileges and position-based budgeting have disadvantaged high-poverty and high-minority schools.[22] Under this system, principals in high-need schools have little leverage to reallocate resources toward staffing to attract and retain teachers.

Much of the interest in within-district resource allocation has been driven by a well-publicized push (by the Fordham Institute, among others[23]) for large districts to allocate resources using weighted student funding (WSF), in which resources are allocated from districts to schools based on the number and characteristics of enrolled students, as well as features of the schools themselves, such as grades served or size. In general, WSF systems propose that schools receive a baseline per capita allocation that is adjusted (weighted) for students who have specific educational needs or who are economically or academically disadvantaged.[24]

New York City's Allocation of Revenues Across Schools: Historical and Fair Student Funding

Historically, NYC's budgeting process for its schools has been opaque, although it has yielded patterns similar to those found in other cities (in the studies reviewed above). Before Bloomberg/Klein and mayoral control, the city schools were administered through thirty-two community school districts (CSDs) responsible for elementary and middle schools, five high school divisions, one citywide special education division, and several other occasional ad hoc divisions, such as the Chancellor's District.[25] In this system, funding flowed from the DOE through the CSDs and came with various program mandates or constraints.[26] Funding teacher positions was the largest constraint on reallocating resources, although school funding did vary from what would have been predicted either on the sole basis of the teachers and administrators working in schools or the characteristics of students in the schools. Simply put, there was no single strict formula applied to all schools or even all schools within a CSD. Nevertheless, schools with higher concentrations of poor students received some categorical funds (e.g., Title I) and generally received slightly more money per pupil and more teachers (albeit with less experience).

In 2008, the DOE began implementing a version of WSF, titled Fair Student Funding (FSF), distributing funds according to a set of student weights (table 3-1).[27]

TABLE 3-1 **New York City Fair Student Funding weights for the 2008–2009 academic year**

	K–Grade 5	Grade 6–8	Grade 9–12
Grade weights	1.00	1.08	1.03
Need weights			
Academic intervention			
Poverty	0.24		
Achievement—well below standards*	0.40	0.50	0.40
Achievement—below standards*	0.25	0.35	0.25
ELL	0.40	0.50	0.50
Special education			
Less than 20%	0.56	0.56	0.56
20–60%	0.68	0.68	0.68
Greater than 60% (self-contained)	1.23	1.23	0.73
Greater than 60% (integrated)	2.28	2.28	2.52
Portfolio weights			
Specialized audition schools	n/a	n/a	0.35
Specialized academic schools	n/a	n/a	0.25
Career and Technical Education (CTE) schools	n/a	n/a	0.05–0.26
Transfer schools	n/a	n/a	0.40

Source: "See Your School's Budget" on the NYCDOE website.

Note: Achievement weights are only given to fourth- and fifth-graders in elementary schools, although these may be eliminated in future years. Weights are identical to those for the 2009–2010 and 2010–2011 academic years.

We include these factors in our regression models: poverty = % free lunch; ELL = % LEP; special education = % resource room and % full-time special education; and achievement = % level 1 fourth-grade ELA, % level 1 eighth-grade ELA, and % failing the math Regents (high schools only).

FSF was launched with the distribution of a small amount of "new" funds, with the intention of increasing the amount and coverage over time as hold-harmless provisions were phased out. Importantly, FSF was aimed at shifting the allocation of resources across schools, while giving principals autonomy over how funds were spent. For example, a school with higher shares of ELL students would receive additional funds, which the principal could choose to spend on programs or teachers only partly related to enhancing English proficiency.

To examine funding across schools within NYC during the Bloomberg years, we use data from the city's school-based expenditure reports (SBERs), which break down school-level expenditures into detailed categories.[28] We briefly discuss changes in several of these expenditure categories, focusing on changes in four broad categories: overall total, total, direct, and classroom dollars. (See table 3-2 for definitions of each category of SBER expenditure and student type used in this paper.) Overall total dollars are the most comprehensive measure of resources and include *pass-throughs*, the latter accounting for contracted services for special education students and charter school expenditures, plus a few other smaller categories. Total expenditures (without pass-throughs) are a subset of overall total expenditures, and include direct spending as well as various systemwide expenditures, such as debt service and central superintendent office expenditures. That said, we do not include pass-throughs in our analyses of allocations across schools because these expenditures are not allocated to individual schools. Direct spending, in turn, includes funds spent at the school level (classroom instruction, instructional support, leadership, and ancillary and building services). Finally, classroom spending is focused primarily on spending related to teachers, classroom staff, books, supplies, and libraries. In our analyses of allocations across schools in NYC, we use *direct spending*, because it focuses specifically on school-level resources.[29]

Broad Trends in Enrollment and Student Characteristics. To understand whether the cost of education overall has risen in NYC, we first examined changes in enrollment and student characteristics and then analyzed trends in aggregate and per pupil expenditures by the categories outlined in table 3-2.

New York City enrollment has been over a million students since at least 1997, peaking at 1.105 million in 2001 and declining by 70,000 to 1.035 million in 2008. With the exception of growth in the share of special education students, the composition of students varied only modestly over the Bloomberg years. As seen in the top panel of table 3-3, between 2002 and 2008, the total number of general education students declined 8 percent, from 1,016,766 to 936,974 (from 92.5 percent to 90.5 percent of total enrollment), while the number of full-time special education students increased 20 percent, from just over 82,000 to over 98,000 (from 7.5 percent to 9.5 percent of total enrollment). Additionally, the proportion of full-time special education students educated in segregated settings (labeled *citywide* by the DOE) rose between 2002 and 2008, from around 1.9 percent to 2.2 percent of the total

TABLE 3-2   New York City definitions of school-based expenditure report types*

Expenditure type	Description	Specific expenditures
Total	Sum of direct services to schools, district/superintendency costs, systemwide costs, and systemwide obligations	
Direct	Services provided directly to public school students and staff, and that take place primarily in the school building during the school day during the school year	Classroom instruction, instructional support services, leadership/supervision support, ancillary support services, building services, district support
Classroom	School-based direct instructional services provided primarily in classrooms (including professional development and contracted instructional services that impact directly on the quality of classroom instruction)	Teachers, education paraprofessionals, other classroom staff, text books, librarians and library books, instructional supplies and equipment, professional development, contracted instructional services, summer and evening school
Pass-throughs**	Costs in the DOE's budget that are earmarked for nonpublic and private educational institutions	Nonpublic schools (general and special education), Fashion Institute of Technology, charter schools

School level***	Description
Elementary	Schools covering grades kindergarten through sixth
Middle	Schools covering grades six through nine
High	Schools covering grades nine through twelve

Student type	Description
General education	Students on the general education register and special needs pupils (e.g. "at-risk" pupils requiring academic intervention support, related service only, consultant teacher program pupils, resource room)
Special education (all)	Students who have been placed in a modified instructional service, special instructional environment or a hospital setting. These students are on the special education register but may be in general education classes for part of the day
Special education (citywide)	District 75
Special education (full time, not citywide)	Full-time special education number in schools

Source: 2002–2003 SBER.

*These definitions are taken directly from the 2002–2003 SBER and may have changed since that date.

**Pass-throughs are yet another type of spending. They include funding for general and special education students in non-public schools, the Fashion Institute of Technology, and charter schools and are not reported on student type or instruction level reports.

***There is large variation in school grade spans in NYC, so these definitions are somewhat fluid. For example, elementary schools may include 8th graders, middle schools may begin earlier than sixth grade and/or end later than 9th grade, and high schools may begin in seventh or eighth grade and only extend through tenth grade.

student population, outpaced by the growth in students educated in integrated settings, which rose from 5.6 percent to 7.3 percent of all students. Although the classification of students into special education is not entirely discretionary, most analysts argue that districts have some discretion. Put differently, some classification changes are controllable, and districts have some power to determine the exact nature of the integration of special education and general education students and the management of these systems.[30] Other characteristics of NYC students, such as percentages who are poor or ELL, changed only modestly over the Bloomberg years. Overall, the only dramatic change in composition was related to the faster growth of the more-costly-to-educate special education students.

Citywide Trends in Funding. To provide the most complete picture of the resources available during the Bloomberg years, we begin by looking at the overall total expenditures in NYC including pass-throughs (see second panel of table 3-3) When pass-throughs are included, inflation-adjusted overall total spending increased by $5.1 billion between 2002 and 2008, or 34.5 percent (from $14.9 billion in 2002 to $20.1 billion in 2008). Pass-throughs increased by 87 percent, or $816 million. This large growth in pass-throughs was due primarily to charter schools, few of which existed prior to 2002, and to contracted services for special education students in schools outside the NYC public schools: spending on charter schools increased 505

TABLE 3-3   **Trends in New York City enrollment and expenditures, 2002 and 2008**

	2002	*2008*	*Change*	*% change*
Enrollments				
Overall	1,098,832	1,035,406	–63,426	–5.8%
General education	1,016,766	936,974	–79,792	–7.8%
% of total	92.5%	90.5%		
Special education	82,066	98,432	16,366	19.9%
% of total	7.5%	9.5%		
Citywide special education	20,918	22,425	1,507	7.2%
% of total	1.9%	2.2%		
Full-time integrated*	61,148	76,007	14,859	24.3%
% of total	5.6%	7.3%		
Aggregate expenditures (in $'000s)				
Total (including pass-throughs)	$14,928,867	$20,078,756	$5,149,889	34.5%
Total (excluding pass-throughs)	$13,989,318	$18,322,803	$4,333,485	31.0%
Direct services to schools	$12,749,665	$16,047,236	$3,297,571	25.9%
Classroom instruction	$7,651,673	$9,043,461	$1,391,788	18.2%
Teachers	$6,036,507	$7,105,224	$1,068,717	17.7%
Instructional support	$1,546,289	$2,492,917	$946,628	61.2%

	2002	2008	Change	% change
Related services	$530,585	$1,176,577	$645,992	121.8%
Leadership/supervision/support	$1,199,501	$1,649,073	$449,572	37.5%
Ancillary support services	$1,403,095	$1,618,672	$215,577	15.4%
Building services	$916,831	$1,156,769	$239,938	26.2%
District/regional support	$32,276	$86,344	$54,068	167.5%
Regional costs	$494,731	$312,550	–$182,181	–36.8%
Systemwide costs	$356,995	$385,638	$28,643	8.0%
Systemwide obligations	$387,926	$1,577,379	$1,189,453	306.6%
Pass-throughs	$939,549	$1,755,953	$816,404	86.9%
Nonpublic general education	$186,980	$242,955	$55,975	29.9%
Nonpublic special education	$687,479	$1,238,711	$551,232	80.2%
Fashion Institute of Technology	$27,020	$43,943	$16,923	62.6%
Charters	$38,070	$230,344	$192,274	505.1%

Aggregate expenditures (in $'000s) by student type

	2002	2008	Change	% change
General education				
Total (excluding pass-throughs)	$10,965,708	$13,609,597	$2,643,889	24.1%
Direct	$9,887,268	$11,569,620	$1,682,352	17.0%
Classroom	$6,222,848	$6,763,155	$540,307	8.7%
Special education				
Total (excluding pass-throughs)	$2,976,306	$4,669,839	$1,693,533	56.9%
Direct	$2,818,851	$4,434,491	$1,615,640	57.3%
Classroom	$1,395,964	$2,255,604	$859,640	61.6%

Per pupil expenditures

	2002	2008	Change	% change
All NYCDOE public school students: Total	$12,731	$17,696	$4,965	39.0%
Direct	$11,602	$15,498	$3,896	33.6%
Classroom	$6,963	$8,734	$1,771	25.4%
General education: Total	$10,785	$14,525	$3,740	34.7%
Direct	$9,724	$12,348	$2,624	27.0%
Classroom	$6,120	$7,218	$1,098	17.9%
All special education: Total	$36,267	$47,442	$11,175	30.8%
Direct	$34,349	$45,051	$10,702	31.2%
Classroom	$17,011	$22,915	$5,904	34.7%
Citywide special education	$52,598	$65,681	$13,083	24.9%
Direct	$50,820	$63,205	$12,385	24.4%
Classroom	$27,051	$31,971	$4,920	18.2%
Integrated special education	$26,273	$32,710	$6,437	24.5%
Direct	$25,385	$31,477	$6,092	24.0%
Classroom	$13,512	$15,922	$2,410	17.8%

Source: NYC SBERs for 2002 and 2008.

Notes: Dollars are 2008 CPI inflated. Values for full-time integrated special education are obtained by subtracting the share of dollars spent on citywide programs from the overall special education dollars.

percent from $38.1 million to $230.3 million, and spending on contracted services for special education increased over 80 percent from $687.5 million to $1.2 billion between 2002 and 2008.

Since the SBERs do not break down pass-throughs by regional, systemwide, student type, or school level, we rely on the total spending (excluding pass-throughs) available from the SBER public school reports to analyze trends in more detail.[31] Table 3-3, panels 2 and 3, shows that total spending (excluding pass-throughs) on all students increased by over $4 billion from 2002 to 2008 (from $14.0 billion to $18.3 billion). Breaking down these total expenditures more finely, we note that direct expenditures increased $3.3 billion or 26 percent, regional costs decreased $182 million or 37 percent, systemwide costs increased $29 million or 8 percent, and systemwide obligations increased $1.2 billion or 307 percent.[32] Classroom instruction spending, however, increased more slowly, by $1.4 billion or 18.2 percent.[33] Much of the difference between growth in direct versus classroom spending was accounted for by *related services*, which help special education students in particular. Finally, total spending increased roughly 4 percent in elementary schools, 73 percent in middle schools, 61 percent in high schools, and 34 percent in citywide special education schools.

Figure 3-3 and table 3-3, panel 4, show trends in per pupil total, direct, and classroom expenditures. As expected, during the Bloomberg years, total expenditures per pupil (not including pass-throughs) increased greatly, by $4,965 (roughly 39 percent); direct expenditures per pupil increased by $3,896 (34 percent), and classroom expenditures per pupil increased $1,771 (over 25 percent). These aggregate per pupil expenditures, however, hide some important trends across programs and levels of education (see figure 3-4). Comparing special and general education per pupil spending, citywide special education students (in segregated schools) cost the most to educate, with direct spending of $63,205 and classroom spending of $31,971 per pupil in 2008. In comparison, direct spending on integrated full-time special education students was $31,477 per pupil ($15,922 for classroom) and spending on general education students was $12,348 ($7,218 for classroom). These per pupil expenditures have all increased since 2002, with a 27 percent increase in direct expenditures and an 18 percent increase in classroom expenditures for general education and a 31 percent increase in direct expenditures and a 35 percent increase in classroom expenditures for those in special education.

As shown in figure 3-5, expenditures per pupil by school level differ in an important way from most other districts: New York City spends less per pupil on high school students than on elementary or middle school students, with middle school spending falling slightly below elementary school spending. Although some attribute this to class size reduction mandates in the early grades and to higher proportions of special education students in elementary and middle schools than in high schools, we note that lower spending per pupil in high schools is not new; it dates back at least to the mid-1990s, suggesting that other forces may be relevant. Further, in addition

FIGURE 3-3 **New York City total, direct and classroom per pupil expenditures, 1997–2008***

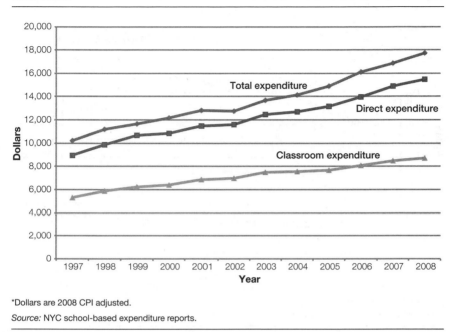

*Dollars are 2008 CPI adjusted.

Source: NYC school-based expenditure reports.

to spending less per high school student, the rate of growth in spending per pupil over the Bloomberg years was lowest for high schools and highest for middle schools.

Spending is not the only measure of resources allocated to students—teacher salaries and pupil-teacher ratios are alternatives. As seen in figure 3-6, inflation-adjusted teacher salaries (total salary plus fringe benefits) increased nearly $18,000 (roughly 25 percent) from 2002 to 2008. This was largely driven by a sizeable increase in fringe benefits (a 69 percent increase), as salary increases were significant but more modest (increases of over 11 percent).[34] At the same time, pupil-teacher ratios remained slightly under 14:1, decreasing somewhat more recently.

Allocations Across Schools: Have They Changed Under Bloomberg?

One of the motivations for Fair Student Funding in NYC was the observation that the variation in funding across schools did not align well with the varying needs and costs associated with student and school characteristics. Thus, we next turn to examining the variation in resources with an eye toward understanding the extent to which the distribution is more—or less—aligned with these needs. To do so, we rely on the factors used in FSF shown in table 3-2, even though it was not introduced until 2008. We use regression analyses to examine whether the distribution of

FIGURE 3-4 **New York City per pupil direct expenditures: General education, citywide, and full time special education, 1997-2008***

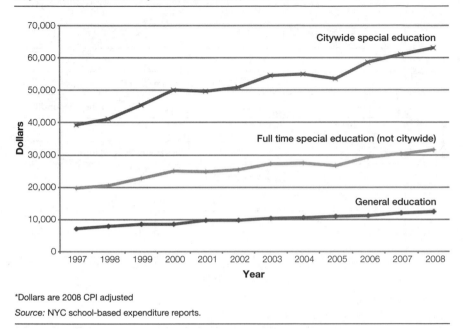

*Dollars are 2008 CPI adjusted

Source: NYC school-based expenditure reports.

resources across schools changed between 2001 and 2008 (a year before Bloomberg and six years after) and complement this analysis by summarizing *changes* in various resources by school poverty quintiles. To be clear, FSF was only in place for a single year within our analysis period, and, on the whole, funds were not actually allocated using these characteristics. Thus, these analyses might be viewed as summarizing a *de facto distribution formula.*

We regress measures of resources per pupil on the five school characteristics identified in FSF. We begin by analyzing 2001 and 2008 separately. We then pool the two years, estimating an interacted model to examine the extent to which the coefficients on the characteristics changed between 2001 and 2008. The regression coefficients provide a sense of the ex post weight given to each characteristic, and the R^2 provides a measure of how well these characteristics describe the distribution. A low R^2 indicates that other characteristics or, perhaps, random events determine much of the variation in school resources; a high R^2 indicates that variation in these characteristics explains much of the variation in resources.[35] We analyze each level of schooling (elementary, middle, and high) separately, since the characteristics were (or, at least, were proposed to be) weighted differently across levels. To summarize, in these regressions we examine the relationship between FSF characteristics and school level

FIGURE 3-5   **New York City per pupil direct expenditures, by school level, 1997–2008***

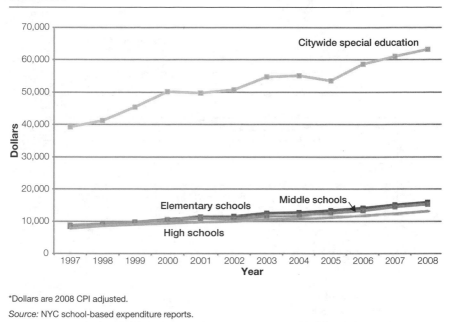

*Dollars are 2008 CPI adjusted.

Source: NYC school-based expenditure reports.

expenditures. These provide a descriptive framework of the effects of FSF character-istics even though they were in place for only one year.

We also explore the extent to which resources for poor students changed from 2001 to 2008 by analyzing changes in resources between the two years by quintile of school poverty in 2001.[36] Note that some schools changed poverty quintiles between 2001 and 2008, but an analysis of these changes showed that the majority did not, and those that did generally only moved one quintile up or down.

Direct Expenditures per Pupil. The results of our regression analyses of direct expenditures per pupil and analysis of changes in direct expenditures per pupil by poverty quintile for NYC elementary schools are presented in table 3-4. Recall that direct expenditures do not include money spent on regional costs or systemwide costs or obligations, but are intended to measure resources going directly to the schools.[37] While the cross-section regressions for 2001 and 2008 show that many of the regres-sion coefficients (hereafter called weights) changed between years, the fully inter-acted model in column 3 indicates that only three of those changes were statistically significant at the 10 percent level or below (percent resource room, percent full-time special education, and percent at level 1 on the reading test). Consistent with the aggregate trends shown earlier, the special education weights increased, both for

FIGURE 3-6 New York City teacher salary, fringe benefits, and class size, 1997–2008*

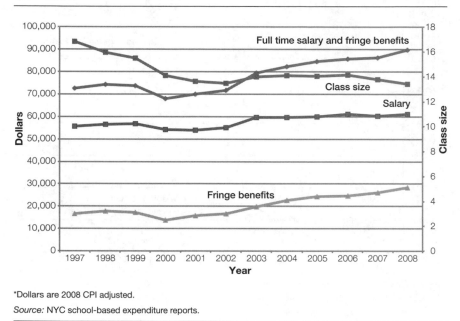

*Dollars are 2008 CPI adjusted.

Source: NYC school-based expenditure reports.

resource room (part-time special education) and full-time special education. The weight also increased for low-performing students, but did not increase significantly for poor students and ELLs. These results demonstrate that on some measures, but not others, spending on students with greater needs increased over time, aligned with the intentions of FSF. In addition, the R^2 increased ten percentage points from 53 percent in 2001 to 63 percent in 2008, indicating that over these years, school expenditures were better described by the FSF characteristics. Nonetheless, more than one-third of the variation across schools remains unexplained by the regression.

The change in expenditures by 2001 poverty quintile (column 4) shows an increasing amount of resources devoted to higher-poverty elementary schools, although the differences between the third, fourth, and fifth quintiles are only marginally statistically significant.[38]

Results for middle schools are similar.[39] Two weights increased at a statistically significant level between 2001 and 2008—those for full-time special education and for the percentage of students scoring at the lowest reading level. The explanatory power of the five FSF characteristics increased more than for elementary schools, with the R^2 increasing from 48 percent to 64 percent, although 35 percent is still unexplained. More resources went to schools in higher-poverty quintiles over these years, although the differences among the top three quintiles cannot be distinguished statistically.

TABLE 3-4 Regressions (columns 1–3) and poverty quintiles (column 4), direct expenditures per pupil, New York City elementary schools

	2001 cross-section (1)	2008 cross-section (2)	Interacted model (3)	Changes by poverty quintile (4)
% free lunch	11.727*** (3.392)	15.603*** (3.268)	11.727*** (3.574)	
% resource room	192.824*** (31.696)	265.059*** (16.091)	192.824*** (33.400)	
% full time special education	292.088*** (15.065)	399.440*** (18.020)	292.088*** (15.875)	
% LEP	-3.225 (6.413)	1.641 (5.763)	-3.225 (6.757)	
% level 1 fourth-grade ELA	-0.193 (8.205)	28.922** (13.197)	-0.193 (8.646)	
2008 * % free lunch			3.876 (4.753)	
2008 * % resource room			72.235** (36.789)	
2008 * % full time special education			107.352*** (23.461)	
2008 * % LEP			4.865 (8.728)	
2008 * % level 1			29.116* (15.323)	
2008			953.805** (427.973)	
1st poverty quintile				3,962.376*** (204.271)
2nd poverty quintile				4,451.185*** (190.024)
3rd poverty quintile				4,706.828*** (186.822)
4th poverty quintile				5,237.026*** (189.700)
5th poverty quintile				5,272.945*** (198.001)
Constant	7,970.507*** (300.490)	8,924.311*** (300.343)	7,970.507*** (316.646)	—
Observations	617	695	1,312	612
R^2	0.531	0.628	0.771	—

Standard errors in parentheses (***$p < 0.01$, **$p < 0.05$, *$p < 0.1$).

Note: Regressions are weighted by school enrollment. The model including poverty quintiles (column 4) is weighted by 2001 enrollment. There is a statistical difference for schools in the third, fourth, or fifth quintiles in 2001 ($F = 2.80$, $p > F = 0.062$), but not between schools in the fourth and fifth quintiles ($F = 0.02$, $p > F = 0.896$). Elementary schools are schools reporting scores on the fourth-grade ELA test. Dollars are in 2008 CPI inflated dollars. Variables are as defined in the note to Table 2.

As to high schools, the changes in our estimated weights for school characteristics are largely insignificant, except for the achievement weight, which moved in the same direction as elsewhere.[40] Here, the explanatory power of the FSF characteristics (18 percent to 28 percent) is very low, and only changed ten percentage points between the two years—spending differences do not seem to be driven by FSF factors. The analysis of poverty quintiles shows that higher-poverty schools did, however, receive more money, although there is no statistical difference among the top three quintiles.

In summary, over the Bloomberg years, the characteristics in FSF formulas explained an increasing share of the variation in expenditures per pupil across elementary and middle schools, and higher-poverty elementary and middle schools received more funding compared with lower-poverty schools over time. At these school levels, the weight given to special education students and students with low reading levels increased from 2001 to 2008, but the weight of other characteristics (e.g., ELL students) did not change significantly. At the high school level, expenditure distributions are still largely unexplained by the FSF characteristics, although spending per pupil increased more for higher-poverty high schools from 2001 to 2008. In addition, student performance played a larger role in spending distributions for high schools in 2008 than in 2001.

Distributions of Other Resources per Pupil. To supplement our analysis, we examine three other resources (classroom expenditures per pupil, teacher salaries, and pupil-teacher ratios) by school level. Classroom expenditures are generally considered to be "closer" to the student and thus are another means of exploring how funds are spent; teacher salaries are important because they make up a large component of district and school budgets; and pupil-teacher ratios are a proxy for class size, which is often considered a valuable nonfinancial resource. For each, we discuss the regression estimates of the changes in the implicit weights on FSF characteristics and we show the changes in resources per pupil by poverty quintile.[41]

Beginning with elementary schools, weights on school characteristics differed more for classroom expenditures per pupil than they did for direct expenditures per pupil. In fact, all but the weight on resource room students are statistically significantly higher in 2008 than in 2001. The R^2 increased twenty-one percentage points to 56 percent, indicating resources directly reaching students in classrooms were better distributed according to FSF after the Bloomberg/Klein administration began. Additionally, higher-poverty schools in 2001 (table 3-5, top panel, column 1) received more classroom expenditures per pupil over this time period compared with lower-poverty schools, with a statistically significant difference among the top three quintiles, but not between the top two.

A related question is whether this change is associated with teacher salaries or pupil-teacher ratios. While higher-poverty elementary schools and elementary schools with larger shares of full-time special education students had higher teacher salary weights in 2008 than in 2001, schools with higher percentages of resource

TABLE 3-5   **Resources by poverty quintile, NYC public schools by level**

	Classroom experience (1)	Teacher salary (2)	Pupil-teacher ratio (3)
Elementary schools			
1st poverty quintile	1,750.61*** (110.65)	22,190.94*** (749.42)	−0.27 (0.17)
2nd poverty quintile	2,226.81*** (102.92)	24,528.35*** (697.15)	−0.49*** (0.15)
3rd poverty quintile	2,340.80*** (101.19)	23,473.79*** (685.40)	−0.58*** (0.15)
4th poverty quintile	2,774.38*** (102.75)	22,825.21*** (695.96)	−0.82*** (0.15)
5th poverty quintile	2,834.53*** (107.25)	22,076.55*** (726.42)	−0.72*** (0.16)
Observations	612	612	612
Middle schools			
1st poverty quintile	1,473.19*** (329.58)	19,012.20*** (1,149.37)	−0.11 (0.28)
2nd poverty quintile	1,945.05*** (310.39)	20,035.99*** (1,080.04)	−0.19 (0.26)
3rd poverty quintile	3,380.42*** (351.87)	21,178.33*** (1,224.36)	−0.92*** (0.30)
4th poverty quintile	3,270.01*** (334.21)	20,225.5*** (1,162.90)	−1.00*** (0.29)
5th poverty quintile	2,986.93*** (449.32)	19,109.62*** (1,563.44)	−0.96** (0.38)
Observations	194	193	193
High schools			
1st poverty quintile	718.50*** (200.85)	23,199.50*** (1,469.17)	0.71** (0.27)
2nd poverty quintile	1,409.69*** (218.66)	23,404.59*** (1,599.40)	−0.50* (0.30)
3rd poverty quintile	2,562.66*** (294.02)	25,690.27*** (2,150.59)	−1.22*** (0.40)
4th poverty quintile	2,102.32*** (320.33)	22,298.35*** (2,343.09)	−1.31*** (0.44)
5th poverty quintile	2,035.63*** (373.58)	24,290.51*** (2,732.58)	−0.84 (0.51)
Observations	153	153	153

Standard errors in parentheses (***$p < 0.01$, **$p < 0.05$, *$p < 0.1$)

Note: These quintiles are derived from regressions that are weighted by school enrollment in 2001. Elementary schools are schools reporting scores on the fourth-grade ELA test. Middle schools are schools reporting scores on the eighth-grade ELA test. Dollars are in 2008 CPI inflated dollars. There is a statistically significant difference for classroom expenditures per pupil for elementary schools in the third, fourth, and fifth quintiles ($F = 6.87$).

room students and students scoring at the lowest level of the reading tests had lower weights. Teacher salaries in elementary schools thus do not follow the pattern seen for classroom expenditures per pupil. These equations do not explain much of the variation in teacher salaries across schools either—the explanatory power declined from 16 percent to 13 percent. Interestingly, the second-lowest quintile witnessed the largest increase in average teacher salaries compared with the lowest and higher quintiles (table 3-5, column 2).

Finally, for the pupil-teacher ratio, there are almost no changes between 2001 and 2008 (except for a lower weight for resource room students), although combined the factors explain a higher percentage of the variation (the R^2 increased significantly).

Thus, while individual factors did not change significantly, as a group they worked to better explain the distribution. By poverty quintile, the two highest-poverty levels had the largest decrease in pupil-teacher ratios compared with the lower-poverty quintiles over the time period (table 3-5, column 3). One explanation is that pupil-teacher ratios improved for high-poverty schools due to the influx of teachers at the beginning levels, perhaps from Teach for America (TFA) and the New York City Teaching Fellows program, since average salaries did not change across the quintiles.

In middle schools, classroom expenditures per pupil are qualitatively the same as direct expenditures per pupil in their coefficient weights and distributions by quintile (middle panel, table 3-5, column 1). In contrast, average teacher salaries show higher (significant) coefficients on poverty and lower (significant) coefficients on resource room, with a lower R^2 in 2008 than in 2001. Pupil-teacher ratios, while higher in high-poverty schools and lower in schools with larger percentages of poorly performing students, decreased more in higher-poverty quintile schools than in lower-poverty quintile schools between 2001 and 2008 (table 3-5, column 3).[42] Thus, as in elementary schools, it appears that more teachers were placed in higher-poverty schools, although not more highly paid ones.

Finally, for high schools, classroom expenditures per pupil show an increased weight on poverty, low achievement, and the share of ELL students, with a meaningful seven percentage point change in the R^2. As before, classroom expenditures per pupil also show a pro-poverty change (bottom panel of table 3-5, column 1). With respect to average teacher salaries, two weights differ in 2008 compared with 2001, although only in a positive direction for schools with higher percentages of full-time special education students.[43] The R^2 increased twenty-four percentage points to 42 percent. Salaries changed across poverty quintiles, although the difference between the top three quintiles cannot be distinguished statistically (table 3-5, column 2). Finally for the pupil-teacher ratio, weights on three factors changed significantly between 2001 and 2008 (schools with larger percentages of full-time special education students had slightly higher pupil-teacher ratios and those with higher shares failing the math Regents exam and higher shares of ELL students had lower pupil-teacher ratios) with a 4.5 percentage point change in the explanatory power and some reduction in the pupil-teacher ratio in the higher-poverty schools (table 3-5, column 3).

In summary, while there was some change in the weights on student factors identified in the FSF allocation formula for these alternative resources, there was variation in the significance across school levels. In elementary schools, for example, the changes in weights of FSF characteristics were more significant in explaining classroom instruction expenditures and teacher salaries than in middle or high schools. Further, schools in higher-poverty quintiles appeared to have larger changes over time in classroom instruction spending and larger decreases over time in pupil-teacher ratios compared with lower-poverty quintile schools. Teacher salaries did not follow this trend, suggesting that perhaps poorer schools received more teachers, but they were not more highly paid.

Private/Philanthropic Funding for New York City Public Schools

Although the vast majority of the financial support for public education is provided by federal, state, and local sources, philanthropic support and voluntary contributions are also noteworthy and a potentially important part of the school finance picture in New York. In this section, we provide a brief overview of that support, without assessing its success or impact, which is outside the scope of this paper.

The Fund for Public Schools

In 1982, the New York City Board of Education created The Fund for Public Schools (the Fund, or FPS), a 501(c)(3) nonprofit organization, as a fiscal agent responsible for accepting donations on behalf of the school system. After Bloomberg and Klein took office, the Fund was relaunched and its objectives repositioned to facilitate and strengthen public-private partnerships and to solicit funding from foundations and individuals for systemwide reforms. According to the 2005 FPS annual report, this restructuring was predicated on a need for "greater leadership and accountability . . . to create meaningful partnerships with the private sector."[44]

The Fund concentrates its efforts on two broad initiatives: securing private funding for education reform and raising awareness about the needs of public schools. Private funding can serve as a catalyst for publicly sustainable work and could allow the DOE to invest in and explore innovative strategies, in spite of budget constraints and without public funding.[45] According to the Fund, the relatively small dollar amounts they raise compared with the entire DOE budget are particularly valuable because of their flexibility, allowing the DOE to implement new or innovative ideas that might not be funded through the public budget. Further, the public-private partnership sees itself as a vehicle to align specific DOE needs with donors. The Fund measures its success by its "ability to leverage public investment for projects with demonstrated success," and its materials stress the importance of collecting and measuring results in numbers (for example, dollars, numbers of schools and students impacted, or benchmarks reached).

The Fund raised nearly $245 million between fiscal years 2003 and 2009, much of which has been invested in research, development, and capacity building across the following categories: teaching, learning and school based-gifts, accountability, empowerment, human capital, internal capacity building, and outreach and communication. For example, by the close of fiscal year 2007, the Fund had raised over $80 million for the NYC Leadership Academy, whose mission is to train principals skilled in leading NYC's schools. During the Leadership Academy's early years, all program expenses were supported through private funding, largely from the Fund; however, once the program proved successful, the DOE made a commitment to support it, awarding the Leadership Academy a five-year, competitively bid public contract.[47]

The second half of the Fund's mission—to raise awareness of the city's schools and encourage New Yorkers to get involved—began early in its relaunch, when Caroline Kennedy joined efforts with the DOE and the Fund. Over the years, corporate partners have sponsored citywide events and campaigns, increasing awareness and donations to initiatives including school libraries and arts education.[48] While the total funds raised amount to a small share of the overall budget (for example, in 2007 FPS funds accounted for 0.18 percent of the total DOE budget), the administration and DOE leadership frame the the Fund contribution as indispensible in supplementing limited discretionary spending and supporting innovations across the system. For example, Mayor Bloomberg states: "We could not have achieved all of our education reforms without the Fund's help."[49]

More Details on Select Private Funding

The FPS efforts make up only a small portion of the larger philanthropic community's contributions aimed at NYC public schools and school-aged children. There are many intermediary organizations (for example, the Urban Assembly) and service providers (for example, The After-School Corporation), whose programs support school-age children—and in some cases schools—across the city. Further, alumni and parent organizations often contribute directly to school resources. To begin to appreciate the scope of private- and nonprofit-sector involvement in public education, we examined the public support and program expenses of select organizations between 2005 and 2007, in addition to several school-centered fundraising groups. This work is *not* intended to be comprehensive; rather it begins to shed light on the private investments in NYC schools and school-aged children unaccounted for in a discussion of FPS fundraising.

Using copies of IRS 990 forms, we probed the contribution by NYC service providers and intermediary organizations to the public school system. The 990 form is submitted by tax-exempt and nonprofit organizations to the Internal Revenue Service each year and contains annual financial information broadly broken down by type of revenue and type of expense. Some of the largest revenue categories include direct public support (contributions received directly from individuals and foundations), government contributions, program service revenue, interest and dividends, and net gains or losses on investments and securities. The program expenses are broken into three categories: program services, management and general, and fundraising.[50] For our purposes, we analyze direct public support (to avoid duplicating any government contributions) and program expenses (to approximate the value of services provided), although we also present total numbers. Note that for the organizations we study, program expenses are between 79 percent and 89 percent of total expenses, while direct public support varies more widely and is between 23 percent and 96 percent of total revenue.

Using our knowledge of NYC and recommendations by the Fund, we examined the following organizations: Achievement First, Good Shepherd, the Harlem Children's Zone, New Visions for Public Schools, Outward Bound, The After-School Corporation, and the Urban Assembly.[51] All of these organizations are dedicated to providing education-related services, operating charter schools, or, in the case of the Harlem Children's Zone, maintaining a comprehensive network of related services for families and children. Between 2005 and 2007 these seven organizations received over $300 million dollars in direct public support. In those same years, their program service expenses totaled over $405 million dollars (see table 3-6). Program expenses for these organizations often include services that do not directly impact public schools; for example, according to form 990, in 2008 Good Shepherd dedicated over $28 million dollars to foster care and residential services. While these dollars are not targeted at schools, they do affect school-age children in New York City. And, to reiterate, these revenues and expenses are in addition to those of the Fund.

Alternatively, we can look at foundations and donors to understand the scope of private funds. For example, one large donor—the Bill and Melinda Gates Foundation—gave over $112 million in grants between 2000 and 2009 to organizations providing education or education-related services, not including grants made to the Fund.[52] In the two years immediately following Bloomberg's inauguration, the Gates Foundation's grants to NYC-based organizations increased dramatically: from more than $1.8 million in 2002 to more than $38 million in 2003. Over the next five years, the Gates Foundation gave over $35 million in support of small high school initiatives separate from monies given directly to the Fund in support of the same initiative. Note that many of these donations likely flowed through the organizations listed in table 3-6, so these are not necessarily additional funds.

The donations and expenses reported in table 3-6 represent only a fraction of the philanthropic support for school-age children in New York City. Accessible public information on the fundraising and spending behavior of other organizations, however, is not always available or comprehensive. For example, as found on the Robin Hood Foundation website, in 2006 Robin Hood reported contributions of $133 million and program expenses of $94 million.[53] While education is one of Robin Hood's core programs, the website does not report what portion of the program expenses go to education-related grants. We do know that in 2002, the foundation announced its Library Initiative partnership with the NYC Board of Education; the initial statement reported a contribution from Robin Hood of $6.94 million, in addition to securing $15 million in in-kind donations and $16 million from the board. Since that date, it appears that over fifty-five school libraries have opened through the initiative, though the total program cost and the locations of the libraries are not readily accessible.

TABLE 3-6 Total revenue (direct public support) and total expenses (program service expenses), select New York City service providers or intermediary organizations, 2005–2008 ($'000s)

		2005	2006	2007	Total	% of rev from direct support
Revenue*						
Achievement First	Total	$7,177	$10,096	$10,955	$28,227	71%
	Direct	($5,099)	($6,168)	($8,660)	($19,926)	
Good Shepherd	Total	$46,832	$59,612	$63,439	$169,884	23%
	Direct	($12,502)	($15,398)	($10,812)	($38,711)	
Harlem Children's Zone	Total	$41,288	$69,422	$61,690	$172,400	83%
	Direct	($29,940)	($60,557)	($52,767)	($143,264)	
New Visions for Public Schools	Total	$26,970	$15,169	$30,297	$72,435	84%
	Direct	($25,282)	($11,395)	($23,827)	($60,505)	
Outward Bound NYC	Total	$4,967	$6,187	$5,609	$16,763	50%
	Direct	($2,739)	($2,768)	($2,874)	($8,381)	
The After School Corporation	Total	$30,058	$29,530	$21,525	$81,113	18%
	Direct	($6,333)	($4,979)	($3,686)	($14,999)	
Urban Assembly	Total	$4,574	$7,082	$3,865	$15,522	96%
	Direct	($4,496)	($6,852)	($3,616)	($14,964)	
Total	Total	$161,865	$197,097	$197,381	$556,344	54%
	Direct	($86,391)	($108,117)	($106,242)	($300,750)	
% of revenue from direct support		53%	55%	54%	54%	

Expenses*		2005	2006	2007	Total	% of exp for program services
Achievement First	Total	$4,963	$8,483	$10,303	$23,750	86%
	Program	($4,274)	($7,052)	($9,099)	($20,424)	
Good Shepherd	Total	$42,288	$52,581	$61,706	$156,575	86%
	Program	($36,198)	($44,672)	($53,292)	($134,162)	
Harlem Children's Zone	Total	$33,324	$39,153	$51,058	$123,535	79%
	Program	($26,410)	($30,506)	($41,064)	($97,980)	
New Visions for Public Schools	Total	$15,957	$15,625	$20,332	$51,915	89%
	Program	($14,363)	($13,710)	($18,255)	($46,328)	
Outward Bound New York City	Total	$4,562	$4,727	$5,223	$14,512	82%
	Program	($3,720)	($3,847)	($4,286)	($11,853)	
The After School Corporation	Total	$32,066	$34,734	$29,734	$96,534	88%
	Program	($28,587)	($30,561)	($25,623)	($84,772)	
Urban Assembly	Total	$2,876	$3,984	$5,307	$12,167	84%
	Program	($2,412)	($3,258)	($4,523)	($10,192)	
Total	Total	$136,038	$159,288	$183,664	$478,989	85%
	Program	($115,963)	($133,607)	($156,142)	($405,711)	
% of expenses for program services		85%	84%	84%	85%	

Source: IRS 990 tax forms for each organization, www.guidestar.com, May 2010.

*Revenue including direct public support, government contributions, program service, interest on savings investments, dividends and interests from securities, etc. Direct public support only in parentheses. Expenses including program service expenses, management and general, and fundraising. Program service expenses only in parentheses.

In addition to the activities of philanthropies and nonprofits, frequent media attention is given to the role of direct contributions to schools by alumni or parent organizations, particularly schools in wealthy neighborhoods or with successful or famous former students, like Brooklyn Technical High School. We looked at several NYC elementary and high schools likely to have highly effective alumni or parent associations and found anecdotal evidence suggesting that while individual schools may be able to supplement their funding through private donations, alumni and parent associations, and other fundraising efforts, the magnitude of these resources is dwarfed by the public resources.[54]

Importantly, the DOE views these additional funds—provided through the Fund, private foundations, or school fundraising—as indispensable to efforts to reform the DOE management (e.g., the NYC Leadership Academy, Project Home Run, ARIS) and change systemwide programming (e.g., career and technical education, multiple pathways to graduation). By strategically aligning fundraising efforts with specific projects, the DOE has tried to increase accountability to donors and, in doing so, encourage more to give. Once innovations have proven successful, fiscal responsibility has shifted away from the Fund, as illustrated by the experience of the Leadership Academy. Will this approach work in other large urban cities? Those without large pockets of local philanthropic support may be unable to leverage the necessary capital. Furthermore, systemwide reform may not be possible in districts whose revenues are not as high as, or have not, increased at the same rate as, NYC's.

Summary and Conclusions

Summary

Resources available to the Bloomberg administration increased significantly between 2002 and 2008. Per pupil revenues grew almost $5,800, and per pupil expenditures, excluding pass-throughs (mostly charter schools and contracted special education services), grew almost $5,000. This was a larger increase than that experienced by other districts in New York State, and NYC was one of the top three spending districts in the country, at approximately $20,000 per student. At the same time, the composition of the city's students changed, with much faster growth in costly-to-educate full-time special education pupils compared with general education pupils. Moreover, teachers received large increases in compensation (including both salaries and fringe benefits). Finally, NYC's practice of spending less on high schools than elementary or middle schools continues and differs from that of other districts.

Several of the factors included in the FSF formula received more weight between 2001 and 2008, as the Bloomberg reforms were implemented. For example, elementary and middle school expenditures were more closely aligned with FSF principles in 2008, although this was not seen for high schools. It does appear that more resources have been channeled to schools in the highest-poverty quintiles, particularly with lower pupil-teacher ratios in high-poverty elementary and middle schools.

Finally, private philanthropy, although not a large amount or percentage of the DOE budget, may have played a role in allowing the administration to reform both management and programming. Additionally, many nonprofit organizations which fund education and education-related services received significant amounts of philanthropic support during these years.

Conclusions

What, then, can we conclude about the role of resources in the Bloomberg education initiative, what we can expect in the future, and what lessons are there for other districts? First, large amounts of additional public money were available to Bloomberg that are unlikely to continue postrecession or be available in other districts. For many years, New York State operated with a structural deficit, where recurring expenditures exceeded recurring revenues. This situation may continue—financed by borrowing from offline agencies, one-time sales of assets, or some other way—however, increased public awareness may force state-level action to prevent growing deficits. If so, budget cuts are probable, as it is unlikely that New York State's citizens will support large tax increases, particularly given the already high state tax rates. Which services will slow in growth? Health? Education? Education spending is already very high (first or second in the nation) and may be the most likely candidate for cuts or slowdown. Moreover, *Campaign for Fiscal Equity* money is unlikely to be fully implemented (restored) at inflation-adjusted dollars, and this will not fill gaps opened by slower growth in education spending. As for federal revenues, the federal government will also need to cut deficits; however, education initiatives may remain high priorities. Even if spending stays where it is, federal dollars do not make up a large percentage of NYC revenues. Finally, NYC's local revenue share is below the state average and could increase. However, NYC's financial sector is not where it was prerecession, and local tax revenues are unlikely to grow rapidly for many years. Additionally, there are many other demands for local resources. All of this indicates that public resources will not grow as quickly in the coming years as they did in the past.[55]

Growth in the special education population is troubling financially, although the shift to integrated rather than segregated classrooms has the potential to reduce the growth in per pupil expenditures for this group of students. This growth, along with large increases in teacher salaries, accounted for much of the spending by the administration since 2002. The DOE contends that the size of and amount of spending on the special education population (especially for contracted services) is not controllable, but many analysts think it is, at least to some extent.[56] Additionally, it is an open question whether the teachers' union would be as cooperative with new initiatives without significant salary increases. Finally, the continuing shift to FSF and the concomitant authority and accountability given to principals could potentially result in fairer and even more effective use of public dollars, but without increases in public dollars, it is unclear whether the initiative can be sustained.

Philanthropic money, even if it does continue, cannot substitute for public dollars, although it could be helpful to the education-related nonprofits and for more innovations in programming. There are questions, however, about whether reliance on private money has led to lack of transparency or mission drift. Although assessing the success and consequences of private resources is outside the scope of this paper, future research in this area seems well warranted.

The changes and innovations already made with public resources will probably have to fuel future improvements for NYC's students. If an adequate base of new management systems and programming has already been incorporated into public spending, then the initiatives could continue to have an effect. If more resources are needed, however, they are unlikely to be forthcoming to the degree they have been since 2002.

Finally, what can we learn from NYC about resources that could be useful to other U.S. districts? Answering this question conclusively would require establishing a causal link between the additional funding available to Bloomberg and important educational outcomes. Our aim in this chapter has not been to establish causality, but instead to provide a clear, descriptive portrait of the changes in available resources and how these funds were distributed. As a result, our conclusions are qualified and focused on the role of resources in enabling the observed reforms.

To begin, the New York City experience suggests that private money (nongovernmental revenues) directly coordinated with the district's mission may have provided resources and flexibility key for innovation. These dollars, however, amounted to less than 0.5 percent of the DOE's annual budget. Further, it is unclear whether (or to what extent) the effectiveness of private resources depends on corresponding substantial increases in public dollars that can be used to implement reforms systemwide. That said, relatively small amounts of unrestricted resources may be particularly important in using public funds effectively and efficiently, and other districts might follow NYC's example by establishing similar unrestricted funding pools—perhaps allocating a percentage of resources to a small innovation fund. At the same time, this might be viewed as an argument for federal or state provision of unrestricted grants that school districts can use according to their own discretion.

Second, to the extent that garnering support from teachers and unions was important for implementing reform, NYC benefited by being able to renegotiate teacher contracts and award raises. While raises may not have been necessary in implementing reform and are likely to be infeasible in districts that have not received large increases in public revenues, the importance of teacher and union support should not be underestimated.

Finally, much of the growth in NYC's revenues was directed toward the full-time special education population. Clearly, decisions about the appropriate level of spending on special education are key to understanding the financial resources puzzle and, to the extent possible, other districts will want to ensure they are providing these services as effectively as possible, particularly if they have not received large increases in public dollars.

New York City was blessed with a large amount of additional public and private money. Bloomberg and Klein may have been instrumental in encouraging growth in these sources by clearly defining their mission for reform and revitalizing an organization (The Fund for Public Schools) to attract private resources. These actions could be applied more broadly by policy makers and education leaders in other districts to influence and stimulate increased revenues aimed at educational reform.

Appendix: Summary of Special Education Reforms Under Bloomberg

In 2000, the NYC Board of Education approved a series of special education reform initiatives commonly referred to as the New Continuum. The Continuum provided a menu of special education services stressing that all children should be educated in the least restrictive environment possible and emphasizing collaborative team teaching (CTT), which allows up to 40 percent of students in a classroom to be special needs.[57] The Continuum has been updated several times over the years. In April of 2003, Mayor Bloomberg announced a series of comprehensive reforms to the special education system in New York City. Crucial to his reform strategy was improving the capacity of general education classrooms and teachers to better serve and include students with disabilities, through the appointment of instructional specialists, professional development, services and incentives, and accountability. A 2005 evaluation for the NYC Department of Education's Special Education Program found that, compared with other large cities (Los Angeles and Chicago), New York City devoted a higher level of resources to its special education program, particularly in related services. This report also suggested that while the DOE was clearly committed to inclusion, special education students were still overly segregated in classes and programs.[58]

Once eligibility for special services has been established, the Individualized Education Program (IEP) team meets to determine placement in one of seven possible classroom environments: general education, general education with related services, general education with special education teacher support (SETS), CTT/integrated coteaching, special class services, day and residential placement, or home/hospital instruction.[59] All special education placements must adhere to the least restrictive environment rule as closely as possible. Students receiving CTT, SETS, or related services remain in general education classrooms with a mix of special needs and non–special needs students. Special class services, day and residential placement, and home/hospital instruction serve students whose needs cannot be met in a general education classroom on a part-time or full-time basis. In addition, there are specialized public schools for students with significant disabilities or District 75 schools. District 75 students may receive services in a general education classroom, in special classes in community school buildings or in specialized schools, in agencies, or in hospitals.[60]

PART II

Teaching and Learning

4

Managing for Results at the New York City Department of Education

Stacey Childress, Monica Higgins, Ann Ishimaru, and Sola Takahashi

Managing for results can be a treacherous tightrope walk for school districts. The popular cry calling for a combination of "pressure and support" remains easier said than done.[1] When schools are failing children, the natural impulse is to ratchet up accountability, adopt a no-excuses policy of one kind or another and increase the pressure on those closest to the students—principals and teachers. However, like most performance-appraisal systems, if implemented in isolation, this approach runs the risk of crowding out capacity building just when it is needed most. Indeed, the schools that are penalized for low performance are often the ones staffed with the educators most in need of development. Though some schools might have a critical mass of staff who simply do not believe improvements in their practice would have an effect on student learning and who therefore resist accountability, most reformers operate on the assumption that the vast majority of educators are motivated to serve their students well. As one long-time urban superintendent says, "If low-performing schools knew how to fix themselves, they would do it."[2] This implies that simply adding more pressure on schools without a concurrent effort to increase capacity runs the risk of undermining the ultimate goal of improving performance; with low self-efficacy or a lack of confidence in their ability to successfully adopt new approaches, principals' and teachers' prospects of improving their students' learning may be hindered. At worst, these professionals might engage in undesirable strategic behaviors that undermine learning.[3]

How, then, can school districts walk the high wire in service of improving results for all children? The New York City Department of Education (DOE) has an approach that has sparked interest from policy makers, practitioners, and researchers worldwide.

This paper attempts to describe this approach. We begin by describing the history behind the DOE's evolving theory of action for how to improve student performance at scale. We include a summary of their efforts to, as Chancellor Joel Klein often said, "change the facts on the ground" to support implementation of the theory between 2002 and 2009. To do this, we cover some of the ground by Paul Hill (chapter 1 in this volume), but focus more specifically on the strategic and structural choices that are relevant to the performance management system. As we will show, the perspective that the DOE took on performance management was unique at the time: rather than granting autonomy as a reward when schools achieve high performance, the DOE granted schools autonomy outright in return for high levels of accountability.

Following this historical overview, we offer a brief summary of research on *organizational learning*, an idea that is reflected in the ways in which the DOE attempted to build capacity in schools. Next, building on this historical and theoretical backdrop, we describe the details of the DOE's performance-management system and the ways in which schools have been held accountable while at the same time being provided with a variety of supports to do their work. Finally, we offer insight from some exploratory analyses we performed based on a large-scale survey of New York City teachers to investigate the DOE's theory of performance management in action. We investigate teacher perceptions of school culture along the dimensions of accountability and organizational learning and explore whether and how these aspects of a school's culture relate to school performance. Suggestions for future research and implications for practice conclude our paper.

New York's Theory of Action and Related Organizational Changes

Between 2002 and 2009, Chancellor Joel Klein and his team implemented an evolving theory of action at the DOE based largely on the premise that if given autonomy for decisions about resources and instruction, school principals would improve the performance of their students more effectively than if those decisions were made for them at the central office. In exchange for this autonomy, principals and their schools would be held more accountable for results than in previous administrations. Klein's theory development was heavily influenced by the work of scholars and thought leaders such as William Ouchi, Paul Hill, and Michael Barber, as well as by his observations of a number of high-performing charter schools in the city.[4]

In order to put their theory into practice, Klein and his team implemented a two-phase strategy. In the first phase (roughly 2003–2006), the team sought to consolidate control by moving the oversight of New York's approximately thirteen hundred schools from thirty-two separately governed and managed community districts and a high school division to ten K–12 regions, a special education district, and a district for alternative schools and programs (for a total of twelve entities), all reporting to the chancellor and governed by Mayor Michael Bloomberg. These new structures were designed to support schools' operational and instructional needs, enforce standards, and implement reforms. Dubbed Children First, this first phase also instituted a common math and literacy curriculum for grades K–8, ended social promotion, created 150 small schools to replace large low-performing high schools, and added a parent coordinator and math and literacy coaches to every elementary school. Reflecting on this phase in 2007, Klein said the purpose was to gain control of a "chaotic and dysfunctional organizational structure" and to "lock the system down, establish some control, and bring coherence to the system." Required curriculum, standardized promotion policies, and a more centralized reporting structure seem incongruous with a theory of action premised on greater autonomy. Klein and his team have argued that in order to eventually put more control in the hands of school leaders they had to first disrupt the entrenched bases of power in the thirty-two community districts, and transferring those districts' authority to the new regions was one way to accomplish this.

After the first two years of Children First, Klein and the senior team began laying the groundwork for phase 2, which would eventually turn the system on its head by moving power from the twelve entities to the leaders of nearly thirteen hundred schools.[5] Klein believed that empowering highly competent principals and giving them the resources needed to make decisions about solving their schools' performance problems would ultimately be in the best interest of students. In order for empowerment to be effective, he also believed that principals needed to be held accountable for student performance. Klein described his theory of action for phase 2, saying: "If we empower principals and hold them accountable for school results, we'll do two things—shift the locus of power from central office to the schools and shift the organizational culture to a focus on results. However, I know that autonomy in and of itself is not going to guarantee success. But it will lead to innovation. And I suspect that if we're tight on accountability and instill an intense focus on student outcomes, we can also build into the equation some variability in terms of problem solving at the school level and learn from it."

The first wave of phase 2 was a pilot called the Autonomy Zone, which school leaders could opt into by signing performance contracts in exchange for freedom from many of the mandates of the Children First reforms, including their reporting relationship to a regional superintendent and the districtwide math and reading curriculum. Other large urban districts, including Chicago, Boston, and Philadelphia, were experimenting with such zones, but in those cities, schools *earned* autonomy by meeting performance thresholds. In New York, the senior team developed a fundamentally different assumption: autonomy was not something to be earned by performing well; rather, it was a *prerequisite* for high performance. Any school leader could choose to participate in the Autonomy Zone ("the Zone"), regardless of the school's current performance.

Twenty-nine schools volunteered to join the Zone, more than half of which had recently launched as new small schools. Each principal signed a five-year performance contract that specified targets for a variety of indicators, including state test scores, attendance figures, and graduation rates. As part of the agreement, principals assumed control over all budgetary and decision-making authority that previously resided with regional offices. Zone schools that met their performance targets were left alone, while those that missed more than a certain number of targets entered into what the DOE called the *ladder of consequences*. The timeline for these consequences was more aggressive than those in No Child Left Behind or the New York State accountability system. The first year a school missed its targets, the school's leadership team was required to develop specific action plans for the following year. If a school missed its performance goals for a second year, the principal could be removed. If things did not improve by the third year, the school could be closed. The principals answered to the Zone chief executive officer, Eric Nadelstern, who was responsible for all Zone schools and worked directly with those who failed to meet their targets. At the beginning of the second year, 19 additional schools joined the Zone. At the end of the second year, 2 of the 48 Zone schools failed to meet their performance goals. In fall of 2006 the number of Zone schools, renamed Empowerment Schools, grew to 332. Klein heralded the increasing interest in the autonomy-accountability exchange as a shift in the fundamental culture of the school system, saying, "I think if you don't change the culture of public education, you're not going to change the outcomes materially. A culture that doesn't focus on performance is a culture that won't work. And now these principals are saying they want to be held accountable for their performance. It's quite a thing to have [332] principals, over the objection of their union, sign performance agreements saying, 'If I don't hit the ball, they'll be sending me to the minors.' It's a big, big deal given the objections from the union and the good relationships many of these principals have with their regions."

Building on what they learned in the pilot, the senior team unveiled a new three-pronged organizational structure that went into effect in fall 2007. The special education district remained intact, but the regions were disbanded and every school leader was given the choice to affiliate with one of three types of School Support Organizations (SSOs):

1. *Empowerment Support Organization (ESO):* The Empowerment Zone converted into the ESO, and additional schools could become Empowerment Schools by signing performance contracts and forming self-managed networks.
2. *Learning Support Organizations (LSOs):* Most similar to the old regional structure but not organized geographically, four Learning Support Organizations offered schools service, support, and oversight through four centers run by the DOE.
3. *Partnership Support Organizations (PSOs):* Schools that partnered with external nonprofit organizations for support and services were part of this structure and signed performance contracts. A number of schools were already partnered with

external organizations, and the new structure would formally give those organizations additional support responsibilities, hold them accountable for school results, and open up the option to additional schools and nonprofits. PSOs had the same level of autonomy granted to the school operators in the ESO.

The autonomy-accountability exchange was at work regardless of which support organization school leaders chose. Though the ESO included the most freedoms, principals' choices about which support organization to affiliate with were framed as acts of autonomy, and regardless of which choice they made, every principal signed a five-year performance contract. Principals also had the option to transfer to another support organization during an open enrollment period every two years. Klein's team believed this new level of autonomy would attract people to school leadership positions who would be more likely to innovate.

As part of the autonomy equation, Klein and Bloomberg negotiated mutual consent hiring with the United Federation of Teachers (UFT), the largest local bargaining unit in the United States. As described by Diane Ravitch in the *New York Sun* at the time,

> The new agreement restores important managerial authority to school principals. It abolishes seniority transfers, which allowed teachers with seniority to transfer into a school by 'bumping' junior teachers, whether the principal wanted the senior teacher or not. Seniority transfers promoted the clustering of the most experienced teachers in highly desirable schools, which was not equitable to low-performing schools in poor neighborhoods. Principals will also have more authority over hiring their staff, which will allow the leaders to shape their team around common goals.[6]

Klein considered this change a pillar of the autonomy-accountability exchange— if principals were to be held accountable for the commitments they made in their performance contracts, they needed the flexibility to build school teams they felt best positioned them for success.

In order to make the autonomy-accountability exchange work at scale, a set of coherent systems and structures were necessary to capture the benefits of principal autonomy and at the same time exploit the advantages of being a large, integrated system. The next section describes some of the key accountability and organizational learning mechanisms that together make up the performance management system in NYC.

Designing a Performance Management System

Jim Liebman had been a respected civil rights attorney, legal scholar, and teacher at Columbia Law School before joining the DOE in 2005 as the chief accountability officer. Klein recruited him with a mandate to lead the design and implementation of a performance management system. Liebman often described the system his team created as an attempt to strike the right balance between instilling accountability for past results and encouraging continuous improvement toward future outcomes. A key goal of the system was to help schools develop into organizations in which professionals were constantly learning with one another about how to solve performance problems. Liebman described his thinking this way:

> Accountability isn't entirely or even mainly about incentives. It's about capacity building, which to me means adult learning based on self- and team evaluation of what's working and what's not, and knowledge management, meaning spreading what works from one student or school to another. If we want the lever of accountability to be as powerful as possible, we have to provide ways for schools to build their capacity to be relatively self-sufficient in evaluating themselves every day and in solving their unique performance problems and, when necessary, in asking for the specific help they need. This will never work if the central bureaucracy behaves as if it has all the answers. Our role is to help professionals in schools ask better questions so that they can craft customized answers based on their own evaluation of their performance problems.

Organizational Learning and Accountability: A Theoretical Backdrop.

The DOE's approach to capacity building is consistent with relatively new approaches to school reform that include the idea of organizational learning. Rather than providing training to implement a specific curriculum or instructional technique, the DOE focused on increasing school teams' capacity to learn from data and adjust their behavior based on this learning. Organizational learning refers to a collective or a more macro-level learning than that which occurs at the individual level.[7] There are many excellent reviews of the organizational learning literature and its application to the context of education, including a recent 2008 special issue on organizational learning in the American Journal of Education.[8] Rather than provide yet another review, we offer instead a very brief overview of the literature, highlighting specific aspects of this work that are present in the design of the DOE's performance management system.

In general, we note that despite the espoused merits of bringing organizational learning theory to the field of education, many education scholars concur that empirical evidence in this arena is lacking and that explicit approaches to building capacity for organizational learning in schools remain in their infancy. One reason that this has remained an elusive phenomenon may be that the concept of organizational learning has become burdened with multiple interpretations. The term *organizational learning* was first noted by March and Simon in 1958.[9] Their research, along with that of their doctoral students, focused primarily on the cognitive processes of information search, acquisition, integration, and assimilation. Much of this work was on private-sector organizations and centered on how knowledge and information could be resources to help organizations "learn" and thereby improve performance.[10]

In contrast, a second approach to organizational learning has emerged over the years that scholars such as Meredith Honig describe as *sociocultural learning theory.*"[11]

Here, rather than emphasize the rational, cognitive processes that govern information management and complex problem solving, the focus has been on how individuals co-construct meaning with those around them. From this vantage point, learning cannot be considered without a close examination of the social embeddedness of individuals in organizations. This research stream has focused on how individuals learn through interactions with others in practice and on the social processes of learning.[12]

Recently, education scholars have called for greater integration between these two perspectives on organizational learning.[13] Research in the adjacent field of organizational behavior has adopted a perspective that takes such an integrative stance. In 2008, Garvin, Edmondson, and Gino introduced several "building blocks" that they argue are critical to organizational learning: a supportive learning environment in which individuals feel "psychologically safe" to speak up and ask for help; concrete learning processes and practices that enable the collection, analysis, and transfer of valuable information; and leadership that reinforces learning by supporting those closest to the organization's core work.[14] Although much of these scholars' work has focused on healthcare and other industries, the conceptual underpinnings of their research and the integrative stance they take has caught the attention of reformers such as Liebman.

Today, many scholars and practitioners, like Liebman, view organizational learning as one side of a productive tension. The other side is accountability. Since the advent of standards-based reform in the 1990s, scholars have been writing about its implications for accountability. This research stream has definitional and interpretation challenges similar to the organizational learning literature cited above. Jennifer O'Day's work draws a distinction between bureaucratic and professional accountability that helps to distinguish between the often top-down pressure an organizational system puts on educators and the mutual responsibility educators have to one another to live up to the quality standards of their profession.[15] Richard Elmore categorizes the different dynamics as *internal accountability*—the shared expectations for teaching and learning and a means to meet these expectations—and *external accountability*—a system for holding people responsible for producing certain results.[16] Elmore also writes about the notion of *reciprocal accountability*, which he sums up in the following statement: "For every unit of performance I demand of you, I have an equal responsibility to provide you with a unit of capacity, if the performance I require of you requires knowledge and skill that you do not possess."[17]

Bringing multiple research streams together, organizational behavior scholar Amy Edmondson recently proposed that work environments characterized by high levels of organizational learning as well as high levels of accountability enable superior performance.[18] This proposition has yet to be empirically tested. Still, it echoes the present-day thesis among education leaders that it is important to balance "support and pressure" in order to reach high performance in schools and districtwide. When communicating the DOE's performance management tools to internal and external audiences in the early days of implementation, Jim Liebman would often quote Elmore's reciprocal accountability concept, and the particular form of capacity he emphasized was the ability of school teams to learn together how to solve their performance challenges. This framing is consistent with Edmondson's proposition that high levels of both accountability for results *and* organizational learning will lead to higher performance than the presence of only one or the other.

Implementing Systems for Accountability and Organizational Learning

Consistent with the theoretical frame described in the previous section, Liebman and his team in the Office of Accountability developed learning tools and processes to help schools build their capacity to problem solve and self-evaluate, even as they ratcheted up the accountability pressure for results. The organizational learning and accountability tools together formed a performance management system with a number of key components, including school Progress Reports, Quality Reviews (QRs), periodic assessments, inquiry teams, and a new technology system.

In this section, we focus specifically on the design, implementation, and evolution of Progress Reports as an accountability tool and QRs as an organizational learning tool, as well as some of the interactions between them. Other chapters in this volume discuss other aspects of the performance-management system (e.g., Talbert's examination of inquiry teams—chapter 6). We primarily cover the first three school years of implementation (2007, 2008, and 2009) and refer to changes implemented in the 2010 school year only when they are useful in illuminating challenges encountered in the preceding years.

Progress Reports

The Office of Accountability created a Progress Report to evaluate and communicate school performance internally and externally. The reports were designed to provide a historical account of a school's overall success in improving student academic outcomes. Progress Reports for all schools included four main subsections, each with different weights that would add up to 100 points to determine a school's overall letter grade, as discussed in more detail below.

To account for differences in curriculum and targets by grade level, two versions of the report were created, one for elementary and middle schools and another for high schools. In 2006–2007, letter grades were assigned based on how schools performed relative to one another on the 100 point scale: the top 15 percent received As, the next 40 percent received Bs, the next 30 percent received Cs, the next 10 percent received Ds, and the bottom 5 percent received Fs. After a baseline was established the first year, each September the DOE published the cut scores that would correspond to letter grades on the Progress Reports at the end of the year.

The cut score for various grades increased a few points each year in order to continuously raise the bar for systemwide performance. The goal was to push out the performance horizon so that schools with good letter grades had incentives for continuous improvement.

The following sections describe the four basic subsections of the Progress Reports—school environment, student performance, student progress, and additional credit—and how they are calculated to produce a score on the 100-point scale and a letter grade.

School Environment. The school environment section evaluated schools based on attendance figures and survey data from parents, teachers, and students in sixth through twelfth grades. The 15 percent weight for this subsection was the sum of 5 percent for attendance and 10 percent for the survey results. The surveys covered four areas, each of which contributed equally to the 10 percent weight: safety and respect, academic expectations, engagement, and communication. Liebman's team designed the surveys but a vendor delivered them, collected the data, and provided anonymous results back to the DOE. Administering approximately 1.5 million surveys posed significant implementation challenges, but from the first year the response rates were large enough to allow for reliable data, and the response rates grew each year, as shown in table 1.

Student Performance. The student performance section graded the school according to the percentage of students scoring at level 3 or 4 on that year's state mathematics and English language arts exams. On the high school Progress Report, this section scored performance on Regents exams and graduation. In 2007, this subsection was worth 30 percent of the total score, and was reduced to 25 percent in subsequent years.

Student Progress. To distinguish the new Progress Reports from previous accountability reports distributed by the city and state, the DOE emphasized individual student growth year to year much more than the average absolute performance of a school's students at a point in time. This section started with a weight of 55 percent, which increased to 60 percent after the first year of implementation. Beginning

TABLE 4-1 **Environment survey response rates**

	2007	2008	2009
Teachers	44%	61%	73%
Students (grades 6–12)	65%	78%	80%
Parents	26%	40%	45%

Source: Author analysis of publicly available progress report results for 2007, 2008, and 2009. New York City Department of Education, *Progress Report Results for all Schools Citywide*, 2007, 2008, and 2009, http://schools.nyc. gov/Accountability/tools/report/default.htm.

in 2008, for elementary and middle schools the progress section measured the change in individual students' performance with four indicators:

- Percentage of all students making at least one year of progress on state exams
- Percentage of students in the school's lowest third making at least one year of progress on state exams
- Average change in proficiency for students scoring at level 1 or 2 in prior year
- Average change in proficiency for students scoring at level 3 or 4 in prior year

Instead of rewarding schools for attracting students who already performed well, the DOE hoped the heavy weight of this subsection would reward what schools brought to their students—in other words, giving schools credit for "adding value" to their students' performance trajectory. In order to account for movement within a proficiency level, the DOE converted the state's range of raw scores to a proficiency rating for English language arts (ELA) and math from third through eighth grades. Table 4-2 includes illustrative conversions for eighth-grade ELA and math scores.

For example, if a student started the school year with a proficiency rating of 2.25 and ended the year at 2.50, the school would receive credit for the gain even though the student did not advance from level 2 to level 3. On the flip side, a school would lose points if a student's proficiency rating went down. If a student's proficiency rating stayed the same from one year to the next, that was counted as making one year of progress. To account for student mobility within the city, a transfer student's progress was split between the sending and receiving school in the year of the transfer, based on the time of year the state exams were administered. A student's ELA progress was allocated 60 percent to the sending school and 40 percent to the receiving school, while math progress was allocated 40 percent to the sending school and 60 percent to the receiving school.

For high schools, the student progress section was calculated according to how students performed relative to the probability they would pass or fail the Regents exams

TABLE 4-2 Conversion of New York state proficiency levels and raw scores to DOE proficiency ratings, 2009

EIGHTH-GRADE ENGLISH LANGUAGE ARTS			EIGHTH-GRADE MATH		
Level	Raw score	Proficiency rating	Level	Raw score	Proficiency rating
4	715–795	4.00–4.50	4	701–800	4.00–4.50
3*	650–714	3.00–3.99	3*	650–700	3.00–3.99
2	602–649	2.00–2.99	2	616–649	2.00–2.99
1	430–601	1.00–1.99	1	470–615	1.00–1.99

Source: NYCDOE Office of Accountability.

*Level 3 is considered proficient for NCLB purposes.

given their eighth-grade scores on state standardized tests. This section also scored the average pass rate for Regents exams and credit accumulation. Liebman included credit accumulation based on historical data that showed a strong correlation between the number of credits a student had in specific semesters (especially in ninth and tenth grades) and the probability of graduating on time. Student progress was calculated on a semester basis in order to account for mobility—the student's progress was used to calculate the score of the school awarding credit in a particular semester.

Additional Credit. Elementary and middle schools are awarded additional credit if they raise proficiency levels by half a level or more for students in the lowest third of performance citywide. The comparable section on the high school version gave additional credit to schools based on the number of students in the same group that attained at least a quarter of the credits needed to graduate in each of their first three years of high school.

Overall Grade. In all but the additional credit subsection, schools received two scores: one showing how well the school performed in relation to all NYC public schools, and another demonstrating how the school performed relative to a group of forty peer schools with comparable students. No school had the same forty peer schools. To determine the overall grade, the city and peer comparisons for each sub-section were weighted 25 percent and 75 percent, respectively, to derive a total sub-section score (which was also converted into a subsection letter grade). The subsection scores were then summed for a total score on the 100-point scale. Any points from the additional credit subsection were then added and the resulting score was converted into a letter grade as shown in table 4-2.(For a technical explanation of the calculation of each subsection and the overall grade, see the *Educator Guide*, available for elementary and middle schools as well as high schools on the DOE's website.[19])

Challenges: Fairness, Fit and Reliability

The Progress Reports quickly became the primary vehicle for assessing and communicating school performance. Even as they were embraced around the city as an accountability tool, their implementation generated a number of challenges related to their fairness, fit with the state's accountability system, and reliability.

Questions of Fairness. Opening new schools was a major pillar of Klein's improvement strategy, and the DOE opened hundreds between 2006 and 2009. New elementary and middle schools did not receive a Progress Report until they had two years of data, and high schools did not receive them until their first cohort graduated. This meant that the new schools strategy went largely "ungraded" in the first years of the Progress Reports. In addition, various stakeholder groups asserted that the Progress Reports did not account well enough for special situations. The DOE eventually responded to these concerns by developing separate reports for schools serving only K–3 students in which only third graders took state exams, for schools serving only special education students taking alternative assessments, and for high schools serving students who were at risk of "aging out" of the school system without graduating.

Some school communities argued that they were disadvantaged in an evaluation system with a 60 percent weight on student growth because they already had high levels of student achievement. But the DOE leadership team was firm in its belief that schools should be rewarded for what they added to their students, and resisted calls to create a customized version of the report for the city's perennially high-performing schools. However, a new rule would go into effect in 2010 so that no school in the top quartile of the performance subsection citywide could receive a Progress Report grade below C regardless of its score on the progress subsection.

Fit with State Accountability System. The DOE's timeline for imposing consequences on underperforming schools was more aggressive than the state's, but the state evaluated schools on absolute performance, not growth rates. As a result, schools with low absolute performance and rapid growth rates received As and Bs on their DOE Progress Reports but showed up on the state's watch list for underperforming schools. This mismatch contributed to public confusion about how to assess school quality.

Another tension was related to the state's annual decision about the cut scores used to define proficiency levels on the state exams. For instance, the state lowered the cut scores for each level in 2009, making it much easier for students to reach the proficiency bar. Because of the heavy weight on year-over-year growth in the Progress Reports, 84 percent of schools received an A or B on that year, as shown in table 4-3. The dramatic uptick in letter grades called into question the usefulness of the Progress Report in determining the real state of performance in the city's schools.

By fall 2009, when the scores were public, Shael Polakow-Suransky had succeeded Jim Liebman as head of the Office of Accountability. He posited that if the leadership team had been able to predict in September that such a large jump might occur, they might have raised their own cut scores even higher so that the letter grades would have been a more accurate reflection of the relative performance of schools.[20] However, he also noted that the DOE would have had to raise the cut scores more than a

TABLE 4-3   **Percentage of schools with each progress report grade, 2007–2009**

	A	B	C	D	F	No score
2007 (n = 1,261)*	23%	39%	26%	8%	4%	n/a
2008 (n = 1,493)	35%	37%	13%	4%	2%	9%
2009 (n = 1,527)	68%	16%	5%	2%	<1%	8%

Source: Author analysis of publicly available progress report results for 2007, 2008, and 2009. New York City Department of Education, Progress Report Results for all Schools Citywide, 2007, 2008, and 2009, http://schools.nyc.gov/Accountability/tools/report/default.htm.

*In 2007 the DOE did not include schools without scores in its progress report data file.

standard deviation from the year before, which would most likely have created questions about the fairness of the decision.[21]

Concerns About Reliability. Perhaps the most significant criticism came from measurement experts such as Harvard professor Dan Koretz, who pointed out that New York State exams were designed to provide a snapshot at a point in time, not as a way to track individual student growth from year to year.[22] Therefore, they were not appropriate for the task of measuring progress at the school level. Another criticism was that the unpredictability of changes in student scores from year to year suggested high levels of measurement error in the state exams, which accounted for 60 percent of the Progress Report grades in elementary and middle schools. High school reports were based on a more diverse set of measures and therefore were more stable.

After years of analysis and discussion of this issue, as well as the concern that those schools with high absolute scores were disadvantaged in the scoring system, the DOE announced that for the 2010 school year it would discard the four indicators it used to calculate the progress subsection in favor of a growth percentile for every student. While maintaining that the four indicators used from 2007 to 2009 had created an appropriate incentive for schools to maximize the growth of every student, the DOE acknowledged that they did not fully account for the relationship between the performance and progress metrics. Going forward, the progress section would use only two indicators: the median growth percentile for all students and the median growth percentile for the bottom third of students on the prior year's proficiency rating.

The new method would account for the fact that low-performing students were more likely to show one year of progress on state exams than high-performing students whose absolute scores were already at the top of the range. The approach was modeled on a methodology developed by the state of Colorado and took into account students' beginning proficiency levels when calculating their yearly progress for state and federal accountability purposes. The underlying assumption was that growth percentiles would control for the probability that students would make one year of progress relative to their starting proficiency. The percentile would indicate what percentage of students had less growth than an individual student. For instance, a student who had a 3.0 proficiency rating on the fifth grade exams would be in the thirty-fifth percentile if he or she maintained a 3.0 rating on the sixth-grade exams. A student who maintained a 4.2 rating from year to year, however, would be in the fiftieth percentile, because fewer students at that rating had historically made a year's worth of progress the following year. In the past, these two students would have contributed the same amount to a school's progress grade. In the new system, the student who began at a higher level would contribute more because of the higher percentile ranking.

In July 2010, as we were writing this chapter, the state of New York released exam scores for the prior school year, which had been calculated based on a new, much higher cut score for proficiency. As a result, scores around the state dropped dramatically. New York City's scores fell at a lower rate than the rest of the state, but nevertheless were a significant drop from 2009. Suransky and his team were recalibrating all scores back to 2006 based on the 2010 cut scores in order to create a better picture of what the growth rates had actually been over the years and were analyzing the implications the sudden change at the state level would have on Progress Report calculations.

Quality Reviews

The leadership team described the Progress Report as a *lagging* indicator because it provided a snapshot of how students performed relative to the year before and how schools scored relative to other schools in the city at a point in time. However, school teams needed different, timelier data that could serve as a *leading* indicator of how their students might perform in the future so that they could adjust their instructional approaches and management systems in order to continuously improve. For this task, the Office of Accountability designed a quality review process to communicate and reinforce a set of behaviors and practices it believed would drive improvements in student achievement.

Beginning in the 2007 school year, every public school in New York City participated in an annual Quality Review (QR), modeled loosely on public school inspections in the United Kingdom and Hong Kong. Every school received a one- or two-day visit from an outside reviewer who observed staff meetings, examined documents, and asked teachers, parents, and the principal a series of questions about a number of the school's practices.

The Office of Accountability partnered with Cambridge Education, a UK-based school-review firm, on the design and implementation of the QR protocols for three years. The rubric that reviewers used to observe schools was focused primarily on the school's use of data to adjust teaching practices in order to improve student outcomes. Liebman and his team created five overarching quality statements, each of which had seven indicators that guided reviewers' observations:

- *Gather data:* School leaders consistently gather and generate data and use it to understand what each student knows and can do, and to monitor students' progress over time.
- *Plan and set goals:* School leaders and faculty consistently use data to understand each student's next learning steps and to set suitably high goals for accelerating each student's learning.
- *Align instructional strategy to goals:* The school aligns its academic work, strategic decisions, and resources—and effectively engages students—around its plans and goals for accelerating student learning.
- *Align capacity building to goals:* The development of leadership, teachers, and other staff capacity is aligned to the school's collaboratively established goals for accelerating the learning of each student.

- *Monitor and revise:* The school has structures for monitoring and evaluating each student's progress throughout the year and for flexibly adapting plans and practices to meet its goals for accelerating learning.

Because the rubric focused heavily on the process by which school teams used data to improve instruction, it reinforced other organizational learning tools that are not discussed in this paper. These include the periodic assessments that every student took five times a year to map their progress toward mastery of the state standards, as well as the teacher-led inquiry teams that were established to spread a culture of data use throughout the schools. Liebman explained the rationale behind a rubric focused on the use of data:

> I looked at all of the rubrics that are out there for school reviews and instructional walkthroughs. They all have one section on the use of data to drive strategy and facilitate frequent adjustment, and many other sections on inputs such as specific teaching practices and curricular materials. As I thought about what we are trying to accomplish, I realized that what we needed to change most was the emphasis in our schools from "teaching inputs" to "learning outcomes." Until we instill a culture of data-driven instructional differentiation in our schools, I'm not as interested in the parts of these rubrics that are about inputs. Secondly, we are not pushing a particular educational philosophy or professional development strategy. The last thing we want to do is to convey the sense that we have an idea in our heads at the central office about what the "right" answer is for each school.

Liebman sometimes described the rubric as a way to determine the degree to which schools were on the way to becoming "autonomous problem-solving units."

In spring 2006, the DOE worked with Cambridge Education to pilot the process in one hundred schools, which led to modest changes to the rubric and review process based on feedback from principals and reviewers. For instance, the pilot used three rating categories: underdeveloped, proficient, and well developed. Pilot schools overwhelmingly scored in the middle category, but principals and reviewers reported that they had seen a wide range of practices within the category. As a result, the Office of Accountability expanded it to five rating categories:

- Underdeveloped
- Underdeveloped with proficient features
- Proficient
- Well developed
- Outstanding

Before going through the QR process, every principal went through approximately forty hours of training on the process through a program called Children First Intensive (CFI) developed and run by Irma Zardoya. CFI familiarized principals with the QR process, the five quality indicators and thirty-five subindicators, and the associated team behaviors reviewers would look for during the QRs.

Throughout the 2007 school year, Cambridge Education consultants performed all of the QRs, but a number of New York principals and administrators observed reviews so that they could conduct the process without consultants in the future. By June 2007, approximately 140 consultants had conducted QRs across more than 1,400 schools; at the end of 2008 they had conducted 2,900 reviews over the two years.

The process was costly; the three-year Cambridge contract was $19 million, and schools spent an enormous amount of time prepping for QRs every year.[23] Beginning in 2009, the DOE no longer reviewed every school annually. Schools that received an A or B on the Progress Report combined with a QR rating of proficient or better were only scheduled for review every third year as long they maintained or improved their letter grade. Schools with other grade and QR combinations remained on the annual cycle. In addition to freeing up time at the school level, the reduction in the number of schools reviewed annually meant that the DOE could accomplish all QRs with internal reviewers rather than expensive outside consultants. At the same time, the DOE made changes to some of the subindicators, tightening some general language to more concrete statements of behaviors. Because only the lowest-performing schools now received QRs, and these were conducted by insiders who were on the lookout for more specific behaviors, the process felt much more compliance oriented than the DOE intended. Shael Polakow-Suransky and his team were considering ways to counter this perception.

Interactions Between the QR and Progress Report

The Progress Reports and QRs were independent tools; for instance, the QR rating appeared on the Progress Report but was not used in the calculation of the school's letter grade. However, Liebman and his team believed that, viewed together, they provided a picture of how the school had performed in the past and how it was likely to perform in the future. This view could be useful in making decisions about positive and negative consequences for schools. Figure 4-1 is a consequences matrix based on schools' Progress Report grades and QR ratings.

In practice, the matrix was not used as an absolute determinant of a school's future, but rather helped identify schools for further attention from the chancellor and the accountability office. For example, a principal in a school that received both an F and an *underdeveloped with proficient features* rating was not automatically fired, but instead was flagged so that the senior team could examine other relevant information about the principal and school in order to make a decision about the school's future.

Plotting schools on the consequences matrix as in figure 4-2 provides an additional layer of information about how schools with various letter grades rated on their QRs. Eventually the DOE hoped to have enough data to determine whether the review was truly a predictor of future performance.

FIGURE 4-1   **Consequences matrix**

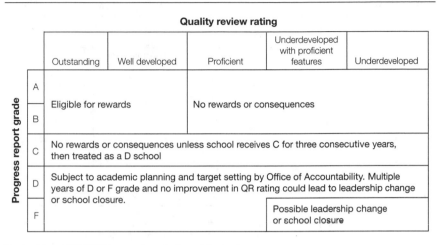

Quality review rating

		Outstanding	Well developed	Proficient	Underdeveloped with proficient features	Underdeveloped
Progress report grade	A	Eligible for rewards		No rewards or consequences		
	B					
	C	No rewards or consequences unless school receives C for three consecutive years, then treated as a D school				
	D	Subject to academic planning and target setting by Office of Accountability. Multiple years of D or F grade and no improvement in QR rating could lead to leadership change or school closure.				
	F				Possible leadership change or school closure	

Source: Internal NYCDOE documents and primary interviews.

For instance, would the eighteen C and D schools with *well-developed* QR ratings in figure 4-2 move into the A and B categories over the next few years? Would the three A and B schools with *underdeveloped* QR ratings receive a lower grade the following year? At the end of the 2009 school year, the tools were too new and had evolved too often to provide a valid link between the two measures.

Though the locus of accountability and the responsibility for the behaviors assessed in the QR process fell squarely on the school principal, the DOE theory of action eventually included the assumption that teams of teachers would use the various data tools to learn more deeply about students and respond more effectively to their needs. As the theory of action continued to evolve, Klein and the senior team began to talk about the strategy as having three phases. The first phase—consolidation—began in 2002 and was focused on the system. The second phase—the autonomy-accountability exchange—began in 2006, and was focused on schools. In 2009, the team was considering a third phase that was focused on classrooms, since, in order for accountability for student performance and team-based problem solving to become sustainable features of the culture at all levels of the system, they had to become part of the everyday work of teachers in classrooms.

Teacher Perceptions of Organizational Learning and Accountability

Pushing the unit of analysis to the classroom level raises the question of how teachers perceive the accountability and organizational learning cultures in their schools, both of which are critical aspects of the DOE performance management system. This

FIGURE 4-2   **Numbers of schools at each position of the consequences matrix, 2009**

		Quality review rating				
		Outstanding	Well developed	Proficient	Underdeveloped with proficient features	Underdeveloped
Progress report grade	A	18	554	391	37	1
	B	0	105	116	13	2
	C	0	17	51	9	1
	D	0	1	17	3	5
	F	0	0	5	0	0

Source: Compiled from publicly available progress report results (New York Department of Education, "2008–09 Progress Report Results for all Schools Citywide," http://schools.nyc.gov/Accountability/tools/report/default.htm).

Note: Includes data from the 1346 schools that had both a progress report grade and a quality review rating in the 2008–2009 school year. All letter grades are from 2009; QR ratings are from 2008 and 2009, depending on the year of a school's last QR.

section draws on a large-scale survey of NYC teacher perceptions and provides an early look at the DOE's theory in action as reflected in teacher perceptions of organizational learning and accountability at their schools. In particular, we explore the extent to which DOE schools do indeed fall out differently across these two dimensions of organizational learning and accountability, suggesting that differences in school cultures do exist and are worthy of further investigation. Second, we examine correlations between various indicators of performance and where schools fall on an organizational learning and accountability matrix. We stress that these are investigatory analyses; we offer several suggestions for future research at the end of this section to deepen our understanding of DOE's theory in action in schools.

The data we analyzed in this exploratory analysis comes from items we added to the DOE's 2009 learning environment survey for teachers. This survey was launched in February of 2009 to approximately 80,000 teachers, of whom 58,000 responded either on paper or online, reflecting a 73 percent response rate. Our data come from the 26,500 teachers (46 percent of the responding teachers) who took the survey online. When we aggregate teacher responses to the school level in our analyses, we focus on non–special education schools where at least 50 percent of teachers responded to a survey and where at least half of these teachers responded to the survey online. This sample of majority-responding schools includes 19,500 teachers in 586 schools.

Building on a pilot validation study conducted in another large urban district, we investigated the extent to which teachers felt *psychologically safe* in their schools. This measure was adapted from Edmondson for the present context and is one of the core components of the organizational learning building block, "supportive work environment," discussed above.[24] The psychological safety measure was composited from three items and added to the 2009 learning environment survey:

- In this school, it's easy to speak up about what is on your mind.
- People in this school are eager to share information about what does and doesn't work.
- People in this school are usually comfortable talking about problems and disagreements.

Teachers responded to these items on a 4-point response scale that ranged from *strongly agree* to *strongly disagree*. A principal components analysis (PCA) indicated that these three items are facets of a single construct.[25] We calculated the arithmetic mean of the items to produce a single value capturing each teacher's sense of psychological safety in their school.

The construct of *accountability* was composited from seven items on the teacher survey, four of which were existing measures on the learning environment survey (first four below) and three of which were new items piloted in other schools prior to being added (remaining three). The items encapsulate many aspects of accountability covered in the literature by capturing teacher perceptions of both internal and external accountability, aspects of the accountability process, and outcomes that serve as accountability targets. Further, and consistent with O'Day's notion of the "new accountability," which places the school at the center of intervention and the teachers as the units for action, these items assessed teacher perceptions of their *school* (rather than their department or some other level of analysis).[26]

- My school has high expectations for all students.
- Teachers in this school set high standards for student work in their classes.
- This school makes it a priority to help students find the best ways to achieve their learning goals.
- My school has clear measures of progress for student achievement throughout the year.
- Our school is focused on improving performance on measures of student achievement for this year.
- Meeting targets for student progress is a priority in this school.
- Helping students reach targets for mastery of important skills and content is a priority for this school.

Conceptually, these items tap into teachers' perceptions of accountability for improving student learning. Together, they offer a new, robust representation of accountability because they cover both the processes and outcomes of accountability for achieving high-performance. This is consistent with many of the theories of action in education reform today, including NYC's theory of action, which has shifted away from a singular emphasis on outputs to one that emphasizes both inputs (e.g., Quality Reviews) and outputs (e.g., performance and Progress Reports).

Empirically, these items hold together as a single construct extremely well.[27] Therefore, as with the psychological safety items, we produced a single accountability value for each teacher by taking arithmetic means of the items.

Our statistical analyses also show that psychological safety and accountability are correlated, but this association is not surprising—nor does it negate the theoretical distinction between the constructs.[28] Both capture perceptions of school culture, which is why they are correlated, and yet they capture different aspects of that culture: psychological safety is about the conditions for adult learning, whereas accountability is about adults focusing on student learning. In fact, 140 schools in our sample were high on one measure but low on the other, suggesting that these two aspects of culture can exist independent of one another.

We aggregated the psychological safety and accountability measures across teachers at each school and reverse-coded them to produce schoolwide values for psychological safety and accountability such that higher values reflect a higher sense of psychological safety and accountability in a school. We used the medians of these school-aggregate measures as the dividing line between high and low values on each measure. The schools that we refer to as *high* on psychological safety and accountability, therefore, are the 223 schools that had values at or above 3.08 and 3.42 on each measure, respectively. The 223 schools that had values below these cutoff points

FIGURE 4-3 **School-level teacher responses regarding accountability/ psychological safety (n = 586)**

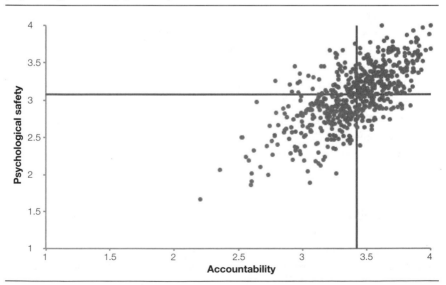

TABLE 4-4 **Descriptive statistics for high psychological safety/high accountability and low psychological safety/low accountability schools**

Performance measure	Min.	Max.		HIGH/HIGH		LOW/LOW	
			n	Mean (s.d.)	n	Mean (s.d.)	t-statistic
2009 progress score	6.7	70	172	47.07 (9.1)	180	42.62 (10.4)	4.28***
2008 performance score	1.5	25	167	16.43 (.34)	177	14.05 (4.2)	5.14***
2009 performance score	7.2	25	172	19.65 (3.9)	180	17.64 (3.9)	4.86***
2007–2008 Quality Review	1	5	168	3.73 (.51)	189	3.44 (.64)	4.67***

*p <. 05; **p <.01; ***p <. 001

on both measures constitute our pool of schools that are *low* on each measure. Figure 4-3 displays the variance that exists between schools regarding teacher perceptions of their school's ability to balance organizational learning and accountability.

To investigate this further, we explored the off-diagonals of the matrix in figure 4-1 to see if there were any apparent differences in performance between the two groups of schools, and we found that there were. As table 4-4 shows, schools with high accountability and high organizational learning environments outperform low-accountability and low–organizational learning environments along a number of performance indicators.[29] We again emphasize that these are preliminary analyses and note, for example, the difference in response rates across the categories. Still, these data do provide some early and suggestive evidence in support of the theory of action regarding the performance benefits associated with creating school cultures in which teachers feel both accountable and psychologically safe to invest in their own learning.

Conclusion

The DOE's performance management system is a distinctive attempt to execute the high wire act of balancing support and pressure that scholars and practitioners have been writing and speaking about for the last decade. The DOE had an explicit theory of action for improving student outcomes—the autonomy-accountability exchange—and attempted to create organizational structures, systems, and culture that were coherent with this theory.[30] For the autonomy-accountability exchange to work at scale, schools had to develop the capacity for adult learning in order to create better learning outcomes for students, given that the central bureaucracy would no longer mandate particular curricular and instructional approaches. This is much more than a psychological contract between the central office and schools, however;

expectations for performance are high and the consequences for not meeting the requirements of the accountability system are serious. Student performance in New York City, as measured by state exam scores and graduation rates, has accelerated since the evolving theory of action was put into practice, but the jury is still out on the specific contributors to that improvement. The state's dramatic upward adjustment to cut scores for 2010 created massive drops in the percentage of students reaching proficiency and reignited the debate about just how much progress students in New York City have actually made during Joel Klein's tenure.

Nevertheless, the approach to performance management, balancing accountability and organizational learning, is already being adopted by other districts. This historical analysis and preliminary empirical work suggest several promising areas for future research. First, we suggest that scholars investigate the ways in which different districts have approached the tensions explored in this paper. Though the DOE's emphasis on the granting of autonomy in exchange for accountability regardless of schools' prior performance is being adopted in other districts, most cities still require schools to earn expanded autonomy. As the demands for improving performance continue and impatience with the status quo increases, it will be interesting to watch how different districts develop and enact their theories of change. How will these theories of action fare and can we create some generalizable principles about what kinds of interventions "work" to produce the results desired? Do different theories of action require different approaches to performance management? Are districts increasingly trying to balance accountability and organizational learning, and if so, do their attempts differ based on their particular theories of action? Investigations of these topics would add greatly to research and practice.

We can also ask, how do these systems impact school culture and what effect does this have on performance? Often, discussions of culture in the education sector are either amorphous ("schools need strong cultures") or descriptive (i.e., long lists of general characteristics such as "collaboration"). If we can identify and more clearly define specific dimensions of school culture (such as accountability and psychological safety) that "matter" in the daily practice of teachers and are predictive of improvements in learning outcomes of students, then we would be better positioned to find points of entry to effect change. If subsequent analyses do support the preliminary findings offered here, and we expect they will, then the next logical question to ask is, why? Why is it that some schools are able to achieve a desirable balance between organizational learning factors such as psychological safety and a sense of accountability? Qualitative data are needed to answer this question and would complement the large-scale survey work that is currently under way in DOE and could provide insight into effects observed.

We hope that the chapters in this volume, including our description of and investigation into the DOE's performance management system and the theories that underlie it, will provide scholars and practitioners with a point of reference for considering their own efforts to cultivate high-performing systems of schools.

5

Improving Instruction in New York City

An Evolving Approach

Jennifer A. O'Day and Catherine S. Bitter

> Our best ideas about policy and management don't *cause* student
> learning to increase. At the very best, when they are working well, they
> *create conditions* that influence what goes on inside the instructional
> core. The primary work of schooling occurs inside classrooms, *not*
> in the organizations and institutions that surround the classroom.
> Schools don't improve through political and managerial incantation;
> they improve through the complex and demanding work of teaching
> and learning.
> —City, Elmore, Fiarman, and Teitel, *Instructional Rounds in Education*

Introduction

Since 2002, New York City schools have been engaged in an initiative of unparalleled scale to improve educational outcomes for the city's 1.1 million students. Over the course of the past eight years, governance structures have been altered, organizational units created and re-created, new monies brought in from both public and private sources, hundreds of teachers and principals recruited and trained, and unprecedented numbers of schools closed and opened. Titled Children First, New York City's initiative under the leadership of Chancellor Joel Klein is undeniably the most ambitious—and one of the most controversial—of such improvement efforts in this city or elsewhere. Much of the controversy—at least currently—centers on particular elements of structural and managerial change, most of which are discussed in specific in other chapters in this volume. The purpose of this chapter is to look behind several of these other reform elements to address the question: *To what extent and in what ways has the New York City Department of Education (DOE) attempted to improve student outcomes by altering what happens in the instructional core of teaching and learning in city classrooms?*

To address this question first requires a definition of what we mean by the instructional core. Building on prior research, Cohen, Raudenbusch, and Ball define instruction as the "interaction among teachers and students around content, in environments."[1] They note that educational efforts often target one or another of these three elements—teachers, students, or content—but that it is in their *relationship* to one another that instruction (and thus learning) actually takes shape. We will return to this definition throughout this chapter.

Second, our focus in this chapter is on the DOE's theory of action (or theories of action) with regard to instructional improvement and the evolution of the strategies and policies that reflect those theories. In their popular 2010 book *Instructional Rounds in Education*, Elizabeth City and her colleagues note that "a theory of action can be thought of as a storyline that makes a vision and a strategy concrete."[2] Carol Weiss describes a reform's theory of change as encompassing the explicit and implicit assumptions about how and why the reform is intended to work.[3] Our goal here is to understand the theory of change that underlies the Children First approach to instructional improvement.

Our discussion derives from document review and interview data collected from February 2009 through May 2010 from approximately sixty stakeholders and participants in the reform efforts. Interviews focused both on general improvement strategies and on specifics related to instructional practice; respondents included current and former officials in the DOE (including four of the five former deputy chancellors of teaching and learning); leaders of the United Federation of Teachers, the NYC Leadership Academy, and nine of the twelve School Support Organizations; additional individuals engaged in providing instructional support to schools and teachers; and other stakeholders. Significantly, we do not include findings about the degree to which classroom instruction has *actually changed* over the course of the Children First reforms. We had neither resources nor time to address this question, and to our surprise have found little or no systematic documentation of instructional changes in NYC classrooms as a result of the strategies we describe. Lacking these data or prior research, we remain agnostic about both the impact to date and the sustainability over time.

Despite the limited parameters of our task, arriving at a clear statement of the DOE's theory of instructional improvement has been somewhat elusive. Several factors contribute to this difficulty. First, the DOE's approach has changed over time as the work has developed, as leaders and participants have learned from their efforts, and as political roles and relationships have shifted. Because prior actions are inevitably understood in light of subsequent events and lessons, trying retrospectively to tease out the degree to which these changes reflect an intentionally staged and coherent approach versus unplanned system learning versus a more fundamental shift in direction is challenging at best. Second, even within a particular phase of Children First, multiple theories of action and interpretations of the reform strategy have coexisted within the DOE and its delegates. The first five years, for example, saw a succession of four deputy chancellors for teaching and learning, each of whom brought his or her own experiences, beliefs, and strategies to the role. Third, the public discourse about the DOE's strategies and intent has not necessarily reflected important streams of instructionally relevant activity that have occurred behind the scenes. As one former deputy chancellor noted, "A lot of the [instructional] work that was taking place would be the centerpiece in any other district, but was subsumed by the political and structural iterations." Finally, the Children First initiative is comprehensive and has many moving parts, many of which are assumed to influence instruction in some—often indirect—way. As the emphasis has shifted to accountability and establishing conditions to support instruction, the intended connections between those conditions and instruction itself have often remained implicit, such that many of our respondents had difficulty articulating the underlying assumptions.

Despite these challenges, a general policy storyline does emerge from respondent reports of how the Children First reforms are, and were, intended to influence classroom instruction. As we have come to understand it, this storyline runs roughly as follows:

- Over the course of Children First, there has been a shift in the DOE's approach from one of centrally managing instruction to one of empowering schools to make instructionally relevant decisions while being held accountable for the results. Strategies in the first phase centered on providing a coherent and consistent system of instructional guidance incorporating common curriculum, instructional resources, and professional learning. Retrospectively, this phase is often described as one of consolidation to ensure equity and overall improvement in instructional inputs.
- In the latter ("empowerment") period of the reforms, the defined role of the DOE vis-à-vis instruction has been to "create the conditions" for instructional improvement. These conditions include not only the three abstract pillars of *empowerment*, *leadership*, and *accountability*, but also a set of more specific and concrete tools and processes designed to focus attention and structure collaborative work around student learning—and around the instructional antecedents and responses to that learning. The underlying assumption is that, with these conditions in place, educators at the school site are in the best position to make instructional decisions appropriate to their particular students and goals. Differentiation, both for individual students and for schools, is an important theme in phase 2, as is the generation and use of varying kinds of information to guide that differentiation.

In the next section we explore this storyline in more detail, delineating the specific policies and tools of each phase of Children First. We then consider the design and implementation of the phase 2 elements in light of similar accountability-based approaches elsewhere, using a framework focused on the generation, interpretation, and use of information for instructional improvement. We end with possible implications of our analysis for future practice.

The Evolution of Instructional Reform in NYC

Change began rapidly in the NYC school system upon the appointment of Joel Klein to the chancellorship in July 2002. Soon after taking office, the Bloomberg/Klein administration embarked on sweeping reforms that touched nearly all aspects of the school system. In this section we focus on the major policies and strategies most relevant to classroom instruction.

Phase 1—Period of "Managed Instruction-Plus," 2002–2006

When Children First began in 2003, deep disparities existed in the quality of curriculum and instruction available to students across the system:

> New York City was a tale of two cities, and there was a thinking curriculum for part of the city, and a nonthinking curriculum for the other part of the city. And the part of the city that was doing well had the thinking curriculum and was more middle class.
>
> *(non-DOE support provider)*

> [When I became] a regional superintendent, I was surprised at how different districts were. A lot of the inequity had nothing to do with money. Because if anything, the poorer districts had more money. What they didn't have access to were the best teachers and best professional development. And in many cases they were left too much alone to make independent decisions, so the kids who needed the most structure or the most thinking curriculum were getting the least.
>
> *(former regional superintendent)*

Among those who had less access to a "thinking curriculum" were traditionally underserved subpopulations, including English language learners (ELLs) and special education students. The same former regional superintendent noted that " . . . up until Children First or No Child Left Behind, it was OK for [ELLs and special education students] not to perform."

The first phase of Children First aimed to address these inequities with a multipronged approach that directly targeted instruction and the capacity of educators across the city. The reform efforts focused on creating instructional coherence within the system, reducing bureaucracy, and reducing inequities in resources among districts and schools to ensure that all students received similar, high-quality instruction and opportunities for learning. Operating as a type of "managed instruction," this phase was characterized by:

- The institution of a common curriculum (mathematics) and instructional approach (literacy) to foster consistency and equity. The DOE mandated the use of a balanced literacy approach and specific mathematics curricula across all elementary/middle schools, common mathematics curriculum in ninth grade, and adolescent literacy classes.
- A clear line of instructional authority, with the DOE at the head. In this first phase, the DOE maintained full oversight of instruction through its department of teaching and learning. Structural changes extended this line of authority through regional superintendents and the local instructional superintendents (LISs) under them.
- The separation of instructional and operational responsibility and authority within the system. Operations were delegated to separate regional centers, to allow regional and local administrators to focus purely on instructional work.
- Significant investment in instructional resources, including professional development, mathematics and literacy coaches, and classroom libraries and textbooks.

Core Curriculum and Instructional Approach

Prior to the Children First reform, upward of seventy elementary school literacy programs existed citywide, with varying levels of implementation and effectiveness. In mathematics, according to a former DOE administrator, they had "just about every program that you can think of, including textbook programs, in the city." Out of these options, the DOE chose one core approach/curriculum for all to implement.

In January 2003, Joel Klein announced that balanced literacy would be the NYC approach to literacy instruction in grades K–8 in all but the most successful schools. Balanced literacy is a meaning-focused, student-centered, and scaffolded approach to the development of literacy skills. Core elements of this approach include modeling of reading skills, flexible grouping based on student strengths and needs, and instructional supports targeting specified skills and levels of text. The choice of this literacy approach was influenced significantly by the histories of those leading the instructional elements of the reform, many of whom had come through Community School District 2. Former District 2 staff and leaders were present throughout the system—as regional superintendents, as central office personnel, and as support providers in schools—and over the years, the system had built its capacity to support this approach to literacy instruction. In addition, Teachers College had been providing professional development for Reading and Writing Workshop for over thirty years, and "the Aussies" also had a strong influence in preparing teachers in the balanced literacy approach.[4] This history gave NYC more internal and external capacity to attempt large scale implementation than many other districts.

Evidence of results for students in several community school districts and from research also influenced the choice of instructional approach. According to a former deputy chancellor, many at the DOE could attest "from experience that using a balanced literacy approach worked for [NYC's] kids, regardless of socioeconomics." Federal program requirements also played a role. To address requirements for the federal Reading First grant, the DOE put in place a phonics program, Month by Month Phonics, which some later described as a "public relations blunder." The new core curriculum met with pushback, particularly from the press and some teachers, and DOE staff spent considerable time defending the choice to the press, to parents, and to others within the system.

In mathematics, a DOE committee chose Everyday Mathematics for K–5, Impact Mathematics for grades 6–8, and Math A for early high school. Like balanced literacy, these programs focused on conceptual understanding, indicating a move toward a student-centered curriculum aligned with the background and experience of those in the DOE at the time. According to a former DOE administrator, the committee used a rubric to evaluate curricular packages, including the ways in which each program supported instruction of ELLs and students with disabilities, the professional development required, and the extent to which the curriculum focused on both mathematics skills and concepts. The selected curricula were rolled out in 2003–2004, with associated professional development provided to regional mathematics liaisons and school coaches citywide.

To support schools' implementation of these new instructional/curricular programs, the DOE invested millions of dollars in instructional support, including new classroom libraries and textbooks for schools throughout the city, professional development provided at both the region and school level (e.g., extensive professional development from Teachers College on balanced literacy), and literacy and mathematics coaches for every school in the city. In addition, specific programs, policies, and resources were targeted at helping underserved and low-achieving students succeed academically. These included policies to end social promotion in grades 3, 5, and 7; mandated Ramp Up to Literacy classes in secondary schools; and extensive professional and materials development (in both English and students' home languages) to support appropriate instruction for ELLs.[5] The professional development, including Quality Teaching for English Learners (QTEL) training, among other programs, focused on instructional strategies to make the core curriculum accessible to ELLs, who in the past may have been excluded from the general curriculum. This significant investment of resources underscored the district's visible intent to influence instruction citywide and to ensure that all students had access to the standards-based curricula.

Restructuring for Instruction

While the central office targeted instruction directly through mandated curricula and instructional resources, it also implemented sweeping structural changes closely tied to its goals for instructional improvement. A major component of Klein's agenda in 2003 was the consolidation of the thirty-two community school districts and the high school division into ten regions, each of which became responsible for both elementary and secondary schools in its geographic domain.[6] Each region was led by a regional superintendent, who reported to the deputy chancellor of teaching and learning. Line authority for instruction was thus centralized.

At the same time, authority for instruction was separated from that for operational management in an attempt to limit distractions and enable regional and school administrators to focus on instruction. Regional operations centers (ROCs) took care of operational issues such as facilities and payroll; regional superintendents were to lead the instructional work. They were aided by subject-area liaisons from the Department of Teaching and Learning and by the local instructional superintendents, who provided direct instructional support and oversight to groups of ten schools within each region. According to one former deputy chancellor, these LISs were put in place because there "needed to be a unit focused solely on instruction."[7]

An additional rationale for the regional structure was to create more equitable educational opportunities. As mentioned earlier, the community school districts reportedly had great disparities in the quality of human capital (both teaching staff and leadership) and professional development. In addition, disparities in the opportunities for teachers from school to school resulted in some schools and districts struggling to attract a strong teaching force. Regions purposively merged higher-performing/higher-capacity districts with their lower-performing neighbors. The task of the regional superintendents, according to one former regional superintendent, was thus "to take the best in the best district we had in our region and make sure the other districts in our region got the same."

Precursors to Empowerment During Phase 1
During this initial period of the reform, the DOE played a strong and visible role in guiding instruction in its member schools. Within this relatively top-down approach to managing instruction, however, precursors to the second, or "empowerment," phase of reform were evident.

Experimenting with Empowerment. From the beginning, there were always schools for which the rules were different. At the outset of Children First, approximately two hundred high-performing schools sought and received waivers from the core curricula in literacy and/or mathematics. Then, starting in 2004, the central office began experimenting with greater school discretion, regardless of prior performance, in exchange for greater accountability for results. From a small Autonomy Zone of 29 schools, the effort had expanded to 332 Empowerment Schools by 2006–2007. The principals of these schools signed performance contracts, committing to specified targets for student test performance, attendance, and graduation rates for all students. In exchange, they received flexibility in the use of funds, instructional programs, and professional development. Equity remained a goal, but for these schools (as for all schools in phase 2) equity became defined as narrowing gaps in student outcomes rather than ensuring similarity in instructional inputs. To reinforce this goal, the schools were subject to consequences, including removal of the principal and closure of the school, if they did not meet targets over several years.

This group of schools became a testing ground for the empowerment-based theory of action that would guide the Children First reform effort in phase 2. They piloted both the general autonomy–accountability exchange and many of the specific tools and processes now integral to the reforms.[8] For example, in 2006–2007, the *inquiry* process was piloted in the Empowerment Schools prior to being implemented city-wide in summer 2007.

Developing School Leaders. During this first phase of Children First, the city also began to invest heavily in leadership development, which would become one of the three central pillars in phase 2 and an important contextual influence on class-room instruction. In summer 2003, the first group of principal candidates entered the Aspiring Principals Program within the Leadership Academy. This program trained new principals to work primarily in lower-performing elementary and middle schools, focusing on their ability to bring the new standards-based curriculum and instructional supports to schools and students that had previously not had access to high-quality instruction. The Leadership Academy later developed programs to train principals to start new schools (the New Schools Intensive), and a coaching program for new principals. Coupled with the replacement of less-effective leaders, these efforts helped lay a foundation for school empowerment. According to one DOE official, "We had by [the start of the Autonomy Zone] trained a lot of the leaders directly . . . and so the level of leadership capacity had gone up a lot."

Investment in Small Schools. At the same time, during phase 1, the number of new small high schools across the city increased rapidly. Instructionally, these schools were characterized by a student-centered curriculum, interdisciplinary approach to instruction, smaller student load per teacher, and integrated time for teacher collaboration—qualities that became more important citywide in phase 2 as many small school leaders moved into administrative positions in the DOE. These schools also served as a training ground for new school leaders entering the system.

Phase 2—School Empowerment, 2007—

In January 2007, Chancellor Klein announced a major shift in the Children First reform that would take the empowerment experiment started in phase 1 and push it out to all schools in NYC. In this new phase, guided by the three pillars of leadership, empowerment, and accountability, the theory of instructional improvement shifted from one of centrally managed instruction to one of generating and using data to inform instruction, empowering all schools to make instructionally relevant decisions, and holding schools accountable for the results. A central tenet of this phase was the belief that empowerment is not an *earned privilege*, but rather a *precondition* for improvement.[9] Thus, all schools, regardless of performance, were granted greater autonomy in exchange for stricter accountability.

With respect to instructional guidance, this new theory of action appeared to many outside of the DOE to be a nearly complete turnabout from the dominant reform model of phase 1. Instead of a mandated common curriculum and instructional approach, every school was granted the authority to decide on an instructional approach for its students. Instead of a clear line of authority for instruction at the central office, the principal was considered the "CEO," with oversight over instruction and supports, and ultimately responsible for student outcomes. Instead of an emphasis on centrally provided professional development for teachers, schools were asked to choose a support organization to provide customized support and professional development. No longer were the leverage points for improvement centrally determined instructional content and teacher development, but rather the provision of and use of information and accountability to focus schools and the system on outcomes.

According to some senior DOE administrators, the 2007 changes were simply an intended evolution from the work accomplished during the first phase of Children First. Phase 1 had laid the base for this new phase 2 theory of action by getting everybody on "more stable ground." As one current DOE leader said, " . . . the introduction of a set of instructional resources . . . and really investing and trying to teach people to use it had a beneficial effect . . . Having that base set of resources available to people and teaching them to use it, it then became much easier to say, okay, well, if you do not want to use it, and you have a better way of doing it, go for it."

Whether evolutionary or an about-face, most agreed that the shift from phase 1 to phase 2 in NYC's approach to instructional improvement was significant. Reported reasons for the change included the difficulty of managing centralized instructional guidance on such a large scale, as well as the broad array of contexts, needs, and perspectives in a system as diverse as New York City. Equally important, however, was the belief that for real change to occur, the attention of the system and its schools needed to be first and foremost on student outcomes, not on a particular instructional approach. According to Klein, good instruction is not inherent to itself; you know there is good instruction when students are engaged and learning—i.e., from the results.[10]

Increased Instructional Autonomy for All

In line with this new theory, in 2007–2008, all schools became "empowered" to choose their own curricular and instructional approach. By moving key instructional decisions closest to the students and schools, reform leaders believed that decisions could be more customized to individual student and school needs and that teachers would be more motivated to work hard and identify creative solutions to instructional problems. In the words of one DOE official, "If you locate the decision making as close as possible to the people that have to implement the decisions, and give enough flexibility and autonomy that they actually can develop a local strategy, that is going to be really powerful and effective in terms of moving student achievement." According to another, "Anywhere where the locus of control is owned at that school level . . . you have a much better shot at those teachers working together, owning their practice, and getting better at it than if you have an external person saying this is how you have to do the work."

Under school empowerment, the role of the DOE regarding instruction shifted to one of *creating the conditions* for schools to make effective instructional decisions appropriate to their students and contexts. While professional development and other capacity-building efforts during phase 1 contributed to these conditions by establishing curricular alignment, building the knowledge and skills of teachers and enhancing classroom libraries and other instructional materials, phase 2 reforms focused on the generation and use of information in a system of empowerment and accountability at the school level.

Tools for Learning and Accountability

To facilitate effective decision making within the empowerment approach, the DOE put in place tools and processes to collect and use relevant data for instructional decision making, promote collaboration among teachers around instruction, and, according to one DOE official, draw "hard lines around student outcomes" for accountability purposes. In chapter 4 in this volume, Childress et al. outline the details of these tools; here we focus on the intended role of each in improving classroom instruction. Later in this chapter, we consider how the collection of tools, taken together, reflect an overall model of information use to improve teaching and learning.

Progress Reports. Issued annually by the DOE, school Progress Reports provide an assessment of a school's performance in three domains—school environment, student performance, and student progress. Schools can also receive additional credit for progress made in closing achievement gaps. Schools are given a composite letter grade derived from the weighted aggregation of these measures and used for accountability purposes. Instructionally, the purpose of the report—particularly the emphasis on progress and gap closure—is to draw attention to the performance of all students in the school (not simply those on the cusp of proficiency) and to motivate instructional responses appropriate to the student population and school context. In economic terms, the Progress Report serves as a lagging indicator representing the result of the efforts of school personnel to improve student learning. Schools with a record of poor Progress Report grades are subject to principal removal or closure.

Benchmark Assessments. More directly relevant for classroom-based instructional decisions, the DOE's Office of Accountability implemented a system of no-stakes periodic assessments for teachers' use in determining students' needs and progress on a regular basis. Responding to requests and criticisms from schools, the DOE worked with vendors to create assessment alternatives that would better meet teachers' needs, and allowed schools to choose from DOE-approved assessments or create their own in mathematics and literacy, as long as they complied with requirements laid out by the DOE.

School Quality Reviews. Starting in 2006–2007, the DOE mandated that all schools participate in an annual Quality Review (QR). This review, conducted originally by outside consultants, and then by trained DOE administrators, analyzes a school's processes along five dimensions, or levers, for change: instructional coherence (curriculum and pedagogy) aligned with state standards, collection and use of data on student learning outcomes, schoolwide planning and goal setting to accelerate student growth, structured professional collaboration to meet school goals, and structures to support continuous improvement processes. Drawn from an instructional framework developed in the Empowerment Schools, the dimensions of the QR rubric can be thought of as leading indicators (in contrast to the lagging indicators of the Progress Reports). That is, they represent elements of a school's conditions believed to be precursors of improved student learning. The rubric has undergone several iterations, and instruction has recently become a higher priority within the rubric. According to a School Support Organization (SSO—see below) representative, "It's much more grounded in what's happening in the classrooms and teacher collaborations."

ARIS. The DOE's Achievement Reporting and Innovation System (ARIS) is an online platform where teachers can access data on their students and school. While it is primarily used as a place to look at test data to inform instruction, the goal is to grow ARIS into a frequently used platform for teachers to share information on effective practices and develop online professional communities.

Inquiry Team. The DOE launched the inquiry team initiative citywide in 2007–2008. This initiative required each school to create a team of teachers and school leaders who met regularly to examine subskills of individual struggling students and identify and test instructional strategies to address the students' needs. By design, the inquiry process not only targets strategies and interventions for specific groups of kids, but also aims to change teaching practice and culture to incorporate consistent collaboration focused on student learning needs and outcomes. Thus, in 2009–2010, the DOE expanded and refined this initiative, setting an expectation that nearly all teachers would engage in collaborative inquiry around instructional strategies, goals, or curriculum—all based on student data.[11]

Restructuring for Instructional Support

Continued restructuring supported the growth of autonomy within the system. The first major structural shift was to dissolve the regions. In place of the line authority associated with regions, the DOE created a system of support for schools, consisting of eleven (later twelve) School Support Organizations (SSOs) from both within and outside the school system. Within the SSOs, the DOE also instituted a system of smaller networks of approximately twenty-five schools each, managed by the SSOs. The SSO structure, like empowerment more generally, reflects the notion that support to schools, as to students, should be differentiated based on need.

School Support Organizations. Each school was expected to select and pay for the services of an SSO. The DOE instituted three types of SSOs: the Empowerment Support Organization (ESO), which supported Empowerment Schools; the Learning Support Organizations (LSOs), which were led by internal DOE staff; and Partnership Support Organizations (PSOs), including nonprofits and university-based centers or departments. The SSOs varied greatly in size and focus. Generally, they helped schools use data to identify areas of improvement, assisted schools in identifying and implementing strategies for improvement, and provided or supported professional development.

Networks. Within the SSOs, schools chose their network or network leader, often basing their choices on existing connections to other schools or to the leader in question. While SSOs varied in structure, network teams generally consisted of four staff—the network leader, achievement coach, business services manager, and student services manager. Beginning in 2010–2011, all networks now also include operations staff.[12] According to one senior DOE official, the network is increasingly considered the targeted unit to build the capacity needed to improve instruction in schools. At this point in time, however, the role of the network is varied and is interpreted in different ways.

In line with the DOE's vision, schools in some networks interact, collaborate, and share learning, facilitated by the network team. As explained by an SSO leader, "The concept of network is really about building strong collaboration and support among the schools within that particular network." Some networks facilitate this type of collaboration through cross-visitation and meetings of inquiry teams among schools and other opportunities for collaboration. However, according to one senior DOE official, only about 10 percent of networks operate in this way.

More often, the network team serves as a support to a set of individual schools. Several SSO representatives noted the challenge that network leaders face in providing support to schools without having line authority over the schools' actions. The network leaders are expected to use their "professional authority" to influence the work in schools. According to one SSO leader, "We became very much aware of the tensions of the role and that we really were not just support . . . We were being asked to . . . manage, in some ways guide—never supervise, but to work alongside to ensure that a principal got done what needed to be done." According to another, "It was hard [asking school staff to do something] because . . . I can't do a thing to you except just keep giving you support."[13]

Building Leadership Capacity

In addition to empowerment and accountability, phase 2 also focused on building school-level leadership, expanding and reorienting the efforts begun in phase 1. Thus, rather than training principals to ensure implementation of the core curricula, Leadership Academy programs focused on developing the principal as CEO, placing particular emphasis on the use of data to determine and manage the improvement process. According to a representative from the Leadership Academy, the principal's role reoriented to "focus on student learning and evidence of student learning, and to create the conditions so that the teacher teams can engage in the work in their classrooms and with each other."

Information and Instructional Improvement in NYC Schools

Our overview of the evolution of the Children First reforms with respect to instruction has been necessarily cursory. We have noted the movement away from a strong centralized instructional guidance system as empowerment and accountability became core elements of the DOE strategy for change. Some respondents outside the DOE lamented this move, arguing that the central office had become "hands-off instruction" and was not "leading educationally." In this section we consider whether this is accurate—at least in intent. Our question: *What is the intended relationship between the phase 2 reforms and the instructional core?* Or, in the words of one cluster leader: "In an environment premised on leadership and empowering accountability, what is the role of central in actually moving instruction?"

To address this question, it is important to begin with the end in mind—that is, with the instructional *goal* of the phase 2 reforms, if there is one. Returning to our earlier definition of instruction as residing in the interaction of teachers and students around content, we would argue that the NYC reforms—including during phase 2— have been very much about changing instruction. Indeed, the objective has been no less than a *fundamental shift in the instructional enterprise*—and in the ways that the system should support it. Instruction under this model becomes not so much about what teachers teach (the presentation of content) as it is about what students learn— or perhaps more accurately, the learning that teachers and students produce together. This concept, of course, is not new, and a number of instructional approaches have long incorporated frequent assessment of student learning and adaptation of pedagogical strategies. The NYC approach seeks to shift the focus even more so onto student learning as the determinant of teaching practice—and to do so at scale, significantly altering the balance between student and teacher in the classroom.

With this goal in mind, the core strategy of results-based accountability and the data it generates take on particular significance. Indeed, much of the focus in the phase 2 reforms is on collecting, assessing, and making available information about student outcomes, school and classroom processes, and school performance. Often when those outside the system—and even many within it—talk about the use of data in the system, it is in reference to the meting out of consequences for schools' failure and grades for school progress. But the collection and use of various types of information is also directed (at least potentially) at classroom instruction—at helping to shape the way that teachers and students interact around content. Our focus in this section is on how the structures and mechanisms of phase 2 reforms are intended to work together to alter classroom instruction and on the design and implementation issues that may hinder their ability to do so.

Given the centrality of accountability and data-based decision making to the current Children First reforms, we have borrowed a framework from O'Day that articulates the conditions under which accountability-based reforms are likely to lead to actual improvements in teaching and learning.[14] She argues that an accountability-based system will produce improvements in instructional practice only to the extent that it (1) generates and focuses attention on valid and relevant information, (2) motivates teachers and others to use that information to improve instruction and student learning, (3) develops knowledge and opportunities for appropriate interpretation and application of the information, and (4) allocates resources appropriately based on evidence of need. Below we discuss each of these dimensions in turn, noting first how the NYC reforms address relevant shortcomings of typical accountability systems elsewhere, and then raising tensions or issues that may reduce the impact of the reforms on classroom instruction—or even contribute to unintended negative consequences. Our focus is on the application of the framework with respect to classroom teaching.

1. *Generate and focus attention on information relevant to teaching and learning and to changes in that information as it is continually fed back into and through the system: In order to alter what happens in classrooms, this focus must occur not only at the school level, but also at the level of individual teachers. Interaction patterns are likely to be particularly important in the generation and spread of such information.*

Typically, accountability systems have had their greatest success in focusing attention on student performance data at the district or school level, but have been less successful in *generating* (or making useful) such data at the classroom level. Weaknesses of most accountability systems include invalid data on outcomes (data that are misaligned with learning goals) and data that are too infrequent or imprecise to be of use in guiding classroom instruction; an overemphasis on outcomes with little attention to data on the processes and other inputs that might have contributed to those outcomes; and a top-down, unidirectional flow of information from the center to the schools, doing little to institute feedback loops or to break down isolation of teachers and other school personnel.

The Children First phase 2 strategies also seek to focus attention on student learning, but the combination of mechanisms described in the previous section address a number of the shortcomings of more typical results-based systems. First, the incorporation of the periodic assessments provides more specific and more frequent information on student learning than is typical in most large systems. Second, the panoply of data sources provides information not only about state test results, graduation, and other student outcomes, but also on a variety of conditions and practices that may be influencing those outcomes (e.g., through learning environment surveys, Quality Reviews, the inquiry process, and ARIS). And third, there are specific mechanisms and tools to help structure teachers' efforts to *connect* the information on outcomes and processes, to identify the likely antecedents to those outcomes, and to develop targeted strategies in response. The most obvious example is the inquiry process, but some SSO respondents noted how the rubrics for the QR could also serve as a general guide for classroom teachers in assessing their own practice.

Despite these positive attributes, the nature of the information generated in the NYC system has been an area of considerable pushback. While most of the criticism has focused on the reliance on what is considered by some to be questionable test score data for school accountability, the questions about assessment validity are equally if not more important at the classroom level. Because of the centrality of information on student performance to the operation of the reforms on classroom instruction, the ability of those tests to validly and reliably measure student performance over time and to align with the goals and standards of the system is critical. If the test results are unreliable or if they systematically overestimate student performance (as the recent recalibration of New York State tests scores implies), then teachers could be drawing false conclusions about the needs of their students or the effectiveness of their instructional efforts. The use of interim tests combined with an emerging emphasis on analysis of student work in some networks and schools could mitigate, but might not erase, the negative effects of an invalid or unreliable summative assessment.

2. ***Motivate teachers and others to attend to relevant information and to expend the effort necessary to augment or change their strategies in response to this information:*** *Motivation must ultimately occur at the individual level but it is likely dependent on the normative structures of the school as well as on the individual characteristics of teachers and students.*

Ostensibly, one of the focal goals of any accountability system is to motivate effort toward improvement on the part of educational personnel. However, typical bureaucratic accountability systems fall short of this mark and often produce unintended negative effects on motivation and staff morale as well. The weaknesses of typical systems include top-down, control-oriented interaction patterns that foster compliance and hierarchy over learning and improvement. Overemphasis on the threat of negative consequences for the adults diverts attention away from student needs toward protecting adults. The end result is often gaming behaviors, curriculum narrowed to testing specifications, formulaic rather than reflective responses to student results, and risk-averse rather than innovative practice. These tendencies can be exacerbated in classrooms and schools where teachers believe the targets are simply unattainable given the resources and knowledge available to them at the time.

The empowerment pillar of the phase 2 reforms seeks to address the negative consequences of accountability by recognizing the professional expertise that exists in schools and classrooms and by providing the authority to school personnel to act on that expertise. The assumption is that this will lead to a sense of ownership that will produce far more dedication and effort than the system would get by imposing a particular curriculum. As a cluster leader notes, "Empowerment really is this idea that if you allow people to own their work, they're much more willing to be responsible and accountable for that work."

Two key implementation issues may severely limit this intended effect. First, it is not always clear exactly *who* is being empowered in NYC schools. While some DOE officials talk about empowering the "school community," including classroom teachers, the emphasis in reform documents and in most of our interviews is on empowering *principals*, with the belief that "if we empower principals, they will empower teachers." According to a leading DOE official, "We share authority with principals; they should do the same with teachers." The following year, however, this same leader admitted, "We've done a good job empowering principals, but teachers don't see a place for themselves . . . principals are not modeling empowerment for teachers." Indeed, teacher union representatives have described the reforms (whether in phase 1 or phase 2) as "revolution from above" with little involvement of teachers, even though it is teachers who are invested with the ultimate responsibility for instruction and student learning.

A second issue lies in the value teachers place on the outcome (e.g., increased test scores) and their perceived ability to attain that outcome. The theoretical and empirical literature on motivation suggests that teachers are more likely to be motivated to improve student performance on measures that they perceive as valid indicators of important learning (raising again the issue of the quality of the assessments) and to the extent that they feel they have the capacity to do so.[15] This perceived capacity is a product of the teachers' beliefs both in their students' ability to achieve and in their own ability to ensure that they do so. Compliance and gaming can derive as much from not knowing how to accomplish a particular goal as from resistance to that goal. This last point closely links motivation and capacity, our next focus in the framework.

3. *Develop the knowledge and skills to promote valid interpretation of information and appropriate attribution of causality at both the individual*

and school level: Learning takes place through the interpretation of information, whether that information is data from a student assessment, research on reading instruction, or observation of a colleague's lesson. Interpretation is dependent on prior learning and influenced by an individual's goals, expectations, values, and context.

Interpreting information about student performance and then acting effectively on that information takes more than motivation; it requires knowledge. There is a vast literature on the kinds of knowledge and skills teachers must have to meet the instructional needs of their students, substantial evidence on the need for supports to go along with any policy pressure to improve, and a growing literature on the influence of interpretation in the implementation of any reform effort.[16]

Typically, capacity-building mechanisms and resources in accountability-based models have been weak, suffering from a reliance on add-on assistance from external agents who often have limited capacity themselves, little understanding of the specifics of the school or classroom, little commitment to the school, and virtually no accountability. Low levels of intensity and transmission models of professional development also combine to reduce the impact most external providers have on instructional practice, particularly in low-performing schools. Widely varying and superficial interpretations of the reforms often lead teachers to incorrectly interpret new practices as "what we are already doing" or to incorporate only the surface elements of the reform without understanding its deeper content.[17]

The approach of NYC schools differs from other systems mainly in its placement of the locus of both learning and expertise squarely in the school itself rather than in the central office. The espoused theory is that the best knowledge about teaching and learning resides in the schools, and the role of the central office, the networks, and the SSOs (now clusters) is to mobilize and grow that expertise. Teachers are to learn from one another in structured opportunities for collaboration and examination of practice and student work, with authority to bring in external providers as appropriate to the identified needs of the school. Principals are to play a key role in leading the learning process, and the central office provides tools and routines to structure that process and keep it focused on student learning.

Several factors may undermine the capacity-building efforts of phase 2 reforms. First, the impact of any tool on teacher learning and instructional practice is dependent on interpretation and understanding of the tool itself. Network leaders and SSOs have varied greatly in their own understanding of tools like the inquiry process and thus in their ability to support teacher teams in using them effectively. Our interviews with SSO leaders suggested that some had made inquiry a central element of their capacity building efforts, closely tied to recent curriculum mapping initiatives, while others were much less familiar with or focused on its use.

Second, the tools that are intended to scaffold teacher learning and change are themselves subject to frequent change. Protocols and measures for the school Quality

Reviews, the inquiry process, and the Progress Reports have all undergone or are undergoing substantial transformation. On the one hand, such changes reflect the DOE's attempt to learn from and respond to feedback from the field. Changes to the QR, for example, have prioritized a focus on coherent curriculum and aligned pedagogy in the school. One external support provider noted that the QRs "just keep getting better and better." Despite these improvements, if the tools that teachers are to use are constantly undergoing revision, teachers have limited opportunity to develop consistent practice that would lead to expertise. Such constant change can also undermine motivation. Stability is an important element to learning, and it is an elusive one in NYC schools. While DOE educators with a long history and considerable expertise in evidence-based practice can see the connection of one version to another, this may not be the case with many of those who are newer to the practice.

Finally, research on teacher knowledge and professional communities suggests that overreliance on teachers' own identification of instructional problems and on each other's expertise may not result in improved practice.[18] Content knowledge and curricular and pedagogical coherence are still essential. Yet multiple informants reported that content-based professional development has declined significantly. Said one support provider, "I am still working with 150 principals. No one is doing professional development in curriculum." By contrast, some networks appear to have increased attention to curriculum and curriculum mapping recently, often as an outgrowth or focus of their inquiry work. Indeed, understanding where one's instruction is headed (e.g., the standards) and how a student's performance maps onto that goal and onto expected learning progressions (e.g., curriculum) can provide the needed substantive context for identifying and effectively addressing individual student needs targeted through the inquiry process.

4. ***Allocate resources where they are most needed***: *While often thought about at the level of the school and system, allocation of teacher resources (time, attention, effort) within the classroom is often critical to the impact of information on student learning.*

From its inception, a core goal of the Children First initiative has been to foster greater equity across schools and regions of the city with respect to their access to high-quality instructional resources. The managed instruction approach of the first phase of the reforms was designed to address these inequities and infuse instructional capacity and consistency across schools of the city, while taking sharper action in the consistently lowest-performing schools. In phase 2, differentiation based on outcomes seems to be the goal both for students in classrooms as well as schools, and woven throughout the accountability measures are mechanisms to motivate and support attention and resources to the lowest-performing students. Several of the mechanisms described earlier focus on data that allow the identification of students requiring additional attention, and processes like inquiry teams structure teachers' attention toward meeting the instructional needs of those students who are outside the "sphere of success."

What is not clear from the efforts in phase 2 is who is monitoring the relationship between classroom *instruction* and student outcomes across city schools.[19] One purpose of such monitoring would be to identify and make available practices and curricula that appear to be more effective. Right now, that task is located specifically in the role of the network leaders, but their purview is limited primarily to the twenty-five schools in their charge. Cross-network sharing of information on instruction is reportedly more hit and miss, though the newly formed clusters as well as cross-network analysis of QR reports could provide an opportunity for such if directed toward this goal. ARIS also presents an opportunity for teachers to share their work, but this aspect of the system is still fairly inchoate.

Another purpose of monitoring instructional offerings would be to create a running picture of the *distribution* of instructional resources and approaches across the city in order to assess whether equity in access to those resources is increasing over time. When asked how they will know whether the goal of more equitable access to high-quality instruction has been met, the answer from DOE officials was consistently that they will know by the outcomes. But relying solely on the lagging indicators of test scores can be problematic. By the time persistent failure is evident from test scores, students will already have missed out on opportunities. In addition, changes in test score measurement over time may make it difficult to track trends in outcomes accurately. For example, the recent recalibration of state testing results based on a higher cut score for proficiency led to questions in the media about the degree to which achievement gaps in NYC schools had indeed narrowed.[20] This in turn has raised questions about the extent to which inequities persist in instructional quality and resources. One area in which the DOE is stepping in to ensure greater equity is instruction for ELLs and special education students, led by the newly established Division for Students with Disabilities and English Language Learners.[21]

Conclusion and Implications

What might this discussion suggest for moving the instructional reforms forward in NYC and elsewhere? For one thing, it suggests that New York City has indeed, as part of its accountability-based reforms, put in place a set of tools and structures that have the potential for influencing classroom instruction in ways that such reforms elsewhere have often failed. At the same time, the implementation challenges discussed above imply some potentially needed refinements in specific areas to realize that influence. Here we focus on four such refinements, all within the context of the DOE's overarching theory of action. We end with considerations for other jurisdictions looking to the NYC model.

Suggestions for Moving Forward in New York City

As this volume goes to press, Joel Klein has just announced his resignation as chancellor of New York City schools, opening up a window of opportunity for the system to consider modifications and new directions in the reform agenda he initiated. It is unclear how much of that agenda will remain, although current indications point to a continuation of central tenets rather than a major overhaul. It is within that context that we offer the following suggestions.

Clarify and amplify messages about the role and nature of instructional improvement in Children First. The current iteration of Children First emphasizes the conditions for improvement on the one hand and student outcomes on the other. Between these two, however, lies the instructional core of teaching and learning. As we gathered data for this chapter, we were struck both by the claims from stakeholders *outside* the system that the reforms were only about test scores, and by the difficulty that many respondents *inside* had in explaining exactly how the reform mechanisms were intended to affect classroom practice. Descriptions of specific reform tools and their purposes also varied from respondent to respondent (sometimes within the DOE itself), and conflicting reports about whether instructionally relevant initiatives were mandatory, encouraged, or voluntary were commonplace.

We concluded that the storyline about Children First with respect to classroom instruction is unnecessarily disjointed, vague, or even absent from the broader representation of the reform goals and strategy. The lack of a clear and reinforced message about how the mechanisms implemented through Children First will improve what happens inside classrooms among teachers and students makes it difficult to counter criticism that the reform is only about accountability and consequences. It may also inhibit teachers and principals from understanding the bigger picture in relation to their daily work, thus undermining coherence and a sense of common direction as well as long-term sustainability.

Capture, analyze, and use systemwide information on instruction and curriculum as well as on student outcomes. Although the targeted unit of change in NYC is the school, the central office still has a role to play in ensuring equal access to high-quality curriculum across schools, identifying and disseminating effective practices, and coordinating learning across practice communities and networks. One strength of Children First has been its development and deployment of tools to collect information on structures and processes relevant to instructional improvement. But to date the DOE has not taken full advantage of the opportunity these tools present to track and analyze what is happening instructionally across schools. Systematic analysis of QR data, incorporation of instructional rounds and similar mechanisms within networks, and regular convening and focused inquiry of network leaders are among the available avenues for collecting and monitoring information on instruction.

Slow down and consolidate. The rapid pace and scale of change throughout the period of Children First was a consistent theme across respondents. In particular, frequent restructuring of the system, rapid and multiple introductions of new initiatives system-wide, and annual changes to many of the tools and requirements related to instruction have contributed to a sense of constant change and uncertainty among many with whom we spoke. When measures change frequently, it is difficult for participants to assess progress in their practice or to gain enough experience with a process to determine what is useful from it, for what purposes, and under what conditions. When structures change frequently, it becomes more difficult to establish or maintain professional relationships and communities of practice—or sometimes just to know who to go to to get things done. The type of deep cultural shift sought by the reforms requires consistency and time to take root, as suggested by Talbert in her treatment of mature inquiry teams in the next chapter. And without deep roots, sustainability across time and administrations—particularly in the heart of instructional practice—is unlikely. DOE leaders may thus want to resist the temptation to continually tinker with the tools, even if they perceive the changes as clear improvements.

Focus on building capacity. The human capital demands in a system of empowerment are substantial. Principals must not only understand but also lead a cultural shift in the very conception of sound instructional practice, while network leaders are expected to develop principals' knowledge and skills to do so. Cluster leaders, in turn, must enable this process, coordinating learning and managing knowledge across the networks, yet the clusters operate with very lean staffing. And of course, the need for capacity building clearly extends to teachers, especially in the areas of content knowledge, curriculum, and pedagogy, as these are essential for interpreting data on student learning and devising differentiated and relevant strategies for moving students toward meeting challenging standards.

How can the DOE address these issues? We believe that the state's adoption of the Common Core State Standards (CCSS) provides an excellent opportunity and useful frame for taking the instructional work to a new level. Planning along these lines has already begun in the DOE. A clear danger is that the CCSS will be seen as yet another new initiative rather than a way to deepen and connect the instructional work already well underway. For example, integrating the CCSS into the inquiry and curriculum mapping processes could provide a common basis for collaboration and calibration not only within but also across schools while maintaining the commitment to school empowerment. It could generate the assignment and analysis of more complex student work than is produced in any of the current standardized assessments. In addition, bringing teachers into the development and roll-out work associated with the CCSS could provide additional opportunities for instructional capacity building and for motivating deeper buy-in and commitment to the reform direction, which will be critical to sustaining the Children First reform beyond the current administration.

Lessons for Other Jurisdictions

The problems addressed by the Children First reforms—including how and what to centralize and what to leave to the discretion of schools, how to ensure access for all children to high-quality teaching and opportunities for success, and how to motivate and sustain improvements over time—are issues common to all urban systems. Understanding the DOE's theory of action can pose alternatives for leaders elsewhere to consider, as well as specific tools that could be incorporated into other efforts. A few cautions are in order, however. The first is that New York City had a wealth of instructional capacity in the form of strong instructional leaders in many of the community school districts and support provider organizations on which to draw. Second, everyone with whom we spoke noted that the first phase focus on instructional coherence laid the necessary foundation for an empowerment approach. To the extent that other districts lack either the capacity for instructional support or school-level coherence, empowerment may not lead to improvements instructionally. Third, the DOE's accountability-based approach is unusually comprehensive in its generation and use of information on both leading and trailing indicators and in its structures to support professional collaboration. Piecemeal adoption of particular tools may not be strong enough to produce meaningful change. And finally, it is important to remember that many of the fundamental tenets of the reforms are as yet unproven. Scores and graduation rates have risen, but we do not know why, and we do not know whether this growth will be sustained over time.

6

Collaborative Inquiry to Expand Student Success in New York City Schools

Joan E. Talbert

Developing school capacity to continuously improve student achievement is essential to the success of New York City's strategy to empower schools and hold them accountable for results. The Inquiry initiative is the New York City Department of Education (DOE)'s approach to developing this capacity. Its goal is to develop school administrators' and teachers' skills in using multiple forms of student performance data to diagnose and close achievement gaps and to create school cultures in which educators collaborate in using evidence as the basis for instructional decisions to expand student success.

New York City's focus on building professional capacity for evidence-based practice stands in sharp contrast to conventional district approaches to improving student achievement. Most feature teacher professional development in content instruction and/or the implementation of curricula with fidelity. They promote particular standards for teacher performance in the classroom. An inquiry approach shifts the focus to student performance and calls on teacher teams to bring all students up to grade-level standards. Teachers are asked to diagnose the learning needs of struggling students and design instructional responses and system changes that meet their learning needs.

This chapter's three purposes are to:

- Describe the evolution of NYC's Inquiry initiative
- Illustrate how the inquiry model works to improve student achievement
- Point to challenges and dilemmas system leaders face in promoting and sustaining inquiry-based school reform

The description of NYC's evolving inquiry design and resources draws on interviews and conversations with reform leaders inside and outside the system during 2006 to 2010. Illustration and analysis of school outcomes and implementation challenges draws on longitudinal research in NYC high schools.[1] The discussion of system challenges captures issues that have surfaced in NYC and in other districts pursuing inquiry-based school reform.[2]

Evolution of NYC Inquiry Initiative

NYC's Inquiry initiative takes a continuous improvement frame on the problem of educational reform. In the long run, the system's capacity to significantly improve student achievement depends on each school's use of data to address all students' learning needs. The problem of change, in this view, is that every school has a *sphere of success*—a group of students with whom it is currently successful. The challenge is to bring more and more students into this sphere.

The Inquiry initiative assumes that every school has a particular student population and pattern of skill gaps, as well as programs and policies that systematically limit the pool of successful students. It thus asks each school to analyze student performance data to determine why some students do not succeed—what skill gaps are not being addressed by the curriculum and how the instructional decision making systems limit success—and to respond effectively to accelerate their learning. This approach may seem straightforward. However, it challenges the conventional assumption that some students will fail to meet standards regardless of teacher efforts, and it brings into question a school's established instructional culture. A design for inquiry therefore must be strategic in shifting teachers' and administrators' thinking about why students struggle and what can be done to ensure that they meet their potential.

The DOE modeled its original design for school inquiry after one created in a local administrator credentialing program called SAM (Scaffolded Apprenticeship Model), currently in its fifth iteration. Developed through a 2004–2005 pilot, SAM marries inquiry-based school reform with leadership development.[3] The DOE piloted SAM's design in over three hundred Empowerment Schools in 2006–2007 and launched the Children First Intensive (CFI) inquiry initiative systemwide in 2007–2008. In 2009–2010, the initiative was refined and renamed *collaborative inquiry*. Table 6-1 provides an overview of the evolving inquiry design and resources through 2009—2010.

The Inquiry Team Model

The inquiry team (IT) design features *teams* that collaborate to improve student learning; *tasks* of examining student work and data, identifying learning targets and instructional strategies, and using assessments to evaluate outcomes; and *tools* that scaffold

TABLE 6-1 Evolution of NYC's inquiry initiative design and resources: 2006–2010

Design and resources	2004–2010 SAM program (Baruch College—New Visions (NV); four iterations)	2006–2007 DOE's ESI pilot (Empowerment Schools; N = 300)	2007–2008 CFI inquiry team initiative (all NYC schools)	2008–2009 CFI inquiry team initiative (all NYC schools)	2009–2010 CFI collaborative inquiry initiative (all NYC schools)
Who's involved?	Teacher team in certification program (involving twenty-eight schools, four in multiple iterations)	School team of principal and teachers	School team of principal, instructional leadership team (ILT) members, other staff; school data specialist	Two (or more) school teams of ILT, teachers, staff; school data specialist; two-year 90% goal identified	Teacher teams at grade-level and by content/ SLC (90% goal); cross-cutting school team
Inquiry model	Team uses data to select up to fifteen target students and identify skill gaps and learning targets; designs and assesses instructional response to move students; makes system changes; spreads inquiry	SAM model	SAM model; target students from lowest-performing third of student population	SAM-DOE model expanded to target students who were not successful but not necessarily lowest third	Team examines student work/data and teacher work; identifies, implements, and evaluates an instructional strategy. Core team uses results to lead schoolwide change and capacity building
Inquiry tools and resources	Low-inference transcripts (LITs) of target students' classes; coaching protocol; NV data platforms	SAM tools	Inquiry target tool ; periodic assessments; ARIS tools; progress report; puality pview (QR); CFI Sharepoint site (website containing training materials shared between SAFs and SSOs); Inquiry Team Interface (early version of inquiry spaces)	Handbook with SAM tools and guidance; same tools and resources as 2007–2008.	Same, with revised inquiry diagram and QR rubric; collaborative inquiry resources and inquiry spaces (online work spaces located within ARIS)

continued

TABLE 6-1 *continued*

Design and resources	2004–2010 SAM program (Baruch College—New Visions (NV); four iterations)	2006–2007 DOE's ESI pilot (Empowerment Schools; N = 300)	2007–2008 CFI inquiry team initiative (all NYC schools)	2008–2009 CFI inquiry team initiative (all NYC schools)	2009–2010 CFI collaborative inquiry initiative (all NYC schools)
On-site resources	Tuition support; school funds for dedicated inquiry time	Per session allocation for team members to meet before and after school	Per session allocation for team members to meet before and after school	Reduced monetary allocation to support inquiry work	Reduced monetary allocation to support inquiry work
Inquiry team support/ training	Weekly seminars and coaching with SAM facilitator; weekly facilitator training	Support from ESI network leader and achievement coaches; monthly network leader training Two three-hour workshops for principals preparing for the introduction of inquiry work and roll-out of the accountability tools	Support from network, SAF; monthly SAF/SSO training; monthly principal network meetings; monthly data specialists training	Same support; SSOs designed training for network teams, and SATIFs Stipends for principal and teacher leaders to support the inquiry professional development in each school networks	Support from principal/ team leaders, citywide monthly cluster institutes Support from network, SATIF, achievement coaches; network sharing Stipends as per 2009

the inquiry work. The model was designed to develop teachers' skills in using student work and assessment data to analyze and address particular skill gaps, thus challenging assumptions that not all students can succeed. It empowers them to make decisions about what and how they are teaching and, in turn, to influence schoolwide decisions.

The CFI model replicated SAM's design. However, it was implemented without the credentialing program's rigorous assignments, weekly seminars, and ongoing feedback and support from an instructor well prepared to facilitate inquiry-based school reform. The IT model did include support from a senior achievement facilitator (SAF) who was an experienced educator/administrator trained to lead inquiry, as well as an evolving set of assessments and online tools to support teams' inquiry work.

Inquiry Team. During the first year of implementation (2007–2008), a school inquiry team comprised the principal and several teachers and staff who represented a broad range of expertise. IT members were responsible for collaborating to use data to improve the success of struggling students. In addition, they were expected to lead colleagues to use instructional responses effective with struggling students, to identify and improve instructional decision making systems, and to spread inquiry practices in the school.

Targets. The model emphasizes "getting small in order to go big" with inquiry-based improvement.[4] This means focusing on a small group of target students and a specific learning target as a starting place for school reform. DOE guidelines for practice instruct the IT to first identify a content area that most needs improvement according to the data and then to identify a target population of struggling students (the lowest-performing third) and select a small group of twelve to fifteen students as a focus for their inquiry. The team then is to use multiple assessments to identify a skill gap prevalent among the target group, such as reading, and then to home in on a subskill (e.g., comprehension) and a particular learning target relevant to that gap (e.g., topic recognition or using context cues).

The approach of beginning inquiry with small learning targets emerged from the early experience of SAM facilitators. School teams were overwhelmed by the need to analyze large amounts of data and translate the data into ways of helping students meet grade-level standards. The facilitators responded by focusing the work on specific targets for intervention. They reasoned that this made the work manageable in scope and potential for improving students on a given skill. Absent a push to stay small, some teams gave up on what they perceived as the need to bridge very large skill gaps, doubting that they could make a difference.

Tasks. The IT model specifies three broad inquiry phases imported from the original SAM model. As described in the DOE's 2008 *Inquiry Handbook*, the phases and steps are:

- *Phase I. Identify Focus, Students, and Targets:* Use data to identify a focus area in which the school is not doing well (e.g., ELA or mathematics), identify a schoolwide target population of students with which the school has not been successful historically, define a small group of target students, set a long-term goal, define learning targets and short-term goals.

- *Phase II. Move the Students:* Analyze conditions of learning for the target students, design and implement an instructional change strategy, evaluate and revise based on interim progress measures.
- *Phase III. Move the System:* Analyze instructional decision making systems that produce conditions of learning, design and implement a system change, evaluate and revise based on interim progress measures.

The tasks are meant to guide the work of a school team and to provide a pathway for continuously bringing more students into the sphere of success. Both SAM and the DOE model have moved incrementally toward spreading the inquiry model to multiple teams across a school.

Tools. Resources and tools designed to support school teams' inquiry include data platforms with results of periodic assessments, formative assessments and protocol for their development, and protocol for looking at student work. The DOE has developed an arsenal of tools over the course of the Inquiry initiative, many of which are housed in ARIS (see table 6-1).[5]

One tool developed through SAM and built into the IT process is the *low-inference transcript* (LIT) in the classrooms of target students. The LIT is a means of documenting the class experience of students by writing a verbatim script of classroom talk and activity. It discourages observers from making inferences about "quality of instruction," or promulgating the idea that a student is "lazy." It is meant to provide valuable data for understanding the school curriculum as taught and experienced by students—rather than as it exists in a plan or in teachers' minds. LITs from multiple classrooms allow a team to identify cross-class trends that help to inform their next steps. As discussed in the next section, , inquiry teams have found this to be a powerful resource for their work because it shifts their focus from instructional delivery to student learning.

Launching the System's Inquiry Team Initiative

The DOE asked all NYC schools to implement the IT model in school year 2007–2008. Every school was required to establish an IT that included the principal and key school leaders and staff. The team was to designate a data specialist who would attend monthly meetings to learn how to use NYC's data systems and to share effective practices with other schools, as well as to lead data analysis in the school team.

Two major and concurrent system changes compounded the challenge of getting the systemwide IT initiative off the ground and running—restructuring from regional authorities to School Support Organizations (SSOs) and networks, and the initiation of the Progress Report and Quality Reviews by the Office of Accountability.[6] As a consequence, the DOE faced substantial resistance as it pushed to develop systemwide capacity for inquiry-based school improvement.

Resistance. Resistance came from the perceptions by principals and some SSO leaders that the IT initiative was a top-down mandate for change in school practice. Principals were reeling from major changes in system organization and accountability demands at the time they were asked to launch the IT initiative. A DOE leader commented: "We found a lot of angry people who . . . were very upset that Regions [regional authorities] were going away after all the buildup of the Regions and all of that work. They just didn't understand why this was happening."

Given their role as service organizations, some SSOs shied away from pushing the implementation of IT practices, fearing that school leaders would see them as an arm of the Office of Accountability. As a result, as one DOE leader put it: "We had different, mixed messages being sent out to the network leaders . . . In some cases [when the Senior Achievement Facilitator was a strong inquiry facilitator], network leaders were very supportive. In other cases, not . . . So it was an interesting first year."

In turn, school leaders received varying messages and levels of support for developing an effective inquiry team. Many principals did not understand how inquiry would help them increase student achievement and complied only minimally with the IT requirement. SSO leaders, SAFs, and network leaders could help schools make connections between inquiry and student outcomes only if they understood and bought into the model themselves. Because the inquiry initiative pushed against more conventional approaches to instructional improvement, such as teacher professional development in content instruction, many of those charged with supporting the inquiry work were not on board or lacked the skills to push the reform, or both.

Capacity Building. Although the DOE was developing a robust data system to support school inquiry, the system was not up and running when the inquiry initiative was launched. To compensate, the DOE developed a tool that was essentially an Excel file of student data that was not very user friendly.

Training was a major challenge during this phase of the initiative. In contrast to schools' voluntary participation in SAM and the DOE pilot in Empowerment Schools, the rest of NYC schools had not opted into the inquiry team initiative or its training. Moreover, a top-down approach to school improvement ran counter to the rhetoric of school autonomy and accountability.

In addition, the inquiry model included many facets and phases. A DOE leader commented that trainers were challenged "to make the work less theoretical and embed it in the actual work that people are engaged in . . . so that it becomes *practical* and they see the connections . . . That's always the biggest challenge."

The range and diversity of school readiness for inquiry posed yet more training challenges. A key factor was the principal's level of comfort with distributed leadership and willingness to collaborate and share decision making with teachers. A further readiness issue was the fit between inquiry practice and the school's culture.

According to one DOE leader, "Some schools were in crisis. Other schools had their own things in place and were moving very nicely and felt this was now a mandate—like 'Who needs this? I'm doing fine with my school'."

Nevertheless, some schools embraced the IT model and took advantage of DOE resources designed to support development of inquiry practices. According to an external evaluation of the first phase of the CFI inquiry initiative, 54 percent of school teams had completed a full inquiry cycle by the end of 2007–2008 and 75 percent by the early months of the 2008–2009 school year.[7] (It should be noted, however, that these statistics do not distinguish between ritual inquiry practice and deep inquiry cycles that boost target students' performance. Research on inquiry-based reform in NYC and elsewhere points to a qualitative difference between implementing surface features and embracing principles and "stance" of inquiry to improve student achievement.)

Implementation Challenges. The DOE used feedback from network and school leaders, along with its internal evaluation, to identify three major implementation challenges that shaped the 2009–2010 revisions.

First, although the DOE considered the Inquiry Team model relevant and valuable for all schools, some principals perceived it as out of sync with their school culture and implemented it in name only. For example, educators in some small schools that embrace a whole child philosophy of education regarded the use of fine-grained data to diagnose and address student skill gaps as inconsistent with their beliefs about how to improve student achievement. In such cases, the principal rejected data-based inquiry as a model for school improvement. Yet school empowerment and accountability hinge on leadership by principals, and their buy-in to the inquiry model was crucial to its success as an engine for school reform.

Second, it appeared to district leaders that some teams were spending too much time on data analysis. Many never moved to making fine-grained evidence-based inferences, formulating hypothesis, and testing those hypotheses in practice. One DOE leader framed the problem in these terms:

> We saw that as teams got together, as they began to look at the data, they spent a lot of time looking at the data trying to identify their target population or what they wanted to do—their learning target—and they didn't get to the real work. And so we had to put some deadlines in, at least some benchmarks—"You should be at this stage"—and [try] to prod them along and push them along . . . and [work] very hard with the Design Team [SAFs and SSO leaders] to help them understand inquiry and the entire process and then help them facilitate the teams in moving along the process. And that was really difficult the first year.

Some of those teams lacked sufficient guidance for assessing student skill gaps and designing effective instructional responses, and may have needed more time and support for moving to an action phase that could make a difference for struggling students.

Third, among teams that *did* design and implement an instructional response, many created responses that may have made a difference for individual students but did not impact classroom instruction (e.g., tutoring, after-school sessions, Saturday classes). Some in the DOE viewed this as not meeting the goals of the inquiry initiative. Yet SAM facilitators came to regard such responses as "trying out" or piloting potential schoolwide interventions and found that teams sometimes needed support in applying what they learned in out-of-classroom settings to the instructional core.

The DOE revised its inquiry initiative in 2009–2010 to address these challenges, with changes designed to make the model more manageable and embedded in instruction. One DOE administrator explained the thinking this way:

> You actually need to simplify the task significantly in order for it to take root and spread . . . When [we] boiled down what the intention of that original model was, it involved looking at student work and student data and looking at the corresponding teacher work and practice and developing a theory about why some portion of the kids are not succeeding in that environment, and a strategy to help them succeed that you then monitor through the use of common assessment tools. And with that feedback loop, make adjustments to some key levers that are at your disposal . . . What's being taught, how it's being taught, how you're assessing what's being taught[, and] how adults are learning in the school . . .
>
> You have to start at the point where people are getting into the habit of looking at student work seriously . . . And part of the habit we're trying to develop is a way of thinking and a cultural shift. So it actually doesn't have to be perfect. Like it's okay for people to be focusing at a more generic [skill] level if the habit is actually forming. Because . . . if you get good at this, you do get driven down to the more specific."

The revised inquiry model and guidance for school implementation were intended to spread and deepen inquiry within NYC schools.

Refining the School Inquiry Model

The DOE introduced a refined *collaborative inquiry* model in the 2009–2010 school year (see figure 6-1 for a graphic of its current design).

Refinements call for quantitative and qualitative changes in schools' inquiry practices from the earlier IT model.

First, each school is asked to involve most teachers in collaborating on inquiry with a team of colleagues—for example, a grade-level team, a subject department or course group, or a house or small learning community (SLC) in restructured high schools.[8] School administrators are called on to establish inquiry teams across the school, schedule their common meeting time, and designate and support a teacher facilitator for each team. This change seeks to spread inquiry across the school and to expand teacher leadership.

Second, the model specifies that the principal's goals for school improvement are the starting place for teacher teams' inquiry. A set-up phase asks principals to lead a schoolwide self-assessment process and then galvanize staff toward common work for the year. The focus for common work is to be informed by data and information

FIGURE 6-1 Collaborative Inquiry process (DOE, 2009–1010)

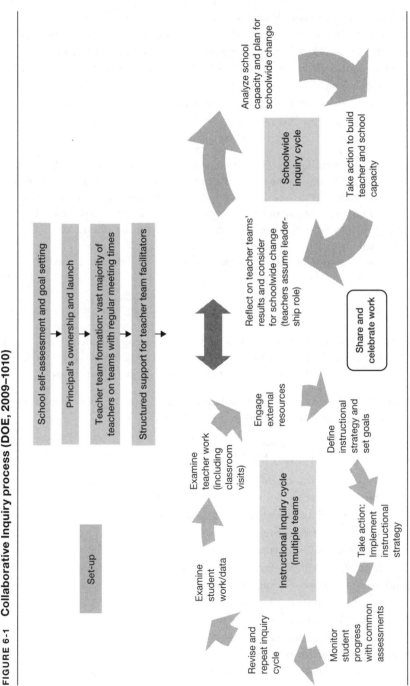

previously gathered and examined as areas of need. This change responds to principals' push-back on the original design and seeks to leverage their buy-in and support for inquiry-based reform.

Third, guidelines for inquiry practice place greater emphasis on classroom instruction than the original inquiry model. Teacher inquiry teams assess student performance against grade-level standards in a content area and in relation to their instruction. The model specifies these steps in the cycle: examine student work/data, examine teacher work (including classroom visits), engage external resources, define instructional strategy and set goals, implement instructional strategy, monitor student progress with common assessments, and revise and repeat the inquiry cycle (see figure 6-1). It continues the original guidelines for focusing on a small group of target students not meeting their potential and staying small to address particular learning targets using an instructional strategy. Because inquiry is conducted by grade-level teacher teams, the work is essentially embedded in instruction. This redesign is intended to deepen inquiry and bring it into classroom practice. Principals and the inquiry team leaders they designate are expected to facilitate the development of inquiry practice and norms.

Consistent with these changes in inquiry guidelines, the DOE revised its Quality Review (QR)—the primary tool for giving schools feedback on their progress toward an inquiry culture (see Childress et al., chapter 4 in this volume). Quality Review ratings on multiple dimensions of school culture and practice provide evidence of whether a school is developing capacity for improvement, potentially counterbalancing a weak Progress Report. Revisions changed language and scoring from what some system leaders regarded as "narrow, quantitative" criteria (e.g., the school has at least four teams doing X focus on inquiry) toward a more descriptive rubric (e.g., teachers are working to improve their X instruction). This aimed to avoid the tendency of some schools to jump through hoops to meet quantitative measures, as well as to prompt a more holistic assessment of the school's instructional and professional culture.

A DOE staff member explained changes in the QR in these terms: "We've spent three years building a data culture. And this tool, the Quality Review, has been a leverage point [along with the Progress Report]. It seemed that the time had come to push on making instruction and instructional coherence as sort of our organizational program, to really be the point of the Quality Review. [We're] no longer building a data culture of the school."

Training demands for implementing the new rubric during 2009–2010 were considerable, particularly since this was the first year that external reviewers were not conducting the QRs. The DOE provided monthly training sessions for a new cadre of internal reviewers, as well as network leaders who opted to attend, to "build a deeper understanding of the quality that we've defined in the rubric with its twenty indicators." The learning curve had to be steep, since the DOE conducted five hundred QRs during 2009–2010.

New Challenges

Extending collaborative inquiry to all teachers in NYC schools posed new challenges for system leadership. Principals and network leaders are responsible for leading schoolwide inquiry, yet some lack the commitment, understanding, and skills to do so. In some schools, the original IT design developed a cadre of inquiry leaders, but this was not true across the board. DOE leaders are challenged to address increasing inequalities in inquiry leadership capacity at all system levels so that all students get the benefits of teachers' collaborative inquiry.

Developing broad inquiry leadership at the school level is critical to the initiative's success. Research and practice testify to the fact that principals and team facilitators play key roles in leveraging and supporting school culture change.[9] In leading change, they prompt teachers to rethink beliefs and assumptions about students, colleagues, and their own abilities that constrain progress on inquiry to expand student success.

In this new phase of inquiry-based reform, system leaders aim to develop a critical mass of teachers in each school who can facilitate the work of their teams in ways that bring about culture shifts to improve student learning. As one DOE administrator commented: "You can put a structure in place, but if there isn't a facilitator in that team that's going to push and keep it focused—and if that person doesn't have a place to reflect and process to get support themselves—it's much harder to make it successful."

Some networks have made strides in training teacher leaders to facilitate collaborative inquiry with their colleagues. The DOE is challenged to develop all networks' capacity to play this role in developing school-based inquiry leadership.

NYC's Inquiry initiative is intended to transform schools' professional culture toward internal accountability for continuous improvement. As a DOE administrator put it: "The inquiry team structure isn't just intended to facilitate getting good at the habit of inquiry. It's also intended to facilitate the breaking down of isolation between teachers, developing teacher leadership, and accelerating the spread of effective practice within the schools."

Our research in NYC high schools has addressed the questions of whether and how school professional culture shifts in schools that implement the inquiry model, as well as what conditions affect implementation. We find that the inquiry model works, when well implemented, to change teacher beliefs and practices in ways that improve student outcomes. However, the challenges of implementing the model are considerable, particularly in high schools, and some teams have lacked essential resources for change.

How Inquiry Works and Implementation Challenges

New York City high schools have implemented collaborative inquiry to widely differing degrees. At one extreme are a small number of schools with nearly five years of experience developing robust inquiry practices through the SAM credentialing program. At the other end of the spectrum are schools that have lacked administrator and/or network support for implementing the inquiry model, and that only ritually carry out inquiry in team meetings, if at all. In between are the majority of schools that have been making steady progress, in good faith and with principal and facilitator support, over the first three years of the DOE's inquiry initiative.

Variation in schools' implementation of inquiry allows us to investigate the questions:

- Does the model work to change school culture and expand student outcomes when it is well implemented?
- What challenges do schools and teachers face in implementing the model and what resources make a difference?

Our research bearing on these issues includes (1) a two-year study of fourteen high schools involved in SAM's second iteration (2005–2007), including seven Autonomy Zone/Empowerment Schools, and (2) a subsequent ongoing study of inquiry work in over seventy New Visions Partnership Support Organization (PSO) schools, most with no experience in the SAM program. Included in both studies are four schools that have participated in SAM continuously beginning in 2005–2006 (dubbed *mature inquiry* schools for their work on implementing the model beyond the three years of the system initiative).[10]

To address the first question, we use five-year longitudinal case studies of the four mature inquiry schools. Evidence from their track record offers existence proof of the theory of change and predicts that inquiry-based reform will pay off in the long run for most NYC schools. Each of these schools developed an inquiry culture, shifted instructional perspectives and practices to address the needs of struggling students, and brought more students into the sphere of success. These schools represent an intersection of strong inquiry support and challenging school contexts. On one hand, teacher teams from these schools received intensive support in implementing the NYC inquiry model through the SAM program; on the other hand they are high schools—two large and two small—that present special problems for change (see Siskin, chapter 8 in this volume).[11]

To address the second question, we use two years of survey data for all New Visions schools and case studies of twelve schools that represent contrasts in SAM experience, high school size, and grade level (most schools in the New Visions PSO are high schools, but we purposely included two elementary schools). Quantitative analysis identifies predictors of school progress in developing an inquiry culture. Qualitative case study data point to challenges that cut across schools that differ in their experience with inquiry and in school organization.

These broad and in-depth analyses of school inquiry practices and culture change offer insight into the developmental arc and phases, as well as hurdles, entailed in developing a school culture of continuous improvement. Most fundamental is whether a team makes the qualitative shift from ritual enactment of surface activities and so-called single-loop learning to authentic collaborative practice and double-loop learning, in which members share habits of mind and practices of using evidence to diagnose and address student learning needs through instruction and system changes.

All school inquiry teams encountered technical, organizational, and cultural challenges in implementing the model for data-based decision making. Managing them depended on a skilled facilitator, assessment protocol, and principal commitment to inquiry-based reform and teacher leadership.

Inquiry Changes School Culture, with Tipping Point in Third Year

Annual faculty surveys in the four schools involved in SAM since 2005–2006 document the schools' steady progress toward a culture of inquiry-based improvement. Each school shows step increases on a measure of "culture of assessment use" for the first three years, followed by a plateau (see figure 6-2).[12] In the two large high schools organized into SLCs, SAM graduates lead inquiry with colleagues in their SLC, and the survey data capture development of inquiry cultures within and across these units. In the two small high schools, a school team including several SAM graduates leads inquiry with grade-level and content-area colleagues. Over time, increasing proportions of teachers were collaborating on using multiple assessments to focus instruction for struggling students. Much of this work focused on student skill gaps in literacy, such as identifying the main idea in a text or knowing academic vocabu-

FIGURE 6-2 **School culture trends for mature inquiry schools: Teacher reports on assessment use**

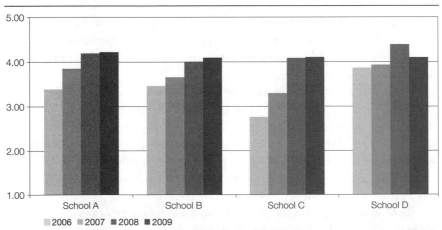

lary in or across a subject area. Teacher teams shared with school colleagues instructional responses for which they had evidence of success with their target students.

These schools' inquiry practices were a radical departure from the past. Three of the four schools began SAM with weak assessment cultures (note 2006 levels of assessment use for schools A, B, and C in figure 6-2). Their data use was limited mainly to reviewing standardized test results, particularly scores on Regents exams. Each teacher and subject department had considerable latitude in deciding whether and how to use finer-grained interim assessments. The 2006 baseline data show that teachers were about as likely to disagree as to agree that assessments were being used to inform instruction. The fourth school (school D) had a tradition of assessing individual student performance through portfolios submitted twice a year, so teachers' initial ratings of their assessment use were relatively high. Through SAM, however, the school made a qualitative shift toward using fine-grained skill assessments to identify and home in on learning targets for their struggling students, primarily recent immigrant English learners with weak academic preparation.

Survey results for spring 2009 show a plateau on the measure of assessment use after three years of change. New inquiry norms and practices were being sustained, and the schools were deepening their inquiry work in ways not well captured by the assessment use survey measure.

Further, in each school we observed particular kinds of culture shifts that accompanied teachers' developing inquiry practice. They illuminate both challenges for change and outcomes of inquiry:

- *Shared accountability:* As teachers worked in teams to diagnose and respond to specific learning needs of struggling students, they began sharing responsibility for the success of all students. Teachers moved from thinking about "my" students to "our" students, as well as shifting their attention from successful students to struggling students.
- *Norm of evidence-based practice:* Faculties developed the habit of using evidence of student performance to evaluate and improve instructional decision-making systems. Teachers moved from (1) relying on their intuition and past practice to using data to drive their instructional decisions and evaluate student learning, and (2) using summative assessments to measure student outcomes to using formative assessments to diagnose student learning needs.
- *Distributed leadership:* As teachers began taking leadership roles in their inquiry teams, ideas and norms about school leadership shifted from administrator decision authority and prerogative to widespread agency and responsibility for improving student success. Teacher teams became leaders of inquiry-based decision making for school improvement.

These fundamental shifts in professional norms and practices established conditions for sustainable inquiry-based improvement in the school.[13]

As expected, these mature inquiry schools evidence greater success in bringing struggling students into the sphere of success. Using 2008 "on track"/"off track" data for students in the 2009 graduation cohort who had scored below proficient in ELA in eighth grade—students who were struggling academically before entering the high school—we found that a significantly higher percentage are "on track for graduation or college readiness" in the four mature SAM schools than in non-SAM schools in the New Visions PSO (68 percent versus 34 percent). Further evidence comes from regression analyses that estimate the effect of a school's inquiry implementation on student outcomes. We found that a school's mean on the "culture of assessment use" survey measure predicts the percentage of its 2009 cohort students who are on track in 2008, with controls for the percentage of those students who entered with below-proficient eighth grade ELA scores.[14]

To what extent might these strong positive results be due to the fact that the four mature inquiry schools were early adopters? We know from decades of research that early adopters do better with any kind of innovation because their decision to adopt an innovation signals motivation and readiness to engage it. Perhaps the schools were already on their way to inquiry-based reform, and supports from SAM and the DOE initiative made little difference. Nonetheless, they offer existence proof that inquiry can be a vehicle for school culture change and improved student outcomes. They moved significantly beyond our baseline measures of their inquiry practices. The facts that teacher teams had intensive support from SAM facilitators and the principal endorsed their work point to resources that make a difference for school progress on the initiative.

Significant improvement in student outcomes reflects the gradual shifts in school culture we documented. These in turn reflect the shifts in teachers' beliefs and perspectives on struggling students and classroom practices that come about through inquiry practice.

Inquiry Changes Teachers' Classroom Practices

The substantive work of collaborative inquiry and leadership is unique to each school and team. Each encounters particular skill gaps of struggling students and facets of their school's instructional culture and systems that keep the students outside the "sphere of success." Yet just as collaborative inquiry engenders certain kinds of school culture changes across diverse schools, so too does it prompt particular shifts in teacher perspectives and classroom practices. Our research suggests that some shifts occur within the first year of implementing the inquiry model:

- *Shift in focus from teaching to student learning:* Most teachers in the inquiry teams we studied said that they had made a big shift in their thinking about classroom instruction. In their own classroom and in observing others, teachers' focus moved from how the curriculum is being taught to what students are learning. They experienced this shift as an important benchmark in the development of their inquiry skills and teaching practice. Many told us that doing LITs in their target students' classrooms prompted this change in perspective. The tool prompted them to see instruction through the lens of struggling students. They learned that their ideas about "high-quality" teaching did not always mesh with struggling students' learning needs. Teachers became aware that students had often missed critical segments of content instruction that state standards prescribed for earlier grades and that this content was not being offered to them in high school courses geared to grade-level standards.

- *Shift from summative to formative assessments of student learning:* Teachers moved from testing for grading purposes to using formative assessments to diagnose student learning needs and develop an instructional response. Going small in assessments to identify misconceptions and gaps in student understanding helped them create responses that accelerated the learning of struggling students. Further, teachers moved to better scaffold learning objectives for their lessons and ask students to give them information about their learning and struggles with particular content.

- *Shift from external attributions of student failure to instructional efficacy:* Teachers stopped perceiving student failure as something beyond their control. Explanations shifted from "miserable family circumstances" or "personal troubles" to skill gaps resulting from prior and current academic experiences. Addressing the gaps became the main concern. As teacher teams designed effective responses and saw the academic gains students were making, they developed a sense of instructional efficacy that carried over into their classrooms.

- *Shift toward on-demand professional development in content instruction:* In some schools, inquiry teams converged in their efforts to address skill gaps prevalent among struggling students, prompting a schoolwide instructional response. For example, after three years of SLC-based inquiry work, team leaders across a large high school reached consensus that student writing was a high-leverage skill domain. As a consequence teachers were eager for professional development (PD) to support their instructional responses. The principal brokered a series of on-site PD days with a literacy/writing expert whose work was enthusiastically received. This teacher learning agenda grew out of their diagnosis of student learning needs, rather than from the judgments of administrators about what teachers needed to know. Interestingly, as a baseline, the same literacy expert had come to the school several years earlier (before inquiry had shown the need for this kind of PD) and, by all accounts, teachers paid little attention. Demand for PD generated through inquiry into student learning needs made all the difference in teachers' readiness to learn and to make changes in their classroom practice. Teachers came to the PD eager to learn from the expert and eager to try out new practices in their classroom.

Such shifts in teacher perspectives and instructional practices interact with changes in school culture. For example, developing team norms of shared accountability for using inquiry to meet the needs of struggling students helped individual teachers shift their focus from delivering curriculum to diagnosing students' learning needs, while individual experiences of making a difference for struggling students helped tip the school toward an inquiry culture.

School Change Entails Technical, Organizational, and Cultural Challenges

We find that progress on data-based inquiry is not linear. Rather, it is bumpy and cyclical. As teachers move outside their comfort zone to develop new assessment and instructional practices, they grapple with the tug of old habits and mind-sets. Teachers report moving two steps forward and one step back, needing to relearn new practices and perspectives. They experience an "Aha!" only to encounter a new challenge. Some teams get stymied by the roadblocks they encounter and never get beyond superficial routines of data use; others become highly skilled in using data to continually improve student learning and success.

The resources a team can draw on for tackling the technical, organizational, and cultural challenges for change matter a great deal. Table 6-2 summarizes the challenges and resources that have made a difference in teams' progress on inquiry-based school improvement.

Technical Challenges. Schools began their inquiry work, whether through SAM or through the DOE's Inquiry initiative, with little prior experience in using student assessment data to design and evaluate their instruction Most teams struggled to use multiple indicators of student performance, use assessment data and student work to identify prevalent skill gaps, and develop and use formative assessments to evaluate the success of an instructional response.

A team's ability to get up and running on inquiry cycles depended on having an assessment-savvy person to lead the work. The designated IT data specialist was a key resource in many schools. Through their monthly network meetings, these specialists learned the ins and outs of the DOE data system and how to analyze periodic assessment to identify specific skill gaps in student performance. Networking with colleagues from other schools also pointed to effective ways of leading school teams and innovative ways of organizing data.

Yet all teams struggled with the push to go small and identify a specific, manageable learning target that they could teach to and use to improve their instructional decision making. Not only did they need skills in looking closely at assessment data and student work but, to many teachers and administrators, the idea of going small to make a big difference was counterintuitive.

TABLE 6-2 **Using inquiry to improve student achievement: Technical, organizational, and social-cultural challenges and resources**

Challenge for change	Facilitating conditions and resources
Technical: Developing inquiry practice	
Using available system data to identify students outside the "sphere of success" and formative assessments to identify skill gaps	Assessment-savvy person on team Data system and summaries that include multiple measures and fine-grained data Data specialist meetings and network
Getting small: Focusing on target group of struggling students and homing in on a learning target for instructional response	Skilled facilitator to address resistance and keep the work focused
Assessing student learning outcomes of instructional responses in order to refine them	Skilled facilitator to guide development of pre/post assessment and provide or point to resources for instructional response
Organizational: Developing leadership	
Creating and protecting time for collaboration on inquiry	Principal commitment and priority for collaborative inquiry
Distributing leadership and developing teachers' capacity to lead inquiry in teams and the school	Principal delegation of authority to teacher leaders and inquiry teams
Social-cultural: Challenging constraining beliefs and habits	
Developing shared responsibility for student success	Administrator focus on results by teacher team; a press for team success
Shifting focus from teaching and curriculum delivery to student learning and skill gaps	Low-inference transcripts (LITs); administrator assurance that LITs are not for teacher evaluations
Shifting teachers' attribution of student failure away from external factors; developing their sense of instructional efficacy	Evidence of team success in accelerating student achievement; team presentations to colleagues and impact on schoolwide decisions

In some schools, the external facilitator (SAF or SAM instructor) helped the team get past frustrations of learning to implement the inquiry model. As one teacher put it: "The process was so frustrating at times that I think if there wasn't an outsider pushing you, we just would have said: 'No. It's not working.' Or, 'These are just the types of kids we get. And we're not going to be able to move them.' Just having an outsider to keep pushing you and still *be* there was critical."

Organizational Challenges. An inquiry team needs regular dedicated time for its work. Yet site administrators manage competing priorities for teachers' time and work outside the classroom, and schools vary widely in both frequency and reliability of time designated for teacher inquiry. Some teams floundered because their scheduled meeting time was often co-opted for another purpose, such as planning for summer school or professional development for a curriculum project. Absent a school priority for collaborative inquiry and protection of the schedule, the work stalls and teachers see it as a DOE mandate and take a compliance mentality.

In order to support collaborative inquiry, principals need to understand the *principles* and believe that it is an effective vehicle for instructional improvement. In schools where the principal was on board and strategic in involving teacher leaders, teams became effective. Using two years of data from our annual survey of IT members in New Visions PSO schools, we found a positive statistical effect of "principal support" on growth in "team functioning."[15] This does not imply that the primary change agent was the principal. Principals rated high on the inquiry team support scale included those who delegated leadership almost entirely to teacher leaders on the team. Indeed, broadly distributed leadership is fundamental to inquiry-based reform. A principal's willingness to share decision authority is essential if collaborative inquiry is to take root.

Professional Culture Challenges.   Reform leaders face opposition and constraints on change that stem from long-standing norms in teaching. Yet schools varied in how extensive and ingrained traditional norms were, since their reform histories or founding cultures may have pulled teachers away from conventions. Nevertheless, all schools are challenged to address constraining professional beliefs and habits.

The Inquiry initiative's call for *teacher collaboration and shared accountability* for student success pushes against norms of privacy and individual responsibility for classroom instruction. The inquiry model's clear focus on students appears to be a useful vehicle for building trust and "deprivatizing" classroom practice. Facilitators who made a difference held this focus when teachers retreated into privacy. Administrators pushed for teachers' shared accountability by focusing on grade-level, department, and SLC performance in reviewing school progress.

Shifting teacher focus from curriculum delivery to student learning requires a reframing of high-quality instruction to focus on outcomes for struggling students. As noted, teacher teams point to the practice of LITs in classrooms of target students as a key lever for change. For example, after diagnosing target students' gap in academic vocabulary, a team was taken aback to see in all its LITs teachers' frequent use of terms such as *summarize, analyze, synthesize,* and *interpret*—realizing that the students could not comprehend such directions or access instructional content. School administrators and team facilitators play important roles in implementing this tool. Success depends on administrators making clear that the classroom observations are not being used for purposes of teacher evaluations. Facilitators support the developing teachers' skill of scripting classrooms verbatim so that student experiences become accessible and available for developing instructional responses. The use of protocols to analyze the LIT allows teachers to track progress in their instructional responses, e.g., use of academic language by students versus by the teacher.

Developing teachers' sense of efficacy or confidence that they can meet student learning needs is a significant challenge for culture change. Convention has it that student failure often is rooted in difficult family conditions, personality traits like "laziness," and personal troubles that derail their academic progress. Such accounts of poor student outcomes are common among teachers in teams that lack a solid design and support for inquiry. Related are assumptions that student learning is linear and that a student performing well below grade level can never catch up. According to teacher reports, the greatest resource for changing their beliefs was the students themselves. Once a team had succeeded in improving target students' performance on a specific skill or academic practice, such as writing a coherent paragraph, they saw that the students could learn to be successful and that their instruction had made a difference. Team presentations of results to colleagues helped to discredit attributions of student failure to factors outside school and move the culture toward a sense of collective efficacy and empowerment to make a difference.

Promising school outcomes for NYC's inquiry model encourage the system's continued investment in this capacity-building strategy. Evidence of particular challenges schools face in implementing the model frame an agenda for network and school leadership development.

Challenges and Issues for System Leadership

Leaders at all system levels—the DOE, cluster, network, and school—must navigate challenges to staying the course with inquiry-based reform:

- The pull of competing paradigms
- Balancing top-down guidance with bottom-up initiative
- Learning and change in an accountability environment
- Diversity in school readiness
- Accountability demands from state and federal authorities

DOE leaders have been thoughtful and strategic in navigating these challenges over the first four years of the inquiry initiative. Their experience offers important lessons for other districts. First, the inquiry approach to instructional improvement has been given top priority as an engine for school change. School administrators and teachers are empowered and held accountable for making instructional decisions based on evidence of student learning—without distractions of top-down curriculum mandates or professional development initiatives. Second, NYC provides teacher teams with a tested model for inquiry and supports the practice with a rich data system and websites for sharing effective practice. Third, system leaders are attuned to the challenge of balancing guidance and accountability for inquiry with care and respect for professional judgment, innovation, and leadership at the school level; and they have developed mechanism for learning from school practice. Fourth, the DOE has reallocated much of its central office staff and professional development resources toward network leaders and facilitators skilled in developing an inquiry culture.

In sum, the system's significant ambition to develop school capacity to use data for improvement is being implemented with coherent, strategic efforts to support this change. Nonetheless, NYC system leaders grapple with challenges entailed in sustaining momentum on this system reform agenda.

Pull of Competing Models and Paradigms for Instructional Improvement

System leaders encounter strong pressures to pursue well-established alternative approaches to instructional improvement. Prominent among them are curriculum mandates, professional development to promote particular pedagogical content knowledge and skills, or programs focused on whole child development. Each has historical roots and proponents in NYC, as well as in other districts pursuing inquiry-based reform.

Acknowledging that inquiry-based reform competes with other improvement strategies is important to building buy-in at all system levels. Proponents of the inquiry initiative need to communicate often why this reform strategy has priority over popular alternatives. In what ways is this approach coherent with the broader NYC reform strategy of school empowerment and accountability? What is the evidence that it works to build school capacity for continuous improvement? What long-term vision warrants significant investment in the inquiry approach to school improvement?

Investing in collaborative inquiry as the leading school reform strategy means backing off from other approaches in the short run, but not in the long run. Indeed, evidence from mature SAM schools suggests that teacher readiness for professional development for instruction is generated through inquiry and that teacher learning under these conditions is more likely to be translated into practice.

Balance Between Top-Down Guidance and Initiative at the Bottom

The success of a system inquiry initiative depends fundamentally on the commitment of school leaders and their ownership of the initiative. Leading school reform from the top of the system runs the risk of engendering compliance responses and ritual conformity to "requirements." This possibility is especially troublesome for an initiative aiming to change school culture. How school administrators and teachers perceive and understand the policy intent and how well it fits with their reform preferences and leadership make all the difference. Also important is whether or not school and teacher leaders have adequate learning opportunities and resources to lead inquiry-based change in the school.

NYC administrators and staff are pursuing a "professional" over a "bureaucratic" approach to system change.[16] They avoid mandates, requirements, and accountability mechanisms that are likely to engender a compliance stance or resistance among school staff. Instead they convey in communications and meetings their respect for, and interest in, educators' views on many facets of the broader reform effort. Several times since rolling out the inquiry initiative in 2007–2008 DOE leaders have organized dialogue sessions with school leaders about the approach and resources.

The idea of *reciprocity of accountability* guided the Inquiry initiative's early roll-out. When the DOE began to hold schools accountable, they at the same time asked school leaders to hold the DOE accountable for providing support for their efforts. In particular, when the Quality Review was introduced to evaluate how well schools were using data in making decisions about instruction and system change, the DOE emphasized that the tool was giving the school valuable information about what was and wasn't working well and why. In turn, the DOE has organized numerous meetings with principals over the years to get their feedback and input on the Inquiry initiative.

System leaders face a dilemma. How do they keep the ballast of a clear reform model while ensuring ownership at the school level? How do they weigh the importance of keeping a strong reform model to leverage change against the risk of losing school commitment by over-specifying reform guidelines? If system reform leadership is mainly a problem of teaching and learning, then leaders have to engage the schools where they are. Yet a constructivist approach to policy formation that starts out by accommodating a wide diversity of school readiness could fail to define a strong enough curriculum to leverage and support change. This would increase school ownership but weaken the scaffold for inquiry practice. The challenge for sustaining an inquiry initiative is being clear on its first principles and supporting consistent adaptations.

Accountability Threats to Learning and Change

The DOE's accountability system calls for results, while its Inquiry initiative calls for learning (see chapter 4 for discussion of tensions). For the purpose of this analysis, it is important to note that designs for collaborative inquiry pull teachers away from the comfort of their closed classroom doors and instructional routines and ask them to take the risks of working with colleagues and committing to turning around struggling students. A natural response to performance pressure is to stick with the tried-and-true—to work harder and longer rather than better and smarter with struggling students. The demands of collaborative inquiry may seem entirely too risky to some teachers or they just may feel that they can more efficiently meet demand for improved student outcomes on their own.

The DOE's collaborative inquiry tools are designed to support teacher learning and change in this accountability context. They provide exemplars of team inquiry, evidence of its success, and all sorts of guidelines for team practice. By providing teams with control over access to the information they post about their own practice, the website provides a safe place for sharing across schools and conveys that the site is in no way designed for teacher evaluation purposes.

NYC principals may feel especially exposed and vulnerable to the risk of failing with a new reform model, particularly if their school's professional culture is weak in social trust. Principals may need incentives and assurance of safety in taking this work on seriously.

The QR is designed partly for this purpose, in that high ratings on leading indicators of a school inquiry culture offer some buffer against sanctions for low Progress Report ratings on student outcome indicators. In such instances, the principal and school are rewarded for moving in the right direction.

Diversity in School Readiness

Readiness to implement collaborative inquiry in teacher teams, and the level of support required, varies widely across schools. Quality Reviews and network leader ratings on the DOE's inquiry capacity measures help to define school readiness and progress. However, it is not clear that school differences on these measures as currently constructed capture the developmental stages or trajectories of school change. Nor is it clear how the information should be used to strengthen inquiry in a given school context.

Research offers little guidance on these issues. Although we have documented the broad arc of change in the way a team works together and how deeply and well they diagnose and address student learning needs, we know much less about what it takes to bring about qualitative shifts toward successful collaborative inquiry. What specific facilitator moves or supports from a principal or tools can move a team beyond the plateaus and roadblocks they encounter? Through what stages and strategies does a school reach a tipping point where inquiry norms overtake resistance to change? Answers to these questions would provide a knowledge base to help focus school leaders' strategic approaches to facilitating inquiry-based reform for schools at different developmental stages and to help define a central office role in fostering school culture change.

Accountability Demands from State and Federal Authorities

New York City's inquiry approach to building capacity for school improvement is in some ways out of sync with the state and federal reform model, and schools experience tensions in the dual accountability systems. The DOE's investment in developing teachers' capacity to use data to improve instruction means that QR ratings (leading indicators) can compensate for negative No Child Left Behind accountability indicators (trailing indicators). Further, a school scoring high on the progress report can be in *schools under registration review* (SURR) status according to New York criteria for subgroup gains, as was the case in one high school we followed. This disjuncture may or may not pull a school away from collaborative inquiry, depending on whether the principal sees it as an effective strategy to improve student test scores, but it certainly narrows attention to test results.

At the national level, rollout of Common Core State Standards (CCSS) may pose a threat to NYC's collaborative inquiry initiative, at least in terms of competing demands for teachers' focus and learning. In theory, national standards could enrich the assessments and student performance data that teacher teams use to identify and address student learning needs. However, the CCSS initiative will require that teachers learn and understand the new set of standards, design or use curricula that promote the new learning outcomes, and learn how to assess student learning under them. If not managed well, this agenda has the potential to shift attention from student learning back onto adult learning and derail a district's inquiry initiative. NYC has designed a rollout of the Common Core standards and training that articulates with teachers' work in grade-level inquiry teams, calling on some teacher groups in each school to take the lead. It aims to marry grade-level inquiry that empowers teachers' instructional decisions with some teacher teams' development of new standards-based assessments. Both will drive inquiry-based reform in NYC schools.

System leaders committed to sustaining and deepening collaborative inquiry in NYC schools are challenged on several fronts. They navigate internal reform politics that threaten to dilute the effort, grapple with technical and organizational complexities of supporting school change, and respond to multiple accountability and reform demands from broader policy contexts. Whether the system stays the course, or is pulled away from its approach to developing schools' capacity for continuous improvement, depends on how the DOE and other system leaders contend with these considerable challenges.

7

Recruiting, Evaluating, and Retaining Teachers

The Children First Strategy to Improve New York City's Teachers

Margaret Goertz, Susanna Loeb,
and Jim Wyckoff

"No reform is more critical to closing the nation's shameful achievement gap than boosting the quality of teachers in high-poverty schools."

—Joel Klein, *Houston Chronicle*, February 20, 2010

"Poor and minority students will never get their fair share of educational opportunity—and are far more likely to lead unsuccessful lives—until administrators and political leaders commit to fundamentally changing the way teachers are recruited, rewarded, and retained."

—Joel Klein, *Huffington Post,* May 8, 2009

Improved outcomes for children have been the oft-stated goal of the reforms that characterize the last eight years of education policy in New York City, collectively known as the Children First reform movement. From the outset, Children First reforms have targeted classroom teaching as an important mechanism by which to improve student achievement. Many of the reforms have specifically addressed the recruitment, assignment, development, and evaluation of teachers in an effort to improve teaching quality. In addition, there have been a variety of new and altered policies affecting resource allocation to schools, school leadership, accountability systems, school supports, school curriculum, and even school buildings. The intent of these policies, at least in part, has been to create incentives and an environment that lead to improved teaching.

A main focus of the Children First reforms has been to grant schools increased autonomy in exchange for increased accountability for outcomes. Over time, principals were given authority over hiring, staff development, and budget allocations, and then held more accountable for improved student outcomes. As part of the reform, the New York City Department of Education (DOE) has also put in place a common curriculum in English language arts (ELA) and mathematics (first required, and now available as a resource) and structures and policies to build capacity of staff and leaders throughout the system. Specifically, for teachers, Children First has established new policies and structures to improve teacher recruitment and assignment, school working conditions and teacher retention, and teacher evaluation processes and supports for improvement. Attention to these elements shows awareness of the labor market forces that prior research has identified as important for teacher quality. For example, recruitment efforts can meaningfully change the pool of teacher candidates, and working conditions strongly influence teachers' decisions about whether to stay in a particular teaching job.[1] However, while there is ample evidence concerning the general dynamics of teacher workforces, little research provides evidence on the effectiveness of the specific interventions used to improve teaching in New York City. The evidence that is available suggests that the DOE initiatives have met with some success.

In this chapter we describe the policies of the DOE that intended to directly and indirectly improve the quality and effectiveness of teachers. Our intent is to assess whether these Children First policies made a difference in student outcomes. To this end, we utilize existing research to evaluate the potential effectiveness of these strategies, and we identify policies for which evidence is currently weak. Two of the authors have worked with colleagues over the last eight years to explore the implications of a number of policies intended to improve the quality of teachers and teaching in NYC schools, and a good portion of this chapter includes a summary of this work. That research employed data from a variety of sources, but primarily relied on individual-level data on teachers and students in NYC from 2000 through 2008. In addition, we integrate similar research by other authors. Whenever possible, we employ research that links policies related to teachers and teaching to their effects on student achievement. As a result, this chapter differs from the others in this volume in that we primarily synthesize existing research. We begin by describing the environment for teachers and teaching in NYC prior to 2002. We then review the reforms undertaken as part of Children First and the evidence of the effectiveness of these reforms. We conclude with a discussion of the overall approach.

Background

In the years leading up to 2002, the environment for teacher recruitment and retention in NYC was bleak. Much of the city's difficulty in teacher recruitment is evidenced by the statistic that from at least as early as 1995–1996 through 2001–2002 roughly half of all new teachers were temporarily licensed (uncertified).[2] The proportion of uncertified teachers in NYC was far greater than in any other school district in New York State and likely greater than most districts nationally. Other measures of teacher qualifications were also notably weak. For example, 25 percent of newly hired teachers in 1999–2000 had failed the New York State certification exam on the first taking, 26 percent had attended undergraduate institutions rated by Barrons as uncompetitive, and, on average, newly hired teachers had average math and verbal SAT scores of 466 and 477, respectively.[3] (These averages do mask great diversity within New York's teaching workforce, as many new teachers had strong academic ability and preparation.) These statistics do not necessarily imply that these newly hired teachers were not strong teachers—the relationship between teachers' background characteristics and their effectiveness is weak. However, they do raise flags concerning the ability of the district to attract and hire more-qualified teachers.

Weak teacher recruitment and retention policies and practices have important implications, especially for poor, nonwhite, and low-achieving children. Within school districts like NYC, teacher salaries vary only modestly, if at all, depending on school working conditions. Therefore, schools with disproportionate shares of poor, nonwhite, and low-achieving students struggle to attract effective teachers. Table 7-1 describes how teaching qualifications were distributed by the free lunch status of their students across NYC elementary schools in 2000. Although the average qualifications of teachers in the least poor schools are not impressive, they are consistently better than those of teachers in the schools with high concentrations of poor students. As one example, only 4 percent of teachers were uncertified in the 10 percent of elementary schools with the lowest percentage of poor children. In contrast, over 20 percent of the teachers in the poorest decile of schools were uncertified. Similar differences exist for most of the other qualification measures.

New York City also had a weak record of teacher retention, especially in the most challenging schools and among their most qualified teachers. For example, between 1996 and 2002, only 20 percent of new teachers in the top quartile on the certification exam left high-achieving schools following their first year, but 34 percent of those teaching in low-achieving schools left after one year. By contrast, 14 percent of teachers in the *bottom* quartile on the certification exam left high-achieving schools after one year, and 17 percent left low-achieving schools.[4] Thus, while it is likely that many NYC schools were staffed by able teachers, it is equally likely that many schools, especially those serving students most in need of strong teachers, were not.

TABLE 7-1   **Qualifications of teachers by percentage of students eligible for free lunch in schools in which they taught in 2000**

Teacher attribute	Lowest 10%	> 10th–25th percentile	2nd quartile	3rd quartile	> 75th–90th percentile	Highest 10%
Percent with fewer than three years of NYC teaching experience	14.7%	18.6%	20.8%	22.9%	25.1%	25.4%
Percent who failed Liberal Arts and Science Test on first attempt	12.2%	16.8%	23.5%	29.6%	35.3%	34.2%
Percent who attended least competitive undergraduate institutions	23.5%	22.9%	23.5%	25.3%	27.5%	27.4%
SAT verbal score	506	487	481	472	465	461
SAT math score	490	477	468	461	451	447
Average expenditures per pupil (real 2005 dollars, using CPI)	$8,002	$8,335	$8,338	$8,738	$9,093	$9,479
Percent eligible for free lunch	21.6%	50.4%	67.6%	81.6%	90.5%	96.3%

Source: Donald Boyd, Hamilton Lankford, Susanna Loeb, Jonah Rockoff, and Jim Wyckoff, "The Narrowing Gap in New York City Teacher Qualifications and its Implications for Student Achievement in High Poverty Schools," *Journal of Policy Analysis and Management* 27, no. 4 (2008): 793–818.

These patterns in teacher qualifications and attrition rates are, at least in part, the result of structural features—including regulations, policies, and processes—that influence the overall supply of teachers to NYC and the distribution of those teachers across schools. In the years leading up to 2002, these structures often worked against the development of a highly qualified and effective teaching workforce. Below we discuss four of these features:

- Teacher compensation
- School working conditions
- Recruitment and transfer systems
- Teacher evaluation and supports for improvement

Teacher Compensation

In 2000, the salary for starting teachers with a BA was $33,186 ($40,303 when adjusted for inflation to 2008). Real salaries at nearly all steps in the schedule remained relatively flat during the 1990s and were somewhat lower than they had been in 1989. In 2000, starting salaries in NYC were about 20 percent lower than the average starting salaries in the NYC suburban school districts at that time. The differential for experienced teachers was even greater. In addition, the differential between real teacher salaries in NYC and its suburbs had grown for both novice and experienced teachers since 1989.[5] Thus, for the twelve years prior to 2002, teacher salaries in NYC lagged inflation and lagged salaries paid by suburban competitors, disadvantaging recruitment and retention efforts.

School Working Conditions

Teachers value working conditions other than salary, both in their initial search for schools and in job retention.[6] A variety of research, including surveys of teachers as well as analyses of teachers' job market decisions, suggests that three components of working conditions are particularly important—the attributes of students, school leadership, and the supports for teachers.[7] While the salary schedules for teachers were constant across schools within NYC, schools clearly differed in their student populations. Since most teachers have been shown to appear to prefer teaching higher-achieving students, schools serving lower-achieving students were at a disadvantage. Another problem stems from the fact that higher-quality school leaders disproportionately served in higher-achieving schools.[8] Schools with low-performing students were thus at an additional disadvantage in attracting and retaining teachers, since the quality of school leadership affected teachers' job decisions. An important piece of evidence as to the inadequate level of resources in some NYC schools comes from the *Campaign for Fiscal Equity v. State of New York* court case. In 2001 New York's highest court found that educational resources were not evenly distributed across NYC's schools and not adequate for a sound basic education.

Teacher Recruitment and Retention

Prior to 2002, the DOE employed a byzantine set of rules and policies regulating teacher recruitment and retention and an inefficient, paper-based means of processing transactions. As a result, the city, like many large urban districts, was losing qualified teacher candidates because they were not given job offers until late August, and then they often still were not sure of their school assignment.[9]

Prior to 2005, NYC teacher transfers occurred under what is commonly called a *seniority-based* transfer policy. Such policies provide teachers who have certification in the relevant license area priority in application queues, based on their years of experience. They also allow *excessed* teachers (those displaced from their positions because of falling school enrollments, budget declines, programmatic changes, or school closures) to *bump*, or displace, less-senior teachers in other schools. School leaders often then have little control over which teachers teach in their school. In addition, the net effect of this system of transfers and excessing is that vacancies do not emerge until late in the summer, well after many qualified candidates have taken other positions.

The transfer policy in NYC prior to 2005 was not a pure seniority-based system, however; it allowed some schools to work around the regulations in their hiring processes. Specifically, as part of the 1995 collective bargaining agreement, schools were given the annual option of determining transfer hiring by a hiring committee composed of a group of teachers and the principal. Schools could opt into this *school-based option*, conditional on a favorable vote of UFT members in that school. The bargaining agreement specifically noted that ". . . a less experienced applicant may be selected if the committee determines that the application possesses extraordinary qualifications." This process was used in filling all teacher vacancies in schools opting into the school-based option and was an important first step toward the elimination of seniority-based transfers, which would be part of the 2005 bargaining agreement. From 2004 to 2006, 35 percent of schools chose to adopt the school-based option.[10]

Even in schools subject to seniority-based transfers, not all transfers were based on seniority. In the non-school-based-option schools, regulations governed the definition of vacancies and the mechanisms by which those vacancies could be filled. At least half of all vacancies were subject to seniority-based transfers.[11] The remaining hires, though, were not posted on vacancy lists but were filled through other arrangements, often word-of-mouth networks. Thus energetic principals could find ways to hire some teachers using criteria other than seniority. Less-energetic principals or those new to the system, typically those leading schools whose students were disproportionately poor and low performing, had more difficulty locating and hiring effective teachers.

Teacher Evaluation and Accountability

The Bloomberg/Klein administration increased the focus of the NYC school system on student achievement and developed accountability policies to increase effort toward these goals at the classroom level. Prior to Bloomberg/Klein, in 2000, the New York State Board of Regents adopted an accountability system that established school performance standards based on student test scores on elementary, middle, and high school exams. Failure to meet the standards triggered a mandatory planning process for the school. Continued failure to meet the standard resulted in designation as a school in need of improvement and could lead to designation as a *school under registration review* (SURR). Poor performance by a SURR school could result in its dissolution. These provisions augmented the school report card system that had been in place since 1998–1999. These performance and accountability standards were generally seen as tough.[12] However, unlike some states, New York had no direct consequences for principals or teachers, and only the lowest-performing schools ever received a SURR designation. As a result, the incentives created by this accountability system were muted for school-level personnel.

As an indication of the relatively weak accountability consequences for teachers, fewer than 2 percent were denied tenure in New York City.[13] The process to remove incompetent teachers was extraordinarily time-consuming and uncertain, deterring many principals from initiating such actions.[14] Many teachers likely held themselves to high standards, and many principals may well have worked with teachers to identify strengths, weaknesses, and plans for improvement, but there was little systematic attention paid to measuring and improving teacher quality.

New York City was by no means unique in the human resource challenges it faced. Nor was it alone in crafting responses to these issues. A few superintendents, with the support of national organizations such as The New Teacher Project, Teach for America, and The Broad Foundation, had begun to undertake new initiatives to address these challenges in other urban districts. These initiatives included developing alternative recruitment and preparation routes for teachers; restructuring hiring, transfer, and assignment policies; and strengthening induction and other professional development programs.[15]

The Children First Agenda for Improving Teacher Quality

While the prior administrations in the DOE made some progress addressing the teacher workforce issues outlined above, the Children First reform agenda developed a strategic approach to changing the regulations, policies, and practices to allow the DOE to recruit and retain more-effective teachers, especially in classrooms with poor, nonwhite, and low-achieving students. The changes that occurred during the last eight years may have been part of a grand vision originating with the initial development of the Children First reform effort. Alternatively, they may represent an evolution of strategies and tactics resulting from experience during the rolling out of Children First. Regardless, what has emerged is a series of initiatives that together make up a coherent approach for improving the quality of teachers and teaching in New York City.

With respect to the Children First reform effort, the DOE views its responsibility as (1) ensuring a pool of qualified teachers through alternative certification routes, higher salaries and other financial incentives, and better (and eventually research-based) screening of prospective candidates; (2) creating a cadre of school leaders who have the skills to select, develop, evaluate, and manage teachers; (3) providing these leaders with the tools they need for effective human capital management, including altered transfer regulations, online placement posting and application tools, and support for beginning and veteran teachers; (4) improving the working conditions in schools by altering resource allocations, providing schools with access to important supports, closing a large number of schools judged to be particularly ineffective, and opening more than four hundred smaller schools; and (5) holding schools and their leaders accountable for improvements in student outcomes. The DOE reform efforts with respect to teacher quality evolved over the years: as with other Children First initiatives, the DOE held tight central control of human capital activities in the early years and then, as the necessary expertise and supports were developed, devolved control and responsibility to the schools. Taken together, these reforms created *the flexibility*, *capacity*, and *incentives* for principals to alter the teaching workforce to improve student achievement.

Many of the rules and policies governing teachers have been determined by the bargaining process between the DOE and the UFT and were agreed on in various

DOE-UFT contracts. Some of these policies, and others that have been proposed but not yet codified in bargaining agreements, have been a source of disagreement between the district and the union. We make no attempt to describe these debates or the motivation behind the positions of the DOE or the union. Rather we describe the policies and, when available, the evidence of their effects.

Assessing the extent to which the Children First reforms led to improved quality of teachers and teaching presents challenges. Most of these reforms were either initiated simultaneously throughout NYC or targeted to specific schools to address particular problems. As a result, there are few good counterfactuals with which to compare the reforms. Pre-/post- comparisons, while suggestive, are often confounded by other changes that occurred simultaneously, such as policies associated with the implementation of No Child Left Behind or more general economic changes affecting the supply of teachers. In addition, separating the effects of one reform from those of others occurring simultaneously is also difficult. For example, isolating the effects on the distribution and retention of teachers resulting from the substantial increases in teacher compensation from the effects of the open market reforms is extraordinarily difficult because both were rolled out over roughly the same period of time throughout New York City. Thus, executing clean evaluations of individual policies, or even separating these policies from the effects of state and federal initiatives, is problematic. Nonetheless, while we are unaware of any studies that attempt to comprehensively examine the effects of the Children First reforms on teacher quality, there are several studies that employ rigorous and systematic analysis to examine the effect of the various aspects of reforms on teachers and students. Most of these studies are best described as descriptive, and some are highly suggestive, but very few provide direct causal estimations.

In the next section we describe in more detail the policy changes in NYC intended to affect the compensation, the recruitment of qualified teachers, working conditions and retention, and the assessment and development of teaching talent. We summarize existing evidence on the success of these initiatives at improving student outcomes.

Teacher Compensation

Teacher recruitment and retention were facilitated by increasing teacher salaries. Salaries for a teacher with a BA and no prior experience increased by over 35 percent from 2000 to 2008, so that by 2008 starting salaries were $45,530. This translates to a 13 percent increase after adjusting for inflation.[16] Teachers throughout the salary schedule received similar or slightly smaller percentage increases. These salary increases net of inflation made NYC somewhat more competitive with neighboring suburban districts.

In addition to salary increases, the DOE used other financial incentives to attract new and veteran teachers to work in high-need schools and shortage subject areas such as mathematics, science, and special education. For example, the Housing Support Program, started in 2006, offers up to $15,000 to experienced mathematics, science, and special education teachers employed outside of NYC who agree to teach for at least three years in the city's high-need schools. Started in 2008, the School-wide Performance Bonus Program offers teachers in high-need schools bonuses equivalent to $3,000 per full-time teacher based on the school's ability to meet performance targets and improve student achievement. In 2006, the DOE introduced the Lead Teacher Program, which provides teachers identified as excellent with a $10,000 supplement to mentor and coach other teachers. Lead teacher status is determined by a variety of attributes, including a record of outstanding classroom teaching, improving student achievement, working successfully with students with greatest needs, and developing and facilitating effective professional development.[17] Finally, the Conversion Program for Supplementary Classroom Teacher Certification provides tuition reimbursement, at the City University of New York tuition rate, to New York State teachers who are certified in nonshortage areas so that they can become certified and teach in designated shortage areas in NYC schools.

These NYC-initiated programs added to programs administered in all New York districts by the state's department of education. For example, the Teachers of Tomorrow Program, a state initiative begun in 2000, offers newly hired certified teachers the opportunity to earn a tax-free grant of $3,400 for each year of satisfactory service (up to four years) if they teach in qualifying high-need schools.

These DOE compensation policies have not been evaluated in a systematic way. We are unaware of any evaluations of the large increases in salaries or of the several programs targeted to attracting teachers to schools with poor and low-achieving students (and retaining those teachers). A notable exception is the schoolwide bonus program that was evaluated in the first year of implementation, when eligible schools were randomly assigned to treatment or control. A study found that the incentives made little difference in student achievement in mathematics or in student, parent, or teacher evaluations of the learning environment. However, the program had only been in effect for three months when the outcome measures were collected.[18]

Some of the work described below cannot be isolated from at least some of the compensation policies (e.g., the analysis of teacher recruitment efforts on student achievement).[19] In addition, prior research suggests that higher salaries can improve both the supply of new teachers and the retention of existing teachers.[20] The implication is that these salaries played a role in the improved teacher qualifications.

Teacher Recruitment

Since 2000 the DOE has initiated two substantial efforts to improve its teacher recruitment policies and practices. First, following a state policy change requiring all classroom teachers to be certified, the DOE developed the New York City Teaching Fellows program. Second, the DOE altered its recruitment processes, including its selection model and timing of offers.

More-Qualified Teachers. In 1998 the New York State Board of Regents passed a regulation abolishing temporary licenses for uncertified teachers, effective September 1, 2003. In 2000, the Regents created alternative certification routes that would allow school districts to hire teachers participating in approved alternative preparation programs as long as they are able to pass required teacher certification exams. In response to these changes, the DOE collaborated with The New Teacher Project to develop the New York City Teaching Fellows program, and in 2000 selected its first cohort of fellows, who became teachers in the fall of that year. The Teaching Fellows Program is highly selective, often attracting early career changers. In 2008, the program attracted nineteen thousand applicants, of whom about one-third were invited for interviews and 15 percent were selected to join the program.

During the summer prior to teaching, teaching fellows participate in a seven-week intensive preservice training program that includes university and DOE-developed coursework and student teaching in the city's summer schools. Teaching fellows are assigned to a master's degree program in one of several colleges and universities across NYC according to the location of their school and their subject area. The DOE pays for approximately 60 percent of the tuition for the master's degree programs. In the fall, teaching fellows enter the job market, but take positions primarily in high-need schools (mainly in the Bronx and central Brooklyn) and in high-need subject areas, including mathematics, science, bilingual education, Spanish, and special education. The DOE-designed Math Immersion program within the Teaching Fellows program helps career changers meet New York State certification requirements in math education, and in most years supplies roughly 50 percent of all new math teachers in NYC middle and high schools.[21] In 2008, 25 percent of math teachers, 20 percent of special education teachers, and 28 percent of Spanish bilingual and ESL teachers in the NYC schools had entered the system through the Teaching Fellows program.

Figure 7-1 shows the rather remarkable changes in the pathways for newly hired teachers in NYC that resulted from this set of changes. In the 1999–2000 school year, over 50 percent of all new teachers were uncertified, 35 percent entered teaching from traditional teacher preparation programs, and the Teaching Fellows program had not been created. By 2003–2004, fewer than 5 percent of teachers lacked a valid teaching certificate, 44 percent had attended a traditional teacher preparation program, 34 percent were teaching fellows, and about 5 percent were Teach for America (TFA) members.

The transformation in the pathways of teachers represented a dramatic shift in NYC's approach to the recruitment and selection of teachers. As shown in table 7-2, the qualifications of teachers in the schools with the greatest proportion of poor students improved dramatically between 2000 and 2005, resulting primarily from the changes in teacher recruitment, especially the selection of teaching fellows. As a result, the gap in teaching qualifications between low- and high-poverty schools substantially declined across all measures of qualifications. Teaching fellows and TFA teach-

FIGURE 7-1   Number of first-year New York City teachers by pathway, 1998–2008

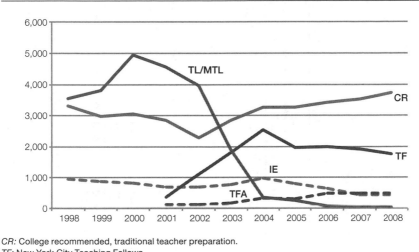

CR: College recommended, traditional teacher preparation.
TF: New York City Teaching Fellows.
TFA: Teach for America (included in TL/MTL prior to 2001).
IE: Individual evaluation, transcript review by NYSED.
TL/MTL: Temporary license/modified temporary license, uncertified.

ers have test scores and academic experiences that are, on average, stronger than those of other teachers, and substantially stronger than the temporary license teachers they replaced. For example, in 2005 newly hired teaching fellows and TFA teachers had average math SAT scores of 541, while newly hired teachers from traditional teacher preparation programs averaged 493. In 2002, newly hired temporarily licensed teachers averaged 460 on the math SAT, which is 80 percent of a standard deviation below the mean of the teaching fellows and TFA teachers who replaced them.[22]

Changes made to teacher recruitment practices are the most studied components of the Children First reforms' approach to improving teacher quality. Several studies have compared the effectiveness of NYC teachers as measured by statistical estimation of the value added by various teacher preparation pathways.[23] Although there are some modest differences in analysis results, the pathways studies consistently find that teachers entering through Teaching Fellows or TFA become more effective than the uncertified teachers they replace and typically as effective as the traditionally certified teachers. In middle school math, TFA teachers appear to be more effective than either traditionally certified teachers or teaching fellows, while both TFA teachers and teaching fellows are slightly less effective in elementary reading. Finally, consistent with the design of the program, TFA teachers in NYC have much higher attrition than either teaching fellows or traditionally prepared teachers, reducing net value-added gains in simulations that account for teacher retention.[24]

TABLE 7-2 Average school qualifications of teachers by student poverty, 2000 and 2005

	2000			2005			Change from 2000 to 2005		
	Lowest 10%	*Highest 10%*	*Gap: Highest 10%– lowest 10%*	*Lowest 10%*	*Highest 10%*	*Gap: Highest 10%– lowest 10%*	*Lowest 10%*	*Highest 10%*	*Change in gap*
% with less than three years of NYC teaching experience	14.7%	25.4%	10.7%	15.1%	21.7%	6.6%	0.4%	–3.7%	–4.1%
% who failed Liberal Arts and Science Test on first attempt	12.2%	34.2%	22.0%	13.4%	24.7%	11.3%	1.2%	–9.5%	–10.7%
% who attended least competitive under-graduate institutions	23.5%	27.4%	3.9%	26.7%	24.3%	–2.4%	3.2%	–3.1%	–6.3%
SAT verbal score	506	461	–45	503	485	–18	–3	23	–26
SAT math score	490	447	–43	495	471	–23	5	24	–19

Source: Donald Boyd, Hamilton Lankford, Susanna Loeb, James Rockoff, and Jim Wyckoff, "The Narrowing Gap in New York City Teacher Qualifications and Its Implications for Student Achievement in High Poverty Schools," *Journal of Policy Analysis and Management 27,* no. 4 (2008): 793–818.

A study of the Teaching Fellows Math Immersion program found that Math Immersion teachers had stronger academic qualifications (e.g., SAT scores and licensure exam scores) than their traditional-teacher-preparation peers, although they had weaker qualifications than math teachers from Teach for America.[25] This study also found that Math Immersion fellows taught in some of the most challenging classrooms in New York City. In this respect, the program has succeeded in attracting large numbers of teachers with stronger academic backgrounds to teach in high-need schools. However, despite stronger general academic qualifications, Math Immersion teachers were responsible for slightly smaller gains in math achievement for middle school math students than were teachers from traditional preparation programs, although in some cases these differences were not statistically significant. In addition, both Math Immersion teachers and traditionally prepared teachers demonstrated substantially smaller gains than TFA teachers.

Boyd et al. explore the overall effects of changes in teacher qualifications between 2000 and 2005 on student achievement.[26] As described in table 7-2, between 2000 and 2005 the gap in teacher qualifications between the most and least poor schools in NYC substantially narrowed. Most of this gap-narrowing resulted from changes in the characteristics of newly hired teachers and was largely driven by the virtual elimination of newly hired uncertified teachers, coupled with an influx of teachers with strong academic backgrounds in the Teaching Fellows program and TFA.[27]

The improvements in teacher qualifications, especially among the poorest schools, appear to have resulted in improved student achievement. Based on estimates from value-added models, researchers found that improvements in the observable qualifications of teachers resulted in average achievement improvement for students in the poorest decile of schools of .03 standard deviations, about half the estimated difference in outcomes between students being taught by a first-year teacher and students being taught by a second-year teacher. If the analysis is limited to teachers in their first or second year of teaching, where changes in qualifications are greatest, the gain equaled two-thirds of the first-year experience effect. Boyd et al. suggest that even greater achievement gains are possible if the DOE can recruit more teachers with strong qualifications.[28] However, this research does not account for aspects of the reforms beyond readily measured teacher qualifications, and ends in 2005. There is also evidence from NYC that selecting teachers based on content knowledge, cognitive ability, certain personality traits, self-efficacy, and scores on a commercially available teacher selection instrument can produce modest achievement gains in students.[29]

Recruitment Processes and Timing. As part of Children First, the DOE created an array of hiring tools to facilitate the matching of new teachers and schools. For example, an online search system, the New Teacher Finder tool, allows principals to post requests for résumés as well as review applications and Teacher Insight Interview responses for prospective teachers who have passed the central screening process. The district also hosts job fairs for candidates and schools.

When reviewing applications, recruiters from the Office of Teacher Recruitment and Quality look for candidates who demonstrate the background, skills, and attitudes likely to make them effective teachers. This central screening process is focused especially on teachers eligible to teach in shortage areas (including math, science, special education, Spanish, ESL, and bilingual education) or willing to teach in hard-to-staff areas of the city. The most qualified applicants—decided according to the district's selection rubrics—are interviewed. Until 2009, if they were judged to have strong potential to be effective teachers, candidates were offered *central commitments*—a guarantee of employment within the NYC public school system with certain terms and conditions. Until the fiscal crisis of 2009, Teaching Fellows, TFA members were also guaranteed jobs in the NYC school system. All new teachers with commitments from the DOE needed to find their own positions, although Teaching Fellows were assigned to search within specific boroughs to focus their job searches. Since 2009, when a hiring freeze was imposed, DOE has not made central commitments. However, the Office of Teacher Recruitment and Quality designates a small group of teachers as TRQ Select, which is similar to central commitments and provides them preferential listing in its New Teacher Finder database. The New Teacher Finder is a searchable database of qualified teacher applicants who have met basic screening criteria that principals may employ to search when hiring teachers. Because searches could yield the names of many candidates, the system returns the TRQ Select, Teaching Fellows, and TFA corps members at the beginning of the list.[30]

The DOE made several changes to address the frequent loss of talented new teacher applicants owing to late hiring. First, budgets are now established in the spring, enabling schools to determine how many new positions they might have open the following school year. Second, hiring of new teachers is no longer delayed until after transferring and excessed teachers are placed. The DOE has established a time-frame, generally April through early August, for teachers seeking transfers to search for jobs. Schools can hire new teachers during this same time period. Excessed teachers can be hired following the April to August window as well as during that period. Third, as described above, the district makes central commitments throughout the spring to teachers in shortage areas or those willing to teach in hard-to-staff areas to provide certainty to candidates who might otherwise take an offer from outside NYC. Lastly, new teachers are hired directly by schools, so candidates know their placement when school begins.

In summary, the DOE has put in place a number of programs and processes to improve the recruitment and selection of teachers. This is the first step in developing a stronger teaching workforce. The research provides consistent descriptive evidence that the changes in teacher recruitment and selection in NYC have substantially changed the qualifications of its teachers and that these changes have had at least a modest impact on student achievement in the city's most-difficult-to-staff schools, contributing to a narrowing of the achievement gap. This does not necessarily imply that recruitment processes or timing are responsible for these outcomes; however, these changes were viewed by the DOE as important components to improve teacher recruitment and placement in difficult-to-staff schools.

Working Conditions and Teacher Retention

The DOE developed several initiatives intended to improve school working conditions and teacher retention. These initiatives have targeted school leadership, teacher salaries, the school learning environment, and teacher supports.

School Leadership. There is substantial survey and case study analysis documenting that school leadership is important to teacher retention.[31] For example, Boyd and coauthors report that second-year NYC teachers who considered leaving, as well as their peers who left following their first year of teaching, identify school leadership and leadership support for teachers as the most important factors in their decisions. They also find that teachers' perceptions of administrative support are strongly associated with teacher transfers and teacher attrition.[32]

Improving school leadership is viewed as a crucial component of the Children First approach to improving the working conditions in schools.[33] The DOE envisioned that effective principals would use increased local discretion and funding to recruit, retain, and develop an effective teaching workforce by creating an environment that was attractive to teachers and providing them with the supports they needed to be successful, and that principals would employ rigorous standards to evaluate teachers and retain only the effective ones.[34] The launching of the Leadership Academy is an important part of this strategy. The Leadership Academy is an independent, nonprofit organization created in 2003 that aims to improve the supply of high-quality principals, especially for low-performing schools.[35] Although initially funded by private foundations, the Leadership Academy is now primarily funded by the DOE. Its Aspiring Principals Program, which trains new principals to work in lower-performing elementary and middle schools, currently accounts for 13 percent of DOE principals.[36]

Recent research has found that elementary and middle school students in schools led by Leadership Academy graduates outperform students in comparison schools led by principals who have not attended the Leadership Academy.[37] The mechanisms for these improvements are unclear, however. And particularly relevant for this chapter, it is unclear whether these principals have increased the retention of effective teachers.

Mentoring. In 2004, the State of New York Board of Regents modified the teacher certification regulations, requiring all teachers with less than one year of teaching experience to receive a "quality mentoring experience" prior to receiving full certification. New York City implemented this requirement with a $36 million teacher mentoring program that was intended to "increase teacher retention, enhance classroom instruction, and improve student achievement."[38] New York City had traditionally provided mentors only for uncertified or alternatively certified teachers, but this program provided all beginning teachers with a full-time mentor throughout their first year. Each mentor was expected to work with approximately seventeen new teachers. The DOE developed the mentoring program in collaboration with the UFT, the Council of School Supervisors and Administrators (CSA), and NYC universities, although the DOE and the UFT were primarily responsible for both the planning and implementation stages of the mentoring program.[39] New York City contracted with the New Teacher Center to implement this program. The mentoring program had four key components: (1) a rigorous mentor selection process, (2) mentors whose full-time job was mentoring, (3) intensive mentor professional development, and (4) regional rather than school-based assignments.[40]

The initial version of the DOE mentoring program appears to have had limited success. Rockoff finds only weak evidence that NYC mentors affected teacher absences, teacher retention, or student achievement.[41] However, he does find that teachers who had mentors with prior experience working in their school or who spent more hours with their mentor had students with better reading and math achievement than the students of teachers whose mentors had no prior experience in the school or who spent less time with their teachers. Another examination of the mentoring program, using a survey of all first-year teachers in 2004, found that those teachers who already felt prepared to teach received the most help from their mentors.[42] The study also found that a focus on instruction and on addressing the needs of student subpopulations during mentoring was associated with greater teacher retention; however, the quality of school administrators was a stronger predictor of new teacher retention than was mentoring.

In 2007–2008, the DOE devolved responsibility and funding for mentoring to the schools, enabling principals to tailor mentoring to the instructional and performance expectations of their schools. Each school, however, was required to form a New Teacher Induction Committee composed of administrators, teachers (a majority of the committee), and representatives of the union. This committee is intended to support teacher development, including the development of a mentor plan. Although each school customizes its mentoring program, the DOE expects that in all schools, experienced teachers will work with new teachers on a regular basis, observing lessons, providing feedback and coaching, and helping to improve instructional practice. School Support Organizations (SSOs) support the development of school mentoring plans and the capacity of school-based mentors through a new position: lead instructional mentor (LIM). A LIM is assigned to each SSO network team and receives training in the New Teacher Center's mentoring model.

The DOE has developed additional supports for mentoring programs, including an online tracking system for mentoring interactions called the New Teacher Induction Mentoring System, and a mentoring program quality rubric devised for Quality Reviews (QRs), a process to assess school quality for the DOE accountability program to evaluate the extent to which the school's mentoring program is successful.

The UFT Teacher Center provide additional professional development for novice teachers. We are unaware of any efforts to empirically evaluate the more recent mentoring efforts.

Open-Market System. In addition to implementing strategies aimed at increasing the appeal of teaching in NYC schools, the DOE also increased schools' authority over hiring, which, as outlined below, has the potential to increase retention, particularly of more-effective teachers. In 2005 the DOE and the UFT agreed to a new contract, effective for the 2005–2006 school year, with provisions that included a new system commonly referred to as the *open-market transfer system*. This policy changed the staffing process for teachers and schools in three key ways. First, it protected the right of schools to choose which teachers they hired, regardless of seniority. Second, it ended the bumping of novice teachers out of their positions by more-senior teachers claiming these positions without input from principals or school staff. Finally, it established a more open hiring process for excessed teachers.[43]

The change in transfer policy in NYC represented a dramatic departure from traditional practice and was intended to alter the teaching and learning environments in schools. Seniority-based transfers had been criticized for contributing to a mismatch between a school's needs and teachers' talents, shuffling ineffective teachers among schools, discouraging novice teachers and causing some effective new teachers leave the profession, and contributing to late hiring.[44] The open-market transfer system allows principals to shape the school workforce and, in so doing, has the potential to change the distribution of teachers across schools, as well as to alter who enters teaching in NYC and who stays. Inexperienced but effective teachers now have much greater ability to transfer, which, if viewed in isolation of the other reforms, increases the likelihood that inexperienced but effective teachers will move to schools with more desirable working conditions. However, as described above, several other reforms are targeted at improving the desirability of schools that educate poor, non-white, or low-achieving students. We are not aware of research that assesses the net effect of these reforms on the distribution of teacher quality across schools, but this clearly has implications for similar reforms that have recently been put in place or are being considered in other urban districts.

One product of the open-market system was the creation of the Absent Teacher Reserve (ATR) pool of more than one thousand excessed teachers—those teachers who have not found another permanent position in the city's schools and generally serve as day-to-day substitute teachers until they find a permanent position. It has been estimated that paying the salaries of teachers in the ATR costs the district $100 million per year.[45] Whether the ATR is a policy problem depends on a better understanding of the teachers in the ATR. Historically the DOE and UFT have disagreed about several aspects of the ATR, including the effectiveness of teachers in the pool, the willingness of ATR teachers to seek new positions, the incentives under the new funding formula for principals to hire ATR teachers (who tend to be more expensive than new teachers), and the amount of assistance needed from the DOE.[46] In a November 2008 memorandum of understanding, the DOE and the UFT agreed to change the financial consequences of hiring teachers from the ATR pool. Until that point schools contemplating hiring ATRs assumed the full salary of these typically more experienced, and thus more costly, teachers. The UFT argued that this put these teachers at a disadvantage in competing for positions with less-experienced and less-expensive new teachers. The agreement virtually eliminates this disincentive. When schools hire a teacher from the ATR they pay only the starting teacher salary, with the DOE assuming the difference in cost between actual salary and the starting salary. There is no evidence on the effect of this policy.

The open-market system for teacher transfer has the potential to influence teachers' decisions about leaving their jobs. In particular, by allowing schools more control over their workforce, the system might improve school working conditions and thus retention. Principals are theoretically now able to match the needs of their students and schools to the characteristics of teachers, ensuring a better fit that is likely to be more stable. In addition, prior to the introduction of the market system, relatively ineffective teachers might leave one school only to take a position in another.[47] This churning of ineffective teachers was at least partially a consequence of the rules and processes governing transfers prior to the open-market system, including the seniority requirements.

There is no guarantee that moving to an open-market transfer system will necessarily increase the retention of effective teachers, but principals certainly now have the ability to reject ineffective teachers. It is conceivable that because principals in schools with relatively fewer poor and low-achieving students now have discretion over whom they hire, that these schools, which are typically believed to be more attractive to teachers, may improve the quality of their workforce at the expense of schools with poor and low-achieving students. However, the balance could shift in the other direction as other reform components of Children First lead to more effective principals (and therefore better working conditions) in previously difficult-to-staff schools. The market system also has the potential to reduce New York's relatively high level of attrition of inexperienced teachers, who previously had low priority to transfer under a seniority-based system and were potentially more likely to simply quit if unhappy with their current placement. However, to date we are unaware of any systematic research that documents the effects of the open-market system and related reforms intended to improve teacher quality. A survey of teachers following the implementation of the open-market system finds that the vast majority of teachers who transfer find their new schools satisfying and that transfer rates are not meaningfully higher in high-poverty schools.[48] Additionally, there is evidence from the early years of this new system and from other districts that principals can recognize effective teachers and that they will hire more effective teachers when given the option.[49]

In sum, teacher retention remains an issue in NYC, especially in lower-performing schools. However, as shown in figure 7-2, there has been a modest decrease in attrition among more recent cohorts of entering teachers, especially following their first year. Of teachers entering teaching in NYC in 2001–2002, 17 percent left following their first year; by 2007–2008 that figure had declined to about 11 percent. There are a variety of factors that could be responsible for the improvement in retention, some of which are beyond the control of DOE policies (e.g., national economic trends). Nonetheless, this improvement is at least consistent with the goals of a set of policies implemented by the Bloomberg/Klein administration. Additionally, teachers, parents, and students have the opportunity to complete learning environment surveys that represent 15 percent of the school Progress Report grade. As an indication that teachers find schools more attractive workplaces, teacher ratings of their schools have steadily increased across each of the domains from 2007 through 2009.[50] It should be noted, however, that a steady increase in response rates over this period may be confounding this result.

Teacher Evaluation

Improving teacher quality by shaping the composition of the teaching workforce through evaluation is another important component of the Children First strategy.

FIGURE 7-2 **Teacher attrition following first four years of teaching**

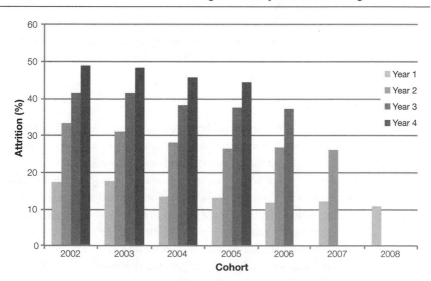

Note: For cohorts beginning in 2006, insufficient time has elapsed to calculate attrition for all four years.

Principals conduct an annual performance review of each teacher. These reviews are intended to provide an assessment of strengths and weaknesses of teachers for the purposes of professional development and as a means of evaluating teachers for tenure. In recent years the DOE has made efforts to make the evaluation of teachers a more rigorous process. Principals have been encouraged to treat the years leading up to the tenure decision (usually in the third year) as an important opportunity to assess a teacher's strengths and weaknesses and work with teachers who are struggling to receive the support they need to improve. Between 2005–2006 and 2007–2008 the number of teachers denied tenure increased from 25 to 164, and those whose probationary period had been extended increased from 30 to 246 over the same period.[51] These are both a small portion of those being considered for tenure, but signal more demanding standards.

Legislation enacted in May 2010, in support of the state's Race to the Top application, creates a statewide comprehensive evaluation system for teachers. Teachers receive one of four ratings—"highly effective," "effective," "developing," or "ineffective"—based on an evaluation that includes several components. Student improvement as measured by a combination of state and local standardized exams counts for 40 percent of the evaluation. The remainder of the evaluation reflects locally negotiated items, such as rigorous classroom evaluations and other measures. The ratings inform a variety of decisions for teachers, including participation in professional development and tenure decisions. Teachers rated as ineffective for two consecutive years may be subject to dismissal.[52] The DOE has provided principals with value-added measures of teacher effectiveness as information for their evaluations, including teacher tenure decisions. The DOE's efforts to more rigorously evaluate teachers for the purposes of more targeted professional development and, failing improvement, of removing teachers from the classroom, are too recent for any systematic evaluation.

Summary

In the years leading up to 2002 there is evidence to suggest that the quality of NYC's teachers varied significantly. The evidence is largely circumstantial—based on measures of teacher qualifications, teacher attrition, and case study or individual reports. However, this evidence is consistent with a simple theory of teacher labor markets that predicts that, conditional on equal compensation, lower-quality teachers will be disproportionately found in schools with poor, nonwhite, and low-achieving students. Of course, determining the overall level and distribution of teaching quality in NYC is somewhat more complicated than this, as we have tried to describe above. However, teacher preferences regarding the attributes of their jobs have a major influence on teacher quality in New York City and elsewhere.

Indeed, we believe that many of the Children First reform efforts evidence an understanding of factors that influence the supply of higher quality teachers. Based on the reforms that occurred immediately prior to and during the Bloomberg/ Klein administration, it is clear that there has been a concerted effort to alter regulations, policies, and practices to improve the overall quality of NYC teachers, and ensure that the students most in need of effective teachers are more likely to get them. Reform efforts such as improving teacher compensation, especially for entering teachers, improving school leadership, attempting to enhance both financial incentives and supports for teachers, and making human resource processes more transparent and tied to measures of performance all demonstrate the application of principles of labor supply.

There is some evidence that efforts to recruit and select more effective teachers, primarily through the Teaching Fellows program, have been effective. However, other initiatives, such as the open-market transfer reforms, have not been examined in any detail to date. Still other changes, such as more rigorous evaluation of teachers, are still emerging, and thus too new for us to understand how they may have affected student outcomes.

We believe the Children First reforms have provided much-needed improvements to teacher recruitment, evaluation, and retention in NYC. Many of these changes have provided a foundation that provides administrators and teachers the capacity to improve the quality of teaching, especially in low-performing NYC classrooms. Other districts can learn from the ways NYC has reengineered its teacher recruitment, evaluation, and retention systems.

Although the qualifications of teachers in NYC, particularly in its lowest-performing schools, have improved, more needs to be done to strengthen the quality of instruction. Unfortunately, the evidence on effective practice is not well developed yet. New models of teacher preparation may well hold promise. Some recent research finds evidence that aspects of teacher preparation tied more closely to the work that teachers ultimately do in classrooms can have meaningful effects on student achievement.[53] This suggests that models of teacher preparation built around clinical experiences may prove more effective. Indeed, New York State's successful Race to the Top application provides an opportunity for organizations other than institutions of higher education to prepare and certify teachers. This process would emphasize more extensive clinical experiences that are integrated throughout preparation. Additionally, efforts to develop rigorous, broad-based teacher assessment systems that are linked to specific professional development show promise. We believe these collaborative efforts are more likely to yield gains in teacher quality than pay-for-performance systems that rely solely on monetary incentives.

PART III

High School Reform

8

Changing Contexts and the Challenge of High School Reform in New York City

Leslie Santee Siskin

The election of Michael Bloomberg, the advent of mayoral control, and the appointment of Chancellor Joel Klein launched a set of complex and often controversial changes in the New York City school system, in everything from politics and governance to promotion policies and classroom assessments, many of which are explored in the chapters of this book. This chapter focuses on strategies employed by the new New York City Department of Education (DOE) under the Bloomberg/Klein administration to improve high schools citywide.

First, the chapter situates NYC's high school reform effort within the broader national and state contexts. In the three decades following *A Nation at Risk*,[1] three waves of reform have created a sea change in expectations for high schools. These waves have targeted: (1) achievement (raise test scores), (2) student attainment (reduce dropout rates), and (3) aspirations (ready all students for college). These efforts have been widely attempted, highly visible—and largely disappointing—creating a daunting context both for high schools and for those who take up the challenge of high school reform.

Second, it locates the Children First high school reforms within the historical context of NYC schooling, also a rather daunting context. New York City has been featured prominently in stories of educational crisis: low test scores and graduation rates that make it an epicenter of the dropout crisis, chronic turnover in chancellors, reports of political corruption and professional incompetence, and tales of 110 Livingston—the home of the former NYC Board of Education—that made the address a nationally recognized symbol of bureaucratic inertia. At the same time, however, NYC has also been recognized as a cradle of reform, creating exemplars of successful schools and strategies—such as the small schools movement—that have been widely influential across the country, and in the new DOE.

Third, the chapter looks at the ways in which this new regime has taken up the challenge of high school reform in NYC within these contexts, and how the reforms have in turn changed the context of high schools within the system. Drawing on data provided by the DOE and interviews with current and former DOE staff and high school principals, this chapter identifies seven key changes:[2]

1. The pace of change has changed.
2. The profile of the high school principalship has changed, with large numbers of new principals playing new roles.
3. Partners from outside the system play an increasingly central role in the design, operations, and support of high schools.
4. The portfolio of high schools is actively managed, with the phasing out of old schools systematically connected to the phasing in of new ones.
5. The process of choice has been extended to all high schools, and all students.
6. New options offer "multiple pathways" to graduation and new models of high school.
7. Professional development and school support have shifted from the district to intermediaries and networks, but high school–specific support in operations and instruction has become hard to find.

While there is no single strategy for high school redesign in NYC and no one distinctive new model for high schools, these changes represent a considerable and concerted effort to reform the system. They attempt to alter the quality (as well as the quantity) of high schools by transforming the conditions that have produced so many failures. As the chancellor explained in a public forum on high school reform, "high school strategies alone will fail." The challenge, he continued, is to "get the system building capacity." As another DOE official put it, "You can't change the schools if you don't change the system." The ultimate question is whether identifying and changing the conditions that produced failure can create, and sustain, a context for success.

The National and State Contexts of High School Reform

High schools have been high on the educational reform agenda for politicians, policy makers, and practitioners for the past thirty years. That heightened attention began, in many ways, when a national commission proclaimed the very "nation at risk." That report was based on a study of high schools, where the commission found "a cafeteria style curriculum," with too many students missing the main course and prepared "neither for college nor for work." Despite declarations of economic and educational crisis, the authors concluded with remarkable optimism. Confident that "America can address this risk," they dedicated the report to children born that year, the class of 2000, who would be prepared for "far more effective lives in a far stronger America."[3]

In the decades that followed, report after report echoed the language of crisis, confirming the mediocrity of high schools in national studies and international comparisons. Reform after reform followed, with new pressures, policies, and programs. The United States set forth the ambitious Goals 2000, and then promised No Child Left Behind. Federal grants encouraged expanded offerings of Advanced Placement and International Baccalaureate courses to upgrade the high school curriculum. They supported new Comprehensive School Reform designs, promoting new high school curricula and structures that would, for example, create "high schools that work" or provide "success for all."[4] While similar in many ways to prior achievement-centered reforms—from the so-called Age of Standards of the 1890s to the Committee of Ten to Conant—what marked this wave as exceptionally challenging was the new emphasis on high standards for *all* students and the introduction of new structures to hold schools accountable.[5]

States moved even more quickly to introduce standards-based accountability, with standardized exams, sanctions for failing schools, and diplomas dependent on test scores—and New York State was no exception. It was exceptional, however, in two ways. First, rather than designing new standards-based tests, it built its new system around existing tests—the Regents exams. These tests, used since the Civil War for college-bound students, were made mandatory for all students. Second, New York required students to pass not just English and math tests, but exams in five subject areas to receive a diploma. In the early years of that policy shift, there was considerable fear that there would be a "lost generation" of students who could not meet the requirements and that in some schools "there would be not one student who could graduate."[6] That fear is increasing again as many worry that the raising of the passing score for the class of 2012 presents a "looming crisis" in graduation rates that could drop by as much as one-third in NYC high schools.[7]

Prompted in part by such concerns, a second wave of reform began, focused on *attainment* rather than achievement. As worries rose that high-stakes testing produced higher dropout rates, a new set of reports and statistics claimed the headlines:

- 1.2 million students each year fail to graduate; seven thousand drop out every day
- Of every hundred students who begin ninth grade, only sixty-eight will graduate and only eighteen will get a college degree
- "One-third of a nation" drop out[8]

What the Gates Foundation called a "silent epidemic" was broadcast loudly as *Time* magazine's cover proclaimed America a "Dropout Nation."[9] What had been normal for most of the twentieth century was redefined as a national crisis at the beginning of the twenty-first. These new expectations for attainment created a sharp change in the demands on high schools, which were now accountable for ensuring that every child would graduate. For many struggling schools in NYC, the idea that they could prepare all students—including those who entered high school with fourth grade reading scores—to graduate in four years seemed an impossible task.

At the same time, a third wave of reform was surfacing, focusing on rising *aspirations* of students and expectations of employers. Reforms and policy pressures called for college readiness for all, signaling a profound shift from the idea of high school as the "people's college" to high school as the people's *ticket* to college. In the midst of new economic crises, students gave new answers to the question of what they wanted from high school—that is, "to graduate and to go to college."[10] According to National Center for Educational Statistics data, the percentage of sophomores aspiring to college jumped from 41 percent in 1980 to 80 percent in 2002—a huge increase in aspirations, where actual achievement and attainment showed little change.[11] It had become normal for ninth graders to expect not only to go to high school, but also to graduate and go on to college. The question of whether high schools could adapt to get them there remained to be seen.

Indeed, the question of whether and how high schools could change, or be changed, in the face of these new demands has found few optimistic answers.[12] Results in all three areas have remained resoundingly disappointing, relentlessly flat. After three waves reform, after three decades of standards and testing, after an entire generation of students (including that class of 2000) had passed through the new systems, there was no evidence—at least no credible evidence at scale—of improvement. Indeed, in state after state, test after test, it seemed that high schools had failed to make any significant progress at all. National Assessment of Educational Progress (NAEP) scores, for example, which many argue give the best indicator of academic achievement, showed long-term trend lines for high school scores that were almost unbelievably flat. Average scores on the math assessment were 302 in 1986, when the students in the Nation at Risk studies were still in high school. By 2004 they had risen to 307, only 5 points. Reading scores were even more intractable: in 1971 the average was 285; in 2004, it was—285. Like the test score data, graduation rates also seemed to have flatlined. High school completion rates rose sharply during the first half of the twentieth century; then they stabilized and stalled. There has been much debate recently about how to calculate graduation rates or count dropouts (June or August? GED or not?), and different research studies have reported different figures. New York State and New York City, for example, counted dropouts differently, which led to politically contentious debate every year when numbers were released. But nationally, and in NYC as mayoral control began, no method of calculation showed the numbers changing substantially, or the curve rising at a significant rate anymore.

That sense of high school crisis, of what Arne Duncan called "educational emergency," has been prevalent and persistent for more than thirty years, and there are few signs of the optimism with which the *Nation at Risk* authors concluded their report. The pressure to improve achievement, attainment, and aspirations remains high, and NYC schools, as they often have, feature prominently on the national agenda: "There isn't one urban school district in the country—Chicago, L.A., New York, D.C., Philly, Baltimore—there's not one urban system yet where the dropout rate is low enough and the graduation rate is high enough. There has been a lot of progress, including in Chicago, but no one is satisfied. We have to get better faster."[13] The question of how to get high schools "better," however, remains a daunting challenge for those working in high schools and those who attempt to reform them.

The Historical Context of New York City

New York City schools have been featured frequently in the discussions about educational emergency. Low test scores have made headlines across the country, as have low graduation rates. *Education Week* identified NYC as an "epicenter" of the dropout crisis, "with nearly 44,000 students slipping away each year." In part, it notes, this is a problem of scale, since NYC has more students and more graduates as well as more dropouts.[14] But the problem has been anything but evenly distributed across the range of NYC high schools. Some schools had persistently produced dropouts at remarkable rates (e.g., only about 10 percent of students who entered ninth grade made it through to twelfth grade)—leading DOE staff to compare them to "dropout faucets" (table 8-1).

Large high schools, with high poverty rates and low performance, provided prime examples of the urban education crisis. Attendance and violence issues (including student shootings on campus) earned one school the headline of "high school from hell" in the popular press, but there were other contenders for the title. As a NYC student portrayed his high school in a video documentary, the most troubled of the city schools were dehumanizing environments, where students—if they stayed—learned

TABLE 8-1   **Numbers of ninth graders and twelfth graders four years later**

School	Entering ninth graders (fall 1996)	Twelfth graders (spring 2000)
Adlai Stevenson	1,199	121
Evander Childs	1,020	134
JFK	1,407	308
South Bronx	282	103
Theodore Roosevelt	1,278	180
Taft	1,013	100

Source: "Comparative Analysis of the Organization of High Schools," New York State Education Department website (nysed.gov).

All of these schools have since been closed or broken up into small schools.

to become "predators or prey."[15] Achievement, attainment, and college aspirations all seemed far away. Both of these schools would be among those closed in the early years of the DOE administration.

Frequently, the problems were attributed to system failure: classic tales of bureaucratic inertia at 110 Livingston Street, with administrators confident that they could just wait out new reforms; chronic turnover in the chancellor's office that repeatedly proved them right. Repeated and widely publicized incidents of political corruption and professional incompetence gave rise to "narratives of helplessness" and fears that reform efforts were hopeless.[16] In a widely quoted statement, former mayor Rudolph Giuliani characterized the school system as "dysfunctional," "just plain terrible," and "no good and beyond redemption." He went on to say, "The whole system should be blown up, and a new one should be put in its place."[17]

But the system has also served as a cradle of reform, giving birth to an "astonishing variety of approaches to leadership, curriculum, school, and policy design."[18] Pockets of success and professional capacity existed, often at the perimeter of the system in individual schools or community school districts, or within the division of alternative schools. Small in scale, slow to grow, and vulnerable to district changes, new models were developed by innovators often working at the margins or under the radar, devising a strategy of "creative non-compliance."[19] District 4 opened a small number of small high schools in what became known as the "miracle in Harlem."[20] A new International High School opened in Queens in 1985, devising effective strategies to serve students new to the country and to embed learning English in learning academics; there are now eleven such schools in NYC, and their design is spreading to other districts. The prominent success of schools like Central Park East Secondary School (CPESS) helped give birth to a new small schools movement across the country.[21]

In addition to new schools, new *strategies* for high school reform emerged. Starting in 1992, the Coalition Campus Schools project phased out two large comprehensive high schools with patterns of poor performance: Julia Richman in Manhattan (with a graduation rate of 36.9 percent) and James Monroe in the Bronx (26.9 percent). At the same time, eleven new small start-up schools were phasing in to take their place and share campus space, with support from networks of well-established small schools like CPESS, Urban Academy, and International High School.[22] With negotiated support from the unions, that project also set up a new system where school-based decisions, rather than seniority, determined hiring. Middle College High School, located on a community college campus, linked its students into college courses, a strategy currently encouraged by the Gates Foundation. A Critical Friends group experimented with adapting school inspection strategies from England, an early precursor of the DOE's Quality Review. New Visions for Public Schools (New Visions) worked with Baruch College to develop a program of scaffolded leadership development that would become the model for the DOE inquiry teams several years later (see Talbert, chapter 6 in this volume). Several high schools joined forces in the

Performance Standards Consortium, which developed performance-based assessments with a reputation for being rigorous, reliable, and valid—albeit labor intensive.

At slightly larger scale (though still characterized as boutique), the New York Networks for School Renewal (NYNSR) project began in 1994, with funding from the Annenberg Challenge grant and support from the chancellor, the mayor's office, and the United Federation of Teachers (UFT).[23] Despite three rapid transitions in the chancellor's office, NYNSR developed a Learning Zone, a virtual district within the district; created more small schools of choice and networks of support; and promoted systemic change—including greater autonomy in exchange for accountability. NYNSR also entered into partnerships with organizations from within education (Center for Collaborative Education (CCE)), intermediary (New Visions), and external community groups (ACORN). Experimental, small in scale, and often as marginal and fragile as the successful schools, such strategies served as precursors to the Bloomberg/Klein reforms and provided a ready resource of professional capacity among NYC educators.

Closer to the center of the system, just prior to the arrival of the Bloomberg/Klein administration, the New Century High Schools initiative began an effort to take high school reform in NYC to larger scale. With New Visions as intermediary and facilitator; with funding from the Bill and Melinda Gates Foundation, the Carnegie Corporation, and the Open Society Institute and with support from the unions and the central office, this new initiative began an experiment (or set of coordinated experiments) to transform NYC high schools. While its central aim was to "create new small schools to replace large failing high schools," the initiative also attempted turnaround strategies with existing large schools, such as small learning communities and inquiry teams.[24] Most notably, New Century issued RFPs inviting organizations outside the system to enter into lead partnerships in the design, development, and ongoing work of the new small high schools—including acting as fiscal agents in managing the start-up monies that external funders would provide.[25] Proposals came in from a range of city organizations, including more than two hundred church, corporate, and cultural institutions, which were screened in a competitive review process. The first twelve New Century schools opened in 2002, with ambitious plans to develop more each year to build a critical mass of successful high schools. In some ways they set the stage for the DOE's high school reform efforts.[26] Like the preceding pockets of success in schools and strategies, however, this initiative was still new, small, and fragile as the Bloomberg/Klein administration began.

The New Regime—Changing the Context

Shortly after Mayor Bloomberg took office, he issued a press release announcing the appointment of Joel Klein as chancellor, an outsider who would take a "fresh look at the problems plaguing the school system, which have been thought of as intractable."[27] In the context of national pressures on achievement, accountability, and college aspirations, high school reform was high on the list of intractable problems. In the local context of the city system, the persistent problems of the most dysfunctional high schools were seen as intolerable. As several of the staff involved in the early years recalled, their fresh look would focus on "bringing the bottom up"—on the "totally failing" high schools with the lowest performance records, and on students with the lowest scores and graduation rates. While they may not have gone so far as to "blow up" the system, as Giuliani had suggested, they took strong, highly visible, and often contested steps to dismantle it and put a new system in place.

Clear and concrete signals of change came quickly when the administration disbanded the old Board of Education and established the DOE, moving it from 110 Livingston to the Tweed building near the mayor's office. Changes in policy followed soon thereafter, as the new DOE convened a set of community engagement meetings to present their agenda of putting "children first" and new set of reforms centralizing authority and increasing accountability, aimed at "taming the system" (press release 2006).A second phase of reforms, a few years later, would shift direction toward decentralization and empowerment in an effort to encourage innovation, "to elevate schools from adequate to outstanding."[28]

Across the two phases, amid the many changes in policy and practices implemented by the new DOE, some (like standardizing K–8 curricula or charter schools) have had relatively less impact on the high schools. Others (like school closing) have had a disproportionately high effect on high schools. Throughout both phases, however, high schools would be high on the agenda as the DOE pledged to close down low-performing high schools and open two hundred new small schools to take their place, and to create a "system of great schools."

That focus on high schools came across clearly across interviews with DOE staff,. So too did a relatively consistent underlying theory of action—what this chapter argues is a theory of *changing the context*. While the words might differ across interviews, the same theme was commonly expressed: "The system we had produced the results we got; if you want to change the results, you have to change the system." System change here is cast as a means, not an end in itself, as the chancellor's frequent refrain emphasized: "What we are seeking is a system comprised of great schools, not a great school system." But what the interviews suggest is the idea of system change as a high school reform strategy: if the DOE staff could identify the conditions that had long produced failure in too many NYC high schools and change those conditions, they could create conditions for success. The following section looks at seven key areas or what they called *levers* of system change where DOE actions have worked to profoundly change the context of high schools, and high school reform, in NYC.

1. The pace of change has changed.

While the old system might have been characterized by bureaucratic inertia, the new DOE is widely regarded as a system of rapid change. Both the speed and scale of reform have increased dramatically—whether credited as iterative change or criticized for instability. Interviewed staff spoke often of their sense of urgency, particularly in the early days. This urgency was due in part to the larger context—national and state pressures, and the sense of "educational emergency" in high schools. In addition, being responsible for the largest school system in the country and operating under mayoral control made the new DOE both very visible and vulnerable. The pressure of elections on the DOE's work was exacerbated by the possibility that mayoral control would sunset in 2009 (it was extended after a temporary eclipse of legislative control). While they hoped for large and lasting effects, the Bloomberg/Klein administration needed "to make a big difference in a little time." It was also, in part, a deliberate design strategy. As one DOE official observed, crediting the business literature, "Sometimes you have to tear [organizations] apart and create chaos. That chaos creates a sense of urgency, and that sense of urgency will ultimately bring improvement."

At the system level, organizational structures that had divided schools by geography (into thirty-two community school districts, or CSDs) and grade level (the high school district) were taken apart, and replaced by shifting configurations of regions, School Support Organizations, and then networks (Hill, chapter 1 in this volume). New people, new titles, and new offices of supervision and support were introduced, and sometimes rearranged as the DOE sought to "set up structures of success." New high schools opened at unprecedented speed and scale—"like doing small schools on steroids" according to a DOE official. School closings, which had been rare before the new administration, rose at a steep curve, changing the landscape of NYC high schools in dramatic ways.[29] Performance measures were revised, and then revised again, with new strategies, like the Quality Reviews, and new structures, like the Achievement Reporting and Innovation System (ARIS), used not only to determine school closings, but also to make data available to administrators, teachers, and even parents (Childress et al., chapter 4 in this volume). With new monitoring capacity in the DOE, pockets of success and promising strategies such as Inquiry teams could be identified, taken to scale quickly, and spread through the system (Talbert, chapter 6 in this volume).[30] Another striking example of this change of pace came with the iZone, as an experiment with "time and staffing and technology" organized around digital technology grew from one site to a small pilot to eighty-one schools in just two years.

At the high school level, staff joked about the new "structure of the month," or about the 2010 restructuring of the system as "Klein 4.0." But they also struggled to keep up with the pace of system change and new demands. One principal commented at a network meeting that "we're all doing things we weren't trained for," and that within the new structures he was not sure who should be providing the training. Another suggested that frequent restructurings required principals to be so "flexible" that "I'm like a contortionist now."

The pace of change has increased throughout the system, but for the high schools, long characterized as an intractable and immovable object, the shift is particularly stark.[31] When literally hundreds of new high schools are opening and trying to find their place in a moving system, the stress can be particularly high. The new pace of change creates particular challenges for the principals.

2. The profile of the high school principalship has changed,
with large numbers of new principals playing new roles.

Much of the NYC reform effort rests on what DOE documents often describe as the three pillars of leadership, empowerment, and accountability, and much of the weight of those pillars falls on the shoulders of principals. To build a system of great schools requires strong principals, and what Klein described as a rejection of "the idea that principals should be told what to do rather than given discretion to act as they think best."[32] Instead, high school principals in the new system are *empowered*, with new roles and responsibilities in operations and budgets; in recruiting, hiring, and supervising staff; in contracting new kinds of partners to provide instructional and operational support; in analyzing and raising test scores and graduation rates; and in marketing their school to prospective students and families (and then being held accountable for the results). For principals in the new high schools, the responsibilities also include a role in developing the design, creating partnerships, managing the start-up process, and engaging in "space wars" to find facilities for their schools—and often sharing that space with other brand-new schools. These are all new roles they typically weren't trained for, and as one principal succinctly summarized, "empowerment is exhausting."

With normal retirements, the heightened turnover that accompanied the new administration, and the opening of some two hundred new schools, a striking number of the people taking on these new roles are new to the principalship. As a *New York Times* study reported in 2009, almost 80 percent of NYC principals became principals during the Bloomberg/Klein administration.[33] Many are not only new, but young.[34] Unlike the Coalition Campus or the NYNSR new schools described above, which were often opened by teachers with experience in the earlier generation of small high schools, approximately 20 percent of the new NYC principals were under forty, and almost the same percentage had fewer than five years of teaching behind them.[35] Like those identified as the "next generation of teachers," this next generation of new young principals is likely to bring different norms and expectations into their roles, but it is likely to need different kinds of support as well.[36]

One source of support developed by the DOE has been their partnership with the Leadership Academy, which provides preparation and support for "Aspiring Principals," and the New School Intensive, which offers design assistance and mentoring through the planning and initial year of new high schools. The intensity of needs and the scale of demand, however, have made it difficult to "get traction on the problem," as one DOE staff member observed. In new configurations and reconfigurations of the DOE organizational structure, such as the regions and networks, district staff say they are "continuously adapting" to try to meet that need, but much of the responsibility for supporting schools and principals has been reassigned to external or intermediary partners.

3. Partners from outside the system play increasingly larger and more central roles in the design, operations, and support of high schools.

Partnerships between schools and community organizations had been an early experiment of the NYNSR, and a core strategy of the New Century high schools initiative, but what distinguished the DOE high school reform effort was the rapid expansion of scale as it embraced the idea that *latent capacity* across the city could be tapped for new ideas and resources. Partners were brought in not only at the system level, where School Support Organizations (SSOs) took on many of the roles of the dismantled CSDs (Childress et al., chapter 4 in this volume), but also at the level of the school. Following the New Century model, the DOE mandated partner participation in new school planning and design. DOE staff talked of trying to "attract different people to the system." They spoke of being "open to everything," including charters, to "get every partner you can find to help build capacity." Health organizations, for example, might provide medical services to a school—and prepare students to enter medical careers. Youth development partners could offer new strategies for supporting at-risk students. Corporate and cultural institutions, sports and community-based organizations came forward. The willingness of external groups to take on an extraordinary challenge surpassed the expectations of many: "They came through when we needed them."

Partners, DOE staff suggest, played another crucial role in system reform as well. As people who "don't work for the system" they could bring not only a new perspective and new resources to persistent problems, but also advocacy and useful criticism. One person explained that "they can scream in a way that principals can't" when materials are needed or structures don't work. Another suggested that partners could give early warnings of trouble, acting as "canaries in the coal mine" (a phrase that appeared in more than one interview).

Working with partners, of course, brings additional work as well as additional capacity.[37] While the DOE might be "open to everything," not every potential partnership had the capacity to open, or the commitment to sustain, a high school. DOE staff spoke of having to develop new and more structured processes and procedures to screen and support proposals "after some difficulties" in the early years. As one interviewee concluded, "It's a lot of work to manage, but it's changing the tone" of the system. High school staff and principals, too, have had to develop new processes and procedures as they have brought partners closer to the core of instruction and operations. Despite the ongoing challenges, however, partnerships have become a standard feature of the context for new high schools, increasing not only the resources available but also the range of options in the portfolio of NYC high schools.

4. The portfolio of high schools is actively managed, with the phasing out of old schools systematically connected to the phasing in of new ones.

Expanding the portfolio of high schools has been a high priority for the DOE, reflecting major change not only in terms of sheer numbers of schools but also in the role of the central office. New York City, like most cities, has long had a range of high schools—including exam schools, small themed schools, career and technical schools, and alternative schools as well as the traditional geographically zoned comprehensive schools. The portfolio model, however, is a more recent idea in high school reform, where districts act as managers of a *portfolio* of schools, rather than managers *of* schools.[38] They are responsible for creating and sustaining a "deliberate mix of different kinds of high schools."[39] In 2005, the DOE introduced an Office of Portfolio Development charged with managing that mix through the creation, closing, and reconfiguring of schools; in the process the DOE has dramatically altered the landscape—or marketplace—of NYC high schools.[40]

Managing the mix at the speed and scale of the DOE's high school reform has become a logistically and politically challenging process in which the closing of schools and deciding what new ones will open, and where they will open, are interconnected and interdependent. DOE staff talked of the need to "open enough so you can close enough," or of being "committed to identifying schools that continue to fail kids and replacing them with better options." As another explained, the opening of hundreds of new small high schools was a highly visible part of the reform effort; the other side of that process was the dismantling of existing schools—more than forty high schools in all. While few schools had been closed under earlier administrations, the pace of decisions to close high schools picked up considerably under the new DOE (table 8-2).

Many were large high schools with large concentrations of over-age and under-credited students—the "dropout faucets" that the DOE had early identified as their top priority, although some small schools were in the mix. Sounding like a stock portfolio manager, one staff member involved in that process explained, "If something doesn't work, don't ride it to the bottom." He went on to describe what he called a "very deliberate approach" of central office staff to identifying the lowest-performing ten to fifteen schools, analyzing data (including performance measures, academic progress, graduation rates, student choice, and learning environment surveys),

TABLE 8-2 High school closings announced

Year	2002	2003	2004	2005	2006	2007	2008	2009
High schools	8	5	3	2	5	5	2	15

Source: Data from DOE records.

and then making "pragmatic choices" to begin the politically difficult and expensive strategy of phase-out and phase-in.

On the DOE website, that link between opening and closing schools is explicit where it solicits proposals for new schools. "To develop an academic program to best replace a failing school," it explains, "new school applicant teams should meet one or more of the following criteria. The DOE's goal is to open the highest-quality new school—district or charter—to meet specific community need."[41] For May 2010, those criteria for high school planning teams included, for example:

- High schools in Manhattan and Brooklyn with programs or a model that serves current high school students with fewer than ten credits;
- Pairs or groups of high schools that can collaborate to offer complementary schools or programs on a campus to meet the needs of specialized populations (e.g., special education, English language learners (ELLs), Career and Technical Education pathways).[42]

Managing the portfolio of high schools implies more than closing failing schools and finding new options. It raises questions about the full mix of schools, and as the portfolio expands, it increases not only in numbers but in variation. The DOE has invested considerable attention to what staff describe as bringing up the bottom, where they have been "changing the landscape" largely by closing the lowest-performing schools with the lowest graduation rates.[43] And there is compelling evidence from recent MDRC studies that the "bottom" has indeed been brought up, that new schools are providing better options and better results in both achievement and attainment for those students most in need.[44] DOE data comparing new small schools against the ones they had replaced showed graduation rates rising sharply for the class of 2009; percentages at seven of eleven "phase-out campuses" had more than doubled (at one site rising from 22.7 percent to 71.7 percent). Staff speak, however, of the inherent difficulty of managing a portfolio this big. Selecting sites to phase out and managing that process for students, staff, and community has aroused questions, conflict, and even a lawsuit; staff speak of "needing to do a better job of letting the community know" or "letting parents know" what is, and will be, in the mix.[45]

More recently, the DOE has turned its attention to expanding the portfolio at the "outer limits." Using new digital tools and new organizational models, the iZone schools stretch "to innovation, to rethink technology, to rethink what a good high school could be." The DOE is reaching for ideas "very different from the old [high school] models," with increasing interest in early college programs and increasing numbers of schools serving grades 7 to 12. A new single-sex school opened to target the "appallingly low" graduation rates of African American males in New York City. One person who had been involved since the early days described a shift in focus as the process evolved a stronger portfolio management model from "replacement of schools that should be closed [to] RFPs, with more thinking about the kinds of schools we think we need."

The DOE has focused less on the high school challenges at the top—deferring, for example, the issue of exam schools where student demand far exceeds supply and where the demographic distribution of enrollment creates heated debate every year (Corcoran and Levin, chapter 9 in this volume). Questions remain about the effects of these changes on the middle, where there can be collateral damage—that is, the small school strategy may be exacerbating problems in large high schools that are left "overcrowded, oversized, and overlooked."[46]

One of the striking changes in the portfolio has been the shift away from *zoned* comprehensive high schools (schools that took all students within a geographic attendance area), which were for many years the predominant model. In 2010, according to the NYC high school directory, there are now none in Manhattan, five in Staten Island, three in the Bronx, seven in Brooklyn, and seventeen in Queens. But closing schools is not the only way to change them, and many have been reconstituted into small learning communities or reconfigured into different programs in the same building. So, for example, one high school still houses a large number of students (2,650), but now hosts three separate programs (only one of which is zoned). While the portfolio has expanded to provide more good options for the most underserved through creating more small high schools and more programs in large schools, students' ability to exercise those options depends heavily on the mechanism of choice.

5. The process of choice has expanded to all high schools, and all students.

In the 1970s, NYC's specialized exam schools offered a form of choice for high-achieving students who competed for qualifying scores on a citywide exam. In the 1980s and '90s, in District 4, the Coalition Campus Project, and then the NYNSR, choice became a strategy of school reform, asking students to make an informed choice about particular and distinctive programs and offering schools the distinct advantage of working with students who had chosen to be there. As Corcoran and Levin describe in detail, participation in the choice process is now mandatory for all high schools and students.[47] High schools post descriptions and admission criteria on their websites and in a massive high school directory, students rank up to twelve choices, and then a complex algorithm, managed at the central office, matches students with programs or schools. In each year since 2004, when this new process was implemented, students have increasingly been matched with schools they have chosen, and fewer (though always some) have not been matched at all. The new choice system was characterized by the chancellor as a "work in progress," but "a work that reflects a lot of progress."[48] DOE staff characterized it as an essential mechanism to move high school reform to scale and to begin to break up attendance patterns that had "segregated high schools academically" as well as demographically and economically.

While other reports have studied the progress of choice systems and how well they work for which students, a choice process involving all students and all high schools changes the context of high schools in two important ways. First, schools have to be "in the business" of recruiting students and marketing their schools. That adds responsibilities for staff and may shift their priorities and practices.[49] This is especially the case when, as in NYC, the data on numbers of applicants per seat for each school are published, and factored into the DOE's assessment of schools. Seeing "five or ten students for every seat," staff say, is considered a sign of demand that indicates a "healthy" school.

Second, that factor of health, or what we might call *chosenness,* varies tremendously across NYC schools. In some "wildly popular" schools, the ratio is far higher; other schools attract only a tiny number of applicants—fewer than one per seat.[50] As early proponents of small schools of choice argued, having students who were informed about the choice they were making, and who made the choice to attend a particular school, creates an extraordinary advantage for a school as well as for students. While teaching in a classroom full of ninth graders is never easy, problems are eased when the room is full of students who feel they chose, or were lucky enough, to be there. The contrast with *unchosen* schools and classrooms, in which students did not want to be and might not stay, can be stark. Despite the progress that has been made with matching, between 2002 and 2008 there were still enough oversubscribed schools—and enough students who did not get their choice—that MDRC could treat the process as a lottery in their study of achievement and graduation in NYC's small schools.[51] And indeed, students who were matched in that choice lottery were more likely to go to, stay in, and graduate from the schools they had chosen. But there are still a substantial number of undersubscribed schools and unlucky students—a problem not only for those schools and students, but for the system.

6. New options offer multiple pathways to graduation and new models of high school.

The problem of students who were unlucky, or underserved, in their high schools, could in part be addressed by closing schools, shutting off the "faucets" through which dropouts were flowing out at the greatest rate, and replacing them with "better options." But there were system capacity limits on how many, and how fast, new schools could be opened. There were also limits to the capacity of what a new small school could do. Yet there were also high numbers of students with high needs, who were highly likely to drop out: an estimated 138,000 over-age and undercredited youth between age sixteen and twenty-one; 70,000 still in school, 68,000 already dropped out. The gap in graduation rates for African American and Hispanic males was described as "distressing." The DOE commissioned a study to look at "prevention, intervention, recuperation, and recovery" of dropouts, identifying key characteristics of both these students and schools (convergence of large size with large numbers of off-track students) where the problems were most concentrated.[52] Many staff at the DOE cite that report, and credit it with influencing their decisions not only to close particular schools, but also to open new kinds of schools and programs that would serve students with the lowest odds of graduating.

The Office of Multiple Pathways to Graduation (OMPG) opened to "focus on students who for a variety of reasons were performing well below what they would need to graduate," explained one DOE administrator. This division "functions in some ways as an R&D operation" for educating over-age, undercredited students, experimenting with design elements, and devising new schedules, teaching tools, types of internships, and credit recovery strategies.[53] Their pathways include Young Adult Borough Centers (evening programs offering flexible hours) and full- or part-time GED programs in more than one hundred sites. A new Learning to Work component integrates career exploration and job readiness activities, including extensive internships, into the academic programs at twenty-five schools. A growing number of *transfer schools* provide an option for students who have been enrolled in high school for at least one year ("though some have never actually entered the building") but have accumulated few credits. Transfer schools point with pride to a graduation rate of 56 percent, versus 19 percent for similar students who have remained in comprehensive high schools (although they worry about the "misalignment" between their population and NCLB's demands for four-year graduation rates). Like other new small schools, transfer schools work with partners, often from youth development fields, who provide services like workshops, tutoring, internships, and individual support as well as collaborating in school operations. DOE staff describe establishing "real partnerships," ones that are "not just after-school programs but woven into the full fabric," as essential to the success of transfer schools, while acknowledging that some have had some difficulties in learning to work with partners from outside the education sector. Unlike other schools, however, since they are relatively small in number (forty in 2010), transfer schools can receive considerable attention and direct professional support from their DOE office.

7. Professional development and school support have shifted from the central office to intermediaries and networks, but high school–specific support in instruction and operations has become hard to find.

Professional development and support are areas of high need for school administrators and teachers who are "all doing things we weren't trained for." In high schools, where the context of work has changed dramatically, staff need to learn how to work with partners or to share campus space, how to manage the process of phasing in new schools or phasing out closing ones, how to navigate new performance measures—the list could go on and on. And there are different issues at the high school level. The DOE measure of attendance, for example, is monitored through ARIS on a daily basis—but high school students often attend (or not) class by class. Yet it is not clear where high school staff should turn for answers in the shifting structures and restructuring of regions, support organizations, and networks—none of which have been organized around high school-specific needs. Some support organizations and networks have more high school expertise than others, but it is up to the school to find the resources that fit—and sometimes, staff worry, "you just leave a school out there by itself."

Most worrying is the problem of instructional support, when the pressure on high schools to raise graduation rates, Regents scores in five content areas, and college readiness can seem overwhelming. The challenge of reaching teaching, or improving instructional practice at the high school level has been notoriously and consistently difficult for reform efforts.[54] DOE staff talk of "still struggling" with ways to deal with the persisting challenge (see O'Day and Bitter, chapter 5 in this volume). Despite new structures, as one administrator noted, "The structure makes it easier to get to instruction, but it doesn't make instruction better." This was a commonly expressed concern among DOE staff: "We have to confront the challenge of how to teach the adults we have." Those we interviewed spoke of early experiments with coaches or literacy curriculum, but also of the limits on what they can do from the central office. With ARIS, for example, promoted as a way to move teachers toward data-driven and differentiated instruction, it is "astoundingly difficult to impact day-to-day classroom practices," and "the real challenge is helping teachers use this data to inform instruction," according to an administrator involved with its development. Another made a similar observation: "We can now produce a twenty-five-page binder on any student. But how does that become actionable in the classroom?" They spoke more hopefully of inquiry teams as another experiment aimed more directly at changing instruction, where small groups of teachers are charged with working together to look at data, identify "targets," and try out new instructional strategies. However, as the DOE rolled the inquiry effort out as district policy for all schools, high schools had a harder time implementing the new structures, and linking inquiry to instruction.[55] Moreover, high schools with high needs often have low internal capacity to meet rising academic standards.[56] Still, as one DOE administrator cautioned, it's "still too early to tell." The DOE has hopes for differentiated instruction strategies as well, but here again, it was noted, "we have a harder time doing it than saying it." Reaching teaching remains hard, particularly in the high schools. New structures like intermediaries and networks move decisions about school support and professional development down to the building level, but the DOE and the high schools still struggle to find professional development with the kinds of content knowledge that high school teachers need—and that Regents exams demand. With hundreds of new teachers in the new high schools, higher Regents requirements looming and pressures for college readiness rising, professional support and development aimed at high schools and high school teaching remain a high need and a persistent challenge.

Summary and Conclusion

Persistent challenges to high school reform in NYC are hardly surprising; decades of reform efforts across the country have confirmed that this is a daunting task. Policies at the national and state levels calling for high schools to raise test scores, reduce dropout rates, and ready all students for college—all at the same time—keep

the pressure high. Yet examples of large-scale success are all too rare. As one person involved with the NYC high school reform effort since the beginning recalled, "We said, 'no one has ever done this before.'" And DOE staff are quite consistent in declaring that they have not done this yet, although they have been, and are still, making what they see as considerable, even unprecedented, progress.

Instead of attempting to answer the question of what a good high school could be and imposing one answer or design on high schools, what DOE staff describe is a concerted effort to rethink the conditions that produced failing high schools and to create conditions under which more schools will rethink—and become—what a good high school can be. This approach is distinctively different from so many high school reform attempts that have focused on school change, but foundered on context effects—often on "incompatibilities with district systems."[57] Operating instead from the premise that "you can't change the schools if you don't change the system," they seek, adopt—and adapt—what they see as levers that can change the system and set up structures of success.

DOE staff stress that these strategies are not silver bullets: some are more strongly developed than others, and each has its own limitations. They point to "disruptive innovations" as accelerating the pace of change and displacing institutional inertia, but worry that "you have to watch for that kind of thinking to creep back in." They talk of the importance of leadership, but finding and keeping enough new principals remains a challenge. External partners bring new resources into the system, but questions about how to hold these partners accountable, or to ensure they have the expertise required (particularly in high schools) remain unresolved. Many of what they saw as the "totally failing" high schools have closed, but too many high schools still produce too many dropouts or prepare too few students to meet Regents requirements. Expanded choice gives students more options and schools new incentives, but historic patterns of academic, demographic, and economic sorting still persist. New pathways to graduation exist, but there are more students in need than they can serve, and second chances come too late for too many. No single lever, on its own, is sufficient to meet the challenges of high school reform. Instead, the DOE sees the potential in their combination, in how these individual (and interdependent) levers can be linked in a synergy of strategies to change the conditions that had produced failing high schools, and to create conditions for success.

High school reform remains, as Joel Klein described the choice system, "a work in progress," but work "that reflects a lot of progress." Through levers like those discussed above—pace of change, profile of principals, role of partners, portfolio of options, process of choice, pathways to graduation, and professional development and support—the DOE aims to change the context of high schools, and high school reform, in New York City.

9

School Choice and Competition in the New York City Schools

Sean P. Corcoran and Henry M. Levin

The Bloomberg/Klein era of school reform from 2002 to the present has been characterized by many breaks from tradition. The strategy of providing considerable school choice, however, is not such a sharp break, given NYC's long history as a laboratory of school choice. What have become more prominent are the expansion of choice to all families and school levels and the simplification of choice to make it easier for parents and students to identify and apply to schools. The district has also significantly expanded the number of schools—especially high schools—from which families can choose. Incoming freshmen can now choose from nearly seven hundred high school programs citywide. In 2004, the district implemented a complex new system of high school choice that requires *all* eighth graders to rank up to twelve preferred school programs. Bloomberg and Klein have also capitalized on the charter school movement by promoting the growth of such schools in the city and encouraging charter-friendly legislation at the state level.

There are two arguments for expanding student and parental choice. The first is that a given school is not always optimal for a child. Some children need structure in their learning, while others need leeway; some learn through applied activities, while others learn through traditional pedagogy; some learn best through connection to a particular academic specialization or theme, while others are comfortable with a broader curriculum. Some require higher degrees of challenge than other students. School choice opportunities enable families to match their children to the best and most suitable learning opportunities for them.

The second argument is based on the goal of competition among schools for students. Choice schools compete for enrollment and receive resources and recognition according to their academic results and ability to attract students. Schools with insufficient demand risk losing their student base as applicants seek other schools perceived as more successful. In the spirit of competitive markets, it is assumed that choice will improve the overall efficiency of the educational system.

The goal of this chapter is to describe the history of school choice in NYC and its recent expansion, with particular attention to the Bloomberg/Klein era. Because the high school admissions process represents one of the most substantial innovations of this administration, we devote considerable effort to describing this system. High school choice balances many objectives, from a better matching of curricula to student needs to raising student and parental engagement, promoting innovation, limiting travel time, and improving academic outcomes. To date, little is known about this system's success in meeting these goals. Using student-level data provided by the New York City Department of Education (DOE), we provide a descriptive overview of the inputs and outcomes of the high school matching process. Space constraints prevent us from addressing many of the potentially interesting questions raised by this complex system. Thus, we focus on a few broad questions, such as: (1) How many high schools do students apply to under this system? (2) What kinds of programs do students rank as their first choice? and (3) Where are students matched? We are especially interested in how the answers to these questions vary with students' race, gender, and poverty status; residential location; and academic ability.

In the next section, we provide a brief history of school choice in NYC that sets the stage for the present reforms. The following section portrays the current landscape of school choice in NYC and describes how the Bloomberg/Klein administration has altered this landscape. We then move to an overview of the current high school admissions process, and present the results of a descriptive analysis of high school matching during the 2005 to 2008 period. After a discussion of the growth of charter schools in the city, we conclude with a summary and insights related to school choice in NYC and other jurisdictions.

A Brief History of School Choice in New York City

Although choice has become a prominent feature of education reform in NYC, it is important to note that the district has long been a laboratory for school choice innovations. With the opening of Stuyvesant High School in 1904, the city quickly became known for its selective specialized high school programs. Two other specialized high schools, Brooklyn Technical High School and The Bronx High School of Science, opened within the next thirty-five years, and in recent years the number has expanded to eight such schools.[1] A ninth specialized school, Fiorello H. LaGuardia High School of Music & Art and Performing Arts, the successor to the reknowned Music & Arts High School, is a highly selective school that evaluates students' academic record as well as an audition. In addition to its specialized schools, the city has long offered a wide variety of vocational institutions, now known as Career and

Technical Education (CTE) schools, providing training in fields ranging from printing to textiles, auto mechanics, and aeronautics.

New York City was a forerunner in promoting school choice in the desegregation era following the 1954 *Brown v. Board of Education* decision. In 1963, the Open Enrollment Program and Free Choice Transfer Policy allowed students from high-minority schools to attend any school in the city with an available seat.[2] These and other desegregation programs were largely declared as failures in a seminal report by State Commissioner of Education James Allen Jr., in part because they relied solely on voluntary transfers and were poorly publicized.[3] Among other things, the report recommended that the district adopt universal citywide high school choice and restructure the lower grades into primary (pre-K through grade 4) and middle schools (grades 5–8).

A key message of the Allen report was that parents desired school improvement in their own neighborhood, not simply an option to send their children elsewhere. In response to a grassroots decentralization movement and desire for systemic reform, the administration in 1969 opted to decentralize the school system into thirty-two community school districts with locally elected boards responsible for K–8 education. High schools remained the responsibility of the citywide board.

One product of decentralization was the opportunity to innovate at the district level. Community School District 4 in East Harlem, perhaps the most well-known example of this innovation, used its newfound freedom to introduce a radical system of school choice.[4] The district encouraged new small middle schools to open, providing a portfolio of options for families both inside and outside District 4. The plan was slowly and methodically expanded until attendance zones were eliminated altogether, and all students were required to choose a middle school.

In the 1980s, career magnet high schools grew in popularity through what is known as the *educational option* program.[5] Career magnets—established to provide students with preparation for employment or further study—often existed as programs within a larger comprehensive high school. At the time, magnet programs were promoted heavily by the city in its high school application process, and in 1988 roughly one in three high school students were enrolled in a career magnet.[6]

The educational option program was the forerunner of a class of high school programs that continue to exist today, described below. These programs' most interesting feature is their explicit attempt to maintain a diverse mix of students based on ability. Since 1986, the city has required that half of all students in educational option programs be chosen at random and the other half selected from among applicants ranked by the school, as long as in both groups 16 percent of students were high scorers on the state reading test, 16 percent were low scorers, and 68 percent were in the middle.[7]

Partly in response to the success of District 4, Chancellor Joseph Fernandez proposed a citywide school choice plan in 1993. This plan allowed parents to choose any elementary or junior high school in the city for their child.[8] While this policy formalized the opportunity to attend any school, the process was complex, did not provide transportation, and was poorly advertised.[9] Though the Fernandez plan failed to be an effective operational design for school choice, it was viewed as an important "symbol of change."[10] As such, it set the stage for an era of expanded choice.

In response to the belief that very large high schools (in many cases NYC's high schools enrolled up to six thousand students) undermined educational success by depersonalizing the academic process, the late 1980s and 1990s saw a period of downsizing large schools. New small high schools, often housed within larger schools, were created with distinctive themes, and students were encouraged to choose among these. Many of the smaller schools were established through the leadership of private organizations such as New Visions for Public Schools and the Center for Collaborative Education, with financial support from the Annenberg and Diamond foundations. The rationale for this downsizing was that small themed schools would be more engaging for students, more effective, and less costly.[11] A second wave of small high schools opened under Bloomberg/Klein (discussed further below), with support from the Gates and Carnegie Foundations and the Open Society Institute.[12]

One cannot discuss school choice in NYC without acknowledging the role of private schools. The city has traditionally been rich in private alternatives, and nearly nine hundred nonpublic schools were operating in 2009–2010—more schools than the public school systems of Baltimore, Washington, D.C., and Philadelphia combined—with an enrollment of close to 250,000.[13] Twenty-two percent of these schools were nondenominational independent schools, while the remainder were religious in orientation. Catholic schools accounted for 34 percent of private schools in the city, but Catholic enrollment has experienced a rapid decline in recent decades, mirroring a nationwide trend. In 1969, there were more than 419,000 students in NYC Catholic schools (which by comparison represents 38 percent of public enrollment). This dropped to 323,000 by 1974 (30 percent of public enrollment), 216,000 by 1986 (23 percent), and 160,000 by 2008 (16 percent). While many Catholic schools have closed, the number of schools has not dropped as precipitously as enrollment. In 1979, there were 287 elementary and 69 Catholic high schools in NYC; today there are 231 and 55.

Finally, NYC has been the site of numerous efforts to promote choice through private school tuition vouchers. For example, in 1997 the School Choice Scholarships Foundation was founded to provide vouchers for low-income children. Over the next three years, voucher students were followed and compared with those who applied for, but did not receive, a voucher. Though voucher recipients on the whole did not show academic gains beyond those of the control group, African American students did appear to benefit.[14] (This finding has, however, been challenged.[15]) Despite the attention these programs received, voucher programs never served more than a very small number of children.

School Choice Under Bloomberg and Klein

The current school landscape in NYC is characterized by considerable choice, which is partly a continuation of historical policies and partly an expansion under the Bloomberg/Klein administration. In addition to a vibrant private school sector, these choices include public school options at all grade levels, charter schools, and a highly developed and mandatory choice system at the high school level. We defer our discussion of charter schools until later in this chapter, but note here that these schools represent a small but growing option for students at all levels, particularly in grades K–8.

Pre-kindergarten and Elementary School

In New York City, school choice begins as early as preschool.[16] Since 1998, the city has offered universal pre-kindergarten (pre-K) to all children who reach age four by December 31 in the year they enroll. Not all public schools offer pre-K, and not all pre-K students attend public programs. A majority of pre-K students attend programs run by state-subsidized community organizations, including churches, daycare centers, and Head Start programs. At last count, there were approximately twenty-two thousand pre-K seats in public schools, while community-based organizations served more than thirty thousand.

Prior to 2008, individual pre-K programs conducted their own registration, a system that reportedly advantaged well-connected or better-informed parents who could navigate the process and secure a desired school.[17] Under Bloomberg/Klein, the DOE centralized pre-K admissions, publishing a directory of programs and providing a common application on which parents may rank up to five choices. Matches to public programs are made by the Office of Student Enrollment, with certain priorities given to siblings of students already attending a school, children applying to their zoned elementary school, and so on. Community-based programs continue to manage their own registration.

Elementary school choice is managed by community school districts under a standardized admissions process implemented in 2009. Parents may apply to any school that appeals to them, and students are enrolled according to sibling and geographic priorities. Students are generally guaranteed admission to their zoned school, although in recent years overcrowding has forced families onto waiting lists, a source of much aggravation within some city neighborhoods.[18]

An important form of choice at the elementary level—at least for high-achieving students—is the city's gifted and talented (G&T) programs. In 2009–2010, there were 136 schools offering districtwide G&T programs and five schools offering citywide programs. Prior to kindergarten, the DOE screens students for G&T eligibility using a standardized admissions test; only students scoring at the ninetieth percentile and above are eligible to apply. The citywide programs have an even higher threshold, requiring a ninety-seventh percentile or higher.

G&T admissions were overhauled in 2008 under Bloomberg/Klein in response to concerns over favoritism and racial and socioeconomic inequities in these programs.[19] Under the old system, districts set their own rules for admissions, and G&T programs were reputed to be havens for middle-class, often white, families who used the programs to gain admission to desired schools.[20] The new standardized admissions criterion—based on a minimum test score—was designed to provide transparency to the process, and it was hoped the new criterion would extend access to previously underrepresented students. Unfortunately, a *New York Times* analysis found that diversity diminished in the first year under this system, with fewer low-income students and racial minorities qualifying for seats.[21] The number of eligible students of all races dropped in half under the new system, from 2,600 to 1,300. Diversity has improved in recent years, and the number of students taking the G&T test and qualifying has grown as parents have found ways to improve their children's scores via tutors and commercial test preparation.[22] In 2009–2010, close to 12,500 students tested for G&T and 3,200 scored at the ninetieth percentile or above, an increase of 45 percent over the previous year. Today, demand for some gifted programs is so high that most seats are filled by children scoring in the ninety-ninth percentile. The DOE announced in summer 2010 that it was seeking a new admissions test.[23]

Middle School

As is the case for elementary schools, middle school choice is governed by the community school districts, but managed by the central office.[24] A directory of middle school choice options is published for each district; the directory lists all schools to which a student living or attending school in that district would be eligible to apply and provides information on each school's location, accountability rating, enrollment, activities and in some cases on open houses and information sessions for prospective families.

As it has done at the pre-K and elementary levels, the DOE has recently sought to standardize middle school enrollment.[25] Again, students are guaranteed admission to their zoned school, but some sections of the city—including large portions of Manhattan and Brooklyn—have no zoned middle schools. In these cases, families must apply to a school using the city's common application, customized with a list of schools their child is eligible to attend. Parents wishing to send their student outside their zone may also apply to do so. Students are then assigned to schools based on priority and eligibility. Roughly fifty selective middle schools recruit students citywide and require an entrance exam, audition, or academic review.

High School

With the matriculation of the ninth grade class in 2004, the Bloomberg/Klein administration inaugurated a significantly modified system of high school admissions. This process, modeled after the system used to match medical residents to hospitals, requires *all* eighth-grade students to submit an application ranking up to twelve high school programs. Selective programs in turn rank applicants, without knowledge of the students' rankings. A centralized matching mechanism then assigns students to programs based on eligibility, admissions priorities and methods, and the preferences of students and schools.[26]

This system replaced an older one in which students could apply to up to five high schools outside of their zone, or attend their zoned high school if one was available. Under the old system, students would receive multiple school offers, and according to the DOE it was not uncommon for students to retain these until matriculation in an attempt to bargain for their most preferred school. Selective schools were allowed to see how they were ranked by the applicant and often used this information as a criterion for admissions. A large fraction of students simply opted to attend—or were defaulted to—their local zoned school.

The reformed high school choice process is lengthy and complex, and we provide only a brief overview here; a timeline is illustrated in figure 9-1.[27] For most NYC students, the process begins in sixth and seventh grade, when students attend admissions workshops and families are encouraged to participate in choice fairs and other admissions events. In the summer following seventh grade, students review the six-hundred-page *Directory of the NYC Public High Schools* published by the DOE and identify schools and programs of interest to them.[28] Basic details—the schools' location, contact information, enrollment, and grade levels—are provided along with information about academic performance, English language learner (ELL) and special education services, and eligibility requirements. Profiles include a one-paragraph description of the school's curriculum, theme, and educational mission ("In Their Own Words"); a list of courses and extracurricular activities; and community, cultural, and corporate partnerships. A variety of Internet resources are also available to aid in the choice process.[29] For students interested in applying to one of the specialized high schools, the specialized high school admissions test (SHSAT) is administered in the fall for eighth and ninth grade students. Schools that require interviews or auditions also conduct these during the fall.

It is important to note that students rank high school *programs*, not *schools* per se. Although the vast majority of schools have only one program, many offer multiple programs within the same building or school.[30] Each program has admissions *priorities* (e.g., priority may be given to students within a defined geographic area) and one of six admissions *methods*, shown in table 9-1. *Unscreened* programs admit students via random lottery. *Zoned* programs give priority to students living in a defined zone. *Screened* and *audition* programs rank students based on test scores, grades, attendance, audition (for audition programs), and sometimes other criteria. *Limited unscreened* programs admit students at random, with priority given to students who attend an information session. Finally, applicants to *educational option* programs are matched half at random and half from among students ranked by the program, so

FIGURE 9-1 **The New York City high school admissions process**

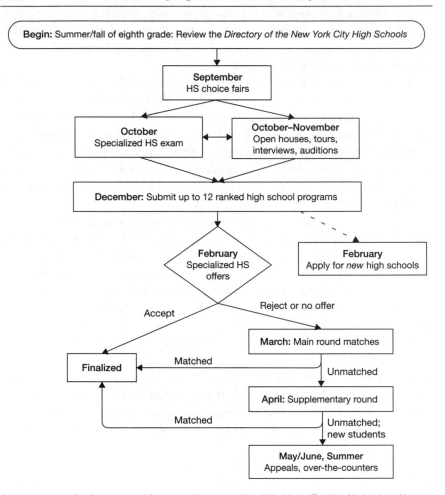

Source: New York City Department of Education; Clara Hemphill and Kim Nauer, *The New Marketplace: How Small-School Reforms and School Choice Have Reshaped New York City's High School* (New York: New School Center for New York City Affairs, 2009).

long as in both groups 16 percent come from the top level of the state reading test score distribution, 16 percent come from the bottom, and 68 percent from the middle. Students scoring in the top 2 percent citywide on the standardized reading test are guaranteed admission to an educational option program, as long as the program is their first choice.

Today NYC students choose from nearly seven hundred high school programs. Figure 9-2 shows trends in the number of programs in 2005–2010 using each of the six admissions methods. In 2010, the three most common methods were screened,

TABLE 9-1   **Public high school program admissions methods**

Method	Description
Screened	Students are ranked by the programs based on their prior year's academic record, standardized test scores, and/or attendance.
Educational option	Structured to yield a particular mix of students based on their seventh-grade reading achievement. Students are matched and distributed among three categories: high (top 16% in reading), middle (mid 68%), and low (bottom 16%). Fifty percent of matches represent students ranked by the school, while the other 50% are matched at random. Students in the top 2% citywide are guaranteed a match to an educational option program if it is their first choice.
Limited unscreened	Students are selected at random by computer. Priority is given to students who attended a school information session or open house.
Audition	Students are ranked based on an audition (e.g., art, design, and performing arts programs) and a review of their academic record.
Zoned	Students living within a specific geographic area are given priority.
Unscreened	Students are matched randomly.
Test	Schools requiring the SHSAT.

Source: New York City Department of Education.

FIGURE 9-2   **Number of high school programs by admissions type, 2005—2010**

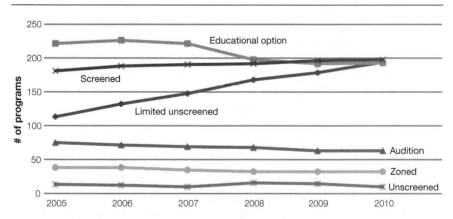

Source: Authors' calculations using DOE high school admissions process data (2005–2008), and NYC DOE data (2009–2010).

Note: For 2005–2008, the number of programs were counted from the universe of school programs that eighth-grade students were matched ("finalized") to. Years refer to the *spring* of the eighth-grade year (and the *fall* in which the student entered high school).

limited unscreened, and educational option, each representing about 28 percent of programs. Audition programs represented 9 percent of the total, while zoned and unscreened programs together represented about 6 percent. Two trends are particularly noteworthy. First, the number of educational option programs has diminished over time. Second, limited unscreened programs have proliferated since 2005, growing from 113 programs in 2005 to 194 in 2010. This trend reflects the efforts of Bloomberg and Klein, who closed many large comprehensive high schools during this period and replaced them with small, limited unscreened high school programs. Indeed, the lion's share of new high school programs opened under Klein have been limited unscreened. In Brooklyn and the Bronx, the fraction of programs that are limited unscreened has risen from 19 percent and 38 percent, respectively, to 33 percent and 49 percent.

In December of eighth grade, students rank up to twelve high school programs on their submitted high school applications. Students designate their interest in one of the specialized high schools and/or LaGuardia on the applications, separate from these twelve. In February, students are informed whether or not they have received an offer to the specialized high schools. Students may accept their offer at the specialized school, or choose to attend their nonspecialized match (from among their twelve choices), which is presented to them at the same time. In March, the vast majority of students (those who did not receive an offer to or did not apply to a specialized school) are matched to one of their twelve choices in the *main round*. Students who do not receive a match in the main round participate in the *supplementary round* by submitting a new set of choices in April. By the end of the supplementary round, nearly all eighth-grade students will have received a high school match. Once students are matched in the main or supplementary round, they may appeal if there are sufficient grounds to do so.[31] Of course, not all entering ninth-graders were present for the high school admissions process. Students who arrive in NYC late—informally referred to as *over-the-counter* students—meet with an admissions counselor at an enrollment office for a high school assignment.

In the next section, we use student-level admissions data supplied by the DOE to provide a broad overview of the inputs and outcomes of the high school admissions process described here. We emphasize that this analysis does not represent a formal evaluation of NYC's high school choice policy. Rather, we wish to highlight interesting and important patterns in school choice behavior and student sorting in the context of a complex, highly decentralized system of school choice. We believe that many of the issues raised here constitute important directions for future research.

A Descriptive Analysis of the High School Admissions Process

As shown above, the high school admissions process implemented by the Bloomberg/Klein administration is both empowering and complex. Students are able to choose from an extensive portfolio of seven hundred programs within schools that range from comprehensive high schools to small themed schools, vocational schools, arts programs, academically rigorous college preparatory schools, and career academies. On the other hand, given so many options, they face an incredibly complex decision process: they must gather information about a large number of programs, attend information sessions and open houses, and make intelligent school choices, with no guarantee in most cases they will receive their top choice. For some students this process will be straightforward, while others—such as children with special needs, those with absent or uninvolved parents, and recent immigrants—may find it considerably more challenging.

In a universal school choice system like NYC's high school admissions process, the decisions students make collectively shape the school environment that every student ultimately experiences. Many families will use information about school achievement to seek out the best fit for their children, but research indicates that parents' idea of a "good school" is more complex than what is revealed through test scores.[32] Parents value a range of school attributes, from peers and curricula to safety and proximity. Households may also have differential access to information about schools or the process of choosing a school. The success of the admissions process will ultimately depend on the choices students make, how families and schools behave in a decentralized system of school choice, and how these choices and behaviors translate into student outcomes.

Space constraints prevent us from performing a comprehensive analysis of student choices and academic outcomes. However, in this section we address a few key questions, focusing primarily on the 2008 application cycle and using application and admissions data provided by the DOE:

- Who participates in the high school admissions process?
- How many high school programs do students apply to?
- What kinds of programs do students rank first?
- When and where are students placed?
- Who applies—and who is admitted to—the specialized high schools?

Who Participates in the High School Admissions Process?

In 2008, more than eighty-eight thousand eighth-graders participated in the admissions process in some capacity (down from more than ninety-six thousand in 2005). A tenth of these (11 percent) were applicants from private schools, many of whom participated to apply to a specialized high school or other academically rigorous public program. More than 47 percent of the private school applicants applied to a specialized high school, although the rate of application to the specialized high schools was very high overall (nearly one in three students applied, even though only 5–6 percent were admitted).

Reflecting the city's student population, the public high school applicant pool was remarkably diverse. Thirty-three percent were African American, 40 percent were Hispanic, 14 percent were Asian American, and 13 percent were white. Close to two-thirds were eligible for free or reduced-price lunches, 11 percent were receiving special education services, 11 percent were ELLs, and 6 percent were recent immigrants.

Of the 2008 participants, most (92 percent) submitted choices in the main round—an important statistic, given that most popular programs are filled during this round. Another 1.5 percent participated only in the supplemental round. The remaining 6.8 percent opted out, applied exclusively to a specialized high school, or were *nonchoosers* (i.e., matched without submitting a choice).

How Many High School Programs Do Students Apply to?

Among those making at least one main round choice, the average number of ranked programs was 7.1 out of a possible 12. Private school applicants ranked fewer on average (6.2); many of these students know they have the option of remaining in a private school if they don't receive one of their preferred choices. Figure 9-3 shows the distribution of choices made in 2008, along with the percentage of students matched in the main round by the number of choices made. There is clearly a positive relationship between the number of designated choices and the likelihood of being matched in the main round. One in fourteen students applied to only one school, and roughly 82 percent of these were matched in the main round. (Many of these are students who applied to an undersubscribed or zoned school, applied to continue in the ninth grade in their own school, or were in the top 2 percent of reading scores and were guaranteed their first choice in an educational option program). For those making two to five choices—about 32 percent—the main round match rate was as low as 71 percent. By a large margin, the greatest share of eighth-graders applied to the maximum number of twelve programs (21 percent). Among those applying to twelve programs, a very high percentage were matched in the main round (93 percent). Interestingly, the average number of choices has fallen over time. This may be attributable to a growing familiarity with the process, better guidance counseling, and/or more targeted searches. The average number of choices in 2005 was closer to eight, and the percentage of students making the maximum twelve choices fell from 35 percent in 2005 to 21 percent in 2008. The percentage of students making *one* choice, however, rose from 5.8 percent to 7.1 percent.

To get a sense of what student or school-level factors explain variation in the number of ranked programs, we conducted a series of descriptive regression analyses for the total number of main round choices.[33] The number of programs ranked by students is important for several reasons. First, it is predictive of successful placement (seen in figure 9-3). Second, it may be indicative of students' perceptions of available and/or viable school choices. Third, it is likely to be related in complex ways to the selectivity of chosen schools. For example, overconfident students may limit their list

FIGURE 9-3   **Number of high school choices in main round, 2008**

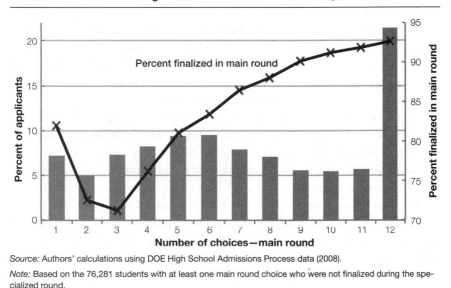

Source: Authors' calculations using DOE High School Admissions Process data (2008).

Note: Based on the 76,281 students with at least one main round choice who were not finalized during the specialized round.

to a small set of selective schools, while less-ambitious students may list nonselective schools with a high likelihood of admission. Finally, it may reflect interventions at the *school* level, to the extent guidance counselors seek to assure placement by encouraging a large number of choices or by completing the forms themselves.[34]

Our analysis finds that the number of ranked high school choices varies in systematic ways with student characteristics above and beyond their association with geography and neighborhood density. Reflecting the role of location, residents of Manhattan and the Bronx on average made 2.5 to 3 more choices than those in Staten Island, and slightly more than those in Queens and Brooklyn. Generally speaking, students in economically and academically disadvantaged groups tended to rank *more* choices than their more-advantaged peers. For example, African American, free-lunch-eligible, and over-age students on average ranked more choices, while white and Asian American students ranked fewer. High-achieving and female students tended to rank more programs, while Hispanic, ELL, and special education students ranked fewer.

This variation likely reflects a combination of factors. White and Asian American students may be overconfident, applying to a smaller number of long-shot selective programs. (They are not necessarily more savvy in their search, as they are also less successfully matched in the main round). The smaller number of choices made by ELL and special education students may reflect a perception of limited options or assistance from guidance counselors who informally place these students. African

American, female, and high-achieving students may be more likely to consider a set of schools beyond their own neighborhood.

We also examined whether and how the number of ranked choices varied systematically across *middle* schools (*feeders*). This pattern could arise if school-level factors—such as guidance counseling, peer effects, or access to information—influence students' behavior in the choice process. Interestingly, controlling for student characteristics (e.g., achievement, race, poverty) and residential area, we observe sizable middle school effects on choices. That is, controlling for other predictive factors, students vary in the average number of choices submitted according to the middle school they attended. We find that the proportion of variation in school choices that is *between* middle schools—as opposed to *within* them—is 0.29. This finding suggests that more research is needed on the role of middle schools in students' high school choices. Recent qualitative research on high school choice in NYC suggests that school resources—and in particular, guidance counselors—play a very important role in the choice process.[35] Counselors are ultimately responsible for submitting applications, and thus may have a high degree of influence on the number of choices. Feeder schools may have established relationships with high schools, perhaps through networks or geographic proximity, which may influence students' choices of schools through the mediating influence of guidance counselors.

What Kinds of Programs Do Students Rank First?

Tables 9-2 and 9-3 provide descriptive statistics for the location, admissions method, and characteristics of students' first choice of high school in 2008. Characteristics of programs and schools are listed across the columns of these tables, while characteristics of applicants are listed down the rows. As seen in table 9-2, a large fraction (39 percent) designate *screened* programs as their first choice. Educational option programs are the second-most popular (29 percent), followed by limited unscreened. Though the city targets about 25 percent of ninth-grade seats to limited unscreened programs, only 15 percent rank these programs first (perhaps because of their relative novelty, or because students perceive quality to be lower in unscreened programs). First-choice admissions methods also vary by student background. For example, 62 percent of Asian students and 47 percent of white students rank a screened program first, versus 33 percent of African American students and 30 percent of Hispanic students. Six percent of white students rank limited unscreened programs first, while 19 percent of African American students and Hispanic students do. Only 6 percent of Queens students rank these programs first, while 32 percent of Bronx students do. High fractions of students in Staten Island (21 percent) and in Queens (13 percent) rank zoned programs as their top choice.

Incoming ninth-graders appear to stick relatively close to home with their first-choice school. Table 9-2 shows the percentage of students from each borough choosing a high school located in the same borough as their residence. This percentage

TABLE 9-2 Number of ranked high school choices, timing of match, location and admissions method of first-choice school, 2008

			FIRST CHOICE: LOCATION			FIRST CHOICE: ADMISSIONS METHOD					
	# of choices: main round	Received first choice, main round* (%)	Same borough (%)	Closest HS to zip code (%)	Distance (miles)	Limited unscreened	Educational option	Audition	Screened	Unscreened	Zoned
All students	7.1	45.9	81.5	13.8	2.50	14.7	29.1	7.1	38.8	1.9	8.5
All public students	7.2	48.3	81.4	13.8	2.48	15.0	29.9	7.1	37.6	1.8	8.5
Subgroup:											
Bottom third reading	6.8	51.5	83.1	13.5	2.32	19.4	37.7	6.6	23.8	2.1	10.3
Top third	7.5	48.0	80.4	13.6	2.65	9.5	21.4	7.4	54.8	1.5	5.4
Bottom third math	6.6	51.0	81.7	13.3	2.38	20.0	38.1	7.2	22.7	2.0	10.0
Top third math	7.6	46.9	82.0	14.0	2.54	8.4	20.2	6.0	58.5	1.3	5.6
Top 2% reading	5.4	64.0	81.4	12.8	2.69	3.8	21.6	4.3	68.1	0.5	1.7
African American	8.2	47.7	78.9	8.4	2.96	19.1	31.4	9.0	33.0	2.5	5.2
White	4.7	47.3	89.3	29.1	1.83	5.8	20.4	6.5	47.0	2.5	17.9
Hispanic	7.6	51.6	78.4	12.7	2.47	18.6	36.1	7.2	29.6	1.1	7.4
Asian	6.0	41.2	89.3	14.7	2.07	3.7	19.1	3.2	61.8	1.4	10.7
Female	7.3	48.5	78.9	13.1	2.64	15.1	29.0	9.9	37.2	1.6	7.2
Free lunch eligible	7.6	49.4	80.3	12.1	2.49	17.3	33.1	6.9	33.2	1.7	7.8
ELL	6.9	52.0	84.1	16.1	1.95	13.8	36.0	4.7	31.2	1.2	13.1
Bronx	8.4	54.0	71.4	10.6	2.66	32.2	31.2	6.6	24.7	0.0	5.3
Brooklyn	7.1	44.9	76.3	12.1	2.33	12.0	31.5	7.2	39.2	2.9	7.2
Manhattan	8.5	45.0	92.6	10.9	2.68	11.6	28.7	8.2	51.1	0.0	0.3
Queens	6.2	39.4	87.4	10.7	2.72	6.6	26.0	7.6	45.8	1.1	12.8
Staten Island	4.0	49.4	94.1	47.4	1.55	8.9	24.5	3.8	32.5	9.1	21.1

Source: Authors' calculations using DOE High School Admissions Process data (2008).

*Represents the percentage of those not placed in the main round who were placed in the supplemental round and received their first choice.

ranges from 71 percent among Bronx students to more than 92 percent in Manhattan and Staten Island. We found that this fraction fell noticeably from 2005 to 2008 for students in Brooklyn and the Bronx as comprehensive high schools were closed, but remained relatively stable in the other boroughs. Among Brooklyn and Bronx students, the second-most-popular destination for a first-choice school was Manhattan, easily accessible by subway.

We calculated the straight-line distance in miles from students' home zip code to their first-choice school. Without exact addresses, we were unable to calculate distances within zip codes, so students choosing schools in their own zip code are assigned a distance of zero. Table 9-2 shows the average distance students were willing to travel to their first-choice school. On average, students were willing to travel an average of 2.5 miles (in Manhattan, roughly 14th to 59th Street, or five to six local subway stops). This likely underestimates students' willingness to travel, given that some students are assigned a distance of zero, and straight-line distance is only an approximation to travel time. Of all applicants in 2008, 14 percent ranked first the school closest to their home zip code (11 percent when excluding Staten Island). Importantly, this share varies by groups of students: almost half of all Staten Island students, 29 percent of white students, 16 percent of ELL students, and 15 percent of Asian students ranked their closest school first. On the other hand, only 8 percent of African American students did so.

Table 9-3 shows the mean characteristics of schools ranked first by students in 2008. For example, among first-choice schools for all students, 22 percent were small schools (<500 enrollment), 47 percent of students enrolled in these schools were eligible for free lunch (a proxy for poverty), the average eighth-grade proficiency rate was 2.95 (on a scale of 1–4), and the average four-year diploma rate was 74 percent. This compares with the average across schools citywide (in the top row) of 49 percent small schools, 62 percent eligible for free lunch, average proficiency of 2.71, and a 68 percent four-year diploma rate. There is considerable variation in the types of schools ranked first across student groups. For example, for high-achieving students (the top third in math), the average top-ranked school had an 80 percent four-year diploma rate, and a 55 percent female and 38 percent free-lunch-eligible student population, respectively. Forty-five percent of these students' top schools had received an A in the city's Progress Report system. In contrast, low-achieving students (the bottom third in math) ranked first schools with an average 66 percent four-year diploma rate, and a 50 percent female and 57 percent poor population. Twenty-nine percent of these schools had received an A on their Progress Report.

Generally speaking, students tended to prefer high schools that matched their own academic, racial, and socioeconomic background. For example, the average top-ranked school for every racial and ethnic group had a student population in which their own race constituted a plurality. White students' average top-ranked school was

40 percent white, even though whites were only 8 percent of city enrollment. Hispanic students' top-ranked school was 49 percent Hispanic, as compared with their 43 percent share citywide.

Descriptive statistics such as these cannot disentangle the complex effects of geography, student preferences, eligibility constraints, and other factors governing school choices. For example, the fact that low-achieving students tend to select schools with lower average achievement may reflect differential access to good schools or a preference for proximity, rather than indifference toward quality. It is clear, however, that students vary substantially in the kinds of schools they choose. On the one hand, this is a key objective of the citywide choice program implemented under Bloomberg/ Klein; with close to seven hundred programs to select from, students can seek one most suitable to their preferences and travel constraints. On the other hand, these patterns suggest that universal choice will be limited in its ability to prevent stratification of students across schools by race, socioeconomic status, and academic ability.

When and Where Are Students Placed?

Of the approximately eighty-two thousand students placed in a high school program through the 2008 admissions process, the vast majority (86 percent) were matched during the main round. The remainder (14 percent) received a match during the supplemental round. Of those finalized in the main round, a large share received their first choice, a proportion that rose over time, from 39 percent in 2005 to 54 percent in 2008. A very high percentage of students matched in the main round received one of their top *three* choices, and this percentage increased over time, from 68 percent in 2005 to 82 percent in 2008. This statistic—frequently cited by the DOE as an indicator of the program's success—is a positive one, as long as students are making optimal choices. The improved match rate could reflect increased sophistication on the part of students ranking schools, better advice from guidance counselors, an increased supply of programs and seats, and so on. On the other hand, students can be assured a match through *undershooting*—that is, purposeful application to less-selective schools with a greater likelihood of acceptance. Students choosing zoned (and are zoned to the school) or undersubscribed schools are virtually guaranteed a match, as are students in the top 2 percent ranking educational option programs first and students choosing to continue in their own school.

Students not placed in the main round appear to be at a distinct disadvantage, in the sense that those matched in the supplemental round are much less likely to receive their first, second, or third supplemental-round choice. About one-third of these students receive their fifth or higher supplemental-round choice. It is unclear why this is the case; it may be due to a lack of information on available seats or a low likelihood of being randomly selected for one of a small number of remaining seats among their top choices.

TABLE 9-3 Mean characteristics of first-choice high school: 2008

	Small school (<500)	Large school (>2000)	Average eighth-grade proficiency* rate	4-year diploma rate	Grade = A	% African American	% Hispanic	% Asian or Pacific Islander	% White	% Female	% Poor**	% ELL	Suspensions per 100
All high schools	48.6	21.8	2.71	68.2	39.8	40.9	42.8	7.8	8.0	51.5	61.8	10.8	12.9
Eighth-grade applicants:													
All	22.4	37.7	2.95	73.5	38.2	29.7	36.0	15.7	18.2	52.3	47.1	8.0	7.9
All public	22.5	38.2	2.93	72.6	36.5	30.2	36.9	15.3	17.2	52.0	48.2	8.3	8.1
Subgroup:													
Bottom third reading	25.8	35.9	2.76	66.5	28.4	34.1	43.8	10.9	10.8	49.3	56.4	10.4	10.0
Top third reading	17.3	39.4	3.13	79.5	45.8	25.9	28.9	19.9	25.0	55.0	38.7	5.4	6.0
Bottom third math	27.3	34.7	2.75	66.4	29.4	35.1	43.8	10.1	10.6	49.9	57.0	10.5	10.2
Top third math	15.7	41.1	3.16	79.8	45.2	24.5	28.2	21.5	25.5	54.7	37.7	5.6	5.7
Top 2% reading	11.0	36.0	3.36	85.8	56.7	20.1	20.8	25.2	33.6	58.9	29.2	3.5	4.2
African American	25.9	33.8	2.87	71.2	30.8	43.9	33.0	11.3	11.4	52.3	52.2	6.6	8.9
White	11.8	53.8	3.10	77.9	52.2	17.4	24.0	18.7	39.7	52.9	30.4	6.0	6.0
Hispanic	27.1	30.8	2.82	69.0	34.0	26.7	49.0	12.0	12.0	50.6	56.1	11.0	9.1
Asian	10.9	55.1	3.21	80.3	40.4	20.6	24.4	31.1	23.6	54.0	33.8	7.1	5.4

Female	23.8	36.6	2.96	74.1	39.1	30.3	36.2	15.2	17.9	55.8	47.5	8.0	7.9
Free lunch	24.8	35.8	2.87	70.4	32.2	32.3	40.6	13.5	13.2	51.3	52.7	9.3	8.7
ELL	26.6	40.0	2.77	67.6	31.5	24.0	49.0	15.1	11.6	49.2	56.8	18.5	9.1
Bronx	40.5	22.6	2.72	65.9	31.0	31.5	56.6	5.1	6.3	51.0	65.3	10.6	10.0
Brooklyn	17.2	44.1	2.95	73.0	29.5	40.4	26.4	13.9	19.0	52.2	45.8	7.3	7.2
Manhattan	36.1	4.2	3.02	78.7	54.2	25.4	45.7	11.6	16.8	56.2	53.3	7.8	7.9
Queens	11.4	48.0	3.12	77.2	38.2	21.6	30.5	29.7	18.0	52.3	37.4	7.9	6.7
Staten Island	8.9	72.4	2.92	74.7	71.4	16.1	19.7	8.9	55.0	50.2	24.8	3.4	8.7

Source: authors' calculations using DOE High School Admissions Process data (2008).

*Eighth-grade proficiency level measured on a scale of 1 to 4, where 1 = below standard, 2 = meets basic standard, 3 = meets proficiency standard, and 4 = exceeds proficiency standard.

**Defined as percent qualifying for free or reduced price lunch.

To gain a better understanding of factors associated with receiving one's first choice, we estimated a series of descriptive multivariate regression analyses for students matched in the main round.[36] A few patterns are worth noting. First, despite making fewer choices, students in self-contained special education classes and English language learners are more likely to receive their first choice, which may reflect a strategy of targeting schools that offer these services. Second, Asian and white students are less likely to be placed in their first choice than nonwhite and non-Asian students, even after controlling for admission method. This shortfall likely reflects the ranking of long-shot selective schools first. Third, students ranking a geographically distant school first are less likely to be matched there (most likely because of geographic priorities). Finally, odds of a first-choice match fall when that program is screened, auditioned, or serves as an educational option school.

With respect to location, students in each borough are about as likely to be matched to a school in the same borough as they are to make their first choice a school in the same borough. An exception is the Bronx: while 71 percent of Bronx residents ranked a Bronx school first, 78 percent were ultimately placed in a Bronx school. On average, students were placed in a high school program about a quarter of a mile closer to their home than their first choice (a distance of 2.25 miles). Sixteen percent were matched to their closest school, and 12 percent were matched to their zoned school.

Another useful way to examine students' preferred and matched schools is to contrast these with characteristics of the middle school they attended. To the extent high school choice provides access to a diverse array of programs citywide, students' high school environments have the potential to look very different from the middle school they experienced. Generally speaking, we find that first-choice schools are on average more advantaged and less racially isolated than students' middle schools by a number of measures, but that students' final school assignment is more similar to the students' feeder school. Examples of this pattern are shown in table 9-4. In this table we show the student composition in students' middle school, first-choice high school, and high school placement for all students and a number of subgroups. For example, the average African American applicant attended a middle school that was 56 percent African American, and ranked first a school with a 44 percent African American population. The average African American applicant's final school assignment, however, was 51 percent African American. Similarly, students in the bottom third of the reading distribution attended a middle school where the average student was 0.24 standard deviations (s.d.) below the citywide average reading score. Their top-ranked school was higher achieving, with an average reading score 0.07 s.d. below average. Ultimately, however, their matched high school looked more like their middle school in terms of reading achievement, with students scoring 0.21 s.d. below average. Of course, it is a mathematical impossibility for all students to attend a more advantaged school in high school than in middle school. These statistics do show, however, that the high school choice process is limited in its success in integrating students by race, ability, and socioeconomic status, beyond what students experience in earlier years of schooling.

Who Applies—and Who Is Admitted to—the Specialized High Schools?

As described above, NYC's academically selective specialized high schools have a long and storied tradition. Specialized high school admissions predate the Bloomberg/Klein administration considerably. However, they remain an important part of the high school choice process. The desirability of these schools is reflected by the large proportion of students who apply for admission. While only a small fraction scored above the minimum cut score on the SHSAT entrance exam required for admission (5.8 percent), in 2008 nearly one in three public school applicants and one in two private school applicants took the exam.[37]

There are stark differences in the population of students who apply to specialized high schools and who ultimately receive offers. Reflecting their highly selective nature, applicants had math and reading scores 0.73 and 0.61 standard deviations above the citywide average, respectively, and were much less likely to be English language learners (3.2 percent vs. 10.1 percent citywide) or recent immigrants (3.5 percent vs. 6.2 percent). Remarkably, Asian students represented 29 percent of specialized high schools applicants, and 53 percent of those were offered seats, though they were only 14 percent of the eighth-grade population. Of course, the race gap in specialized high school admissions primarily reflects differential preparation for and performance on the SHSAT, not favoritism or discrimination per se. Still, this imbalance affects the high school admissions process as a whole and continues to be a concern for the DOE.

In a multivariate regression analysis, we find that—as would be expected—students with higher seventh-grade math and reading scores are much more likely to apply to specialized high schools, to be offered a seat, and to enroll once admitted. This is especially true for those with high math achievement. Interestingly, holding constant seventh-grade achievement, other student characteristics were strongly predictive of application and admission. Controlling for seventh-grade test scores, Asian students' odds of applying were twice as high as those of other students, and their odds of admission more than three times as high. Female, Hispanic, ELL, and free-lunch-eligible students had a lower likelihood of applying (controlling for test scores), and these groups were also less likely to accept an offer if received. Notably, students guaranteed a seat at the educational option schools—those in the top 2 percent in reading—had significantly lower odds of applying to a specialized high school and accepting if given an offer.

TABLE 9-4 Composition of students in applicants' feeder school, first-choice high school, and matched program: 2008

		APPLICANT GROUP						
	All	African American	White	Hispanic	Free lunch eligible	Female	Bottom third reading	Top third reading
Mean % African American:								
Applicants' feeder school	31.8	56.3	13.3	23.5	33.5	32.1	35.3	27.1
Applicants' first choice school	29.7	43.9	17.4	26.7	32.3	30.3	34.1	25.9
Applicants' match	35.2	50.7	20.0	29.8	36.7	35.2	37.6	31.6
Mean % white:								
Applicants' feeder school	13.4	5.9	40.8	8.4	8.9	13.5	8.1	20.6
Applicants' first choice school	18.2	11.4	39.7	12.0	13.2	17.9	10.8	25.0
Applicants' match	12.0	6.4	34.0	8.3	8.9	12.2	8.3	17.2
Mean % Hispanic:								
Applicants' feeder school	40.4	30.1	25.4	57.1	45.1	40.2	46.3	33.3
Applicants' first choice school	36.0	33.0	24.0	49.0	40.6	36.2	43.8	28.9
Applicants' match	40.1	34.4	27.8	51.5	43.2	39.9	44.4	34.9
Mean % free lunch eligible:								
Applicants' feeder school	64.6	67.8	44.9	71.1	71.8	64.2	71.1	56.2
Applicants' first choice school	47.1	52.2	30.4	56.1	52.7	47.5	56.4	38.7
Applicants' match	54.3	58.5	35.3	60.6	58.3	54.1	59.7	47.1

Mean % female:

Applicants' feeder school	50.0	50.6	49.9	49.9	49.9	50.6	49.5	50.7
Applicants' first choice school	52.3	52.3	52.9	50.6	51.3	55.8	49.3	55.0
Applicants' match	50.0	50.3	50.5	49.5	49.6	53.4	48.8	51.8

Mean reading standardized score:

Applicants' feeder school	-0.046	-0.148	0.372	-0.193	-0.157	-0.032	-0.240	0.203
Applicants' first choice school	0.181	0.086	0.406	-0.008	0.058	0.191	-0.076	0.437
Applicants' match	-0.067	-0.123	0.190	-0.164	-0.138	-0.042	-0.211	0.154

Source: Authors' calculations using DOE High School Admissions Process data (2008).

Note: The high school poverty measure is not directly comparable to the feeder school poverty measure (percent free lunch eligible).

The Growth of Charter Schools

With the appointment of Chancellor Klein in 2002, the expansion of charter schools became a top priority in NYC. Under his administration, the number of charter schools rose from 16 to 98 (2002–2009). Enrollment in charter schools grew rapidly, from 1,800 in 2000 to more than 29,600 in 2009 (figure 9-4). Under a planned expansion to 125 schools in 2011, approximately one in ten schools in NYC will be a charter school. However, because of the relatively small size of these schools, charter enrollment will still amount to a very small share of citywide enrollment—about 3 to 4 percent. In 2009, Mayor Bloomberg announced his intention to increase the number of charter schools to 225, and charter enrollment to 100,000.

Given the Bloomberg/Klein administration's strong support for charter schools, it is worth asking whether these relatively new schools have performed as well as traditional schools. National studies appear to show no clear academic advantage in the performance of charters over traditional public schools. Two of the largest studies found that charter students do no better than similar students in conventional public schools.[38] A study from the CREDO organization at Stanford University found that about 46 percent of charters performed at roughly the same level as traditional schools in mathematics; 17 percent performed better and 37 percent did worse.[39]

Importantly, the CREDO report points out that states varied considerably in charter school performance. Differences in state requirements, authorization procedures, and monitoring can make a difference in these outcomes. This is especially relevant in the case of NYC, where three studies have found that charter schools there have outperformed public schools. CREDO conducted a separate study of NYC charter schools and found that in mathematics, about half of the charter schools showed aca-

FIGURE 9-4 **New York City charter school enrollment, 2000–2014**

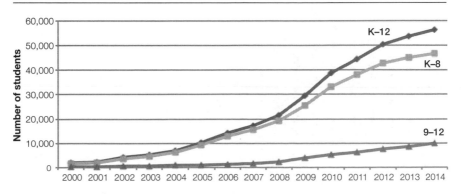

Source: New York State Department of Education. 2010–2014 enrollment is forecasted using school-level planned enrollment from the New York State Department of Education.

demic growth that was statistically greater than would have been attained in public schools; one-third showed no difference, and 16 percent had poorer results.[40] In reading, about one-third of the charter schools did better; about 60 percent had about the same achievement, and 12 percent had worse results.

Strong performance by NYC charter schools was also found in a 2009 study by Hoxby and Murarka.[41] Their study is unique in that it took advantage of the lottery assignment of students to oversubscribed charter schools. Hoxby and Murarka found that, on average, students in NYC charter schools performed better academically than comparable students in traditional schools. Based on an extrapolation from these results, the authors assert that charter schools would close two-thirds of the achievement gap in reading and 90 percent of the gap in math between students in Harlem and those in the wealthy suburb of Scarsdale. She also concludes that more students in charter schools than in traditional schools will graduate with Regents diplomas. However, a formal evaluation of these statistical results found that although there was evidence that oversubscribed NYC charter schools showed an achievement advantage, its magnitude may have been exaggerated by half by the statistical methodology chosen by the researchers.[42]

A third NYC charter study that has received considerable attention addresses results in a single school, the Harlem Children's Zone Promise Academy (HCZ).[43] This study found that HCZ lottery winners were comparable at entry with lottery losers who presumably continued at traditional public schools. However, HCZ students who entered at sixth grade were much more likely to be at grade level or above in eighth grade than the comparison group and had substantially higher achievement scores. Though these results are impressive, the study lacks generalizability for two reasons. First, HCZ students received supplemental health and other services that lottery losers did not. Second, the finding of success for a single school cannot be used to characterize the average effectiveness for all charter schools. Nevertheless, existing evidence suggests that charter schools in NYC are performing better academically than the traditional public schools that charter students are drawn from. It will be important to monitor these findings as the charter sector continues to expand.

Conclusion

In a span of less than eight years, the Bloomberg/Klein administration has made a significant imprint on choice and competition in the city's schools. Although school choice is not a new idea in NYC, this administration has heavily promoted school choice and competition between schools. It has significantly expanded the number of schools from which families may choose and has sought to simplify and streamline the process of application and school assignment. The administration has continually sought ways to make the process more transparent and fair and has demonstrated a willingness to learn from its mistakes. Today, the DOE operates as a kind of market facilitator, providing information about schools and coordinating a standardized enrollment process. In addition to its own school programs, the city has heavily promoted the growth of charter schools that operate independently from the DOE.

In our view, the most remarkable choice innovation of the Klein administration has been its reformed high school admissions process. No longer are students permitted to attend a default zoned school and avoid an active choice. All incoming high school students are *required* to choose a school, ranking up to twelve programs. A complex matching mechanism then assigns students to schools based on their preferences and the eligibility criteria of their schools. In this chapter we provided a cursory analysis of this system, with a focus on the number of programs students apply to, the types of programs they rank first, and where they ultimately enroll. Particular concern was paid to differences in choice behavior across boroughs of the city and by race, ethnicity, gender, and academic ability. Our descriptive analysis shows clear and systematic differences across students and middle schools in the types and characteristics of high school programs applied to and enrolled in. This variation may or may not be a matter of concern. On the one hand, the admissions process is designed to provide maximal choice, permitting students to find the school most suitable to them. On the other hand, it depends heavily on students' access to information and knowledge of the process.

There is little doubt that school choice is more transparent and equitable under Bloomberg and Klein, in the sense that the rules of the game are clearly defined and universally applied. But improved transparency has not necessarily reduced the overall complexity of the system. In fact, in providing universal access to more than seven hundred high school programs, the DOE has shifted the burden of a complex choice decision onto students, their parents, and schools. Of course, this freedom to choose a school is arguably a virtue in and of itself. But whether or not this shift improves academic outcomes in the long run will depend on how students and their families make school choices. If demand is relatively insensitive to academic quality and more responsive to location and/or social influences, even a fair system of choice will fail to provide an impetus for academic improvement. Moreover, to the extent students vary in the values they place on school characteristics, decentralized school choice has the potential to increase stratification by race, academic ability, and socioeconomic status. Unfortunately, the system in New York City is too new for us to evaluate its overall success along these dimensions. But all of these questions represent important topics for future research.

10

How Students' Views Predict Graduation Outcomes and Reveal Instructional Disparities Under Children First Reforms

Ronald F. Ferguson

The New York City Department of Education's (DOE's) reform strategy under Joel Klein's leadership, Children First, emanated from a belief that greater autonomy with greater accountability would inspire school-level professionals to do their best work. Klein's team believed that if school principals, working with other stakeholders, were given appropriate incentives and supports, they would build capacity and would design and implement reforms that would improve student outcomes. Of course, some schools were deemed unlikely to improve and were closed; often multiple small schools replaced one large school that had occupied the same physical space. But generally, the autonomy and accountability strategy for new and continuing schools rested heavily on a system of reports and indicators that school officials and other interested stakeholders monitored to make judgments about progress— not only graduation rates and testing outcomes, but also conditions documented in learning environment surveys and school inspection reports. These progress and performance judgments affected both school- and system-level allocations of personnel, time, and financial resources.

It appears that the approach bore fruit. A January 2010 report from the Alliance for Excellent Education recounts a number of achievements since Children First began in 2002. For example, the city's four-year graduation rate improved impressively, including reductions of 16 and 14 percentage points, respectively, in the African American–white and Hispanic-white high school completion rate gaps. In addition, scores on Regents exams rose, admissions to four-year colleges increased, more students took Advanced Placement exams and scored a 3 or better, and more schools escaped the state's *schools under registration review* designation. Since high schools are the most difficult part of the K–12 system to improve, these are achievements to celebrate.[1] However, much more progress is possible, especially if we listen to our most important stakeholders—our students.

Students experience classrooms for many more hours than any outside observer does. In contrast to secondary schools, colleges commonly take advantage of this fact by surveying students about the quality of the teaching they experience. College officials decide what qualities they seek in teaching, and they poll students using course evaluations to monitor whether these qualities are indeed present. If they are wise, college professors use the feedback to revise their courses and refine their teaching. Often, review committees consult course evaluations to inform personnel decisions. However, at the primary and secondary levels, we seldom ask students for their perspectives. Instead, we treat them as though they lack the capacity to make useful judgments. What a mistake! Fortunately, the DOE is moving in a more promising direction.

New York City has instituted learning environment surveys as an integral part of the reform strategy. Three surveys—one for students, one for teachers, and one for parents—include a variety of questions about teaching, learning, safety, and satisfaction. Responses can inform official decisions about supports and personnel for particular types of schools and for the system as a whole.

In addition to the school-level DOE survey, ten New York City high schools piloted classroom-level surveys from the Tripod Project for School Improvement in 2007 and 2008. While the DOE learning environment surveys allow system-level officials to see inside schools, Tripod surveys allow these officials to see inside classrooms. They enable both school- and system-level administrators to more deeply appreciate and more effectively respond to the variability in teaching quality that remains inside almost every school.

This chapter uses data from both the DOE and Tripod surveys to show the types of information that such surveys can provide to help decision makers not only in NYC, but in any school system. The focus here is on high schools, but the ideas apply in elementary and middle school as well. First we use the DOE learning environment survey and shows that between-school differences in student perceptions of teaching quality help to predict differences in graduation and Regents diploma rates. Then, using data from Tripod surveys, we show that quality varies much more between classrooms inside schools than it does between schools—a fact that has major implications for school-level collaborative inquiry in Children First reforms.

In particular, we use both teacher and student survey responses to show that some teachers are much more effective than others *in the same schools* at eliciting student engagement. Teachers who are impatient, who lack content knowledge or pedagogic skills to clear up confusion, who fail to make learning interesting, or who seem satisfied with mediocre student performance elicit low engagement responses from many of their students, especially students who struggle. Conversely, the very same students—Tripod surveyed many individuals in two different classrooms—may be highly engaged in classrooms where teachers have deep content knowledge, strong pedagogical skills, and unwavering patience.

So far, only a few schools in the NYC system have conducted classroom-level surveys. Consequently, detailed measurements of within-school instructional disparities are generally unavailable and play no strategic role under Children First reforms. This chapter presents a new analysis of instructional quality in NYC schools and classrooms to help stakeholders understand disparities more thoroughly and respond to them more effectively.

Quality Differences Between High Schools

The DOE administers annual learning environment surveys in order to monitor progress on system reforms. Based on the DOE student survey, this section presents data on student perspectives concerning the quality of instruction in their schools. In line with the small schools emphasis of Children First reforms, differences between smaller and larger schools are a special focus. The analysis shows that student perspectives are statistically important predictors of both graduation rates and percentages earning Regents diplomas. Of course, such relationships could merely be correlations if the students most likely to graduate and earn Regents diplomas are just "easy graders" when it comes to judging their teachers. This is a possibility. However, we provide reasons to believe that the patterns are substantially causal, not merely correlations. All of the graduation outcomes are for the cohort of students that began high school as ninth-graders in September of 2005 and who should have graduated in spring of 2009 if they finished in four years.

Basic Patterns

Student perspectives are taken from the DOE learning environment survey administered in the spring of 2008.[2] This was a whole-school survey and the response rate was over 70 percent. The analysis covers 251 high schools for which we were able to match student perceptions of teacher quality with demographic characteristics, enrollment data, and graduation outcomes.[3]

Of the 251 schools, 6.2 percent have enrollments of fewer than 300 students; 45.4 percent serve 300 to 499 students; 19 percent have 500 to 1,000 students; 12 percent serve 1,000 to 2,000 students; and 17.4 percent have between 2,000 and 4,500 students. All variables in this part of the chapter are school-level aggregates.

Student perceptions of instructional quality are captured here using survey items that group conceptually and empirically into five indices.[4] All are quality dimensions that school reformers, including Children First reformers, explicitly value. *Personal Support* is a three-item index measuring whether students perceive that teachers take a special interest in them as individuals. For example, "My teachers give me extra help when I need it." The *Climate of Respect* index combines five items that measure whether members of the school community—both students and adults—treat one another respectfully. For example, "Teachers at my school treat students with respect," and "Students who get good grades in my school are respected by other students." The *Challenging Goals* index combines two items related to support for adopting ambitious goals and working hard to achieve them. For example, "My school helps me to develop challenging goals." The *Stimulation and Relevance* measure is a three-item index capturing whether teachers make learning relevant and inspire students to learn. For example, "My teachers connect what I am learning to life outside of the classroom," and "My teachers inspire me to learn." For each item in each of these indices, we say that students agreed if they checked either "strongly agree" or "agree." The fifth quality index, *Multiple Rigorous Assignments*, is a two-item index. One item asks, "Approximately how often, during this school year, have your teachers asked you to complete an essay or research project using multiple sources of information?" The other asks, "Approximately how often, during this school year, have your teachers asked you to complete an essay or project where you had to use evidence to defend your own opinion or ideas?" Our preliminary analysis established that the major distinction here is between students who responded that they got such assignments five or more times during the school year and those who did not. Thus our formulation of the Multiple Rigorous Assignments index measures the average percentage of students responding that they had such assignments five or more times.

We formed a composite measure by combining all five of the categories above and then, using that composite measure, assigning schools to quartiles of the overall distribution of schools. Therefore, by definition, one-quarter of the high schools that completed the survey occupy each quartile. Since a composite of the subindices are the basis for the quartile definitions, it is not surprising that higher quartiles have higher average values of each index. Nonetheless, it is interesting to examine figure 10-1 to see how agreement varies across quartiles of the quality distribution. Keep in mind that the Multiple Rigorous Assignments category tallies the percentage of students reporting that they had five or more such assignments.

Figure 10-1 shows that the highest agreement levels pertain to items in the personalized support category. Clearly, smaller percentages agree with items in the Stimulation and Relevance and Climate of Respect categories. By far the shortest bars on figure 10-1 pertain to the percentages with five or more rigorous assignments as measured by the Multiple Rigorous Assignments index.

Using the same composite teaching-quality index, figure 10-2 shows the four-year graduation rate within each quartile for students who entered as ninth-graders in September 2005. Similarly, figure 10-3 shows the percentages of the same cohort who graduated with Regents diplomas.

It is interesting to compare the smallest schools (those with less than 300 students) with the largest (those with at least 2,000). In figure 10-2, schools with fewer than 300

FIGURE 10-1   **Average levels of agreement with items in five subindices of school learning conditions, by quartiles of the composite index formed by the average of the subindices**

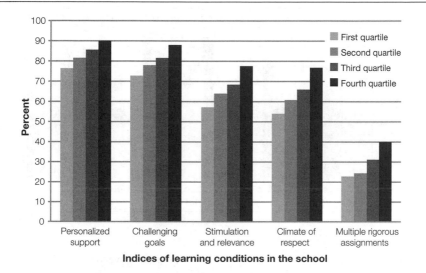

Source: Student responses to NYC DOE student surveys.

FIGURE 10-2   **Four-year graduation rates, by school size and students' ratings of instructional quality**

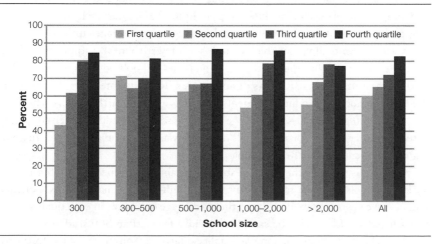

FIGURE 10-3 **Percentages graduating in four years with Regents diplomas, by school size and students' ratings of instructional quality**

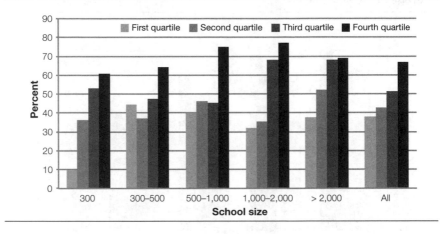

students that are also in the bottom two quality quartiles have lower graduation rates than schools in the same two quality quartiles that serve more than 2,000 students. In other words, the low-quality big schools in this sample graduate a higher fraction of their students on time than the low-quality small schools. The graduation rate advantage that the smallest schools have over the largest schools in figure 10-2 shows up when comparing schools in the top two quality quartiles; for the top two quality quartiles, the small schools have a slight advantage in graduation rates over the big schools.

Comparisons get even more interesting in figure 10-3. Quartile by quartile, large schools with more than 2,000 students have higher percentages finishing in four years with Regents diplomas than schools with fewer than 300 students. Indeed, for both the second and the third quality quartiles, schools with more than 2,000 students have the highest Regents diploma rates. The only categories that outscore the largest schools in producing Regents diplomas are the fourth quartile schools in the 500–1,000 and 1,000–2,000-ranges. Among schools of equal perceived quality based on student surveys, large schools do roughly as well as smaller schools in guiding their students toward Regents diplomas.

But there is more to the story, as shown in table 10-1. Specifically, high-quality large schools are quite rare compared with high-quality small schools. For each school-size category, table 10-1 shows the percentage of schools in each quality quartile. Of sixteen schools in the sample that have fewer than 300 students, 81 percent (13 schools) fall into the top two quality quartiles. Conversely, of the forty-two schools with more than 2,000 students, 81 percent (34 schools) are in the bottom two quality quartiles. Indeed, even among schools serving 1,000–2,000 students, half are rated by their students in the bottom quality quartile.

TABLE 10-1 **Row percentages in composite quality quartiles, by school size, for a NYC sample of 251 non-exam high schools**

	QUALITY QUARTILES FROM THE COMPOSITE INDEX				
	First	*Second*	*Third*	*Fourth*	*Total*
Enrollment range	**Row percentages**				
Fewer than 300	6.25	12.5	37.5	43.75	100
300–499	14.04	22.81	31.58	31.58	100
500–1,000	29.17	31.25	22.92	16.67	100
1,000–2,000	51.61	16.13	12.9	19.35	100
2,000–4,500	40.48	40.48	14.29	4.76	100

Source: Author's calculations using DOE data, as explained in text and notes.

TABLE 10-2 **Average percentage agreement with items in five teaching quality indices among NYC students in 251 non-exam high schools, by school size**

	Multiple rigorous assignments	*Climate of respect*	*Personal support*	*Stimulation and relevance*	*Challenging goals*
Enrollment range					
1. Fewer than 300	35	68	86	70	82
2. 300–499	31	67	86	68	81
3. 500–1,000	29	62	82	64	78
4. 1,000–2,000	27	61	81	64	78
5. 2,000–4,500	23	60	79	63	78
Differences between the largest and smallest schools (row 5 minus 1):					
6. Difference between rows 1 and 5	12	8	7	7	4
7. With controls for student and teacher characteristics	12	8	6	12	10

Source: Author's calculations using DOE data, as explained in text and notes

Table 10-2 unbundles the composite quality index into the five subindices that we used to construct it. The table shows an unbroken pattern: larger schools receive lower ratings. The largest difference between size categories is for Multiple Rigorous Assignments, where the gap between the smallest and the largest schools is eleven percentage points. The smallest gap is for the Challenging Goals category, where the difference is only three points.

To summarize, we defined five instructional quality subindices and an overall composite. We divided the composite into quartiles and showed that higher quartiles have higher values for all five subindices. Students agreed most that they received Personalized Support. But even in the top quartile of the quality composite, fewer than half reported five or more writing assignments during the school year that required using multiple sources and defending the logic of an argument. Next we examined how rated quality relates to school size, and found that schools with more than 2,000 students are rated mostly in the bottom two quality quartiles. Schools with no more than 1,000 students tend to be in the top quartiles, while schools with between 1,000 and 2,000 students rate lowest, with half in the very bottom quartile. However, one-fifth of the schools from this same 1,000–2,000 range occupy the very highest quartile, making this size category the most variable in quality.

Now we ask whether differences in rated quality between large and small schools can be explained by differences in the types of students they serve or differences in teacher experience. We conducted a statistical analysis that controlled for student characteristics and teacher experience. Control variables included the racial, ethnic, and gender composition of the student body, the percentage of students classified as poor, and the percentage who were recent immigrants. We also controlled for the percentage of teachers at the school with five or more years of teaching experience, as well as the percentage who had taught at this specific school for at least two years.

The results are shown on line 7 of table 10-2. Here we see that the difference in student ratings of teaching quality between the largest and the smallest schools stays the same *or increases* when we control for student and teacher characteristics. These differences in teacher-quality ratings are statistically distinguishable from zero at the 95 percent confidence level or better in calculations that control for student and teacher characteristics.[5] These results indicate that differences in how students rate schools of different sizes are almost surely not the result of differences in the makeup of their student bodies.

Predicting Graduation and Regents Diplomas

It is easy to see from figures 10-2 and 10-3 that schools in higher-quality quartiles achieve better graduation outcomes, no matter what their size category. But can school quality differences account for graduation rate differences between schools of different sizes?

The graduation rate in table 10-3 for schools with fewer than 300 students is 79 percent. The rate for schools with 2,000 to 4,500 students is 62.9 percent. Hence, the gap is 16.1 percentage points. Similarly, one can use table 10-3 to compute the difference in graduation rates between any two size categories and see that the difference is greater when there is more of a difference in school size. The 16.1 percentage point gap is slightly reduced to 14.3 after controlling for student and teacher characteristics. However, after controlling for teacher-quality differences, the gap is only 8.7—a drop of 5.6 percent-

TABLE 10-3   Four-year graduation outcomes in a sample of 251 non-exam high schools for NYC students entering high school September 2005, by school size

| | | REGENTS DIPLOMA RATES | |
| | | | |
Enrollment range	Graduation rates	As a percentage of ninth-grade entrants four years earlier	As a percentage of four-year graduates
1. Fewer than 300	79.0	54.5	66.6
2. 300–499	72.0	48.6	65.6
3. 500–1,000	68.4	48.2	67.6
4. 1,000–2,000	64.4	46.5	68.0
5. 2,000–4,500	62.9	46.8	71.6
Differences between the largest and smallest schools (row 5 minus 1):			
6. Difference between rows 1 and 5	16.1	7.7	−5.0
7. With SES controls	14.3	5.7	−5.5
8. With SES plus teaching quality controls	8.7	2.31	−10.5

Source: Author's calculations using DOE data, as explained in text and notes.

age points. Thus, student perceptions of teaching quality predict 5.6 percentage points of the graduation rate differences between the largest and the smallest schools—more than one-third of the differences. The differences in graduation rates between schools of different sizes are no longer statistically significant after we control for school quality.[6]

Can we say the same for Regents diploma rates? Column 2 in table 10-3 shows the percentage of entering ninth-graders in 2005 that finished high school four years later with a Regents diploma, and column 3 shows the percentage of four-year graduates from that same 2005 cohort that received a Regents diploma. The main thing to notice here is that differences across school-size categories are much smaller when the outcome under examination is Regents diplomas. Despite a clear relationship between school size and four-year graduation rates, there is not much of a relationship between school size and success at producing Regents diplomas. How can this be?

The answer appears to be that smaller schools are better at helping struggling students—those unlikely to earn Regents diplomas—to complete high school in four years. These types of students are less likely to finish in four years if they attend very large schools. However, this fact does not necessarily mean that larger schools have a much bigger dropout problem, since many of the students who fail to complete in four years at larger schools were still enrolled in the data we examined. What we know is that a smaller percentage of students at larger schools graduated in four years. And, at least for some of them, their ultimate graduation outcomes remain to be determined.

These school-quality findings may help explain the findings in the highly regarded impact study of NYC's small schools released recently by MDRC. The study, by Howard Bloom, Saskia Levy Thompson, and Rebecca Unterman addressed the effectiveness of what the authors called "small schools of choice" (SSCs).[7] It found that attending SSCs increased students' four-year graduation rates by 6.8 percentage points.[8] This difference in graduation rates is not statistically distinguishable from the 5.6 percentage point difference predicted using teacher-quality measures in the present study.[9] Consistent with our findings above, the MDRC researchers found that any small-school advantage in receipt of Regents diplomas was not statistically distinguishable from zero.[10]

So, is improving teaching quality along particular dimensions—multiple rigorous assignments, a climate of respect, personalized supports, challenging goals, and stimulation and relevance—a worthy strategic focus for Children First reforms? Our analysis indicates that student perceptions of instructional quality on these dimensions predict more than a third of the 16-percentage-point four-year graduation rate gap between the smallest and the largest categories of high schools. This is not trivial; improving instruction along these dimensions appears to be a worthy aspiration.

What should we conclude about the small schools policy under Children First reforms? Based not only on the findings here, but also on the rigorous MDRC study, it appears that the small schools policy has made a positive difference. The findings are consistent with what one would expect if small schools were more successful at the types of Children First collaborative inquiry activities that Joan Talbert discusses in chapter 6 in this volume—activities focused explicitly on finding ways to help struggling students succeed. At the same time, it appears that no school-size category has a clear advantage in producing Regents diplomas. Schools of all sizes have room to improve as NYC reforms go forward.

Measuring Quality Differences Between Classrooms

So far, this chapter has focused on school-level averages. A focus on school-level averages directs attention to the goal of improving weak schools, but may distract attention from the importance of improving weak classrooms. Even the best schools are likely to have classrooms where instruction needs to improve dramatically.

School-level averages mask tremendous variation inside schools. There is much more disparity from classroom to classroom inside most schools than there is from one school to another inside most districts. The section below argues that school- and district-level strategists should design and implement reform measures with an appreciation for the fact that classrooms differ. We will discuss some of the most important types of variation.

Tripod Surveys in NYC

The remainder of this chapter deals with ten NYC high schools that the Tripod Project surveyed concerning classroom-level conditions in 2007 and 2008. To introduce the schools, we show how they compare to other NYC high schools as well as to schools in other districts. The comparisons to schools in other districts respond to interest in New York about how student perceptions in the nation's largest city compare to those of students in other places, but these comparisons are not the focus of the analysis.

Tripod Project surveys were administered in ten NYC high schools in 2007 and 2008.[11] Nine of the ten schools are also represented in the DOE learning environment data examined above. Comparing these nine schools to others using the DOE data provides a basis for judging whether they are representative enough that their responses to Tripod surveys might be of broader interest and relevance. However, before conducting this comparison, a brief introduction to the Tripod Project is in order.

The *tripod* in the Tripod Project name refers to three "legs" of quality teaching: content, pedagogy, and relationships. This model emphasizes teachers' content knowledge, pedagogic skills, and capacity to form and sustain effective student-teacher relationships. The premise is that students will engage more deeply and learn more effectively when they perceive that all three legs of their teachers' tripods are strong. In order to actualize this basic idea, the Tripod Project framework identifies five categories of targets for student engagement that teaching quality engenders. It also identifies seven types of classroom conditions—the *seven Cs*—that correspond to key elements of teaching quality.

The five targets for student engagement are that students should:

1. *Trust* teachers and classmates and feel welcome and safe in their presence, instead of feeling mistrustful, unwelcome, or unsafe
2. *Cooperate* with teachers and classmates, including behaving respectfully, instead of being uncooperative or disrespectful
3. *Aspire* to achieve ambitious learning goals, instead of feeling ambivalent or uncommitted
4. *Persist* in the face of difficulty, instead of becoming discouraged and disengaged
5. *Achieve* success and satisfaction, instead of experiencing failure and disappointment

High-quality teaching can help students to achieve these targets.

Both the underlying theory and actual patterns in the data indicate that teachers are more effective at helping students achieve the engagement targets when their students rate them better on the seven Cs of teaching. Specifically, effective teachers:

1. *Care* in ways that promote trust and constructive teacher-student relationships: *"My teacher in this class makes me feel that he/she really cares about me."*
2. *Control* students' tendencies toward out-of-order, disrespectful, or off-task behavior: *"Our class stays busy and doesn't waste time."*
3. *Clarify* key concepts and ideas that might confuse students (note that this may include allowing students to at least temporarily puzzle over questions as one pathway to clarity): *"My teacher has several good ways to explain each topic that we cover."*

4. *Challenge* students to persist, work diligently, and think rigorously: *"My teacher doesn't let people give up when the work gets hard,"* and *"My teacher wants us to really understand the material, not just memorize it."*
5. *Captivate* students to stimulate interest and hold their attention: *"My teacher makes lessons interesting."*
6. *Confer* with students to elicit their questions and perspectives: *"My teacher encourages us to share ideas with one another in class."*
7. *Consolidate* to help students integrate and retain ideas: *"We get helpful comments to let us know what we did wrong on assignments."*

The seven Cs indices are composites of multiple survey items similar to the ones listed here as examples.

Notice that the first four of the seven Cs represent concepts quite similar to the five indices that formulated above to analyze the DOE surveys:

- Care is similar to Personal Support from the DOE—both concern strong teacher-student relationships.
- Control is similar to Climate of Respect from the DOE—both concern respectful and cooperative behavior.
- Challenge relates to both Challenging Goals and Multiple Rigorous Assignments from DOE—all three concern pressing students to work hard and think rigorously.
- Captivate is similar to Stimulation and Relevance from the DOE discussion—both concern making school interesting, relevant and inspiring.

The other three of the seven Cs—Clarify, Confer, and Consolidate—are less well aligned with the DOE measures. The analysis below will focus on the four measures—Care, Control, Challenge, and Captivate—that align best with the DOE measures. In addition, we include Clarify because the ability to clear up confusion is so important to effective instruction. Certainly, Clarify should be a focus for collaborative inquiry teams in their work with struggling students. Our unpublished findings from other districts show Clarify to be especially important as a predictor of value-added achievement gains.

The NYC Tripod Sample

Are NYC schools that took Tripod Project surveys typical enough of other high schools in the city that their Tripod survey results should be of general interest? In table 10-4, we place schools into four categories: we refer to schools that have from 300 to 1,000 students as *medium-sized*, while *large* schools have from 2,000 to 4,500 students.[12] These two groupings include all of the NYC schools that took Tripod surveys, with half in the medium category and half in the large category.[13] Columns 1 and 2 represent medium-sized and large schools, respectively, that took Tripod surveys; columns 3 and 4 represent the same two size groupings for schools that did not.

TABLE 10-4 **Comparing student ratings of instructional quality and student body characteristics of Tripod and non-Tripod NYC schools in two size ranges**

| | NYC TRIPOD SCHOOLS | | OTHER NYC SCHOOLS | |
	Medium-sized high schools (1)	Large high schools (2)	Medium-sized high schools (3)	Large high schools (4)
Instructional quality				
Personal support	82	83	82	79
Climate of respect	60	61	63	61
Challenging goals	78	81	79	79
Multiple rigorous assignments	28	21	29	25
Stimulation & relevance	65	66	64	63
Student body characteristics				
% poor	58	55	58	41
% Aslan	2	15	7	21
% African American	63	32	38	27
% Hispanic	34	43	45	33
% white	1	9	9	19
Attendance and enrollment				
% daily attendance	79	79	85	84
Enrollment	647	3388	676	3177
Schools in DOE sample	5	4	46	41

Note: Medium-sized = 300–1,000 students; large = 2,000–4,500 students.

It appears from table 10-4 that students attending Tripod schools are somewhat more disadvantaged than the students of the average of NYC high school. Still, we think the answer to the question, "Are Tripod schools typical enough to be of general interest?" is yes. Despite some differences in student body characteristics and attendance patterns, students in the system's Tripod and non-Tripod samples rate teaching quality quite similarly on the DOE school-level survey.

Disparities Between Schools and Classrooms

In this section, we show how much schools differ from one another on teaching-quality ratings. We compare the differences between schools with the differences between classrooms and show that the differences between classrooms are much larger.

To construct table 10-5, we rank-ordered all of the schools in the DOE student survey for each of the indices defined above using the DOE data. We did this separately for each of the five indices. For each index, table 10-5 shows the tenth, fiftieth, and ninetieth percentile values.[14] The bottom line of the table subtracts the tenth from the ninetieth percentile values to show the differences. The smallest difference is for Personal Support in large schools, where agreement with items in the

TABLE 10-5 Percent agreement with items in teaching quality indices at the tenth, fiftieth, and ninetieth percentiles in school rankings in medium versus large enrollment categories

	DOE TEACHING QUALITY INDICES									
	PERSONAL SUPPORT		CLIMATE OF RESPECT		MULTIPLE RIGOROUS ASSIGNMENTS		CHALLENGING GOALS		STIMULATION AND RELEVANCE	
Percentile	Medium (1)	Large (2)	Medium (3)	Large (4)	Medium (5)	Large (6)	Medium (7)	Large (8)	Medium (9)	Large (10)
10th	75	74	51	54	20	19	72	73	55	57
50th	83	79	63	59	28	22	79	79	64	62
90th	89	84	75	73	40	34	87	86	73	69
90–10 difference	14	10	24	19	20	15	15	13	18	12

Source: DOE student survey.

Note: Medium = 300–1,000 students; large = 2,000–4,500 students.

Personal Support index is only 10 percentage points lower at the tenth-percentile school than at the ninetieth-percentile school. The largest differences are for Climate of Respect in both large and medium-sized schools. Percentages agreeing with items in this index at the tenth percentile schools are 51 and 54 percent for medium-sized and large schools, respectively. For this index, the average level of agreement rises to roughly three-quarters at the ninetieth percentile for both medium and large schools.

Table 10-6 uses Tripod Project data to show differences between classrooms by major subject for schools that took Tripod surveys in NYC (the *NYC* columns) and other districts (the *Others* columns). Table 10-6 uses five of the Tripod Project's seven Cs indices. Recall that four of these five—Care, Control, Challenge, and Captivate—are conceptually similar to the measures defined on the NCYDOE data, for which percentile values are shown on table 10-5.

Table 10-6 is structured similarly to table 10-5, but there are several important differences. First, the percentile values in table 10-6 pertain to positions in the distribution of *classrooms* instead of the distribution of *schools*. Second, table 10-6 shows patterns for four different subjects. Third, each pair of columns in table 10-6 represents different school systems (NYC versus others) instead of different school-size groupings inside NYC.[15]

At least two features of the pattern in table 10-6 are striking. First, there is a dramatic similarity between the NYC numbers and those for other districts. The numbers for New York schools versus those from other systems are so close that it seems they could have come from a single community.

A second striking feature, and one that is quite troubling, is that the differences between the tenth- and ninetieth-percentile classrooms are huge. The majority of these gaps are 40 percentage points or more. It might be tempting to believe that the tenth-percentile classrooms are concentrated in a few low-performing schools. That would be incorrect. As we pointed out above, there is much more disparity from classroom to classroom inside most schools than there is from one school to another inside most districts.

For example, see figure 10-4. This figure shows ratings for 130 math and English classrooms in one of the large NYC schools. We began by averaging the five indices on the horizontal axis to get one composite variable. Then we divided that variable into deciles for this particular school. For each of the five measures of instructional quality, figure 10-4 shows the average level of agreement with items that measure that aspect of teaching quality, within each decile of the composite distribution. A comparison of the heights of the bars on the first and tenth deciles for each of the indices on the horizontal axis of figure 10-4 reveals that the numbers are quite close to the tenth and ninetieth percentiles shown on table 10-6, indicating that the spread in quality of the whole Tripod sample can be found in miniature at the school level. This is typical not only in NYC, but in other cities as well.

TABLE 10-6 Percent agreement with items in teaching quality indices at the tenth, fiftieth, and ninetieth percentiles in classroom rankings in medium versus large enrollment categories

| | | FIVE OF THE TRIPOD SEVEN Cs TEACHING QUALITY INDICES | | | | | | | | | |
| | | CARE | | CONTROL | | CLARIFY | | CHALLENGE | | CAPTIVATE | |
Subject	Percentile	Others (1)	NYC (2)	Others (3)	NYC (4)	Others (5)	NYC (6)	Others (7)	NYC (8)	Others (9)	NYC (10)
Math	10th	41	44	29	32	36	41	44	49	30	32
	50th	68	67	51	50	67	69	65	66	55	56
	90th	87	90	70	77	88	92	80	85	79	79
	90–10 difference	46	46	41	45	52	51	36	36	49	47
Science	10th	40	46	28	26	37	42	41	42	27	25
	50th	67	67	50	50	66	70	62	59	57	55
	90th	84	88	70	72	88	88	80	78	80	81
	90–10 difference	44	42	42	46	51	46	39	36	53	56
English	10th	44	52	33	34	39	50	47	49	35	36
	50th	70	73	52	57	68	72	64	67	59	63
	90th	89	89	73	71	88	90	81	83	82	78
	90–10 difference	45	37	40	37	49	40	34	34	47	42
History	10th	45	54	33	31	43	50	43	50	31	37
	50th	69	73	54	55	70	71	61	67	60	62
	90th	90	90	72	77	89	89	79	84	83	84
	90–10 difference	45	36	39	46	46	39	36	34	52	47

FIGURE 10-4 **Average percent agreement with items in selected indices, within deciles of a composite index, for 130 math and English classrooms in one NYC high school**

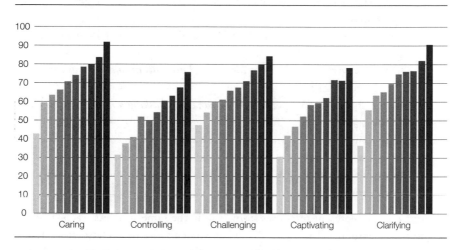

Same Students, Multiple Classrooms

Another way to demonstrate differences between classrooms is to survey the same student in two different classrooms. When we survey the same students in different classrooms we always find differences in how students respond across classrooms, and also find that students in the same classroom together tend toward agreement. In addition, when the same students are surveyed in two classrooms, they tend to report better behavior, higher goals, and more engagement in the classrooms of teachers that they rate higher on the seven Cs indices.

In one analysis, we selected 450 NYC students who had quite different experiences in at least two different classrooms. For each of these students, two classrooms in which they answered surveys differed from one another by at least a full standard deviation on the seven Cs composite index. As an example of how large the differences were on Caring, which is the first of the seven Cs, the same students' average agreement with the statement "My teacher in this class makes me feel that he/she really cares about me" was 76.9 percent in the highly rated class, but only 31.6 percent in the low-rated class.

We examined how well these students met the Tripod student engagement targets in the two classrooms. The following examples show gaps in average responses comparing the higher- with the lower-rated classes for these 450 students. Clearly, students expressed quite different levels of agreement with statements concerning engagement in the two classrooms.

- 44.1 percent versus 12.8 percent for *"I feel close to my teacher in this class."*

- 52.4 percent versus 22.3 percent for *"I care about pleasing my teacher in this class."*
- 82.7 percent versus 63.2 percent for *"For this class, I try hard to be on time and not to be absent."*
- 92.3 percent versus 72.0 percent for *"In this class, it is important to me to thoroughly understand my class work."*
- 88.7 percent versus 69.8 percent for *"One of my goals in this class has been to learn as much as I can."*
- 79.2 percent versus 55.4 percent for *"I don't mind asking questions in this class if I need to."*
- 65.6 percent versus 37.4 percent for *"I am satisfied with what I have achieved in this class."*
- 62.4 percent versus 44.8 percent for *"I have done my best quality work in this class all year long."*

Again, these represent responses from exactly the same students, each surveyed in multiple classrooms. They show that when students and their classmates rate one classroom more highly than another with regard to the seven Cs instructional practices, they also tend to become more engaged in the higher-rated class in ways that their survey responses capture.

Like teaching, student engagement is a classroom-level phenomenon. It varies "within student" from one classroom to another, partly in response to teaching. Obviously, reforms to affect teaching and learning have to reach the classroom in order to make a difference. Many reforms do not penetrate deeply enough. The fact that they do not is indicated by the prevalence of teaching practices such as those that we discuss next—practices that students might reasonably perceive as the teacher giving up.

Teacher Responses Define the "Give-Up" Index

Some of the teachers whose classrooms we surveyed in 2007 and 2008 completed a Tripod survey for teachers. The survey includes roughly seventy questions about pedagogy, thirty about the teacher's opinions of the students in the class, and forty about the school-level professional climate and working relations.

One of the analyses we conducted involved matching student and teacher surveys to analyze an index composed of the following seven items from the teacher survey. We combine these items and call the composite the *Give-Up index*:

1. I tend not to wait for students to answer when called on if they take a long time to start.
2. I call on high achievers more than I call on low achievers.
3. I feel I am boring some students when I go slowly so that others can keep up.
4. It is unreasonable to expect that all students can succeed in my class.

5. I believe that encouraging low achievers to ask questions slows the class down too much.
6. I have so much to cover in class that there isn't enough time to answer student questions.
7. [I tend to disagree with] I believe that almost every student has the potential to do well on a particular assignment.

Only one of the NYC schools surveyed more than half of its teachers in a manner that the teachers' responses could be linked to students' at the classroom level. This particular school had 126 classrooms in which both the teacher and the students completed surveys about the particular class.[16] At this school, negative attitudes among teachers were a bit more common than usual.[17] Variation in attitudes and practices among these teachers produced within-school correlations between the Give-Up index and student perceptions that were large and highly statistically significant.

Table 10-7 shows the correlations between the Give-Up index and selected items representing the seven Cs instructional quality indices for the school in question. The table shows that the higher the teacher's score on the Give-Up index—determined by the teacher's own responses to the items listed above—the less that teacher's students agree with items in the seven Cs indices.[18]

We discovered that the negative correlations were being driven by the top, most problematic, quartile of the Give-Up distribution. As panel A in table 10-7 illustrates, the teachers who fall into the highest (that is, worst) quartile of the index are rated markedly worse by students than the teachers in the other three quartiles. On Clarify, for example, the worst teachers are rated eighteen percentage points lower than the rest of their colleagues.

Individual teachers' propensity to give up on students cannot necessarily be explained by saying that they have troublesome students to start with. Students whose teachers rated worst on the Give-Up index rated their classmates as average. In particular, Panel B of table 10-7 shows that there was no correlation between teachers' responses to the Give-Up index and student responses concerning teasing, stresses outside of class, or the difficulty of the class. At the same time, students did report disengagement in the classrooms of high-give-up teachers. They agreed less with statements such as the following:

- I have pushed myself hard to completely understand my lessons in this class.
- I would ask the teacher for help if I needed it.
- When I work hard in this class, an important reason is that the teacher demands it.
- I can do almost all the work in this class if I don't give up.

This correlation suggests that when the teacher gives up, the students tend to give up too.

TABLE 10-7 **How students' Tripod responses in 126 classrooms at a large NYC high school correlate with their teachers' responses to the Give-Up index**

			Give-Up Quartiles		
			1, 2, 3	4	Difference
	Example survey items	Correlations with the Give-Up Index	Percentage Agreement		
Panel A: Seven Cs indices		(1)	(2)	(3)	(4)
1. Care	My teacher in this class makes me feel that he/she really cares about me.	–0.31*	58	44	–14
2. Control	Our class stays busy and doesn't waste time.	–0.29*	56	43	–13
3a. Clarify	My teacher has several good ways to explain each topic that we cover.	–0.28*	63	45	–18
3b. Clarify	If you don't understand something, my teacher explains it another way.	–0.27*	67	54	–13
4. Challenge	My teacher doesn't let people give up when the work gets hard.	–0.32*	63	47	–16
5. Captivate	My teacher makes lessons interesting.	–0.32*	55	38	–17
6. Confer	My teacher encourages us to share ideas with one another in class.	–0.36*	60	45	–15
7. Consolidate	We get helpful comments to help us know what we did wrong on assignments.	–0.38*	67	51	–16
Panel B: Troublesome classmates?					
	In this class, students get teased if they study hard to get good grades.	–0.01	19	16	–3
	In this class, some students try to keep others from working hard.	–0.03	29	24	–5
	Problems outside of school sometimes keep me from doing work for this class.	–0.04	24	21	–3
	For most students, this class is harder than other classes.	–0.01	32	27	–5

*Indicates statistical significance at the 0.001 level.

Professional Learning as a Response

Everything in the chapter up to this point concerns patterns in survey responses that show differences in teaching quality. The first half of the chapter addressed differences between schools, while the last half has focused on differences between classrooms. The unavoidable conclusion from both parts of the paper is that students in different schools and classrooms experience very different levels of quality of instruction. Most students experience quite noticeable variation every day as they move from one classroom to another.

Learning New Strategies for Clearing Up Confusion

Obviously, there are two basic approaches to improving teaching and reducing this variation. One is to attract additional skilled and committed people into teaching while inducing the least effective teachers to leave the profession, or at least the district. The other is to help teachers improve through professional learning activities. Children First attempts to do both. Both are important, and they are interdependent. There are reasons to believe that skilled and committed candidates for teaching will be most attracted to cultures of continuous improvement. Furthermore, they will contribute to those cultures by investing their own time and energy in ongoing professional learning.

Teachers who engage actively in professional learning will agree more with statements such as "I am using teaching strategies in my class that I've learned in the past year." For shorthand, we will refer to this as the *learning and using new strategies* statement. We should expect that teachers who agree more with this statement will rate better on measures of instructional quality. Table 10-8 is structured around this statement; the data in the table are for the same large NYC high school as in table 10-7. Teachers could respond to the statement in four ways: strongly agree, agree, slightly agree, or disagree.[19]

Column A of table 10-8 focuses on responses to the learning and using new strategies statement among teachers in the top (i.e., worst) quartile of the Give-Up index. The table shows that more than half of all teachers who checked "disagree" in response to this statement—specifically, 53 percent of "disagree" teachers—were in the top quartile of the Give-Up index. Conversely, of the teachers who checked "strongly agree" in response to the learning and using new strategies statement, only one-fifth (21 percent) of these teachers were in the top quartile of the Give-Up index. In other words, at least for this particular high school, teachers who learn and use new strategies are less likely to treat students in ways that could reasonably be interpreted as giving up on them.

Column B suggests a likely reason: it indicates that teachers who engage in professional learning are more likely to have several ways of explaining things that students find difficult to understand. Among teachers who disagree with the learning and

TABLE 10-8   Correlates of: "I am using teaching strategies in my class that I've learned in the past year": How the Give-Up index and multiple explanations relate to agreement with this statement at the same New York City High school represented on table 10-7.

The left column of this table shows four response options for the statement in the title to this table. Of the teachers who gave the response on each particular row, the numbers below answer the questions listed at the tops of columns A, B ,and C.*

	Column A	Column B	Column C
	What percentages are in the top (i.e., worst) quartile of the Give-Up index?	What percentages say they "always" have several ways of explaining things that students find difficult?	What percentages of their students agree that, "If you don't understand something, my teacher explains it another way."
Disagree	53	19	53
Slightly agree	41	33	60
Agree	32	44	65
Strongly agree	21	54	67

Note: Neither the columns nor the rows of this table should add to 100 percent. (See the discussion in the text. Each number on each row is defined in relationship to 100 percent of the teachers who gave the response on that row for the statement about learning and using new strategies.)

Sample sizes are: Disagree (n = 19); slightly agree (n = 44); agree (n = 71); strongly agree (n = 37).

using new strategies statement, only 19 percent agree that they "always" have several ways of explaining things that students find difficult to understand.[20] This percentage almost doubles—to 33 percent—among teachers who slightly agree and almost triples—to 54 percent—among teachers who strongly agree with the learning and using new strategies statement. Of course, there is a chicken-and-egg issue here, since teachers with greater academic skill—developed over a lifetime—might have an easier time explaining things to students and also find professional learning to be more engaging. In any case, there is clearly a correlation.[21]

Are these differences perceptible to students? Column C of table 10-8 indicates that the answer is yes. This column uses an item from the student survey: "If you don't understand something, my teacher explains it another way." This is one of the key items inside the Clarify index of the seven Cs. Agreement is a response of either "mostly true" or "totally true." Slightly more than half (53 percent) of students whose teachers disagreed with the learning and using new strategies statement agreed that their teachers provided multiple explanations, compared with almost two-thirds (67 percent) of students in the classrooms of teachers who strongly agreed with the statement.

Visiting Classes and Discussing Student Work

Two of the most commonly prescribed methods for teacher professional learning are watching each other teach and discussing examples of student work with colleagues.

Panel A of table 10-9 shows the frequencies with which teachers engage in these two practices. It shows that only 24 percent of the teacher respondents at the high school featured in tables 10-7 and 10-8 have had other teachers visit multiple times during the survey year to watch them teach. While a larger percentage (38 percent) has participated multiple times during the survey year in discussions of student work, this is still a minority. Teachers from other NYC schools reported classroom visits from other teachers and conferences about student work at a higher rate—52 percent and 55 percent, respectively—but there are reasons to believe that these respondents are more active on average than other teachers at their schools.[22] As a point of comparison, respondents from outside NYC report both fewer visits and fewer discussions than the NYC respondents.

Panel B of table 10-9 calls into question whether teachers benefit much from all of the visits and discussions. For each cell of Panel A, Panel B of table 10-9 shows the percentage of teachers who agree strongly that they are using teaching strategies learned during the past year. Generally, NYC teachers in this sample are less likely than teachers from outside the city to strongly agree that they are using new strategies. Inspection of Panel B indicates at best a weak relationship between how frequently teachers visit or discuss student work and the use of new strategies.

Toward Effective Collaborative Inquiry

The evidence presented above indicates that professional learning activities are not always effective. Talbert (chapter 6) describes the collaborative inquiry method that is currently the main strategic approach to professional development in the NYC system. Talbert makes it clear that in order to work well, collaborative inquiry has to be more than just teachers visiting one another's classes or discussing student work with no impact on teaching practice. Instead, under the DOE collaborative inquiry strategy, teachers are supposed to learn to analyze student achievement data and focus on a limited number of struggling students. Working together, they strive to understand the students—including by examining their test scores, watching them in the classroom, and studying their work. The idea is for teachers to collaborate to design and implement approaches to help these students find success. What a team of teachers learns from intensively helping a few students is supposed to prepare those teachers to serve other students more effectively and, in a best-case scenario, spread to improve the whole school.

Talbert reports that collaborative inquiry has shown evidence of improving student outcomes when implemented well. But the approach is in various stages of development across the system—and that this development is going well in some schools and departments but not in others. She writes that it is at constant risk of being derailed by competing approaches to school improvement.

A tension, and a reasonable fear, is that a more active focus on evidence of instructional quality of the type that this chapter presents could lead system officials to

TABLE 10-9　Participation in classroom visits and discussions of student work in New York City and other districts

Frequencies	ANOTHER TEACHER VISITED FOR 20+ MINUTES TO "WATCH YOU TEACH"			LOOKED WITH OTHERS AT STUDENT WORK FOR AT LEAST HALF AN HOUR		
	High schools outside New York City (1)	Other NYC high schools in the Tripod sample (2)	The same NYC high school from tables 10-7 and 10-8 (3)	High schools outside New York City (4)	Other NYC high schools in the Tripod sample (5)	The same NYC high school from tables 10-7 and 10-8 (6)
Panel A	Column percentages			Column percentages		
Never	30	10	17	16	13	16
Less than yearly	23	5	12	15	5	9
Once this year	19	13	28	17	13	18
Twice this year	12	20	19	15	15	19
Several times this year	16	52	24	36	55	38
Total	100	100	100	100	100	100
Panel B	Percentages that strongly agree that they are using teaching strategies learned in the past year					
Never	33	6	14	33	15	7
Less than yearly	36	38	19	12	0	19
Once this year	29	41	15	44	35	13
Twice this year	40	30	34	26	43	16
Several times this year	44	31	24	45	30	33
Total	35	30	21	35	30	20
Number of respondents	494	179	172	494	179	172

undermine the collaborative inquiry approach. In particular, it is conceivable that system-level officials might revert to imposing more professional development solutions from the top down, instead of trusting teachers and administrators to craft their own approaches in school-level teams. Such fears may be well founded.

A wiser response than ignoring the evidence would be to acknowledge information such as that provided by the Tripod surveys without blinking and then decide how best to use it. Officials at every level of the system should recognize that perceptions of teaching quality and student engagement are underutilized information resources that can enrich professional learning, including through collaborative inquiry. Just as teams of teachers analyze achievement data, the same teams can analyze student perceptions of the classroom experiences that foreshadow the achievement outcomes. Grounded in rich conceptions of teaching and learning, surveys focused at the classroom level can help guide collaborative inquiry teams toward well-conceived plans and actions to help more students succeed. The same surveys can inform capacity-building priorities at the system level for supporting the collaborative inquiry professional development strategy.

Conclusion

This chapter describes instructional strengths and weakness measured for NYC high schools using student and teacher surveys during Children First reforms. It shows tremendous variation in student perceptions of instructional quality, especially between classrooms, and it shows that school-to-school differences in such perceptions help in predicting graduation rates and Regents diplomas. These school-to-school differences in survey responses are not predicted by students' background characteristics. Instead, they appear to reflect differences in what students experience in classrooms. By comparing highly rated classrooms with lower-rated classrooms, the chapter delineates the gap that exists between current conditions and what seems possible based on what the most effective classrooms in the system are already achieving.

The question now is whether Children First reforms can be successful at helping many more teachers to reach the levels that their most effective colleagues have shown are possible. There are reasons to be cautiously optimistic, but success is far from certain.

A recent report from the Achievement Gap Initiative at Harvard University tells the instructional leadership stories of fifteen high schools that have shown impressive learning gains in math or English language arts.[23] Central to these stories were serious approaches to designing, implementing, monitoring, and refining professional learning. It sometimes took as long as a decade, but leaders at these schools worked hard to achieve broad-based involvement in professional learning—and they succeeded.

Unfortunately, such stories are much more the exception than the rule. Tripod teacher surveys in the past have identified several school conditions that too often lead teachers to avoid participating in or to ignore what they learn through professional development. Top reasons include that leaders pile new initiatives on top of the old, so that the new ideas are "just too much on top of everything else"; that teachers are not held accountable for learning and applying professional development lessons; that there is not enough support and training when a new idea is introduced; and that ideas are not introduced in a manner that inspires teachers to be interested.

There are four clear implications. First, school leaders need to streamline teachers' duties in order to provide the time and mental energy it takes for them to engage ambitiously in learning and applying effective classroom practices. Second, for any important professional development activity, people in leadership positions, including teacher peer leaders, need to monitor implementation in order to support teachers and hold them accountable for participating and then actually using what they have learned. If particular ideas prove to be unworkable or misguided, monitoring may help to reveal this fact and inform midcourse corrections. Teachers' views should be respected—with the understanding that not participating in professional learning or not attempting to implement new ideas around which colleagues have reached agreement should not be an option. Third, leaders need to provide adequate supports and training for teachers to facilitate their success. And fourth, they need to introduce ideas in ways that foster positive anticipation and inspire teachers to engage them. These features are too often absent from the practice of school leadership.

How do these features fit with Children First? Generally, they are not inconsistent with the Children First concepts that other chapters of this volume articulate. But neither is it clear that Children First reforms are reliably on track to achieving these conditions in the majority of NYC high schools. First, as other chapters describe, scheduling remains a problem, such that teachers in some departments of some schools lack sufficient time for collaborative inquiry. Second, ambiguity and ambivalence remain concerning when and how to hold teachers accountable for participating in professional learning. Third, while there is enough capacity to provide the necessary supports for collaborative inquiry in some schools, there is not enough for every school that needs it. In the absence of such supports, some school-level administrators and teachers do not know how to implement collaborative inquiry. Fourth, collaborative inquiry places a heavy emphasis on having teachers cooperate to first discover the problems facing particular students and then either find or create instructional responses. For teachers who have not yet experienced personal success with struggling students, this may seem like a wild goose chase, not a cause for positive anticipation. The system needs capacity to differentiate professional development for school leaders, and school leaders need capacity to differentiate supports for teachers. This applies to individual teachers as well as to collaborative inquiry teams, each with their own strengths and weaknesses.

Student survey responses concerning the widely varying quality of instruction that they receive in NYC high schools confirm this need for differentiated professional learning. Even our best schools have some teachers who need special help, and even our weak schools have teachers with good ideas who can play leadership roles in helping peers to improve. This chapter shows that there is more variation in teaching quality within schools than between them. In response, Children First strategies need to deal effectively with *both* between- and within-school gaps in teaching quality.

Children First reforms over the next several years should use classroom-level surveys to track progress not only in raising average quality, but also reducing the types of within-school disparity that the second half of this chapter documents. There should be school- and system-level goals for progress on the types of classroom conditions that the seven Cs measure as well as on targets for student engagement. One worthy goal would be to raise every classroom in the system above the current bottom quartile of student-rated instructional quality by the year 2015, and over the current median by 2020.

Going forward, students' views concerning classroom-level experiences can be a rich source of information for Children First reforms. After all, no one knows more about life in the classroom than the students and teachers who gather there. Their survey responses tell us that some high school classrooms in New York City provide terrific learning experiences, but others do not. There is much to celebrate, but there is also much remaining to be achieved.

PART IV

Student Outcomes

11

Children First and Student Outcomes: 2003–2010

James J. Kemple

A s discussed in other chapters in this volume, the New York City Department of Education's (DOE's) Children First reforms have evolved over time into a complex set of strategies aimed explicitly at changing the dynamics of school leadership, instructional empowerment, and accountability. The cornerstones of the reforms include new organizational structures, internal and external support mechanisms, and a performance management system that did not exist prior to 2003. The resulting web of initiatives has placed the New York City school system on the cutting edge of educational reform, eventually drawing attention and even imitation from districts across the state and the nation.

The primary bases for assessing the progress of the system at all levels have been measures of student performance in the form of the New York State mathematics and English language arts (ELA) tests for elementary and middle schools and graduation rates and Regents examination results for high schools. Most notably, 85 percent of the annual school Progress Report score is derived from student achievement measures.[1] Each year the DOE releases its analysis of these indicators and maps trends over time. Recent reports from the DOE have indicated that, on average, the city's schools have made significant progress both on test score measures and on high school completion rates.[2] The DOE often cites these indicators as evidence that Children First reforms have had a positive effect on the quality of education provided to the city's children.

To date, however, the field has lacked a rigorous and independent analysis of the extent to which these improved test scores and graduation rates reflect Children First effects per se or are instead artifacts of prior reform efforts or of other influences during the Children First era (2003–2010). Indeed, the decade of 2001–2010 saw an unprecedented array of educational improvement initiatives at the national, state, and local levels. Nationally, the No Child Left Behind Act of 2002 (NCLB) generated an intense focus on state, district, and school accountability. New York State and New York City helped frame this renewed focus on standards-based accountability with the development of more rigorous statewide standards and assessments during the 1990s and early 2000s (prior to Children First) and by instituting reforms aimed at improving opportunities for students to learn and to meet these standards during the Children First years.

To explore the distinctive effects of Children First reforms on student outcomes, this chapter addresses four sets of questions:

- How do student test score trends in NYC since 2003 compare with trends prior to that point? How have NYC test score trends changed compared with other school districts in New York State during the same period? To what extent do these comparisons provide evidence of Children First effects on student test scores?
- How have test score trends changed for key subgroups of students and schools, including students with disabilities and schools serving a high percentage of low-income families?[3] What do these trends suggest about the effect of Children First reforms on high-need populations?
- What is the relationship between students' performance on the New York State assessments and their likelihood of graduating from a NYC high school within four years? How has this changed over time, and what does it suggest about whether these test scores are robust indicators of students' preparation for high school?
- How have high school graduation rates changed in NYC for cohorts of students who began high school after 2002, compared with graduation rates for students who entered high school prior to the Children First reforms? How have graduation rates in NYC changed compared with those of other New York State school districts during the same period? To what extent do these comparisons provide evidence of Children First effects on high school graduation rates?

The key findings in this chapter are derived from what is known as a *comparative interrupted time series analysis*, a method used widely in education research and evaluation to assess the impact of broad systemic policies and interventions on student outcomes.[4] The methodology provides an assessment of the degree to which the unique constellation of reform activities and conditions established in NYC during the Children First era are associated with systematic changes in test score or graduation trends compared with trends prior to 2003 and compared with trends in similar districts and schools in New York State during the same period.[5] This approach allows us to reasonably attribute systematic changes in outcome trends during the Children First era to elements of the reform initiative that mark important breaks with the recent past and that set NYC apart from other urban school districts across the state.

Test Score Trends in Grades 4 and 8: Evidence of Reform Effects

This section focuses primarily on trends in New York State assessments of English language arts (ELA) and mathematics from 1999 through 2010. This analysis will be supplemented by a summary of findings from the National Assessment of Education Progress (NAEP) for NYC between 2003 and 2009.

Data Sources, Analytic Approach, and Analytic Issues

The analyses of test score trends utilize school-level data compiled from the New York State Education Department (NYSED), the DOE, and the Common Core of Data (CCD) from the National Center for Education Statistics (NCES) at the US Department of Education.[6] NYSED data on fourth-grade and eighth-grade ELA and math test scores are available for the school years 1998–1999 through 2009–2010 and include both the average scale score for each school and the percentage of students in each school that scored at designated performance levels aligned with statewide performance standards.[7]

Consistent with the accountability requirements of NCLB and New York State, the analyses of test score trends in this paper focus on the percentages of students who scored at level 3 or 4 on the state assessments, the level at which the New York State Board of Regents considers a student to have met the state's proficiency standards.[8] In addition to their policy relevance, proficiency levels provide a transparent and intuitive benchmark for describing and assessing test score performance trends. However, proficiency rates can be misleading because they focus on a single point in the distribution of test scores. They may thus mask trends in overall performance or neglect increases or decreases in test scores at other points in the distribution. To address this important shortcoming, a future supplement to this paper will include an analysis of trends in scale scores on the state tests; preliminary findings from this analysis are consistent with those discussed in the current paper that focus on the percentage of students who scored at level 3 or 4 proficiency levels.[9]

The sample of schools for this analysis includes 2,141 schools in New York State that tested students in fourth grade between 1999 and 2010, and 922 schools that tested students in the eighth grade during the same period. This sample is divided into three groups: (1) schools in New York City; (2) schools in the four next-largest districts in New York State (Buffalo, Rochester, Syracuse, and Yonkers), referred to as the *Big Four* districts; and (3) schools from all other districts in New York State. For the analysis of fourth-grade test scores, the sample encompasses 609 schools from NYC, 119 schools from the Big Four, and 1,413 schools from the rest of New

York State. For the analysis of eighth-grade test scores, the sample encompasses 204 schools from NYC, 51 schools from the Big Four, and 667 schools from the rest of New York State. Only schools with test score data for a minimum of three years prior to the 2002–2003 school year and a minimum of three years during and after the 2002–2003 school year were included in this sample.[10]

Table 11-1 provides a summary of characteristics of the schools in the test score analysis sample and illustrates similarities and differences among the three groups of schools. As discussed below, the analysis of test score trends must account for the observed differences in order to provide a valid comparison of test score trends.

The findings presented in this section of the chapter are based on comparative interrupted time series analyses. The central strength of this methodology is that it accounts for many factors that may have produced changes in test scores in NYC instead of or in addition to the Children First reforms that began in 2002–2003. The goal of accounting for these factors is to identify the most viable alternative to what actually occurred in NYC; that is, to construct the best estimate of test score trends that were likely to have occurred for NYC schools in the absence of reforms that were instituted during the Children First era. This alternative trend is known as a *counterfactual*. The analyses conducted for this chapter are based on a particularly strong counterfactual in that it accounts for many important alternative influences on student test scores that may have been present over and above the reforms instituted in NYC during the Children First era. A strong counterfactual increases confidence that the findings from the analyses constitute rigorous evidence of effects, or lack of effects, from these reforms. These effects are reflected in the differences between NYC test score outcomes and the estimated counterfactual test score outcomes.

There are several potential influences on test scores that are controlled for by the comparative interrupted time series analysis:

- *Reforms and trends that were under way prior to Children First. For example, test scores in NYC (and across New York State) were improving, virtually linearly, even before the Children First reforms:* Thus, it is possible that these trends would have continued even if the Children First reforms had never been developed or implemented. The interrupted time series analysis isolates changes in test score trends that occurred NYC from 2003–2010 over and above what would have occurred had the pre-2002 trends continued.

- *National or state policies and reforms, such as NCLB, aimed at improving schools across New York State and the country as a whole:* It is possible that the accountability mandates and school improvement initiatives required under NCLB beginning in 2002 produced improvements in student test scores independently of the reforms initiated under Children First. Similarly, there may be other federal or state policies aimed at school improvement that caused test scores in NYC during the period from 2003 through 2010. The comparative interrupted time series analysis isolates changes in test scores that occurred in NYC during this period over and above those that occurred in other districts that were subject to the same federal and state policies, mandates, and reform initiatives.

- *Changes in the state test, scoring methods, or performance criteria and increasing familiarity with the assessments and their frameworks:* It is possible that the state assessments in ELA and math became easier over time or that teachers and students became increasingly familiar with test content, scoring methods, and performance criteria. By comparing test score trends in NYC schools with those of other schools in New York State (schools that used the same ELA and math tests for students in grades 4 and 8 and were subject to the same scoring methods and standards over time), the method can hold constant the independent effect of changes in the test or scoring criteria.[11]
- *Differences in school or district characteristics between New York City and other districts that may influence test scores trends independent of Children First reforms:* As illustrated in table 11-1, there were several differences in the characteristics of schools from NYC and the Big Four districts prior to the introduction of Children First reforms in 2003. These differences may have enhanced or limited the capacity of schools to make progress during subsequent years. A higher concentration of especially challenging schools or of schools highly susceptible to change in NYC could account for some or all the differences in test score performance. The comparative interrupted time series analysis accounts for many of these potential influences by including school characteristics in the statistical models as control variables.

In short, the counterfactual for this analysis is the estimated NYC test score trend for 2003–2010 controlling for: (1) the continuation of test score trends under way in NYC schools prior to 2003; (2) changes in test score trends before and after 2003 in the Big Four districts; and (3) differences in school characteristics between New York City and the Big Four. This counterfactual represents the best estimate of test score trends that were likely to have occurred for NYC schools in the absence of reforms that were instituted during the Children First era. Thus, the best evidence of effects from these reforms is derived from the difference between the test score trends that actually occurred in NYC and the estimated counterfactual trends.

Even with a particularly strong counterfactual, the comparative interrupted time series analysis has some limitations. First, it is possible that other events and initiatives unique to NYC but completely unrelated to Children First reforms produced changes in student outcomes during this period. For example, as discussed elsewhere in this volume, NYC experienced a substantial influx of additional education funding throughout this period, particularly after 2007 when Fair Student Funding formulas were being implemented.[12] However, a large body of prior research finds that

TABLE 11-1 Characteristics of schools with tested students averaged across school years 1998–1999 to 2001–2002[a]

Characteristic	FOURTH GRADE			EIGHTH GRADE		
	New York City	Big Four	Rest of New York State	New York City	Big Four	Rest of New York State
Student demographics						
Race/ethnicity (%)						
African American	34.1	51.9	8.1	34.3	51.4	7.7
Hispanic	37.9	19.2	6.1	34.9	17.9	5.5
White	16.1	25.8	82.6	17.9	27.8	83.8
Asian or Native American	11.9	3.1	3.2	12.9	2.9	3.0
Gender (%)						
Male	50.8	50.7	51.4	51.1	50.5	51.4
Female	49.2	49.3	48.6	48.9	49.5	48.6
Student free/reduced-price lunch eligibility						
Students eligible (%)	76.9	75.0	23.9	74.8	74.1	20.3
Schools with:						
81–100% of students eligible (%)	59.1	43.2	1.5	57.4	47.3	0.9
50–80% of students eligible (%)	26.2	47.5	12.1	27.8	38.9	5.4
0–49% of students eligible (%)	14.7	9.3	86.4	14.9	13.8	93.6
Average student enrollment and students tested						
Enrollment: All grades	831	574	494	1069	759	640
Enrollment: Tested grade (fourth or eighth)[b]	122	76	87	294	134	176
Tested students (fourth or eighth)	118	75	86	275	128	170
Tested students classified for special education (%)	12.7	17.6	12.0	12.2	18.0	13.4

	FOURTH GRADE			EIGHTH GRADE		
Characteristic	New York City	Big Four	Rest of New York State	New York City	Big Four	Rest of New York State
NYS English language arts test performance						
Average scale score	638.8	635.5	662.4	689.6	685.0	704.5
Students scoring at level 3 or 4 (%)	43.7	39.2	68.5	35.0	25.8	52.6
NYS mathematics test performance						
Average scale score	637.8	634.7	663.0	690.7	683.1	716.2
Students scoring at level 3 or 4 (%)	52.6	48.6	80.0	26.8	19.9	51.4
NYS composite test performance						
Average scale score	638.3	635.1	662.7	690.1	684.0	710.4
Percent of schools with:[c]						
Low proficiency rate (%)	25.6	26.0	0.4	36.6	58.6	2.3
Middle proficiency rate (%)	45.2	59.7	9.6	36.8	29.6	15.0
High proficiency rate (%)	29.2	14.3	90.0	26.6	11.8	82.7
Sample size	609	119	1,413	204	51	667

Source: Research Alliance calculations from New York State Education Department test score reports and National Center for Education Statistics Common Core of Data.

Notes: Sample includes all schools in New York State with at least three years of test score data prior to 2003 and at least three years of test score data after 2003.
Student demographic characteristics, average scale scores, and percent of students scoring at level 3 or 4 are weighted by the number of students tested in the grade.
Missing values for percent free and reduced-price lunch, number male, and number female for individual schools were imputed using values from surrounding years and taking the average. In cases where there was only one surrounding year (e.g., a missing value for 1998-1999), the value for the non-missing year replaced the missing value.
a. Characteristics are averaged for schools in New York City, the Big Four, and the rest of New York State, respectively; the characteristics have been averaged across the four academic school years 1998-1999 to 2001-2002.
b. The number of students tested and percent of schools with students scoring at level 3 or 4 come from the mean of both the English language arts and mathematics tests.
c. Proficiency categories were determined by examining the distribution of the percent of students scoring at level 3 or 4 for New York City schools and the Big Four schools in 1999 to 2002. The proficiency categories for fourth grade are as follows: lowest proficiency rate = < 36% of students scoring at level 3 or 4; middle proficiency rate = 36-60% of students scoring at level 3 or 4; and highest proficiency rate = > 60% of students scoring at level 3 or 4. The proficiency categories for eighth grade are as follows: lowest proficiency rate = < 20% of students scoring at level 3 or 4; middle proficiency rate = 20-40% of students scoring at level 3 or 4; and highest proficiency rate = > 40% of students scoring at level 3 or 4.

increases in school spending, in and of themselves, have little impact on student achievement.[13] Much of this research does suggest, however, that specific uses of additional funding in schools may have an effect on student achievement. In the context of this analysis, therefore, it is more likely that the interaction between Children First reforms and the manner in which they influenced specific uses of additional funding could account for changes in student achievement, rather than just the funding itself. Thus, the influence of additional funding may be seen, at least in part, as an artifact of Children First rather than an independent factor that would have occurred without Children First.

A second limitation is that although the analysis can shed light on the overall effect of reforms that occurred during the Children First era, it cannot isolate the specific features of the Children First reforms that may have been most responsible for these effects. As discussed elsewhere in this volume, the reforms have had many components, and these were designed to interact with each other and with other policies and school conditions. By exploring the variation in Children First effects across schools within NYC and by collecting data on the implementation of specific reform activities, further research can expound on the mechanisms that enhanced or limited the impact of Children First reforms; studies of this nature are being undertaken by a number of researchers, including the Research Alliance for New York City Schools.[14]

As a final note before discussing the findings, the paper also presents differences and similarities between NYC and the remaining New York State districts (not including the Big Four) in an effort to provide a further context for interpreting test score trends in New York City. These comparisons control statistically for test score trends prior to 2003 and for differences in school demographic characteristics. However, there are dramatic demographic and prior-performance differences between NYC and the rest of the state; greater caution should be exercised when using these comparisons to infer evidence about effects of reforms undertaken during the Children First era.

Effects on New York State Assessment Test Scores: 2003–2010

In 2010, the New York State Board of Regents made significant changes in the performance levels used to classify students as meeting the state's proficiency standards. Therefore, the scores for school year 2009–2010 are independent from those of prior years rather than a continuation of preceding trends.[15]

School Years 2002–2003 Through 2008–2009. Student proficiency rates in NYC increased substantially from 2002–2003 to 2008–2009. However, some of this increase was likely to have been attributable to influences outside the reforms instituted as part of Children First, such as prior reforms, reforms being initiated at the state and federal level, and a growing familiarity with the tests and scoring rubrics. After accounting for these factors and for the influence of school demographic characteristics, however, the analysis yields persuasive evidence that the reforms instituted during the Children First era did produce improvements in student test scores. These effects persisted and increased throughout the period.

Figures 11-1a and 11-1b illustrate the key elements of the comparative interrupted time series analysis and present detailed findings for fourth-grade ELA test scores. Figure 11-1a shows the average percentage of fourth-grade students who scored at level 3 or level 4 (defined as proficient by state standards) in NYC schools, in schools in the Big Four districts, and in schools in the remaining school districts in New York State. The figure presents these averages for 1998–1999 through 2009–2010. (This figure is nearly identical to those presented by the DOE in its report on test score trends between 2002 and 2009.[16] The proficiency rate increased from an average of 48 percent in 2002 to 71 percent in 2009 (an average increase of over 3 percentage points per year over seven years).

Figure 11-1a also illustrates several of the factors that may account for the increases that occurred in NYC independent of the reforms that were implemented as part of Children First starting in 2003. Most notably, test scores in NYC schools were already on the rise prior to 2003. The figure shows that the proficiency rate increased from 35 percent in 1999 to 48 percent in 2002 (an average increase of just over 3 percentage points per year over four years). This rate of growth during the pre–Children

FIGURE 11-1 **Percent of students scoring at level 3 or 4, English language arts and mathematics, school years 1998–1999 to 2009–2010**

A. Actual percent of grade 4 students scoring proficient on English language arts

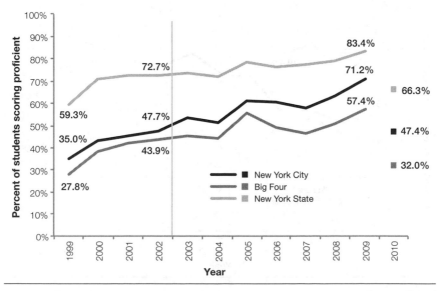

continued

FIGURE 11-1   *continued*

B. Estimated percent of students scoring proficient on English language arts

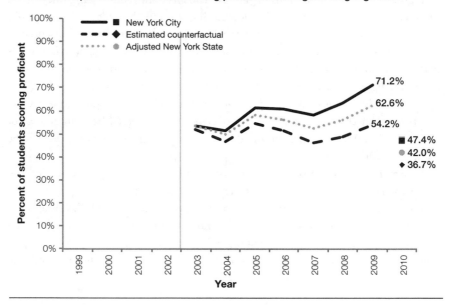

C. Actual percent of students scoring proficient on mathematics

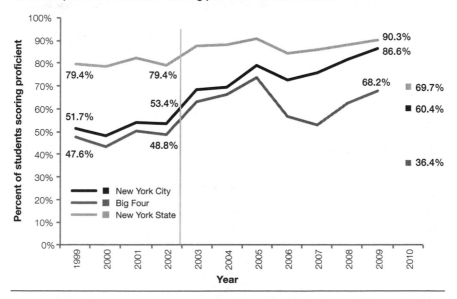

D. Estimated percent of students scoring proficient on mathematics

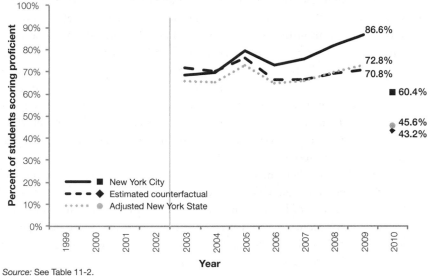

Year

Source: See Table 11-2.

Notes: See Table 11-2.

Percent of students scoring proficient is weighted by the number of students tested in the grade.

The *Estimated Counterfactual* is the regression-adjusted proficiency rate in New York City in 2009 and 2010 after controlling for the continuation of test score trends underway in New York City schools prior to 2003, changes in test score trends before and after 2003 in the Big Four school districts, and differences in school characteristics between New York City and the Big Four. School characteristics include total school enrollment; percent of total enrollment that is Black, White, Hispanic, or other race; percent of total enrollment that is eligible for free or reduced-price lunch; and percent of tested students who are classified for special education. The difference between the actual New York City proficiency rate and the estimated counterfactual is presented as evidence of the effect of reforms instituted during the Children First era (2003–2010) in New York City.

The Adjusted New York State is the regression-adjusted test score trend in New York City in 2009 and 2010 after controlling for the continuation of test score trends underway in New York City schools prior to 2003, changes in test score trends before and after 2003 in the remaining New York State districts (other than New York City and the Big Four), and differences in school characteristics between New York City and the Big Four. School characteristics include total school enrollment; percent of total enrollment that is Black, White, Hispanic, or other race; percent of total enrollment that is eligible for free or reduced-price lunch; and percent of tested students who are classified for special education.

First era is consistent with the increases that occurred in subsequent years. Among the Big Four districts, the proficiency rate increased from 28 percent in 1999 to 44 percent in 2002 (an average increase of 4 percentage points per year over four years), and among the remaining districts the rate increased from 59 percent to 73 percent (3.5 percentage points per year). These annual growth rates are the same as or larger than those exhibited for NYC schools during the same period. The figure also suggests that the growth rates in other districts slowed somewhat after 2002 relative to those for NYC schools (almost 2.5 percentage points per year for NYC versus 1.7 percentage points per year in the Big Four districts and 1.4 percentage points per year in the remaining New York State districts).

The estimated counterfactual for this analysis is shown in Figure 11-1b as the dashed line. The differences between the fourth-grade ELA test score trend for NYC schools and the estimated counterfactual trend provide evidence of effects on test scores from the reforms instituted during the Children First era. The figure shows a widening gap between the actual proficiency rate for NYC schools and the estimated counterfactual. By 2009, the proficiency rate for NYC schools was estimated to be an average of 17 percentage points higher than the average for estimated counterfactual. (This difference is statistically significant at the $p < 0.001$ level.) Although this difference is smaller than the overall increase in proficiency rates in NYC between 2002 and 2009, it provides a more rigorous indication of the increases associated with Children First reforms specifically.

The dotted line represents the remaining New York State districts after controlling for prior trends and demographic differences. It shows that fourth-grade ELA proficiency rates in New York City outpaced the statistically adjusted New York State rates. By 2009, NYC proficiency rates were estimated to be about 9 percentage points higher than the statistically adjusted rates for schools from the remaining New York State districts. (This difference is statistically significant at the $p < 0.001$ level.)

Figures 11-1c and 11-1d show a similar pattern for fourth-grade math proficiency rates. By 2009, the fourth-grade math proficiency rate for NYC schools was estimated to be an average of 16 percentage points higher than the estimated counterfactual. This difference is statistically significant at the $p < 0.001$ level and provides evidence of positive effects on fourth-grade math proficiency rates from the reforms instituted during the Children First era.

Fourth-grade math proficiency rates for NYC schools also outpaced the adjusted rates for schools from the remaining New York State districts. By 2009, the fourth-grade proficiency rate for NYC schools was estimated to be 14 percentage points higher than the adjusted rates for schools from the remaining New York State districts (statistically significant at the $p < 0.001$ level).

In general, the findings for eighth-grade ELA and math test scores were similar to those for the fourth grade. Proficiency rates in both subjects were increasing steadily in NYC between 2003 and 2009. Although some of the increase was likely due to influences outside the Children First reforms, the analysis provides compelling evidence of positive effects on eighth-grade ELA and math proficiency rates from the reforms instituted during the Children First era.

Figures 11-2a and 11-2c show that eighth-grade ELA and math proficiency rates were climbing steadily for NYC schools, schools from the Big Four districts, and schools from the other districts in New York State. At the same time, Figure 11-2b indicates that the eighth-grade ELA proficiency rates for NYC schools outpaced the estimated counterfactual (represented by the dashed line) and that this difference increased systematically over time. By 2009, the eighth-grade ELA proficiency rate

FIGURE 11-2 **Percent of grade 8 students scoring at level 3 or 4, English language arts and mathematics, school years 1998–1999 to 2009–2010**

A. Actual percent of students scoring proficient on English language arts

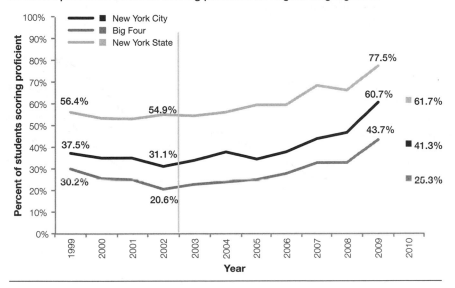

B. Actual percent of students scoring proficient on English language arts

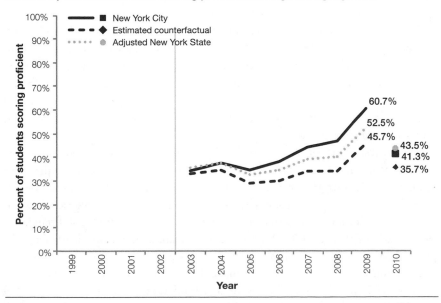

continued

FIGURE 11-2 *continued*

C. Actual percent of students scoring proficient on mathematics

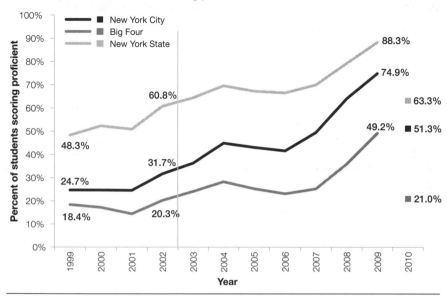

for NYC schools was 15 percentage points higher than the estimated counterfactual (statistically significant at the $p < 0.01$ level).

Figure 11-2d also shows evidence of Children First effects on eighth-grade math proficiency rates. By 2009, the eighth-grade math proficiency rate for NYC schools was estimated to be an average of 20 percentage points higher than the estimated counterfactual (statistically significant at the $p < 0.001$ level). Figures 11-2b and 11-2d show an increasing difference between NYC proficiency rates and the adjusted rates for the remaining New York State districts after controlling for prior trends and school demographic characteristics.

School Year 2009–2010. For 2010, the New York State Board of Regents raised the score that students needed to achieve in order to be classified as meeting the state's proficiency standards (from level 3 to level 4). As a result, many fewer students across New York State were classified as proficient, even though they achieved scale scores that were the same or higher than those that would have met the 2008–2009 standards. Because of this change, 2009–2010 test scores are analyzed independently from the prior school years. The goal of the analysis is to assess whether the effects of Children First reforms were sustained despite dramatic changes in the state testing standards.

Table 11-2 shows estimated differences in proficiency rates in both 2008–2009 and 2009–2010 between NYC schools and the estimated counterfactual. The results in Table 11-2 indicate that for the fourth grade, the effect of Children First

D. Estimated percent of students scoring proficient on mathematics

Source: See Table 11-2.

Notes: See Table 11-2.

Actual percent of students scoring proficient is weighted by the number of students tested in the grade.

The *Estimated Counterfactual* is the regression-adjusted proficiency rate in New York City in 2009 and 2010 after controlling for the continuation of test score trends underway in New York City schools prior to 2003, changes in test score trends before and after 2003 in the Big Four school districts, and differences in school characteristics between New York City and the Big Four. School characteristics include total school enrollment; percent of total enrollment that is Black, White, Hispanic, or other race; percent of total enrollment that is eligible for free or reduced-price lunch; and percent of tested students who are classified for special education. The difference between the actual New York City proficiency rate and the estimated counterfactual is presented as evidence of the effect of reforms instituted during the Children First era (2003–2010) in New York City.

The *Adjusted New York State* is the regression-adjusted test score trend in New York City in 2009 and 2010 after controlling for the continuation of test score trends underway in New York City schools prior to 2003, changes in test score trends before and after 2003 in the remaining New York State districts (other than New York City and the Big Four), and differences in school characteristics between New York City and the Big Four. School characteristics include total school enrollment; percent of total enrollment that is Black, White, Hispanic, or other race; percent of total enrollment that is eligible for free or reduced-price lunch; and percent of tested students who are classified for special education.

reforms on proficiency rates persisted through 2010 despite the drop in rates across the state. The effects on fourth-grade ELA proficiency rates were somewhat smaller in 2010 than they were in 2009, while the differences for fourth-grade math were somewhat larger.

The results for the eighth grade are somewhat more mixed in 2010, particularly for ELA. While Children First effects persisted through 2010 in both eighth-grade ELA and math, the effects for ELA were considerably smaller in 2010 than in 2009. The NYC proficiency rates in eighth-grade ELA and math were higher in 2010 than the estimated counterfactual by 5.6 and 17.4 percentage points, respectively. Both of these differences were statistically significant at the $p < 0.05$ or lower. However, the

TABLE 11-2   **Percent of students scoring at level 3 or 4, fourth- and eighth-grade English language arts and mathematics, school years 2008–2009 and 2009–2010**

Grade, subject, and year	New York City average	ESTIMATED COUNTERFACTUAL[a]		ADJUSTED NEW YORK STATE[b]	
		Average	Difference	Average	Difference
Fourth grade					
English language arts					
2009	71.2	54.2	17.0***	62.7	8.5***
2010	47.4	36.7	10.8***	42.0	5.4***
Mathematics					
2009	86.6	70.8	15.8***	72.8	13.8***
2010	60.4	43.2	17.2***	45.6	14.8***
Sample size	609		119		1,413
Eighth grade					
English language arts					
2009	60.7	45.7	15.0**	52.5	8.2***
2010	41.3	35.7	5.6*	43.5	–2.2*
Mathematics					
2009	74.9	54.5	20.4***	55.3	19.6***
2010	51.3	33.9	17.4***	39.0	12.2***
Sample size	204		51		667

Source: Research Alliance calculations from New York State Education Department test score reports and National Center for Education Statistics Common Core of Data.

Notes: Sample includes all schools in New York State with at least three years of test score data prior to 2003 and at least three years of test score data after 2003.

All values are weighted by the number of students tested in the grade.

A two-tailed t-test was applied to the estimated differences for each year. Robust standard errors are used to account for serial autocorrelation. Statistical significance levels are indicated as: ~ = $p < 0.10$; * = $p < 0.05$; ** = $p < 0.01$ percent; *** = $p < 0.001$.

a. The *Estimated Counterfactual* is the regression-adjusted proficiency rate in New York City in 2009 and 2010 after controlling for the continuation of test score trends under way in New York City schools prior to 2003, changes in test score trends before and after 2003 in the Big Four school districts, and differences in school characteristics between New York City and the Big Four. School characteristics include total school enrollment; percent of total enrollment that is African American, white, Hispanic, or other race; percent of total enrollment that is eligible for free or reduced-price lunch; and percent of tested students who are classified for special education. The difference between the actual New York City proficiency rate and the estimated counterfactual is presented as evidence of the effect of reforms instituted during the Children First era (2003–2010) in New York City.

b. The *Adjusted New York State* is the regression-adjusted test score trend in New York City in 2009 and 2010 after controlling for the continuation of test score trends under way in New York City schools prior to 2003, changes in test score trends before and after 2003 in the remaining New York State districts (other than New York City and the Big Four), and differences in school characteristics between New York City and the Big Four. School characteristics include total school enrollment; percent of total enrollment that is African American, white, Hispanic, or other race; percent of total enrollment that is eligible for free or reduced-price lunch; and percent of tested students who are classified for special education.

eighth-grade ELA difference was nearly 10 percentage points smaller in 2010 than in 2009, and the eighth-grade math difference was three percentage points lower.

Estimated differences in eighth-grade ELA proficiency rates between NYC schools and the adjusted rates for the remaining New York State districts also declined from 2009 to 2010—and in 2010 NYC rates were lower than those for the rest of New York State. The difference in eighth-grade math proficiency rates between NYC schools and the adjusted rates for the remaining New York State districts also declined but continued to be positive and statistically significant.

Thus, the findings for 2010 suggest that, although Children First effects appear to have persisted through the change in proficiency standards, the gains made by NYC schools up through 2009, relative to both the Big Four and the remaining districts throughout the state, were diminished to varying degrees by the move to higher standards. Because the score required to be classified as proficient increased, the smaller differences in 2010 suggest that the effects of Children First reforms may not have been as robust at the higher ranges of the test score distribution compared with the effects for 2009, when the proficiency standard was lower. As noted earlier, additional analyses are being conducted to examine effects across the distribution of scores and at other points in the distribution throughout the Children First era. Preliminary findings from these analyses indicate that the patterns of differences and similarities are similar to those presented here.

NAEP Results for New York City: 2003–2009

The National Assessment of Educational Progress (NAEP) is the only national assessment of student achievement in the United States. Initiated in 1969, NAEP assessments are conducted periodically in reading, mathematics, science, writing, US history, civics, geography, and other subjects. In addition to testing in state-wide samples of schools, the NAEP Trial Urban District Assessment (TUDA) has administered assessments in reading and math in selected large urban school districts including New York City. TUDA has been conducted every two years since 2003 and allows scores for NYC to be compared with scores from the rest of New York State as well as with other urban school districts and the nation as a whole.

Figures 11-3a and 11-3b show NAEP results in fourth-grade reading and math from 2003 through 2009 for NYC, New York State, all urban districts in the TUDA sample, and all of the nation's public schools. Figures 11-3c and 11-3d show the NAEP results for the eighth grade. The figures illustrate trends in the percentage of students scoring at or above proficient.[17]

The figures show that the NAEP results for NYC have been somewhat mixed. In general, NYC has performed below the national average and below the average for the rest of New York State in both reading and math and in both the fourth and eighth grades. However, NYC has scored above the average for urban districts in fourth-grade reading and math and has scored at or slightly above the average for

FIGURE 11-3 **Percent of students scoring proficient on the National Assessment of Educational Progress (NAEP) fourth- and eighth-grade reading and mathematics, 2003–2009**

A. Grade 4, reading

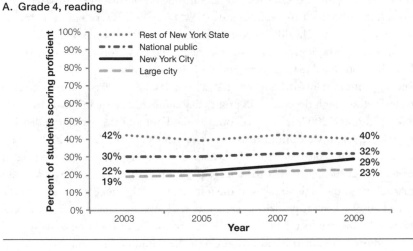

B. Grade 4, mathematics

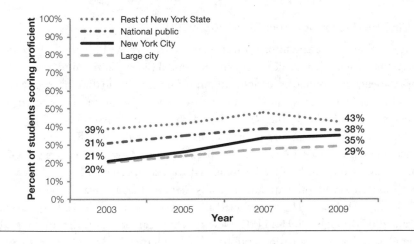

urban districts in eighth-grade reading and math. Fourth-grade students in NYC have shown significant improvements on both reading and math NAEP assessments since 2002. In the eighth grade, NYC proficiency levels have improved only in math. Eighth-grade reading scores have remained flat over this seven-year period, which is consistent with the rest of the country and other urban districts.

C. Grade 8, reading

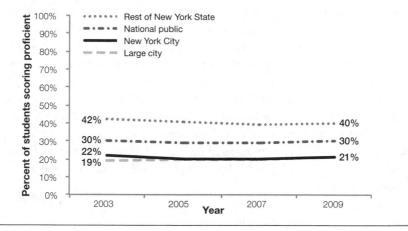

D. Grade 8, mathematics

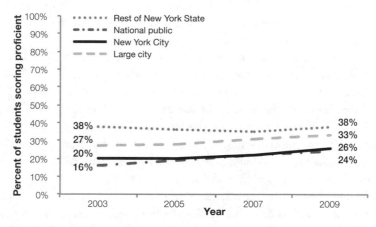

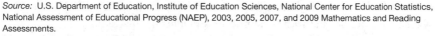

Source: U.S. Department of Education, Institute of Education Sciences, National Center for Education Statistics, National Assessment of Educational Progress (NAEP), 2003, 2005, 2007, and 2009 Mathematics and Reading Assessments.

Because NAEP data do not exist for NYC prior to 2002, they do not allow a comparative interrupted time series analysis.[18] However, NAEP provided us with statistics on differences in changes in NAEP proficiency rates over time between NYC and the rest of New York State, allowing a systematic comparison between the two.[19] This information has the effect of controlling for initial differences between NYC and the rest of New York State in 2003 and then assessing the statistical significance of remaining differences in subsequent years.

Some important cautions should be noted. First and most importantly, NAEP is not aligned with the standards and curriculum frameworks developed by the New York State Board of Regents and so may not be measuring the same underlying constructs as the New York State assessments. In addition, NAEP does not carry negative or positive consequences either for schools and systems or for students, and therefore, schools and students might not take the NAEP as seriously as the state tests. NAEP is also administered only to a small stratified random sample of students within a small stratified random sample of schools within New York City and across New York State. As with assessments based on any sampling strategy, as opposed to a universally administered assessment, the results may be sensitive to sampling variation or to relatively low or high representations of subpopulations of schools or students.

For these reasons and because the NAEP-based comparisons cannot incorporate the features of the comparative interrupted time series analysis, it is not possible to draw any conclusions about the effects (or lack of effects) of Children First reforms on NAEP test scores. Because of the very high profile of NAEP and its nationwide testing program, however, NYC's NAEP scores are discussed briefly to offer an additional framework for understanding test score trends in NYC and how they are situated in both a statewide and national context.

Two notable patterns stand out. First, the overall proficiency rates on NAEP are much lower than on the New York State assessments (compare Figures 11-1 and 11-2 with Figure 11-3). This difference in results is likely due to a combination of differences in the content of the tests, in the standards that are used to designate proficiency levels, and in the consequences attached to student performance. To the extent that the NAEP assessments capture important aspects of what students should know and be able to do, Figure 11-3 indicates that in 2009, less than half of NYC students possessed this knowledge and these skills.

Second, New York City experienced a greater increase in proficiency rates than did the rest of New York State. The differences in increases were statistically significant for fourth-grade reading and math and for eighth-grade math. The difference was smaller and not statistically significant for eighth-grade reading.

Between 2003 and 2009, in fourth-grade reading, NYC proficiency rates increased by 7 percentage points, compared with a 2 percentage point drop for the rest of New York State. This difference of 9 percentage points is statistically significant at the $p < 0.001$ level. For fourth-grade math, NYC proficiency rates increased by 14 percentage points compared with a 4 percentage point increase for the rest of New York State (a difference of 10 percentage points, statistically significant at the $p < 0.001$ level).

Figure 11-3 shows that proficiency rates in eighth-grade reading actually declined somewhat for both NYC and the rest of New York State between 2003 and 2009; the difference is not statistically significant. By contrast, increases in NYC proficiency rates in fourth-grade math (6 percentage points between 2003 and 2009) did outpace the flat trend for the rest of New York State (statistically significant at the $p < 0.01$ level).

Variation in Test Score Trends and Evidence of Effects for Subgroups of Students and Schools

This section of the paper extends the comparative interrupted time series analysis of test scores based on the New York State assessments to explore evidence of Children First effects for subgroups of students and schools in New York City. The first set of analyses considers general education students and students with disabilities. The second set looks at subgroups of schools based on their concentration of students from low-income families. The goal of these analyses is to determine whether effects were widespread or were concentrated among certain subpopulations.

Findings for General Education Students and Students with Disabilities

Since 1999, NYSED has reported state test scores separately for students in general education programs and students enrolled in special education (students with disabilities).[20] Table 11-3 presents results from analysis of the test scores for these two subgroups of students. The table shows the difference in proficiency, as of 2009, between NYC schools and the estimated counterfactual.

The findings in table 11-3 provide evidence of positive Children First effects both for fourth-grade general education students and for fourth-grade students with disabilities. The effects appear to be substantially larger, however, among students with disabilities. For example, by 2009 ELA proficiency rates for students with disabilities in NYC were an average of 35 percentage points higher than the estimated counterfactual. The difference for general education students was 11 percentage points. The differences in effects for math were even larger: 47 percentage points for students with disabilities compared with 12 percentage points for general education students.

Children First also appears to have had positive effects on eighth-grade proficiency rates in each subject for both general education students and students with disabilities. The effects on eighth-grade ELA proficiency rates were similar for general education students and students with disabilities. The effects on eighth-grade math proficiency rates were more pronounced for students with disabilities.

It is not clear what explains the larger effects for students with disabilities. Unlike previous efforts to track student progress in NYC, the accountability framework that

TABLE 11-3   **Percent of grade 4 and grade 8 students scoring at level 3 or 4, English language arts and mathematics, general education and special education students: School year 2008–2009**

Student subgroup, grade, and subject	New York City average	ESTIMATED COUNTERFACTUAL[a]		ADJUSTED NEW YORK STATE[b]	
		Average	Difference	Average	Difference
General education students					
Fourth grade					
English language arts	77.9	66.6	11.2**	71.1	6.7***
Mathematics	90.7	79.1	11.6*	75.0	15.7***
Sample size	609		119		1,413
Eighth grade					
English language arts	65.8	52.4	13.4*	57.1	8.7***
Mathematics	79.4	63.7	15.7**	60.5	18.8***
Sample size	204		51		667
Special education students					
Fourth grade					
English language arts	36.9	2.2	34.7***	9.6	27.3***
Mathematics	65.6	18.8	46.8***	44.0	21.5***
Sample size	609		119		1,413
Eighth grade					
English language arts	21.3	10.1	11.2**	20.0	1.3
Mathematics	41.9	8.0	33.9***	23.2	18.8***
Sample size	204		51		667

Source: See table 11-2.

Notes: See table 11-2.

a. The *Estimated Counterfactual* is the regression-adjusted proficiency rate in New York City in 2009 and 2010 after controlling for the continuation of test score trends under way in New York City schools prior to 2003, changes in test score trends before and after 2003 in the Big Four school districts, and differences in school characteristics between New York City and the Big Four. School characteristics include total school enrollment; percent of total enrollment that is African American, white, Hispanic, or other race; percent of total enrollment that is eligible for free or reduced-price lunch; and percent of tested students who are classified for special education. The difference between the actual New York City proficiency rate and the estimated counterfactual is presented as evidence of the effect of reforms instituted during the Children First era (2003–2010) in New York City.

b. The *Adjusted New York State* is the regression-adjusted test score trend in New York City in 2009 and 2010 after controlling for the continuation of test score trends under way in New York City schools prior to 2003, changes in test score trends before and after 2003 in the remaining New York State districts (other than New York City and the Big Four), and differences in school characteristics between New York City and the Big Four. School characteristics include total school enrollment; percent of total enrollment that is African American, white, Hispanic, or other race; percent of total enrollment that is eligible for free or reduced-price lunch; and percent of tested students who are classified for special education.

formed a central element of Children First reforms explicitly incorporated test scores for special education students into its school Progress Reports. However, this focus was also incorporated into the NCLB accountability requirements that were being implemented throughout the state during this period. Further research is needed to explore ways in which Children First reforms may have placed additional emphasis on services for students with disabilities.

Findings for High- and Low-Poverty Schools

An important goal of the Children First reforms has been to improve schools serving large proportions of traditionally low-performing and high-need, under-served students. One well-documented indicator of these populations is economic status. For this reason, differences in achievement trends for subgroups of schools were analyzed based on the percentage of students eligible for free or reduced-price lunch before the Children First era. As with the previous findings, the results for the school subgroups are based on the comparative interrupted time series method that accounts for pre-2003 test score trends and other demographic differences across schools.

For the purposes of this analysis, schools from across New York State were categorized into three groups:

- *Highest poverty rate:* Schools with an average of more than 80 percent of their students eligible for free or reduced-price lunch between 1999 and 2002
- *Middle poverty rate:* Schools with an average of between 51 percent and 80 percent of students eligible
- *Lowest poverty rate:* Schools with an average of less than or equal to 50 percent eligible

Tables 11-4 and 11-5 present findings for the fourth and eighth grades, respectively, for the three subgroups of schools and for both 2009 and 2010.

In general, the findings for fourth-grade ELA and math suggest that while there is solid evidence of Children First effects across schools with different poverty rates, the reforms do not appear to have substantially narrowed the gap between the highest- and lowest-poverty schools. Table 11-4 indicates that Children First effects on fourth-grade ELA and math proficiency rates are generally consistent across the three subgroups of schools. For example, in 2009, the difference in fourth-grade ELA proficiency rates between NYC and the estimated counterfactual ranged from 16 percentage points for the highest-poverty schools to 19 percentage points for the lowest-poverty schools. Although somewhat smaller than the differences in 2009, the differences in 2010 remained positive. For the highest- and middle-poverty schools, all of the fourth-grade ELA differences in proficiency rates were statistically significant in both 2009 and 2010. The small sample sizes for the estimated counterfactual in the lowest-poverty group of schools contributed to the lack of statistical significance even though the differences were similar to those in the other groups.

TABLE 11-4   **Percent of grade 4 students scoring at level 3 or 4, English language arts and mathematics, school years 2008–2009 and 2009–2010**

Subgroups of schools defined by percent of students eligible for free or reduced-price lunch

Percent of students eligible, subject, and year	New York City average	ESTIMATED COUNTERFACTUAL[a]		ADJUSTED NEW YORK STATE[b]	
		Average	Difference	Average	Difference
81–100% of students eligible					
English language arts					
2009	65.1	49.2	16.0**	30.5	34.6*
2010	39.3	28.6	10.7***	21.1	18.2**
Mathematics					
2009	83.3	65.4	17.8*	37.1	46.2***
2010	52.9	35.7	17.2***	23.3	29.6***
Sample size	360		51		20
51–80% of students eligible					
English language arts					
2009	75.1	58.0	17.1**	54.4	20.7***
2010	52.1	40.8	11.3***	41.1	10.9***
Mathematics					
2009	89.1	72.3	16.8*	75.7	13.4**
2010	65.0	46.5	18.5***	47.9	17.1***
Sample size	159		56		164
0–50% of students eligible					
English language arts					
2009	89.4	70.2	19.3	92.7	–3.2
2010	72.3	60.7	11.6~	69.8	2.5~
Mathematics					
2009	96.0	85.6	10.4	94.7	1.3
2010	82.9	68.8	14.0**	70.0	12.8***
Sample size	90		11		1,175

Source: See table 11-2.

Notes: See table 11-2.

The subgroups of schools were defined based on the average percent of students eligible for free and reduced-price lunch between 1999 and 2002.

a. The *Estimated Counterfactual* is the regression-adjusted proficiency rate in New York City in 2009 and 2010 after controlling for the continuation of test score trends under way in New York City schools prior to 2003, changes in test score trends before and after 2003 in the Big Four school districts, and differences in school characteristics between New York City and the Big Four. School characteristics include total school enrollment; percent of total enrollment that is African American, white, Hispanic, or other race; percent of total enrollment that is eligible for free or reduced-price lunch; and percent of tested students who are classified for special edu-cation. The difference between the actual New York City proficiency rate and the estimated counterfactual is pre¬sented as evidence of the effect of reforms instituted during the Children First era (2003–2010) in New York City.

b. The *Adjusted New York State* is the regression-adjusted test score trend in New York City in 2009 and 2010 after controlling for the continuation of test score trends under way in New York City schools prior to 2003,

The pattern of findings for the eighth grade is more complex and mixed.[21] Table 11-5 indicates that effects on eighth-grade ELA and math proficiency rates were concentrated among the middle- and high-poverty schools. A comparison of the estimated counterfactual proficiency rates suggests that, in the absence of Children First reforms, there was likely to be very little difference in proficiency rates between the middle- and high-poverty schools in New York City. Thus, because the effects for the middle-poverty schools were somewhat larger than those for the high-poverty schools, the achievement gap between these types of schools may have increased during the Children First era. In general, the effects for both ELA and math in the eighth grade declined between 2009 and 2010. Given the smaller sample sizes in the subgroups of schools and the changes in effects over time, further analysis is needed to better understand the nature of these findings.

Student Test Scores and High School Graduation Rates

A critical concern regarding the use of test scores to assess student achievement or to gauge school improvement is that test scores do not necessarily capture the skills and knowledge that students need to succeed in other areas of their education and development. For example, test score improvements may signal that students are becoming more skilled at answering specific types of questions or that teachers' familiarity with the tests enables them to prepare students for specific items rather than give them the underlying knowledge and skills. To the extent such factors drive test performance, increased scores are unlikely to reflect true learning gains. Similarly, they may be unlikely to predict subsequent achievement or school completion.

This section provides an analysis of the relationship between students' eighth-grade test scores and their likelihood of graduating from high school within four years. This analysis utilizes student-level data to shed light on the extent to which students' performance on the New York State assessments of ELA and math indicates their preparation for high school work and their likelihood of earning a high school diploma. This analysis also examines the extent to which the test score-graduation relationship changed over the period before and after Children First reforms began to be implemented.

---

changes in test score trends before and after 2003 in the remaining New York State districts (other than New York City and the Big Four), and differences in school characteristics between New York City and the Big Four. School characteristics include total school enrollment; percent of total enrollment that is African American, white, Hispanic, or other race; percent of total enrollment that is eligible for free or reduced-price lunch; and percent of tested students who are classified for special education.

TABLE 11-5   **Percent of grade 8 students scoring at level 3 or 4, English language arts and mathematics, school years 2008–2009 and 2009–2010**

Subgroups of schools defined by percent of students eligible for free or reduced-price lunch

Percent of students eligible, subject, and year	New York City average	ESTIMATED COUNTERFACTUAL[a]		ADJUSTED NEW YORK STATE[b]	
		Average	Difference	Average	Difference
81–100% of students eligible					
English language arts					
2009	51.4	37.9	13.5*	n/a	n/a
2010	31.0	25.3	5.6*	n/a	n/a
Mathematics					
2009	68.3	46.7	21.5***	n/a	n/a
2010	40.4	24.3	16.2***	n/a	n/a
Sample size	117		24		6
51–80% of students eligible					
English language arts					
2009	65.2	38.8	26.4**	45.7	19.6*
2010	45.9	37.6	8.3	40.6	5.2~
Mathematics					
2009	77.6	48.2	29.4***	52.9	24.7*
2010	56.2	34.8	21.5***	35.9	20.4***
Sample size	57		20		35
0–50% of students eligible					
English language arts					
2009	77.6	n/a	n/a	74.1	3.5
2010	59.5	n/a	n/a	62.9	–3.4~
Mathematics					
2009	87.7	n/a	n/a	73.8	13.9**
2010	70.1	n/a	n/a	56.5	13.6***
Sample size	30		7		607

Source: See table 11-2.

Notes: See table 11-2.

The subgroups of schools were defined based on the average percent of students eligible for free and reduced-price lunch between 1999 and 2002.

"n/a" denotes that sample sizes were fewer than ten and judged to be too small to calculate reliable estimates.

a. The *Estimated Counterfactual* is the regression-adjusted proficiency rate in New York City in 2009 and 2010 after controlling for the continuation of test score trends under way in New York City schools prior to 2003, changes in test score trends before and after 2003 in the Big Four school districts, and differences in school characteristics between New York City and the Big Four. School characteristics include total school enrollment; percent of total enrollment that is African American, white, Hispanic, or other race; percent of total enrollment that is eligible for free or reduced-price lunch; and percent of tested students who are classified for special education. The difference between the actual New York City proficiency rate and the estimated counterfactual is presented as evidence of the effect of reforms instituted during the Children First era (2003–2010) in New York City.

Data Sources, Samples, and Analysis

The data for these analyses cover the period from October 2001 through August 2009 and include information about individual students' eighth-grade test score performance and about their high school completion status four years later. The analysis focuses on two samples of students: (1) those enrolled in a NYC high school for the first time as a ninth-grade student in October 2001 (referred to as the 2001 cohort) and (2) those enrolled in a NYC high school for the first time as a ninth-grade student in October 2005 (referred to as the 2005 cohort). Students from the 2001 cohort were scheduled to graduate in June 2005, and students from the 2005 cohort were scheduled to graduate in June 2009. The key outcomes for this analysis are whether students had earned a local diploma or a New York State Regents diploma by August of 2005 (2001 cohort) and August of 2009 (2005 cohort).[22]

Findings

Figures 11-4a and 11-4b show the high school completion rates for the 2001 and 2005 ninth-grade cohorts, respectively. High school completion rates are shown for the range of scale scores that these students achieved on the New York State eighth-grade ELA and math assessments. The scale scores are the average of each student's ELA and math scale scores. Table 11-6 presents a summary of the distribution of test scores and graduation rates for both cohorts.

There are several notable patterns. First, there is a strong positive relationship between eighth-grade test scores and the probability of earning a high school diploma within four years after entering high school. Figures 11-4a and 11-4b show that across both cohorts of first-time ninth-grade students, those with higher test scores were more likely to have earned either a local diploma or a Regents diploma within four years than those with lower test scores. For example, for the 2001 cohort, the average graduation rate for students scoring at level 3 was 79 percent, compared with only 30 percent for students scoring at level 1. The difference in Regents diploma rates was even larger, with 65 percent of those at level 3 receiving a Regents diploma compared with only 8 percent of those at level 1. Similar differences across proficiency levels can be seen for the 2005 cohort. This suggests that the ELA and math

---

b. The *Adjusted New York State* is the regression-adjusted test score trend in New York City in 2009 and 2010 after controlling for the continuation of test score trends under way in New York City schools prior to 2003, changes in test score trends before and after 2003 in the remaining New York State districts (other than New York City and the Big Four), and differences in school characteristics between New York City and the Big Four. School characteristics include total school enrollment; percent of total enrollment that is African American, white, Hispanic, or other race; percent of total enrollment that is eligible for free or reduced-price lunch; and percent of tested students who are classified for special education.

TABLE 11-6   **Four-year high school completion status by score on eighth-grade ELA and mathematics examinations**

Four-year completion status	PROFICIENCY LEVEL 1		PROFICIENCY LEVEL 2		PROFICIENCY LEVEL 3		PROFICIENCY LEVEL 3 OR 4	
	2001 cohort	2005 cohort	2001 cohort	2005 cohort	2001 cohort	2005 cohort	2001 cohort	2005 cohort
Percent in level (%)	35.9	7.6	28.3	47.8	20.6	37.4	35.8	44.6
Four-year completion status (%)								
Graduated	30.2	28.1	60.1	57.6	78.7	85.5	84.9	87.3
Regents diploma	7.8	6.8	33.4	32.6	64.7	77.8	75.1	80.7
Local diploma	22.4	21.3	26.7	25.0	14.0	7.7	9.8	6.6
GED	2.0	0.6	3.9	2.4	3.1	1.9	2.2	1.7
Still enrolled	45.7	42.9	26.2	27.4	13.9	9.6	10.0	8.4
Dropped out	21.4	25.2	9.6	12.2	4.2	2.9	2.9	2.5
Number of students	16,462	4,070	13,002	25,714	9,468	20,085	16,416	23,986

Source: Research Alliance calculations from New York City Department of Education test score and graduation reports.

Notes: Proficiency levels were determined based on the average of a student's eighth-grade ELA and math scale scores. Cut points for each level were based on the average of the ELA and math cut points for each year.

FIGURE 11-4   **Percent of students who graduate by eighth-grade composite test scores**

A. 2001 cohort

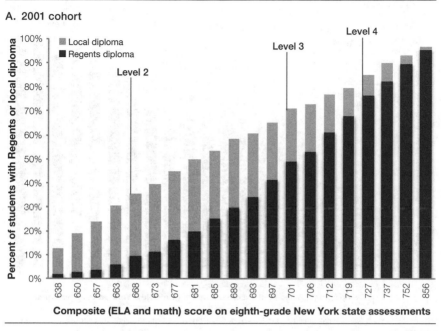

Composite (ELA and math) score on eighth-grade New York state assessments

continued

assessments provide a useful indicator of students' preparation for high school work, particularly at the extremes of the distribution of test scores.[23]

Second, many students who met the state proficiency standards in the eighth grade were unlikely to earn a Regents diploma. The New York State Education Department designates students who score at level 3 or 4 on the eighth-grade assessments as having reached the state's proficiency standards. Yet a substantial proportion of students who meet the state standards do not graduate from high school, and many more do not receive a Regents diploma. For example, Figure 11-4a shows that for the 2001 cohort, less than 60 percent of students who scored at the lower end of level 3 graduated from high school with a Regents diploma within four years, and less than 50 percent received a Regents diploma. This finding suggests that the proficiency standards and the distinctions among performance levels in the middle of the distribution may not be the best indicators of students' preparation for Regents-level high school work. Changes in the proficiency standards in 2010 were designed to address this shortcoming directly by setting the eighth-grade proficiency standards at levels that are associated with passing scores on the high school Regents exams.

Finally, over time, a higher proportion of eighth-grade students were meeting the state proficiency standards, and a higher percentage of these students were earning

FIGURE 11-4 *continued*

B. 2005 cohort

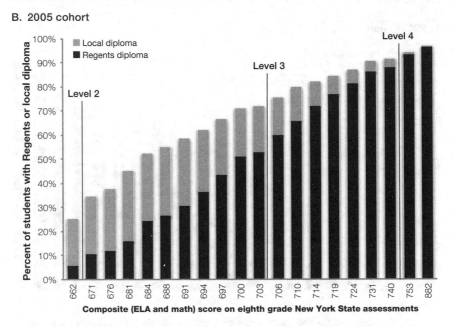

Source: Research Alliance calculations from New York City Department of Education test score and graduation reports.

Notes: Students in the sample include first-time 9th graders in October 2001 and 2005, respectively.

Each bar represents 5% of all students in the sample.

The composite score beneath each bar represents the upper-bound of the range of scores.

Proficiency levels were determined based on the average of a student's 8th grade ELA and math scale scores. Cut points for each level were based on the average of the ELA and math cut points for each year.

a Regents diploma. Table 11-6 shows that the percentage of students scoring at level 3 or level 4 increased from 36 percent for the 2001 cohort to 45 percent for the 2005 cohort. At the same time, Regents diplomas for students scoring at level 3 or 4 increased from 75 percent to 81 percent. This trend may suggest that the ELA and math proficiency standards became better indicators of student preparation for high school work. During this same period, however, the high schools in NYC were evolving, and their improvement may account for some or all of the improvement in graduation rates across the spectrum of eighth-grade ELA and math performance levels.

Trends in High School Graduation Rates

This section examines trends in high school graduation rates for students across New York State who began high school between school year 2000–2001 and school year

2004–2005. These five cohorts of entering high school students span the period during which Children First reforms were initiated in NYC and can offer some insight into whether trends in the city's graduation rates began to change as the reforms were being implemented and whether they were deviating from trends in other school districts across the state.

Data Sources, Samples, and Analysis

The findings presented here are based on a modified application of the comparative interrupted time series analysis that was used for the earlier test score analysis. As with the test score analysis, the counterfactual for this analysis is estimated as the NYC graduation rate trend for post-2003 cohorts of first-time ninth graders controlling for: (1) continuation of graduation rate trends under way in NYC schools for cohorts prior to 2003; (2) changes in graduation rate trends before and after 2003 in the Big Four districts and schools; and (3) differences in school characteristics between New York City and the Big Four. This counterfactual represents the best estimate of graduation rate trends that were likely to have occurred in NYC schools in the absence of reforms that were instituted during the Children First era. Thus, the best evidence of effects from these reforms is derived from the difference between the graduation rate trends that actually occurred in NYC and the estimated counterfactual trends.

However, two important features of the data for the graduation trend analysis make it a weaker analysis and require that more caution be exercised in drawing inferences from this analysis about the effect of Children First reforms on graduation rates.

First, data for this section are available only for five cohorts of students: those who were first-time ninth-graders in October 2001 (and scheduled to graduate in 2005) through October 2005 (and scheduled to graduate in 2009). As a result, the analysis will only be able to include two years of graduation trends prior to 2003 and three years for the Children First era, from 2003 to 2005. Consequently, the comparison with pre–Children First graduation trends will be less robust than the test score analysis, and there will be less information about subsequent trends. Also, the early cohorts of students were progressing though high schools during the period when Children First reforms were first being implemented, yet the analysis treats their graduation rates as a function of pre–Children First circumstances. To the extent that the early features of Children First reforms produced positive outcomes for students who started high school before 2003, the differences underestimate Children First effects on graduation rates.

Second, the unit of measurement for graduation rates is the district rather than the individual school. A major feature of those Children First reforms aimed at high schools involved the closing of low-performing schools and the opening of new small schools, typically in the same or a nearby location. Thus, some schools will have no post-2002 data because they were closed down. Other schools will not have any pre-2002 data because they were opened later. Using the district as the unit of analysis, rather than individual schools, diminishes the statistical power somewhat. Also, because of the closing and opening of schools in NYC and because of the open-choice process that was implemented during this period, there were changes in the composition of the cohorts of students within and across the NYC districts. This analysis attempts to account for these changes by controlling for demographic characteristics of the districts.

Findings

Figure 11-5a shows that NYC graduation rates improved by nearly 12 percentage points between the 2001 cohort of first-time ninth graders and the 2005 cohort. However, just under half of this improvement occurred for the cohorts that entered ninth grade prior to the start of Children First reforms (the 2001 and 2002 cohorts). At the same time, graduation rates for the Big Four districts also improved somewhat over these five years, although they declined slightly from the 2001 cohort to the 2002 cohort. In short, some of the improvement in NYC graduation rates is likely to have been an artifact of prior reforms, and some may be the result of other policies and reforms that resulted in improvements in other urban districts and across the state.

FIGURE 11-5 **Percent of students who graduate in four years, ninth-grade 2001 and 2005 cohorts**

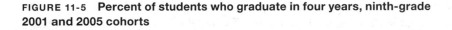

A. Actual four-year graduation rates

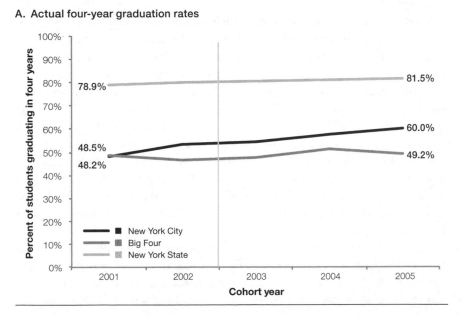

B. Estimated four-year graduation rates

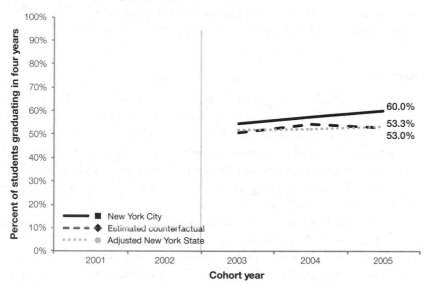

Source: See Table 10.

Notes: See Table 10.

Graduation rates reflect students who graduate with a regents or local diploma. It does not include students who transfer out of the New York City school system.

Actual percent of students who graduate is weighted by the number of students enrolled in the grade.

The *Estimated Counterfactual* is the regression-adjusted proficiency rate in New York City in 2009 and 2010 after controlling for the continuation of test score trends under way in New York City schools prior to 2003, changes in test score trends before and after 2003 in the Big Four school districts, and differences in school characteristics between New York City and the Big Four. School characteristics include total school enrollment; percent of total enrollment that is Black, White, Hispanic, or other race; percent of total enrollment that is eligible for free or reduced-price lunch; and percent of tested students who are classified for special education. The difference between the actual New York City proficiency rate and the estimated counterfactual is presented as evidence of the effect of reforms instituted during the Children First era (2003-2010) In New York City.

The *Adjusted New York State* is the regression-adjusted test score trend in New York City in 2009 and 2010 after controlling for the continuation of test score trends underway in New York City schools prior to 2003, changes in test score trends before and after 2003 in the remaining New York State districts (other than New York City and the Big Four), and differences in school characteristics between New York City and the Big Four. School characteristics include total school enrollment; percent of total enrollment that is Black, White, Hispanic, or other race; percent of total enrollment that is eligible for free or reduced-price lunch; and percent of tested students who are classified for special education.

After estimating a statistical model that accounts for these factors and for the influence of district-level demographic characteristics, the analysis yields evidence that the reforms instituted during the Children First era did produce improvements in graduation rates for the 2005 cohort. Figure 11-5b shows the difference between NYC graduation rates for the 2003 through 2005 cohorts and the estimated counterfactual graduation rates for the same period. Although graduation rates for NYC outpaced those of the estimated counterfactual (60 percent and 53 percent, respectively), the difference was statistically significant only for the 2005 cohort (a 7 percentage point difference, statistically significant at the $p < 0.001$ level).

Conclusion

New York City schools experienced substantial improvements in proficiency rates on the New York State ELA and math assessments and on graduation rates during the Children First reform era. Some amount of this improvement is likely an artifact of reforms and trends that were under way before the implementation of Children First reforms, some is likely due to other reform initiatives at the federal and state level, and some is likely due to a growing familiarity with the assessments and testing strategies across the state.

There is compelling evidence that the constellation of reforms being instated in NYC from 2003–2010 had a positive effect on ELA and math proficiency rates in the fourth and eighth grades and on graduation rates, over and above continuing effects of prior reforms or conditions shared by other districts. These findings are based on a comparative interrupted time series analysis, a rigorous evaluation method designed to account for these other influences on student outcomes. The evidence suggests that the effects on proficiency rates extend both to general education students and to students with disabilities, with especially large effects for the latter. The evidence also suggests that the effects of Children First persisted through 2010, when the New York State Board of Regents substantially increased the threshold required for students to be classified as meeting the state's proficiency standards.

Still, there are a number of important questions that these analyses are not able to address:

- *How have Children First reforms affected the performance of other important subgroups of students, including English language learners, recent immigrants, students who enter their grade already behind or with limited skills, and other students with characteristics often associated with low performance on achievement tests?*

Test score and graduation data for these subgroups are available from the New York State Education Department only after 2002; the comparative interrupted time series analysis requires several years of information prior to the Children First reforms. Nonetheless, a key goal of the Children First reforms has been to close the gaps from groups of students with characteristics associated with a history of low performance to their peers. A scientifically rigorous analysis of Children First effects on these gaps will require a creative application of other statistical methods that can control for alternative influences on test score trends.

- *Which features of the Children First reform are most likely to account for the positive effects on student test scores and graduation rates, and which features are likely to need strengthening in order to bring about further improvements?*

At the school level, Children First manifests itself in structures, leadership and teaching capacities, and supports that vary widely across the NYC education system. This variation is likely to have proliferated even further with the introduction in 2007 of the school-level autonomy and empowerment that have become cornerstones of the second phase of Children First reforms. Thus, it will be impossible to attribute the effects of this complex and interconnected set of reforms to any specific features or groups of features. It is essential, however, that additional research investigates the conditions that have led to improvements in student outcomes, particularly in schools that have experienced the steepest gains during the Children First era. The Research Alliance for New York City Schools has begun this process by identifying groups of historically low-performing schools and collecting data to determine how and why some of these schools have experienced dramatic improvements in student performance while others have remained stagnant or declined further. This effort includes both qualitative inquiry and additional quantitative analysis.

In addition, nearly twenty years of research conducted by the Consortium on Chicago School Research has yielded useful insights into the conditions necessary to bring about significant improvement in student achievement. A recent summary of this research points to "five essential supports" for school improvement: leadership, parent-community ties, professional capacity, student-centered learning climate, and ambitious instruction.[24] The Research Alliance is embarking on a similar line of research to measure these and other supports and to determine the extent to which they are associated with school improvement in New York City.

Other recent studies have also begun to examine key elements of the reforms instated during the Children First era. For example, a study of the many new small schools of choice established during the Children First era shows that these schools have had substantial effects on student performance and progress toward graduation.[25] Building on a naturally occurring randomized controlled trial that results from the NYC high school admissions process, this study found that the small schools increased the likelihood that students would stay on track to graduation and increased graduation rates by nearly 7 percentage points. Further research is planned to identify the features of these small schools that make them more effective and to learn how these conditions can be created in more high schools across the city. Other studies have focused on leadership development and the changes in grade-to-grade promotion standards.[26] Extensions of this work would also shed valuable light on the sources of effects discussed in this chapter.

- *What are the best early indicators of student preparation for and progress toward a high school diploma and ultimately a successful transition to college and work?*

The findings presented here show that student performance on the eighth-grade ELA and math assessments are positively associated with the likelihood that students will graduate within four years of entering high school. The association with earning a Regents diploma is especially strong. The analysis also suggests, however, that these assessments are likely to be incomplete indicators of student preparation for high-level high school work, as many students who are classified as proficient are unlikely to graduate or earn a Regents diploma. In addition, little is known about the degree to which these assessments provide useful insights into students' likely achievement trajectories as they progress toward high school, particularly at the critical transitions into and through the middle grades and pre-adolescence.

The Research Alliance for New York City Schools is conducting studies of these issues by first identifying individual and school factors associated with a student's likelihood of achieving performance levels in the middle grades that are associated with a high probability of success in their first year of high school. This work will provide information for both policy makers and practitioners about early warning indicators that can be used to identify students for special supports and help during the middle grades and during their initial transition into high school. In related work, the Research Alliance is also building on work conducted by the Consortium on Chicago School Research that identified indicators of whether students are getting off track for graduation and preparation for college and careers.[27] This analysis will expand the range of performance and engagement indicators beyond ELA and math test scores and will result in tools that school leaders and counselors can use to target students for special supports and intervention. This analysis will also build on work conducted by the DOE through its Achievement Reporting and Innovation System (ARIS) and its development of graduation on track and college-readiness indicators.

PART V

Themes and Commentary

12

Reflections on Children First

Jennifer A. O'Day and Catherine S. Bitter

Eight years ago, the New York City Department of Education (DOE) embarked on a road that promised fundamental transformation of the largest school system in the land. At the writing of this chapter, Chancellor Joel Klein, the key architect of that reform effort, has just announced his resignation. How will the new leadership of the city's schools sum up, build on, or alter the strategies of Children First? What will be the role of the many constituencies and stakeholders seeking a place at the decision table? And how will evidence—both of what has taken place in the past eight years and of the apparent results of those efforts—inform the reform discourse and direction in the coming months and years?

It is our hope that the individual chapters in this volume and the research on which they are based can shed some light on the core strategies that have constituted the Children First agenda and, by doing so, can help to inform the leadership transition currently under way in the DOE. It is also our hope that lessons from the experiences of New York City schools can help to inform improvement efforts in other jurisdictions, for many of the core issues that the DOE has sought to address—from human capital management to accountability to high school transformation—are shared by other urban systems across the country.

As we discussed in the introduction to this volume, the NYC Education Reform Retrospective review panel chose to ground the commissioned papers in this volume within specific domains of reform activity. Yet many of the issues addressed in particular domains are in fact reflective of more global educational problems, strategies, and themes. To introduce a few of these broader issues, we concluded the introductory chapter with six cross-cutting questions. We return to the substance of those questions here, focusing on the relevant patterns that emerge across the chapters.

In addition, because a key goal of the retrospective has been to contribute to the reform *dialogue*, both in NYC and across the nation, we also incorporate short reflections on the selected themes from stakeholders and observers inside and outside the city. Neither the list of themes nor the list of contributors to these reflections is exhaustive, nor could they be in a short treatment such as this. Indeed, in order to include even these few reflections in the discussion, we had to ask our contributors to be extremely brief and, in some cases, to respond to a narrower question related to the theme. Despite these limitations, we believe the reflections are suggestive of the range of perspectives and experiences that can and should inform the interpretation of these chapters and future improvement efforts.

Theme 1: Defining the Strategy: Complexity, Coherence, and Strategic Evolution

The first question posed in the introduction to this volume is one that has come up again and again in our conversations both with informants inside the system and with stakeholders and observers outside: *Is there a coherent Children First strategy that emerges across time and across domains of reform activity?* In other words, when we talk about Children First, writ large, what reform strategy or approach are we really talking about? Several authors in this collection (e.g., Hill, chapter 1 in this volume; Childress et al., chapter 4; and O'Day and Bitter, chapter 5) note the difficulty—or even futility—of looking for a simple answer to this question, as the approach under Children First has in fact shifted and evolved over time. Even leaders in the DOE make a distinction between phase 1 (consolidation) and phase 2 (empowerment), though they tend to describe these as simply two acts in the same play. Most of the authors appear to agree, as they treat the early years of the reform as a preamble, setting the stage for the core reforms that were scaled up across the system in phase 2, and most focus their primary analyses on those latter core reforms. Nonetheless, O'Day and Bitter argue that while the DOE may have had similar goals during both eras (e.g., to improve classroom instruction), the underlying theories of action about how to accomplish these goals and about the role of the central office in doing so differed substantially. They also point to the disjunction experienced by many practitioners in the system in the transition from one approach to the other—an observation that may have implications for any impending change in direction envisioned by the system's incoming leadership.

The evolution of the reform approach across the eight years of Bloomberg/Klein's administration is hardly surprising, however, as the conditions, understandings, and leadership in the system were also shifting during this time. A related theme emerging from these papers is the rapid pace and scale of change even *within* each reform phase, and the challenge of understanding and implementing the frequent restructuring, the modifications of processes and tools, and the proliferation of new demands and processes. Talbert (chapter 6 in this volume), for example, draws attention to the annual modifications to the collaborative inquiry process and expectations at the school level; Childress et al. similarly note the recent alterations to the accountability metrics; and Siskin (chapter 8) focuses on the challenges high school principals have encountered as a result of the sheer pace of change.

But perhaps even more than the pace and evolution of the reform strategies, it is the comprehensiveness and complexity of the improvement efforts that make simple characterization of the Children First reforms difficult, while they also point to a coherence of the efforts that might otherwise be missed. The intentional interaction of many of the reform strategies is evident from the multiple cross-references in the papers in this volume. Structural changes (Hill; Childress et al.), human capital management policies (Goertz et al., chapter 7), and accountability measures and tools (Childress et al.) are meant to enhance instructional improvements (O'Day and Bitter) and cultural changes (Talbert) as well as to support fundamental transformation of secondary education (Siskin). Broad-based school choice (Corcoran and Levin, chapter 9) and portfolio approaches (Hill) have been designed on the assumption that ineffective schools will be weeded out through the results-based accountability system (Childress et al.) as well as the market. Of course, the simultaneous introduction of many interacting policies does complicate attempts to assess the effectiveness of any given policy or even set of policies (Goertz et al.; Kemple, chapter 11), but one could argue that this is the case in any truly systemic reform effort.

Each of these aspects of the Children First initiative—the evolution of policies, the pace of change, and the comprehensiveness and complexity of the approach—poses challenges as individuals and leaders across varying levels of the system try to make sense of the reforms and use their interpretation to guide their work. To illustrate this, we asked leaders at two distinct levels—the chancellor of the New York State Board of Regents, Merryl Tisch, and high school principal Philip Weinberg—to reflect on the core elements of Children First as it impacts their own work:

> New York State educates three million school-aged children in over seven hundred school districts. New York City is home to more than one-third of those children. The partnership with our largest school district has helped define a broad reform agenda that includes the redesign of teacher preparation and evaluation, the advancement of a statewide accountability system driven by data based on student growth, the adoption of common core standards in both English language arts and mathematics, and the development of a new generation of assessments as part of a multistate consortium. These joint reform efforts, coupled with legislation that secured the expansion of the charter school movement in New York State, have established New York's leadership role in the bold national effort known as Race to the Top.
>
> —*Merryl H. Tisch, New York State Chancellor of Schools*

There certainly has been a great deal of sound and fury surrounding the changes wrought by Children First. From my perspective, the core strategy of Children First was to create an entirely new operating structure for the Department of Education. All of the school system's practices and approaches were examined. The conclusion was that the system as it existed simply did not work, and that the best approach was to start anew. The years in between appear to be a rigorous attempt to define what "new" should look like.

We navigate these changes by ensuring that our school's focus remains on quality teaching and exemplary learning, rather than on political pressures. Accountability and evaluation have changed dramatically under Children First, and because data has been more of a focus than pedagogy, we are often faced with a hard choice between statistical success and instructional improvement. The habitual upheaval associated with Children First has been difficult for schools in very predictable ways, as it would be for any organization in which institutional memory was lost and governance structures were concurrently reshuffled. My job has often been to insulate the community from the constant political turmoil attached to the changes and keep us focused on our school's shared instructional philosophy, which we continually strive to develop and refine.

—*Philip Weinberg, Principal, High School*
of Telecommunication Arts and Technology

A discussion of the interpretations of the Children First reforms would be incomplete without at least some mention of the deep polarization of the public discourse surrounding the Bloomberg/Klein policies. While Hill approaches this issue in terms of interest group politics and changing power relationships among stakeholders, Henig et al. (chapter 2) also note the differing conceptions of engagement that influence individuals' and groups' interpretation of what the DOE has and has not done with respect to engaging parents and community in the efforts. Another influence on the public discourse, which perhaps receives short shrift in this volume, is that of the media. Yet the media have the power to frame public understanding of the reforms both by what they report and by how they do so. Richard Colvin, director of the Hechinger Institute at Columbia University, reflects on this issue:

Complex school reform efforts are difficult to communicate, both for district officials and journalists who work for general-interest news organizations. Journalists often cover education policies only when they generate controversy, and focus on the conflict, rather than the policy itself. That has been particularly true of the Children First reforms in New York City. For example, recently much of the news coverage has been about opposition to giving charter schools space in other school buildings. The general lack of space, and the concerns of parents whose children attend the charter schools, were downplayed. Klein has acknowledged publicly that he and his office have not done a good job of telling the story of the New York City reforms. Journalists often complain about how difficult it is to get even the simplest, most straightforward information out of the DOE, and most teachers and principals say they fear retribution if they are quoted in the media (even though there is no formal policy prohibiting them from speaking). It is also very difficult for reporters to get into buildings to see the reforms as they happen. If journalists could see how the reforms play out in classrooms and schools, and if they were able to talk to teachers and principals, their reporting would more likely be nuanced and explanatory and descriptive, even if they do report on opposition and conflict.

—*Richard Colvin, Director of the Hechinger*
Institute on Education and the Media

Theme 2: Challenging the System: Boundaries, Expertise, and Authority

From its inception, Children First has been focused on system change—not just in terms of reaching all schools in the system but also of fundamentally altering the very way that the system operates. The goal, in Joel Klein's words, is not a great school system but a system of great schools.

A multidimensional picture of system change emerges from chapters in this volume. On one dimension, we see a school system with unusually permeable boundaries, where individuals from other sectors and professions move in and out of leadership positions in the DOE based on their talent and fit with the reform agenda rather than on their background in education or prior position in the city schools (Hill); where teachers and principals are recruited from nontraditional sources and trained through alternative routes and programs (Goertz et al.); and where new organizations inside and outside the system have taken on the work of instructional support and guidance that is typically performed by district offices (Childress et al., O'Day and Bitter, Talbert, and Siskin). On another dimension, we find that the traditional line authority between the central office and the schools has all but disappeared, as "CEO" principals become empowered to allocate resources, hire and manage staff, and make instructional decisions with little oversight or supervision from the DOE or network cluster leaders (Hill; Childress et al.; O'Day and Bitter; and Siskin). From a third angle, we note that traditional conceptions of public accountability and governance by policy-making school boards and the interest group politics so common to urban systems have been replaced by accountability through the ballot box (Hill; Henig et al.), through the market (Corcoran and Levin), and through management by results (Childress et al.). Indeed, even traditional conceptions of teachers' work have been challenged (O'Day and Bitter), as have generally taken-for-granted human resource policies like seniority, teacher placement, and evaluation (Goertz et al.).

We asked three individuals to comment on these system changes from their distinctive perspectives: Leo Casey, United Federation of Teachers vice president of academic high schools; Robert Hughes, president of New Visions for Public Schools, the largest Partnership Support Organization (PSO) working with NYC schools; and Warren Simmons, executive director of the Annenberg Institute for School Reform, which has developed a conception of "smart educational systems" that also challenges traditional district definitions and boundaries, but is quite distinct from the approach of Children First:

Through their many structural incarnations, the Children First reforms have been driven by one article of faith: the idea that public education needs to be remade in the image and likeness of a private sector business. From the massive centralization of the system in ten regions to the wholesale devolution of central Department of Education responsibility for teaching and learning in networks, this corporate conception of education has provided an unchanging foundation. The answer to every educational question was to be found in the promotion of competition and market modes of organization.

Given this foundation, the essential qualification for leadership within Children First has been experience in management, and not professional training as an educator or experience in real classrooms and schools. Once understood as an instructional leader, the principal is now reconceived as an all-powerful chief executive officer of the school. Once understood as a system of supports for the educational work of schools, the central administration is focused on a "bottom line" of quantitative accountability measures derived almost entirely from flawed standardized exams.

A number of negative effects have followed from the introduction of this corporate model. The CEO principal runs up against the culture of collaboration and trust, focused on teaching and learning, which is the foundation of successful schools. When the principal lacks educational skill and experience, he loses the moral authority to lead in the eyes of his staff. The devolution of the central administration into a corporate accountability bureaucracy that no longer provides supports to schools has left many schools—especially those who serve low income communities with concentrations of high need students—adrift and without positive direction. Finally, the autocratic character of the corporate model has undermined the democratic oversight and direction of education, eviscerating the role of the public in public education. The voice of parents, staff, and local communities are routinely ignored and disregarded, leading to widespread alienation from the Children First leadership of New York City public schools.

—*Leo Casey, Vice President of Academic High Schools, United Federation of Teachers*

Recognizing that they inherited a fundamentally broken system, the Bloomberg/Klein administration engaged in a period of bold and unprecedented invention to redesign the system itself. Headlines have rightly focused on the decisions to provide school leaders with increasing degrees of autonomy along with greater accountability for student achievement. But in my view, their legacy resides elsewhere, in the creation of freedom to engage in discipline innovation: establishing data systems and interim assessments that enable educators to develop strategies and test whether they actually improve student outcomes. For example, beginning in 2001, the New Century High School Initiative invited educators and community leaders to create new school models that increased student personalization, changed staffing and curricula, and leveraged community resources. Since then, these groups have created an array of new models—themed high schools, transfer schools and dual language schools-- that build on the collective experience and expertise of educators, youth development agencies, and community leaders. Their impact on student achievement has been validated at scale by MDRC. Similarly, they empowered teams of teachers to examine their own practice and its relationship to the success of students in their classrooms. Thousands of teachers on Inquiry teams now rapidly create, implement, and evaluate strategies to address those specific student needs, maintaining a sharp focus on their teaching's impact on student learning. Over the last eight years, the administration's commitment to "design thinking" at the classroom, school, and district levels may be more enduring than the structural changes they have wrought.

—Robert Hughes, President, New Visions for Public Schools

In our experience, district reinvention is guided by three broad theories of action. Leaders choose to raise student performance and build school capacity by: (1) creating professional learning communities in which teachers and principals collaborate to identify needs and solutions; (2) managing instruction by using a common curriculum or instructional framework in all schools; and (3) creating a portfolio of schools, giving schools the resources and freedom to seek appropriate supports to enhance teaching and learning. While not mutually exclusive, these approaches require major shifts in roles and responsibilities at the central office, intermediate (e.g., regional), and school levels. The DOE has shifted its theory of action at least two times over the past eight years without adequately communicating and clarifying the significant shifts in roles and responsibilities these changes entail. The resulting confusion undermines parents' and educators' ability to use the levers of data, accountability, and choice to promote equity and excellence within and across schools. Moreover, these shifts have occurred in a high-stakes environment where professional compensation and employment are tied to student performance and where chronic school failure can lead to school closure.

Leaders of schools and districts that beat the odds realize that education improvement occurs in a larger political and cultural context that must be understood and, where necessary, changed—sometimes through force of will, but also through strategic and results-oriented community engagement. This more community-centered approach is critical in a city where the relationship between political power and student achievement remains highly correlated with race, ethnicity and income and where the schools have been historical battlegrounds where groups vie for access and influence. While the portfolio model increases levers for parent and student engagement at the school level, it also weakens the levers parents and school leaders use to address systemic failures and inequities, potentially undermining the community support needed to sustain reforms even in the face of promising results. Addressing this shortcoming should be a high priority for the new chancellor, and one that should be addressed collaboratively rather than by fiat.

—Warren Simmons, Executive Director, Annenberg Institute
for School Reform, Brown University

Theme 3: Leveraging Change:
The Autonomy-Accountability-Capacity Challenge

A major challenge in the Children First reforms has been to strike the most effective balance over time among autonomy at the school level, accountability for results, and the capacity of school personnel to achieve those results—and to do so at scale. The third question we posed in the introduction is: *How has the system addressed the dynamic tension between school autonomy, capacity, and accountability, and how has this changed over time?* New York City has approached this balance somewhat differently than many other urban systems.

Several chapters (Hill; Childress et al.; and O'Day and Bitter) discuss the evolution in this balance over time, distinguishing between a focus on building consistency and capacity throughout the system in phase 1, and the granting of greater autonomy to principals, in exchange for increased accountability, in phase 2. Unique to NYC, autonomy is considered a *precondition* for success rather than an earned privilege, and thus principals of *all* schools have been given more authority over spending, curriculum, and professional development. O'Day and Bitter reflect on the way that, in this latter phase of the reform, the focus on empowerment coincides with a shift in the DOE's role to "creating the conditions" for instructional improvement, with the underlying assumption that, given the right conditions (e.g., tools for learning, accessible student data), those closest to the students can make the best decisions to impact their learning. Yet the DOE asserts that for empowerment to truly leverage change, there must be strong accountability for results. While O'Day and Bitter discuss how the Children First reforms address the shortcomings of many accountability systems—for example, by generating and using frequent data on both inputs and outcomes (e.g., School Quality Reviews and Progress Reports)—several authors (Childress et al., Hill, O'Day and Bitter) note that questions surrounding the validity and reliability of the assessments may limit the effectiveness of NYC's accountability system.

We raised this set of challenges with Robert Schwartz, academic dean of Harvard University's Graduate School of Education, who has considered issues of accountability at the local, state, and national levels:

> The present accountability era is in some measure a reaction to an education system that has historically overvalued autonomy, especially in the classroom. In countries with a much stronger professional culture and widely shared norms of practice, there is much less need for formal systems of external accountability. In our setting, however, "professional autonomy" in the pre-standards-movement world was the banner under which teachers (and schools) could close their doors and do their own thing with little or no transparency or public accountability for results.
>
> Autonomy without accountability led to an educational system with huge variability in outcomes from classroom to classroom and school to school. If this is the major challenge the current standards and accountability movement is designed to address, what is the role of school-level autonomy in meeting that challenge? New York's answer is that autonomy is a precondition for accountability: unless I as a principal have control over the resources needed to produce the results for which I am to be held accountable, it's not fair to expect me to accept responsibility for results.

The problem comes in the definition of resources. Even if I get to pick my own teachers—a fight New York has waged heroically, with some success—given the limited training and experience of most of the teachers I would choose to hire, will I have the resources (human and financial) to provide ongoing development and support to build the teaching capacity and collaborative culture required to continuously improve performance across all classrooms? Do such resources (especially instructional and organizational expertise) exist in sufficient supply, even in New York, to make the autonomy-for-accountability bargain viable? Without a much better educated and trained educator workforce and professional culture, will even the best designed and resourced accountability/autonomy strategy get us the results we need?

—*Robert Schwartz, Academic Dean, Harvard Graduate School of Education*

As Schwartz suggests, the human capital demands in a system anchored in autonomy and accountability are indeed substantial. In NYC, principals are taking on additional responsibilities to lead instructional improvement efforts, collect and interpret data, and manage schools as "CEOs," and they require additional skills to do so (Siskin; Childress et al.; Talbert; and O'Day and Bitter). Network leaders are expected to support principals in these roles, and cluster leaders must coordinate this work across the networks they oversee. And teachers need appropriate knowledge and skills to interpret data and develop instructional strategies to meet students' needs in an environment of challenging standards (O'Day and Bitter; Goertz et al.).

While the first phase of Children First incorporated centrally directed intensive professional development in areas such as balanced literacy and instruction of English language learners, the second phase of Children First assumes that the knowledge necessary for improving instruction resides within the schools themselves. Teachers are expected to learn together through the collaborative inquiry process, and principals are expected to facilitate this learning, bringing in external expertise when necessary.

The papers in this volume raise questions about whether the fundamental level of capacity needed for the accountability-autonomy exchange to work exists in NYC under Children First. For example, Ferguson (chapter 10) examines the wide variation in instructional quality, as described by students, both across and within schools, and Goertz et al. provide evidence that, despite improvements in the distribution of teachers, the highest-poverty schools continue to have less-qualified teachers on average than the lowest-poverty schools. Siskin points out that the reform has brought in a large cadre of new and young principals who need additional support in their roles.

In addition, several chapters question the degree to which the tools that aim to build capacity (e.g., inquiry tools, Quality Reviews) do so sufficiently. Talbert describes the time necessary to develop effective inquiry teams and raises concerns about the readiness of all schools to take on this intensive work. Talbert, Childress et al., and O'Day and Bitter also raise questions about the ability of teachers and principals to learn from tools that are subject to varying interpretations and constant change, and note the limited opportunities for content-based professional development.

Ernest Logan, who represents NYC principals through the Council of School Supervisors and Administrators, echoes these capacity issues as he reflects on how Children First has affected principals in the city:

> The Children First reforms have allowed creative school leaders to design their own schools around the needs of individual students without being micromanaged from above. However, when school leaders don't have the expertise or resources to develop schools that meet all students' needs, they are often without an adequate safety net. The supports they require were once provided by district superintendents who could provide course correction when needed. There's more of a sink-or-swim mentality under the current reforms. The support mechanism also changes too often—from regional offices to [School Support Organizations] to clusters. More stability and continuity would be helpful.
>
> —*Ernest A. Logan, President of the Council of School Supervisors and Administrators*

In addition to the level of capacity needed to support the accountability/autonomy exchange, one must consider whether the levels of accountability and autonomy themselves are sufficient to reach the expected end result. When we asked Benjamin Sherman, a high school principal, to reflect on the accountability-autonomy-capacity balance, he brought up this issue as one of the challenges faced daily in schools:

> The small schools movement and the focus on autonomy and accountability within Children First have allowed us to improve outcomes for more children. Fewer children slip through the cracks, and more young people are ready for rigorous college work. I like the accountability aspect of Children First. It does not bother me that if I do not move my kids I lose my job—that's the way it should be. And if my school is not able to function as a cohesive educational unit, it should be closed. Because that is how important education is for our students.
>
> In terms of capacity, however, there are not enough supports for principals. We are facing dwindling school budgets, increasing nonacademic requirements (safety plans, recycling programs, etc.), and significant testing requirements. In small schools, there are fewer hands to do this work. We need more funding to hire support staff to take care of scheduling, test coordination, and data compliance. Right now I am paying teachers to do this, and teachers are not able to do this very well.
>
> Principals are being given autonomy, but yet we are shackled with these new tasks that used to be done by the DOE, and with many other restrictions. I need the ability to hire and fire, yet terminating a teacher is an onerous two-year process, and there has been a hiring freeze for two years. I also need more flexibility in scheduling my teachers and fewer restrictions on where and how I spend money. Since we are being held accountable for academic results, we have to run at the same speed or faster with leg shackles. It is very discouraging, and the challenges are immense.
>
> —*Benjamin Sherman, Principal, The East-West School of International Studies Q281*

Theme 4: Seeking Equity: Inputs, Processes, and Outcomes

Accountability for the outcomes of *all* students, as described in the previous section, aims to focus the attention of school leaders and teachers on the core goal of Children First: to reduce deep inequities in educational opportunities and to close achievement gaps among groups of children in the city's schools. Many of the papers in this volume speak to the multiple approaches the NYC reforms take toward this goal of increased equity. O'Day and Bitter and Goertz et al. describe strategies to improve instruction and the quality of teachers and leaders at all grade levels; a central purpose of these strategies is to level the playing field with regard to educational inputs. At the high school level, a larger and more diverse portfolio of schools has been developed to meet the varying needs of students, particularly those who were traditionally underserved in the previous system. Students have greater opportunity to choose a school that will best meet their needs, and the DOE has created multiple pathways for those who do not meet with success on the traditional path to graduation (Siskin; Corcoran and Levin).

Holding schools accountable for improving the performance of all students also aims to focus the attention of school leaders and teachers on struggling individuals and subgroups of students in their charge. Tools and processes for analyzing and interpreting data aim to foster collaboration around instructional strategies for these students (Childress et al.; O'Day and Bitter; Talbert). Finally, the incorporation of the Fair Student Funding formula facilitates this focus by allocating resources to schools based on student need (Stiefel and Schwartz, chapter 3).

Several chapters point to progress made toward the goal of increased equity. For example, Stiefel and Schwartz provide evidence that resources are increasingly allocated according to the Fair Student Funding formula; Corcoran and Levin note that more and more students are receiving their first-choice school within the high school choice process; and Kemple speaks to increased outcomes for special education students in relation to general education students. However, the authors also note that the road to equity is a long one, and NYC still has far to go to reach this ambitious goal. For example, Kemple's rigorous analyses of test score results reveal continued disparities in outcomes between high- and low-poverty schools; Corcoran and Levin show that, despite the extensive school choice process, students typically end up in high schools with students of similar academic, racial, and socioeconomic backgrounds as those in their middle school; and Siskin concludes that despite the closing of many "dropout factories," many schools still prepare too few students for graduation.

To highlight the progress made toward increasing equity in New York City, as well as the challenges, we asked Pedro Noguera, who has studied issues of equity in NYC and other urban centers, and Chung-Wha Hong, the executive director of the New York Immigration Coalition, a leading advocacy organization for immigrant communities at the local, state, and national level, to reflect on what they have observed in New York over the past eight years:

> My feelings about New York on this issue are mixed. To be fair, I have seen many schools that have been improved, where there is a greater focus on evidence of student learning, and I am seeing fewer schools that are chaotic and disorganized. Given the size of this district, to be able to accomplish that is laudable. I attribute it to the relentless focus on raising student achievement through an emphasis on test scores. The DOE also created transfer schools to serve kids who might otherwise have dropped out. In some cases, these schools have partnered with community-based organizations and have worked well. This is a good thing.
>
> But I also have many concerns. The DOE has allowed the number of screened schools and charters to grow, which has meant that the numbers of schools serving high-need students have shrunk, concentrating them on certain campuses. Schools like the nineteen on the closure list last year are overpopulated with level 1 students, many of them over-age, and these schools are often staffed by inexperienced teachers. We know from research that kids who are farther behind need more-experienced, not less-experienced, teachers. So this is a flawed strategy. We need to make sure that schools that do serve high-need kids get additional resources. And we need to think more creatively about effective interventions to address students' needs. Some schools are doing this on their own; but while resourceful principals are doing well, those who are less resourceful are not.
>
> —*Pedro Noguera, Professor of Teaching and Learning, New York University*

One indicator of equity in the NYC school system is to look at how more than 150,000 English language learners are doing. For immigrant and ELL students, Children First reforms did not lead to improved outcomes. The ELL dropout crisis continues as half of ELLs continue to drop out of high school, and many ELLs do not receive adequate English instruction to achieve college and career readiness. When the DOE was most effective is when it worked together with community groups to account for ELLs in the Fair Student Funding, to support the international schools, or to provide interpretation and translation services to parents who don't speak English. But continuing progress on those efforts must be part of a system-wide vision and program for ELLs that includes scaling up the best teaching practices, allocation of adequate resources, and a deep and sustained engagement with parents and communities.

> —*Chung-Wha Hong, Executive Director, The New York Immigration Coalition*

We also asked Kati Haycock from the Education Trust, a national advocacy organization focused on reducing achievement gaps at all grade levels, to comment on this theme. She reflects on what NYC can learn from nationwide efforts towards reducing achievement gaps:

> For the past decade, many schools and school districts have worked hard to close the gaps that have for too long separated low-income students and students of color from other young Americans. Certainly, we've made some headway. But progress is not fast enough.

Some would argue that this simply proves that it is poverty or culture or parents after all, that until we change all those things, we can't get this job done. Yet all around the country, there *are* schools that are getting the job done and districts that are making a lot of progress, too. What can we learn from them?

- The quality of school leaders matters a lot; if we don't get this part right, we won't get this job done. And nobody, frankly, should take on a turnaround without proving him- or herself elsewhere first.

- It's not just about quality teachers, it's about quality *teaching*. Schools and districts that are making the most progress invest enormous time in agreeing on what should be taught and what level or work is "good enough." Their lessons are thoughtful, well organized, and coherent, and teachers get lots of quality coaching and feedback. They look constantly at data of all kinds; literally nothing about teaching or learning is left to chance.

- When kids come in behind, they need more instruction, not less. Schools that are making the most progress not only provide those extras, but they make sure students get them.

Focus is really important, and the focus in these schools and districts is very squarely on the things they can control, not the things that are beyond their control.

—*Kati Haycock, President, the Education Trust*

Theme 5: Sustaining Reforms: What, Why, and How

The fifth question posed in the introduction to this volume is particularly timely: *what implications do the findings and discussions in these chapters have for sustaining the reforms over time and across changes in city and system leadership?* Michael Bloomberg's election to a third term in 2009 granted the administration more time than originally expected for their sweeping changes to take root. However, the recent turnover in the chancellorship brings the question of sustainability once again to the forefront of the dialogue around Children First.

This volume highlights several factors potentially contributing to or hindering sustainability. Hill and Henig et al. argue that sustainability will depend on the extent to which *constituencies of support* are built to maintain the initiatives of Children First. Hill speaks to the fact that some groups who were prominent in decision making prior to Bloomberg/Klein were disenfranchised in an effort to make change happen quickly, and these groups could be a threat to the reform in the long term. Henig et al. note that a countermovement focused on a different notion of community engagement could threaten the sustainability of the reform effort.

In addition, both chapters note that a fundamental assumption of the Bloomberg/Klein administration is that *improved student outcomes* will help to build new constituencies of support. However, this idea hinges on consistent positive and significant change in student outcomes. While student test scores have increased over the past eight years, Kemple's analysis of student outcomes raises questions about the size and source of the effects. Will these improvements continue, and are they sufficient to gain the support necessary to maintain Children First in its current form into the future?

Sustainability also depends on the extent to which *tools and processes* associated with the reform effort are institutionalized. For example, Talbert highlights schools in which the inquiry process has taken root and potentially changed the school culture for the long term. Yet she brings up several challenges to sustaining the initiative systemwide, including the balancing of top-down guidance and bottom-up initiative, the diversity in school readiness for change, and accountability demands from broader policy contexts. In addition, the fast pace of implementation and frequent changes in tools and processes for improving instruction can limit the extent to which they become integrated into the school's core (O'Day and Bitter).

Stiefel and Schwartz take a different perspective, describing significant increases in per pupil *funding* over the Bloomberg years, including substantial private money that has enabled reform. However, they note that the growth in revenues is unlikely to be sustained due both to the continuing effects of the 2008 recession and New York State's structural deficit.

We asked Charles Kerchner of Claremont Graduate University to reflect on the challenges and possibilities for sustainability in New York City:

> One must make a distinction between regime turnover/stability and institutional change. It is possible for a regime to last long enough that it infuses the culture (e.g., the New Deal) or permanently changes institutions (e.g., by fundamentally altering standard operating procedures). But sometimes regimes—even those that last for a while—don't have any long-term institutional traction at all. For example, it is now hard to find any evidence in San Diego that Alan Bersin's program to fundamentally change everything in the district was ever there.
>
> In New York City, the current regime is lasting longer than it was supposed to. Mayor Bloomberg got an unanticipated third term. The oppositional political forces in the city that had been dampened by the regime's coming to power and taking a monopoly in the public policy space are beginning to find their voice again and to find champions, like Diane Ravitch. A lot of political elements have started to coalesce. The union is getting smarter, and community groups are starting to say that the results are not as good as they expected. Because the regime has been there long enough to be judged by performance and not its promises, it is vulnerable. At the same time, it has also put down roots by way of developing leaders and external support providers, implementing the portfolio notion in a more robust way, and so forth. So maybe when the regime goes away, these elements will stay and there will be substantive institutional change.
>
> —*Charles Taylor Kerchner, Claremont Graduate University*

The question of what *should* be sustained is also an important one. We provide two perspectives on this question below. Kathryn Wylde first highlights the accomplishments of Children First from the business community's perspective. The final reflection comes from one of the most important, yet often overlooked constituencies—the students themselves. We asked representatives from the Urban Youth Collaborative to reflect on what they would like to see continue, and what should be changed, in NYC public schools in the years ahead:

> The New York business community is greatly encouraged by the significant progress in public education that has been achieved during the Bloomberg/Klein administration. Business will be a significant force for sustaining those achievements going forward. Putting in place accountability measures for professionals, for schools, and for the system as a whole are probably the most important accomplishments of Children First from a business perspective. Improved use of data to manage public education, to evaluate professional performance, and to guide policy decisions are long-standing priorities. Parents, prospective employers, and the broader community will not easily give up the accountability measures that have been introduced through Children First. Another highly valued component of Children First is the empowerment of school leaders. While much is still to be done in terms of increasing the authority and flexibility of principals, Children First has introduced a management framework that makes sense to the business world and that they are prepared to support and strengthen. The New York City Leadership Academy has institutionalized reforms in how principals are recruited, trained, and mentored that the business community believes in. The Academy was designed to survive any particular administration, helping to insure continuity in school leadership that is dedicated to the fundamental principles of Children First.
>
> —*Kathryn Wylde, President and CEO, Partnership for New York City*

Many high schools are very focused on test preparation. Every day is focused on learning how to pass tests like the Regents exams, and students do not learn anything else. As a result, students feel underprepared when they enter college. High schools should instead be focused on college preparation. Some programs, like the Student Success Centers, aim to do this through mentoring and academic help, and should be sustained and grow in the future.

The school choice system gives students more options for where they can go to school, which is a good thing, and is better than placing students in local, overcrowded schools. However, at the end of the day, the education system and all schools within it still need to be improved. My local school has metal detectors, but if I go to a different school, it may have the same problems.

The creation of small schools within the reform has advantages. Students can receive more individualized attention, and it feels more like a family environment. However, large schools should not just be phased out. They should be given the support to succeed, and closure should be only the last resort. Also, small schools are often located within a campus that may have some of the same issues as the large schools, such as metal detectors and security guards. This environment is in conflict with the environment that the small schools aim to create. It makes the school feel like a prison rather than a place to learn, and many students are turned off by this environment and drop out of school.

—Robert Moore and Adolfo Abreu, Urban Youth Collaborative

Theme 6: Transporting Reform: Context, Strategy, and Context Again

The chapters in this volume have understandably focused primarily on New York City, both with respect to documenting the specific reform efforts and with respect to identifying potential lessons and implications for future policy and practice. Indeed several of the chapters (Henig et al., Siskin, Corcoran and Levin) provide considerable background on the historical antecedents to the Children First policies—that is, on the specific policy and reform histories in New York City that have formed the basis for many of the strategies expanded or enhanced by the Bloomberg/Klein administration. Both historians and system theorists tell us that all change is history dependent, so understanding these precursors can help explain both what the DOE chose to do and how participants and stakeholders have responded. This history, as well as the current political and governance arrangements (Hill) and the sheer scale of the system, suggest a uniqueness to the context of the New York City system that begs the question: *what lessons and strategies might be transportable to other jurisdictions and under what conditions?*

We raised this question with three current and former superintendents from other large urban districts and conclude this set of reflections on New York with their observations. Andres Alonso, who served as deputy superintendent for Teaching and Leaning in the DOE before becoming CEO of the Baltimore City Schools, talks about what he was able to bring from NYC to his new position and district. Tom Boasberg, superintendent in Denver, addresses the same question from a very different district setting, while Tom Payzant, who led multiple urban districts before retiring from his eleven-year tenure at the helm of Boston Public Schools, notes how his work with aspiring superintendents in the Broad Superintendents Academy incorporates lessons from NYC and other districts managed by nontraditional leaders:

> I do not believe in the notion of a wholesale transporting of reform or transferring a formula for change. The work in school systems is immersed in particular contexts. While certain biases or orientations to the work are transportable, different districts have different structures, different histories, different financial resources, different governance realities. The work needs to be tailored to the children and institutions you are trying to change.
>
> However, there are fundamental principles and orientations to the work that can be transferred. What I drew from New York was an awareness of key levers that all systems should pay attention to, such as:
>
> • The attention to the individual school as the place where important things happen
> • Constant attention to student outcomes

- An almost obsession with the effectiveness of people and teams
- A focus on how systems engineer failure and engineer success
- An impatience with excuses and with justifications for failure at either the school or the central level
- A willingness to move very fast—sometimes without consensus
- An openness to the idea of a portfolio approach to schools that inherently embraces choice and competition

All these are things with which most large urban school systems are currently wrestling.

In addition, what I brought from my experiences in New York City was the orientation to boldness and a belief that many things could be done in a shorter timeline. My team and I have observed that what we do [in Baltimore] in six months, other districts take three to four years to do. This natural timidity that I see in many other places might have imposed itself on me if I had not had the experience in NYC. People here experience this as a surge of energy that was not here before. *That* I learned in NYC, and I am not sure I would have had that confidence otherwise.

—*Andres Alonso, CEO, Baltimore City Schools*

I do not buy the argument that the NYC experience is not applicable to other districts. Districts that don't have mayoral control or that have as much as one-third fewer dollars per student may find some of the NYC strategies harder to undertake, but it is just silly to say that they are nontransferable. Of course, specific district contexts are important. For example, there may be some strategies that might be unworkable in NYC but would be more effective in smaller systems. Conversely, the extraordinary level of decentralization and lack of nonnegotiables on elements such as core curriculum or common assessments in NYC may be right for that system but may not be the right answer for a district of fifty to eighty thousand students.

As superintendent in Denver, I have looked to New York for study and emulation in several areas, such as their coherent turnaround model of phasing out underperforming schools and opening new ones one grade at a time, the systematic nature of the school accountability system, and their talent pipeline strategies for both principals and teachers. We have studied their network structure, which is created by principals and consumer driven for support services, though in Denver we have not gone this far. I also see pros and cons to the notion that principals do not have a boss, as there are some areas in which coherence across the system is a good thing. And while closing the bottom 2 to 3 percent of schools a year is productive, we also need to more effectively implement coherent strategies to change outcomes in the bottom 25 percent.

—*Tom Boasberg, Superintendent, Denver Public Schools*

The challenge of scalability exists in all different sizes of school districts and schools, and New York City is just a special case of this. Some of the lessons learned from Joel are transferable, but context is important. For example, one big piece is whether the teachers' union is interested in being a partner in the reform strategy. In NYC, Joel Klein and Randi Weingarten of the United Federation of Teachers have partnered on a number of things and then are apart on others. Also, in NYC they give autonomy to schools first to enable them to try new things. But I worry about whether the capacity is always there to do the right thing and what's best for children. And in the accountability system, we don't yet have the metrics right to stand up to our principles for individual student growth and equity.

In training the next generation of superintendents, we must focus on getting prospective superintendents up to speed on how to be instructional leaders. They must understand what good teaching and learning is, how to create a talented and effective senior leadership team, and how to build the capacity of the team to carry out the work to ensure that all children have the opportunity to learn and achieve at high levels. In [the Broad Superintendents Academy], part of the challenge is to get nontraditional candidates up to speed on the teaching and learning side. They have good experience on the human capital side, on using data. They are not averse to accountability. This is common practice in the private sector and to some extent in the private nonprofits. This experience serves them well, but they have to have a good chief academic officer or person working on the academic side. This is the key to success.

—*Tom Payzant, Professor of Practice, Harvard Graduate School of Education, and former Superintendent, Boston Public Schools*

Conclusion

Enacting change in a system as large and diverse as New York City is a challenging goal; doing so in as comprehensive and far-reaching way as the DOE aims to through Children First is even more ambitious. The DOE's intentions and theory of change under the Bloomberg/Klein administration, however, have often been overshadowed by the polarized debate and controversy surrounding the reforms. Our hope is that this volume has helped to shed light on the DOE's goals, assumptions, and strategies over the past eight years, and that the cross-cutting themes laid out in this concluding chapter bring out some of the interconnections and patterns among these strategies. The reflections included represent just a snapshot of the wide range of perspectives with respect to this reform effort—yet they demonstrate the diverse opinions and viewpoints among constituents inside NYC and among observers on the outside. This diversity of insights and experiences can enrich learning in the system and field and bring new information to the sense-making process as the new leadership in NYC sets a path for future reform efforts.

Notes

Introduction

1. The supporting foundations include: Bill and Melinda Gates Foundation, Carnegie Corporation of New York, Robertson Foundation, and Michael & Susan Dell Foundation.

2. The members of the Retrospective review panel have shifted somewhat over the course of the project but have included the following individuals: Jennifer O'Day, chair (American Institutes for Research); Stacey Childress (Harvard Business School); Libia Gil (American Institutes for Research); Louis Gomez (University of Pittsburgh); Beverly Hall (Atlanta Public Schools); Susanna Loeb (Stanford University); Charles Payne (University of Chicago); Wendy Puriefoy (Public Education Network); and Joan Talbert (Stanford University). Two members (Hall and Childress) recused themselves from the panel in midcourse when potential conflicts of interest emerged due to changes in their respective situations.

Chapter 1

1. This paper is based on fieldwork done in the course of a study on portfolio school districts, based on a grant from the Carnegie Corporation of New York to the Center on Reinventing Public Education. This thirty-month project involves close tracking of the evolution and results of portfolio-district initiatives in New York City, Washington, D.C., New Orleans, Denver, and Chicago via analysis of public documents and press accounts, and interviews with key actors in the city government, school system, and interest groups. A *portfolio district* pursues a mixed strategy of new-school development (often via chartering) and improvement of existing public schools, under a common performance framework, so that all schools are judged on the same performance standards, and any school's continuation depends on evidence of student growth. For a preliminary report on the study see Paul Hill et al., *Portfolio School Districts for Big Cities: An Interim Report* (Seattle: Center on Reinventing Public Education, 2009).

2. As Susanna Loeb noted in comments on an earlier draft of this chapter, these definitions leave out a third factor that determines the capacities of top management—systems. Data and oversight systems can both enable leadership (by giving leaders insight about what is happening beneath them, helping them identify problems that need attention, and signaling subordinates about what outcomes are valued) and act as governance constraints (e.g., by making leaders and subordinates spend time on issues that top management does not consider important).

3. Editorial, *New York Times*, August 7, 2002.

4. Joseph Berger, "Report Details School Fraud by Custodians," *New York Times*, November 13, 1992, http://www.nytimes.com/1992/11/13/nyregion/report-details-school-fraud-by-custodians.html.

5. Bruce Bimber, *The Decentralization Mirage* (Santa Monica, CA: Rand, 1995).

6. See, for example, Thomas W. Malone, "Making the Decision to Decentralize," *Harvard Business School Working Knowledge for Business Leaders Archive*, March 29, 2004, http://hbswk.hbs.edu/archive/4020.html.

7. See, for example, Michael C. Dorf and Charles F. Sabel, "A Constitution of Democratic Experimentalism," *Columbia Law Review* 98, no. 2 (1998): 267.

8. Charles Sabel, *Learning by Monitoring*, (Cambridge, MA: Harvard University Press, 2006).

9. Mike Schmoker, "Tipping Point: From Feckless Reform to Substantive Instructional Improvement," *Phi Delta Kappan* 85, no. 6 (2004): 424–427.

10. Few other cities adopting features of New York's reforms are so clear about the uses of autonomy. Hartford and the District of Columbia, for example, still treat autonomy as a reward only for the best.

11. Stephen Brill, "The Rubber Room: The Battle over New York City's Worst Teachers," *New Yorker*, August 31, 2009, http://www.newyorker.com/reporting/2009/08/31/090831fa_fact_brill.

12. Charles Sabel, "What To Do about Wicked Problems After Whitehall (and What Scotland May Just Possibly Already Be Doing)," (paper presented to the OECD Conference on Devolution and Globalization Implications for Local Decision-makers, Glasgow, Scotland, February 28, 2000).

13. See Shannon Marsh and Paul Hill, "Multiple Pathways to Graduation: New Routes to High School Completion" (working paper, Center on Reinventing Public Education, Seattle, 2010).

14. Sabel, *Learning by Monitoring*.

15. See Colorado Department of Education, "Associate Commissioner Richard Wenning on the Colorado Growth Model," Colorado Department of Education, http://www.schoolview.org/media/Tutorial/CGM_PubTutorial_01.asp, for a discussion of the new measurements for the school Progress Reports. See Childress et al., chapter 4 this volume, for a more complete description of the results-based accountability system.

16 Similar opposition has arisen in New Orleans, Denver, and Washington, D.C.

17. Diane Ravitch, *The Death and Life of the Great American School System: How Testing and Choice Are Undermining Education* (New York: Basic Books, 2010).

18. Dorf and Sabel, "A Constitution of Democratic Experimentalism."

19. Leaders in both New York and New Orleans cite long waiting lists for new schools opened up under their reforms. New Orleans has extensive survey evidence of parent satisfaction.

20. For evidence that elements of decentralization initiatives persist and accumulate over time despite political and governance changes, see Charles Taylor Kerchner et al., *Learning from L.A.: Institutional Change in American Public Education* (Cambridge, MA: Harvard Education Press, 2009).

21. See, for example, a report by Tulane University's Cowen Institute: *Managing Innovation: Models for Governing the System of Public Schools in New Orleans* (New Orleans: The Cowen Institute, 2010).

Chapter 2

1. We're grateful for the research and editing support provided by Research for Action research assistants, Jesse Gottschalk and Deborah Good, and interns Maggie Larson, Katherine Saviskas, and Matthew Tossman, who assisted with coding the data. Henig is listed as first author to reflect the role he played in coordinating and integrating the process but each of the coauthors made substantial contributions to this article, and the others are listed in alphabetical order.

2. Quoted in Elissa Gootman, "1,200 Parents Prepare to Take on Role as Paid Liaisons in Schools," *New York Times*, August 21, 2003, http://www.nytimes.com/2003/08/21/nyregion/1200-parents-prepare-to-take-on-role-as-paid-liaisons-in-schools.html

3. Dan Jacoby, Democracy for New York City, testimony at the Public Hearing on the Governance of the New York City School District, Queens, January 29, 2009.

4. Beginning more than a year before the planned legislative action, we were engaged in a major research project on the political dynamics around the mayoral control debate. The study, commissioned by the Donors Education Collaborative (DEC), focused especially on the Campaign for Better Schools, a coalition of organizations it had helped to get off the ground in the hopes of ensuring that the governance debates would include a broad range of voices. The purpose of the study was to examine DEC's strategy of support for collaboration among grassroots, advocacy, policy, and research groups to affect education policy, using the Campaign and the mayoral control debate as the lens through which to assess its grantmaking. For that project, which is distinct from and begun prior to our research specifically for this chapter, we conducted ninety-one interviews with a variety of actors, observers, and policy makers and forty-four observations of events and meetings. In addition, we reviewed relevant documents and closely tracked media coverage of the groups, individuals, and issues involved in the mayoral control debate and legislative negotiations.

5. Dennis Walcott, testimony at the Public Hearing on the Governance of the New York City School District, Queens, January 29, 2009.

6. Richard Pérez-Peña, "Albany Backs Mayoral Rule Over Schools," *New York Times*, June 11, 2002, http://www.nytimes.com/2002/06/11/nyregion/albany-backs-mayoral-rule-over-schools.html?pagewanted=1.

7. Michael Bloomberg, speech at the New York Urban League's Dr. Martin Luther King, Jr., Symposium, January 15, 2003.

8. Benjamin R. Barber, *Strong Democracy: Participatory Politics for a New Age* (Berkeley, CA: University of California Press, 2004).

9. Marion Orr, "Community Organizing and the Changing Ecology of Civic Engagement," in *Transforming the City: Community Organizing and the Challenge of Political Change*, ed. Marion Orr (Lawrence, KS: University Press of Kansas, 2007), 1–27.

10. Marion Orr and John Rogers, eds., *Public Engagement for Public Education* (Palo Alto, CA: Stanford University Press, 2010).

11. Lydia Segal, "The Pitfalls of Political Decentralization and Proposals for Reform: The Case of New York City Public Schools," *Public Administration Review* 57, no. 2 (1997):141–149.

12. Ibid.

13. Anemona Hartocollis and Yilu Zhao, "School Boards on the Wane, But Not Without Some Regrets," *New York Times*, June 12, 2002, http://www.nytimes.com/2002/06/12/nyregion/school-boards-on-the-wane-but-not-without-some-regrets.html.

14. Barber, *Strong Democracy*.

15. In 1996, Chancellor Crew formed a new Office of Parent Advocacy and Engagement, later renamed Office of Parent and Community Affairs (OPCA), staffed by seven parent coordinators and with an annual budget of approximately $600,000. In 2000, Chancellor Levy replaced the OPCA with a revamped Office of Parent Advocacy and Engagement (OPAE), in an effort to increase parental involvement and to better respond to parents' problems. Laura Williams, "Crew's New Office Aims to Get Parents Involved," *New York Daily News,* October 14, 1996, http://www.nydailynews.com/archives/news/1996/10/14/1996-10-14_crew_s_new_office_aims_to_ge.html; Carl Campanile, "Levy Expels Board's Chief Parent Liaison," *New York Post,* September 19, 2000, http://www.nypost.com/p/news/levy_expels_board_chief_parent_liaison_c4CDJpKmOgoRXho3S5qodN; and *New York Post,* "No Excuse for Absent Parents," November 9, 2000, http://www.nydailynews.com/archives/opinions/2000/11/09/2000_11_09_no_excuse_for_absent_parents.html.

16. Ibid, Williams, "Crew's New Office Aims to Get Parents Involved"; Campinile, "Levy Expels Board's Chief Parents Liaison"; and *New York Post,* "No Excuse for Absent Parents"; Interview with DOE official, April 2010.

17. Budget figure from *Office for Family Engagement and Advocacy Annual Report 2008–2009,*New York City Department of Education, 2009. Estimate of staffing from interview with DOE official, April 2010.

18. Gootman, "1,200 Parents Prepare to Take on Role as Paid Liaisons in Schools."

19. Interview with DOE official, April 2010; Walcott, testimony, January 29, 2009.

20. Martine Guerrier, testimony at the Public Hearing on the Governance of the New York City School District, Queens, January 29, 2009.

21. City of New York. *Mayor's Management Report:Preliminary Fiscal, 2010*, http://www.nyc.gov/html/ops/downloads/pdf/2010_mmr/0210_idf.pdf.

22. The three reports, all issued by the Office of the Public Advocate, are: Betsy Gotbaum,*Waiting for Your Call . . . : A Survey of New York City Department of Education Parent Coordinators* (New York: Office of the Public Advocate of New York City, 2003), http://publicadvocategotbaum.com/new_policy/waiting_for_call.html; Betsy Gotbaum, *Still Waiting for your Call. . . : A Follow-Up Survey of New York City Department of Education* (New York: Office of the Public Advocate of New York City, 2004), http://www.nyc.gov/html/records/pdf/govpub/2697still_waiting_for_your_call.pdf; and Betsy Gotbaum, *Is Anybody Listening? A Follow-Up Survey of New York City Department of Education Parent Coordinators* (New York: Office of the Public Advocate of New York City, 2008), http://nyc.gov/html/records/pdf/govpub/moved/pubadvocate/2008ParentCoordinatorReportfinal.pdf.

23. Interview with DOE official, April 2010.

24. New York City Department of Education, *Office for Family Engagement and Advocacy Annual Report 2008–2009* (New York: New York City Department of Education, 2009).

25. Interview with DOE official, April 2010.

26. There are about 1.1 million students with about 1.8 to 2 million parents, but some families have multiple children in the system. The 35 percent estimate here uses as its denominator the same estimate of number of families used by DOE in presenting response rates to its annual parent survey (848,500).

27. Interview with DOE official, April 2010; interview with DOE official, May 2010.

28. City of New York, *Mayor's Management Report*, 2009, http://www.nyc.gov/html/ops/downloads/pdf/2010_mmr/0910_mmr.pdf.

29. Walcott, testimony, January 29, 2009.

30. We were told that this is something that may be done in future years.

31. New York City Department of Education, *New York City School Survey: 2009 Citywide Results* (New York: New York City Department of Education, 2009).

32. According to a recent report by the city's Independent Budget Office, more than two-thirds of the city's charter schools are located in public school buildings, and the IBO calculated public support for charter schools in 2008–2009 at $16,373 per pupil for schools in DOE buildings and $13,661 for those not in DOE buildings. New York City Independent Budget Office, "Fiscal Brief: Comparing the Level of Public Support: Charter Schools Versus Traditional Public Schools" February 2010.

33. Interview with DOE official, May 2010.

34. Joel Klein, testimony at the Manhattan Borough Senate Hearing, February, 2009; Garth Harries, testimony at the Aspen Institute NCLB Turnaround Committee, Howard University. Washington, DC, September 2, 2009.

35. Jess Wisloski, "Parent Groups Playing Hooky," *New York Daily News*, May 5, 2008, http://www.nydaily news.com/ny_local/queens/2008/05/06/2008-05-06_parents_groups_playing_hooky_.html.

36. In addition to leadership structures listed below, the state has mandated the establishment of the perhaps more traditional parental involvement structures of parent associations or parent-teacher associations at each school, and requires the principal to consult with these groups regularly on issues related to curriculum, budget, discipline, safety, food services, and special programs.

37. Office of the New York City Comptroller, "Powerless Parents," New York City Comptroller's Office, May 20, 2009, http://www.comptroller.nyc.gov/bureaus/opm/reports/05-20-09_powerless-parents.pdf

38. DOE official, telephone conversation, October 5, 2010.

39. "Regulation of the Chancellor, Number A-655, 2010," New York City Department of Education, http://schools.nyc.gov/NR/rdonlyres/381F4607-7841-4D28-B7D5-0F30DDB77DFA/82007/A655FINAL1.pdf.

40. Dennis Walcott, as quoted in Gail Robinson, "Hanging Up on Parents?" *Gotham Gazette*, May 22, 2006, http://www.gothamgazette.com/print/1860.

41. "Citywide and Community Education Councils, 2010," New York City Department of Education, http://schools.nyc.gov/Offices/CEC/default.htm.

42. Wisloski,"Parent Groups Playing Hooky"; Richard Gentilviso, "Community Education Council Election Process Begins," *Queens Gazette*, March 4, 2009, http://www.qgazette.com/news/2009-03-04/Front_Page/Community_EducationCouncilElection_Process_Begins.html; Julie Bosman, "A Lack of Interest (and Candidates) in New System's School Parent Councils," *New York Times*, April 28, 2007, http://www.nytimes.com/2007/04/28/nyregion/28schools.html; and Guerrier, testimony, January 29, 2009.

43. Jennifer Freeman, "CEC Q&A: Promoting Democracy at Home," http://insideschools.org/blog/?url=http://insideschools.org/blog/2009/02/23/cec-elections-promoting-democracy-at-home/.

44. Rachel Monahan and Meredith Kolodner, "Number of Candidates for New York City School Council Races Plunges,"*Daily News*, April 7, 2010.

45. Some of the city's enlistment of intermediary organizations is traceable to the New Century High School Initiative funded by the Bill and Melinda Gates Foundation, and the Carnegie Corporation of New York, among others, and begun under previous administrations. New Visions, one of the most important of the intermediary groups, was formed at this time. For background on how the Bloomberg/Klein administration drew these groups more directly into a school support role, see Jonathan Gyurko and Jeffrey Henig, "NYC: Strong Vision, Learning by Doing, or the Politics of Muddling Through?," in *Between Public and Private: Politics, Governance, and the New Portfolio Models for Urban School Reform*, eds. Katrina E. Bulkley, Jeffrey R. Henig, and Henry M. Levin (Cambridge, MA: Harvard Education Press, 2010); and Talbert, chapter 6 in this volume.

46. The DOE reports that it has now assigned a point person to each cluster in an effort to encourage more engagement efforts (DOE official, telephone conversation. October 5, 2010).

47. Interview with DOE official, January 2010.

48. Interview with former state official, August 2008.

49. Mark S. Weprin, quoted in Jennifer Medina and Elissa Gootman, "Campaign to Keep Schools Under Mayor's Thumb," *New York Times*, September 1, 2008, http://www.nytimes.com/2008/09/02/nyregion/02control.html?_r=1&scp=1&sq=Campaign%20to%20keep%20schools%20under%20mayors%20thumb&st=cse.

50. Much of the original data collection for the sections on the mayoral control battle was undertaken as part of the two-year study Research for Action, in collaboration with Professor Jeffrey Henig of Teachers College, conducted of the Campaign for Better Schools for the Donors' Education Collaborative (DEC). For more detailed accounts, see report series: Eva Gold et al., *The Campaign for Better Schools: Building a Coalition, Gaining Recognition and Forging a Platform to Influence the Terms of the Mayoral Control Debate in NYC, May 2008–May 2009* (Philadelphia: Research for Action, 2009); and Eva Gold et al., *The Campaign for Better Schools: Outcomes of the Mayoral Control Debate—Changes to NYC School Governance Legislation and Long-Term Effects, May 2009–May 2010* (Philadelphia: Research for Action, 2010).

51. Geoffrey Canada, "Accountability = Achievement, Says Top Children's Advocate," *New York Daily News*, November 22, 2008, http://www.nydaily news.com/opinions/2008/11/23/2008-11-23_accountability__achievement_says_top_chi.html.

52. Carl Campanile, "Gates $4 Mil Lesson Aided School Control," *N.Y. Post*, August 18, 2009, http://www.nypost.com/p/news/regional/item_ekjA6OeXIrxZjDATHPbkuJ.

53. Jesse Gottschalk, *Addendum to Year 2 Report: The Mayoral Debate and the Media: The Campaign for Better Schools and other Actors in the Public Lens, September 2008–May 2010* (Philadelphia: Research for Action, 2010).

54. Interview with journalist, October, 2009.

55. Interview with journalist, October, 2009.

56. Parent Commission on School Governance and Mayoral Control. *Recommendations on School Governance.* (New York: author, March 2009).

57. Gottschalk, *Addendum to Year 2 Report.*

58. For more information on the recommendations of the Parent Commission, see: http:\\parentcommission.org/parent_commission_Final_Report.pdf.

59. Interview with journalist, October, 2009.

60. Eva Gold et al., *The Campaign for Better Schools: Building a Coalition*; Gold et al., *The Campaign for Better Schools: Outcomes of the Mayoral Control Debate*; and Gottschalk, *Addendum to Year 2 Report.*

61. Interview with local official, October 2009. See endnote 3 for a description of the research and interviews.

62. Interview with DOE Official, April, 2010.

63. Including students was and still is important to some members of the coalition. In subsequent discussions, this center has beenmore often referred to as simply a "parent training center." We use that shorthand in the remainder of this chapter.

64. For a much fuller analysis of the question of who won and who lost, see Gold et al., *The Campaign for Better Schools: Outcomes of the Mayoral Control Debate.*

65. Elizabeth Benjamin,"Liu Will Audit DOE's 'Musical Chairs' School Closures," *New York Daily News*, January 28, 2010, http://www.nydailynews.com/blogs/dailypolitics/2010/01/liu-will-audit-does-musical-ch.html.

66. Sharon Otterman, "Judge Blocks Closing of 19 New York City Schools," *New York Times*, March 26, 2010, http://www.nytimes.com/2010/03/27/nyregion/27close.html.

67. Our charaterization of leaders' thinking is based on multiple interviews and observation of Campaign meetings.

68. *New York Times*, "Profile of New York City Voters," November 4, 2009, http://www.nytimes.com/interactive/2009/11/04/nyregion/1104-ny-exit-poll.html.

69. Javier C. Hernandez and Sharon Otterman, "Education Chief Raises Doubts on Pick by Bloomberg," *New York Times*, November 23, 2010. http://www.nytimes.com/2010/11/24/nyregion/24waiver.html.

Chapter 3

We thank Elizabeth Debraggio and Lila Nazar de Jaucourt for their excellent assistance on all parts of this paper, Margaret Goertz and James Wyckoff for helpful comments, William Duncombe for his generous assistance with the state data, and Meryle Weinstein for her extraordinary help with the city data. We appreciate the help and feedback from the New York City Department of Education, Jennifer O'Day, Catherine Bitter, and participants in the Spring Workshop. We alone, however, are responsible for the content of this chapter.

1. Throughout this paper, we refer to 2002–2008 as the *Bloomberg years* and compare these against an earlier time period from 1996 (or 1997) to 2001. While data are available over a longer period for district revenues, they are not for intradistrict (NYC school level) expenditures, and the years were chosen to include both data sets.

2. Our intention is to provide an overview of the primary resources available during Bloomberg's first two terms and the primary drivers of spending as we see them. Thus, we note trends for significant categories of overall resources, but do not focus on smaller categories. We add endnotes when we are aware of a different perspective by the DOE.

3. Unless otherwise indicated, we report dollar figures adjusted for inflation to 2008 dollars.

4. DOE schools do not include charter or nonpublic providers of special education services.

5. New York State Constitution, Article XI, Section 1.

6. Hawaii is the only unitary school district in the nation. All funds flow from the state department of education to schools. See http://www.k12research.com/HawaiiSchoolDistrictContacts.html.

7. The federal share has grown over time in all regions, but is lowest in the Northeast, attributable in part to the federal reliance on poverty-based funding formulae and the relative wealth of the region.

8. We weight all of the district numbers in New York State by the proportion of the state's students in each district to reflect the disparity in the size of districts.

9. Some of these factors would yield ongoing inflows of funds, and some would be received for a finite period of time.

10. Campaign for Fiscal Equity, "*CFE v. State of New York*: A Chronology," http://www.cfequity.org/static. php?page=chronologyoflawsuit&category=resources.

11. The *CFE v. State of New York* ruling was overturned by the Appellate Court in 2002 before the Court of Appeals reversed the Appellate Court's decision in 2003.

12. Adjusted to 2008 using the Consumer Price Index (CPI).

We define pupil numbers using the Duplicated Combined Adjusted Average Daily Membership (DCAADM) used by the New York State Department of Education, which states that this pupil count is the best count of the number of students receiving their educational program at district expense. DCAADM includes the average daily membership (ADM) of students enrolled in district programs (including half-day kindergarten pupils weighted at 0.5); plus equivalent secondary attendance of students under twenty-one years of age who are not on a regular day school register; plus pupils with disabilities attending Boards of Cooperative Educational Services (BOCES) full time; plus pupils with disabilities in approved private school programs, including state schools at Rome and Batavia; plus resident students for whom the district pays tuition to another school district; plus incarcerated youth. Beginning with the 1999–2000 school year, pupils resident to the district but attending a charter school are included. Beginning with the 2007–2008 school year, students attending full-day pre-K are weighted at 1.0; half-day pre-K students are weighted at 0.5. Since residents attending other districts were also included in the CAADM count of the receiving district, this pupil count is a duplicated count.

The other districts include the other *Big Four* (Buffalo, Rochester, Syracuse, and Yonkers), all of which are fiscally stressed, along with rural districts with their own issues, and relatively wealthy suburban districts. These are averaged out in the rest of New York State numbers. Although New York City is only one of approximately seven hundred school districts in New York State, the city educates about one-third of the state's students.

13. Total revenue includes all monies available to a district for the General Fund, Special Aid Fund, and Debt Service Fund.

14. Regression models estimating growth rates for NYC and the rest of the state are not shown, but are available upon request from the authors. These show that the differences are statistically significant.

15. Chris Plotts and Jennifer Sable, *Characteristics of the 100 Largest Public Elementary and Secondary School Districts in the United States: 2007–08*, (NCES document no. 2010-349, Washington, DC: U.S. Government Printing Office, 2010).

16. These per pupil expenditures differ slightly from the state number reported above due to different sources and definitions of expenditures and revenues. Each source is consistent across districts within the source.

17. In part, this low share may be related to the concept of *municipal overburden*, whereby local tax bases may be insufficient to cover the high costs of providing public services in urban areas with large shares of high-need populations. See, for example, Jay M. Stein, "Distributing 'Municipal Overburden' Aid to School Districts," *Urban Education* 14, no. 2 (1979): 205–220; Harvey Brazer and Therese McCarty, "Municipal Overburden: An Empirical Analysis," *Economics of Education Review* 5, no. 4 (1986): 353–361; Harvey Brazer and Therese McCarty, "Municipal Overburden: A Fact in School Finance Litigation?" *Journal of Law and Education* 18, no. 4 (1989): 547–566; and James Knickman and Andrew Reschovsky, "Municipal Overburden: Its Measurement and Role in School Finance Reform" (working paper, National Institute of Education, Washington, DC, 1981). As in many municipalities, the NYC school district is fiscally dependent on the city for local funds and must compete for tax revenues with other needs for public services. Previously the city followed the Stavinsky-Goodman statue (which was intended to protect against disproportionate cuts in school funding). As of 2002 the city was required to meet "maintenance of effort" provisions outlined in Section 2576 of the New York State Education Law, which the city has done successfully. Thus, the city is in compliance with state laws in terms of the local share of revenues.

18. Ross Rubenstein, Amy Ellen Schwartz, Leanna Stiefel, and Hella Bel Hadj Amor, "From Districts to Schools: The Distribution of Resources across Schools in Big City School Districts," *Economics of Education Review* 26, no. 5 (2007): 532–545.

19. See, for example, Margaret Goertz and Leanna Stiefel, "Introduction to School-Level Resource Allocation in Urban Public Schools," *Journal of Education Finance* 23, no. 4 (1998): 435–446; and Leanna Stiefel, Ross Rubenstein, and Robert Berne, "Intra-District Equity in Four Large Cities: Methods, Data, and Results," *Journal of Education Finance* 23, no. 4 (1998): 447–467 for evidence from Chicago and Rochester.

20. Bruce D. Baker, "Within District Resource Allocation and the Marginal Costs of Providing Equal Educational Opportunity: Evidence from Texas and Ohio," *Education Policy Analysis Archives* 17, no. 3 (2009):1–31.

21. See, for example, Marigee Bacolod, "Who Teaches and Where They Choose to Teach: College Graduates of the 1990s," *Educational Evaluation and Policy Analysis* 29, no. 3 (2007): 155–168; Charles Clotfelter, Helen F. Ladd, and Jacob Vigdor, "Who Teaches Whom? Race and the Distribution of Novice Teachers," *Economics of Education Review* 24, no. 4 (2005): 377–392; Eric A. Hanushek, John F. Kain, and Steven G. Rivkin, "Why Public Schools Lose Teachers," *Journal of Human Resources* 9, no. 2 (2004): 326–354; Kirabo C. Jackson, "Student Demographics, Teacher Sorting, and Teacher Quality: Evidence from the End of School Desegregation," *Journal of Labor Economics* 27, no. 2 (2009): 213–256; and Ross Rubenstein et al., "From Districts to Schools: The Distribution of Resources Across Schools in Big City School Districts," *Economics of Education Review* 26, no. 5 (2007): 532–545.

22. Marguerite Roza and Paul T. Hill, "How Within-District Spending Inequities Help Some Schools to Fail," in *Brookings Papers on Education Policy*, ed. Diane Ravitch (Washington, DC: Brookings Institution Press, 2004).

23. Thomas B. Fordham Institute, "Fund the Child: Tackling Inequity and Antiquity in School Finance" (Washington, DC: Thomas B. Fordham Institute, 2006).

24. Jay G. Chambers, Jesse D. Levin, and Larisa Shambaugh, "Exploring Weighted Student Formulas as a Policy for Improving Equity for Distributing Resources to Schools: A Case Study of Two California School Districts," *Economics of Education Review* 29, (2010): 283–300; and Roza and Hill, "How Within-District Spending Inequities Help Some Schools to Fail."

25. This district was formed by New York City Schools Chancellor Rudy Crew to focus on improving the performance of the lowest-performing public schools, which were geographically dispersed across the city.

26. Program mandates include, for example, the requirement that federal Title 1 money serves poor students. An oft-cited budget constraint in schools is the need to fund teacher positions already in existence.

27. New York City Department of Education. "Fair Student Funding: Fair Funding for All," January 2007, http://www.edpriorities.org/Info/CityBudget/Fair_Funding-WEB.pdf.

28. New York City Department of Education "School Based Expenditure Reports" are accessible at: https://www.nycenet.edu/offices/d_chanc_oper/budget/exp01/OLD_YEARS.asp. These reports are nearly unique among large districts, most of which are located in states that do not produce such reports. Some states, such as Texas, Ohio, and Florida, have such reports for all districts in their states—including, of course, the large ones.

29. Central administration expenditures are not part of direct expenditures. They account for a very small share of total expenditures (2.2 percent in 2002 and 1.6 percent in 2008). School administration costs, defined broadly to include not only principals and assistant principals, but also secretaries and support staff, are part of direct costs and are higher (8.2 percent of total expenditures in 2008), but have remained fairly constant over time—increasing only 0.2 percent from 2002.

30. See, for example, Julie Cullen, "The Impact of Fiscal Incentives on Student Disability Rates," *Journal of Public Economics* 87, no.7 (2003): 1557–1559. See also the appendix for a description in broad terms of changes in the provision of special education under Bloomberg.

31. In conversations and related correspondence with the DOE they made clear that these funds (pass-throughs) absorbed some of the growth in available revenues and, thus, that the "significant increase in revenues to the NYC school *system* was [not] fully bestowed upon DOE public school students." (Photeine Anagnostopoulos, chief operating officer; Stephanie Lawkins, executive director, Office of Data & Reporting; Susan Olds, executive director, Financial Strategies Group; and Dominique West, director of operations, conference call and related e-mail correspondence with authors. July 29, 2010.) We present per pupil expenditures excluding pass-throughs for total, direct services to schools and classroom instruction, which provide a more accurate portrait of the dollars going to DOE public school students.

32. Regional costs include instructional support and administration, sabbaticals, leaves, and additions to regular salary; systemwide costs include central instructional support and central administration; and systemwide obligations include debt service and retiree benefits.

The DOE notes that during the Bloomberg years the "financial growth rate of the schools actually lagged the growth rate in the overall financial condition of the department" (Anagnostopoulos, Lawkins, Olds, and West, July 29, 2010.) Our intention is not to examine the validity of these claims.

33. Correctly, the DOE states that a significant share of the increase in direct expenditures was not spent inside the classroom (42 percent of the increase in direct services to schools is captured by the increase in

classroom instruction) and over three-quarters of the money that did go into classrooms went to teachers ($1.1 of the $1.4 billion increase or 77 percent). (Anagnostopoulos, Lawkins, Olds, and West, July 29, 2010.) Renegotiating teacher contracts, however, was a policy decision and our purpose is to descriptively detail the entirety of Bloomberg and Klein's policies.

An additional 20 percent of the increase in direct expenditures is explained by the $646 million (or 122 percent) increase in related services.

34. This increase is an average over all levels of teacher experience and education. Note that average salaries reflect both increases in the salary scale and changes in the composition of the teaching staff. See Goertz, Loeb, and Wyckoff (chapter 7) in this volume, for more information on salary trends before and during Children First.

35. In some sense, these regressions may be best viewed as capturing the ex post distribution—in the sense that they measure the association of each characteristic, holding the others constant, with resource distributions. The regressions do not reveal ex ante intentions or causality, of course, and there are many other factors that might (and undoubtedly do) influence resource distributions across schools. If our interest were in estimating the *causal impact* of these factors on resources, then we might be concerned that their exclusion might lead to bias in the estimates. In this context, however, our interest is to provide *descriptive analyses* and, specifically, to analyze how and in what way resources vary with the FSF characteristics identified as appropriate factors for resource distribution.

36. The fifth quintile is the highest-poverty quintile.

37. Sensitivity analyses show that regression results do not differ when using total versus direct per pupil expenditure (results available from authors).

38. Specifically, we see that direct expenditures per pupil increased $3,962 between 2001 and 2008 for schools in the lowest poverty quintile in 2001. Direct expenditures for schools in the highest-poverty quintile in 2001, however, increased nearly $5,273. The differences in growth between schools in the fourth and fifth poverty quintiles are not statistically different from each other. That is, it is likely that the difference in the magnitude of the increase between schools in the top two poverty quintiles in 2001 is the result of sampling or other statistical error.

39. These results are not shown, but are available from the authors.

40. Performance in high school is measured by the percent failing the math Regents (typically taken in ninth or tenth grade). While FSF uses a student's eighth-grade test scores to determine whether he/she qualifies for the achievement need weight, we note that these test scores (eighth grade and early Regents) are correlated.

41. Results for the interacted coefficients are discussed, but not shown. These are available from the authors.

42. In other words, while schools with larger shares of poor students had higher pupil-teacher ratios in 2008 (controlling for other school-level FSF factors), higher-poverty-quintile schools in 2001 experienced a larger decrease in pupil-teacher ratios than those in lower quintiles. This occurs because the regressions control for characteristics other than poverty that are correlated with poverty, while the quintile analyses do not control for these factors.

43. The poverty weight is negative.

44. The Fund for Public Schools, 2005 Annual Report, "Private Investment in Public Education: Supporting Change in NYC," http://schools.nyc.gov/fundforpublicschools/.

45. Ibid.

46. Jennifer Bell-Ellwanger (New York City DOE); Liz Larson (The Fund for Public Schools); and Susan Olds (Executive Director, Financial Strategies Group), e-mail correspondence with authors, October 7, 2010.

47. The Fund also raised initial support to test or launch other initiatives that have been subsequently scaled up, including the Quality Review pilot program, the ARIS information system, and the Children First Networks. Additionally, the Fund raised money to support projects designed to revamp dated or inefficient DOE infrastructure, such as an overhaul of the Division of Human Resources ("Project Home Run"), with close to $7 million in support from The Broad Foundation, the Michael and Susan Dell Foundation, the Bill and Melinda Gates Foundation, and the Robertson Foundation.

48. For example, in 2004, the Fund partnered with *Real Simple* magazine for Get Organized New York, a citywide tag sale raising over $500,000. Other public awareness efforts have included the Shop for Public Schools initiative and the 2007–2009 "Keep it Going NYC" campaign. See The Fund for Public Schools 2008 Annual Report, "A Shared Investment. Unlimited Returns," http://schools.nyc.gov/fundforpublicschools/.

49. The Fund for Public Schools 2008 Annual Report, "A Shared Investment. Unlimited Returns," http://schools.nyc.gov/fundforpublicschools/.

50. These categories are listed in the following places on the 990 forms. Part I: Revenues, Expenses and Changes in Net Assets or Fund Balances and Part II: Statement of Functional Expenses.

51. To be clear, we relied only on publicly available information, such as printed documents and Web resources. Future work might profitably explore this topic more fully by engaging more directly with funders and support organizations.

52. http://www.gatesfoundation.org.

53. "Robin Hood: Targeting Poverty in New York City," Robin Hood Foundation, http://www.robinhood.org/home.aspx.

54. School-based fund raising (or revenue enhancement) efforts can take a variety of forms beyond the archetypal bake sale—and the amounts are nontrivial. As an example, the *New York Times* reports that for years, public school parents across the city raised hundreds of thousands of dollars to independently hire teaching assistants and aides, although in 2009 Bloomberg put restrictions on this practice, requiring that such hires be done only with school principal input.In another example, P.S. 6, the Lillie Devereaux Blake School on the Upper East Side, raised funds for a new library by hosting an alumni benefit with tickets priced up to $300, and supplemented city funding for a green roof with a $200,000 fundraising drive. In 2007, the P.S. 6 Parent Teacher Association filed a 990 form reporting over $500,000 in contributions. As a final example, in 2008 the Alumni Foundation of Brooklyn Tech received over $1.5 million dollars in contributions in addition to announcing a campaign to raise $21 million from alumni by 2013. While overall this money represents a tiny fraction when compared with the total DOE budget, it is nevertheless illustrative of the often unaccounted for additional funding available to select schools across the city. Other efforts aim to enhance receipt of public funds. At Stuyvesant High School, when faced with budget cuts, parents successfully organized a "full force campaign" encouraging eligible students to enroll and participate in the free and reduced-price lunch program. The school expects to receive an additional $1.5 million in Title 1 funds for the 2010–2011 school year.

55. In fact, budgets have already begun to shrink by 2010.

56. See the appendix for more information.

57. "Special Education Resources," Advocates for Children, http://www.advocatesforchildren.org/resource/specialnyc.php3.

58. Thomas Hehir et al., *Comprehensive Management Review and Evaluation of Special Education* (submitted to the New York City Department of Education, 2005).

59. The term *general education* refers to the curriculum, not the classroom placement.

60. New York City Department of Education, "A Guide to Special Education Services for School-Age Children," http://schools.nyc.gov/Academics/SpecialEducation/KeyDocuments/default.htm.

Chapter 4

We are especially grateful to the Public Education Leadership Project of Harvard Business School and Harvard Graduate School of Education for their support of this work and to Rebecca Holcombe for her research assistance. Portions of this paper are adapted from Stacey Childress and Tonika C. Clayton, *Focusing on Results at the New York City Department of Education* (Cambridge, MA: Public Education Leadership Project at Harvard University, PEL-054, Harvard Business Publishing, 2007). All direct quotes from Joel Klein, Jim Liebman, and other NYCDOE staff are from this piece unless otherwise noted.

1. Penny Bender Sebring and Anthony S. Bryk, "School Leadership and the Bottom Line in Chicago," *Phi Delta Kappan* 81, no. 6 (2000): 440.

2. Quote from Arlene Ackerman in Stacey Childress and Jennifer M. Seusse, *Star Schools Initiative at the San Francisco Unified School District* (Cambridge, MA: Public Education Leadership Project at Harvard University, PEL-039, Harvard Business Publishing, 2006).

3. Brian A. Jacob, "Accountability, Incentives and Behavior: The Impact of High-Stakes Testing in the Chicago Public Schools," *Journal of Public Economics* 89, no. 5–6 (2005): 761–796.

4. For an overview of the relevant work of Ouchi, Hill, and Barber see: William G. Ouchi and Lydia G. Segal, *Making Schools Work: A Revolutionary Plan to Get Your Children the Education they Need* (New York: Simon & Schuster, 2003); Paul Hill et al., *Portfolio School Districts for Big Cities: An Interim Report* (Seattle: Center on Reinventing Public Education, 2008), http://www.crpe.org/cs/crpe/download/csr_files/pub_psdp_interim_oct09.pdf; and Michael Barber, *Instruction to Deliver: Fighting to Transform Britain's Public Services* (London: Methuen, 2008).

5. The number of schools grew to nearly 1,500 by 2009, fueled by new charter schools and the new small high schools that launched to replace large comprehensive high schools. Existing single high schools were often replaced by four to six smaller schools, contributing to the rapid growth in the absolute number of schools.

6. Diane Ravitch, "The UFT Agreement," *New York Sun*, October 4, 2005, http://www.nysun.com/opinion/uft-agreement/20949

7. See, for example, Kenneth Leithwood, Lawrence Leonard, and Lyn Sharratt, "Conditions Fostering Organizational Learning in Schools," *Education Administration Quarterly* 34, no. 2 (1998): 243–276.

8. Chrysan Gallucci, "Districtwide Instructional Reform: Using Sociocultural Theory to Link Professional Learning to Organizational Support," *American Journal of Education* 114, no. 4 (2008): 541–581.

9. James March and Herbert Simon, *Organizations* (New York: Wiley, 1958.

10. See, for example, Daniel A. Levinthal and James G. March, "The Myopia of Learning," *Strategic Management Journal* 14, (Winter 1993): 95–112; and Levitt and March, "Organizational Learning."

11. Meredith I. Honig, "District Central Offices as Learning Organizations: How Sociocultural and Organizational Learning Theories Elaborate District Central Office Administrators' Participation in Teaching and Learning Improvement Efforts," *American Journal of Education* 114, no. 4 (2008): 627–664.

12. See for example, Lev S. Vygotsky, *Mind in Society: The Development of Higher Psychological Processes*, ed. Michael Cole (Cambridge: Harvard University Press, 1978); and James V. Wertsch, "A Sociocultural Approach to Socially Shared Cognition," in *Perspectives on Socially Shared Cognition*, eds. Lauren B. Resnick, John M. Levine, and Stephanie D. Teasley (Hyattsville, MD: American Psychological Association, 1996): 85–100.

13. For example, see Knapp, "How Can Organizational and Sociocultural Learning Theories Shed Light on District Instructional Reform?"; and Honig, "District Central Offices as Learning Organizations.".

14. David A. Garvin, Amy C. Edmondson, and Francesca Gino, "Is Yours a Learning Organization?" *Harvard Business Review* 86, no. 3 (2008): 109–116; and Amy C. Edmondson, "Psychological Safety and Learning Behavior in Work Teams," *Administrative Science Quarterly* 44, no. 2 (1999): 350–383.

15. O'Day, "Complexity, Accountability, and School Improvement."

16. Richard F. Elmore, *School Reform from the Inside Out: Policy, Practice, and Performance* (Cambridge, MA: Harvard Education Press, 2004).

17. E-mail from Richard Elmore to author, June 3, 2010. For more Elmore on accountability, see "When Accountability Knocks, Will Anyone Answer?"and "Building a New Structure for School Leadership," both in Elmore, *School Reform from the Inside Out*.

18. Amy C. Edmondson, "The Competitive Imperative of Learning." *Harvard Business Review* 86, no. 7 (Jul, 2008): 60–67.

19. For a more technical explanation of the calculation of the various subsections and overall Progress Report grade, see the NYCDOE website "Educator Guide: The New York City Progress Report—High School," 2009, http://schools.nyc.gov/NR/rdonlyres/EEE6AEBC-9576-4AED-A176-CE24FA43245B/0/Educator-Guide_HS_1104092.pdf.

20. Shael Polakow-Suransky, *In Defense of High School Progress Reports: Responding to Readers' Comments* (Gotham Schools, 2009), http://gothamschools.org/2009/11/25/responding-to-readers-comments/#more-28138.

21. Shael Polakow-Suransky, conversation with authors, June 17, 2010.

22. For a nontechnical overview of Koretz's criticism, see his guest blog on Eduwonkette from September 17, 2008, *Guest Blogger Daniel Koretz on New York City's Progress Reports*, http://blogs.edweek.org/edweek/eduwonkette/2008/09/guest_blogger_daniel_koretz_on_1.html.

23. New York City Independent Budget Office, "The School Accountability Initiative: Totaling the Cost," 2010, http://www.ibo.nyc.ny.us/iboreports/Schoolaccountability111308.pdf.

24. Edmondson, "The Competitive Imperative of Learning."

25. The eigenvalue for the first component was 2.48, while the second component eigenvalue was well below the 1.0 cutoff point at 0.31. Cronbach's alpha for these three items was 0.89, indicating strong internal reliability. The items were not standardized or weighted, since standard deviations were similar across the three items (0.75 to 0.92), and PCA eigenvectors were nearly identical (0.57 to 0.59). This allowed us to preserve the original scale of this measure for ease of interpretation.

26. O'Day, "Complexity, Accountability, and School Improvement."

27. Results from the PCA indicated that these seven items tap into a single construct, with the first component eigenvalue at 4.71, while the second component eigenvalue was 0.95. Cronbach's alpha showed a strong internal reliability, with a value of 0.92. As with the psychological safety items, PCA weights were not used (eigenvectors ranged from 0.33 to 0.40) and items were not standardized (standard deviations ranged from 0.63 to 0.77).

28. Pearson's r for the psychological safety and accountability variables is 0.69.

29. Notes on the performance measures employed in these preliminary analyses: (a) We used the overall progress report score (a grade of A–F) that each school receives each year. (b) We used the 2007–2008 QR scores because only approximately 30 percent of the schools got 2008–2009 QRs (if a school got an overall Progress Report grade of B or better and a *proficient* or better on their 2007–2008 QR, they were not reviewed

in 2008–2009). The QR scores were based on a 1 to 5 scale, which we reverse-coded so that 5 = excellent and 1 = underprepared (of which there was only 1 school in our sample). (c) Both the progress and performance scores are complex calculations made by the district; we have included the min/max to the side in case this is helpful for contextualizing.

30. Stacey Childress, Richard Elmore, Allen Grossman, and Caroline King, *Note on the PELP Coherence Framework* (Cambridge, MA: Public Education Leadership Project at Harvard University, PEL-010, Harvard Business Publishing, revised 2007), http://cb.hbsp.harvard.edu/cb/web/product_detail. seam?R=PEL010-PDF-ENG&conversationId=143801&E=70507.

Chapter 5

We are grateful to the many NYC stakeholders and reform participants who shared their experiences and viewpoints about the instructional reforms during interviews for this chapter. Our thanks also go to the DOE research staff, especially Jennifer Bell-Ellwanger, for helping to arrange interviews and for reviewing our drafts for accuracy. Thanks to Andres Alonso, Louis Gomez, Claire Sylvan, and Josh Thomases for their helpful feedback on earlier drafts of this chapter. Opinions expressed here are those of the authors and do not necessarily reflect the views of funders or reviewers.

1. David Cohen, Stephen Raudenbusch, and Deborah Ball, "Resources, Instruction, and Research," *Education Evaluation and Policy Analysis* 25 (2003): 119–142.

2. Elizabeth A. City, Richard F. Elmore, Sarah E. Fiarman, and Lee Teitel, *Instructional Rounds in Education: A Network Approach to Improving Teaching and Learning*, (Cambridge, MA: Harvard Education Press, 2010): 40.

3. Carol H. Weiss, "Nothing as Practical as Good Theory: Exploring Theory-Based Evaluation for Comprehensive Community Initiatives for Children and Families," in *New Approaches to Evaluating Community Initiatives*, vol. 1, *Concepts, Methods, and Contexts*, eds. James P. Connell, Anne C. Kubisch, Lisbeth B. Schorr, and Carol H. Weiss (Washington, DC: The Aspen Institute, 1995).

4. AUSSIE (Australian United States Services in Education) provides professional development services to elementary, middle, and high schools focused on improving instruction and data use; see http://www.aussiepd.com/.

5. The mandating of Ramp Up to Literacy for struggling readers represented the first time that literacy work was introduced at the high school level. In some high schools, nearly all students participated in this program. This requirement was a challenge for many high school teachers who were inexperienced in teaching reading and writing. See Siskin (chapter 8 in this volume) for additional efforts, such as the multiple pathways initiative at the high school level.

6. The regional structure was not recognized by the New York State Education Department, and NYC remained composed of thirty-two legislated community school districts.

7. A number of these LISs served as titular heads of other Community School Districts.

8. See Childress et al. (chapter 4 in this volume).

9. See Hill (chapter 1 in this volume); and Childress et al. (chapter 4 in this volume).

10. Joel Klein, private communication, June 29, 2009.

11. Many of the SSO respondents reported that the DOE *required* 90 percent of all teachers to participate in an inquiry team; DOE staff said it was a suggestion or goal. For additional information on the inquiry process, see Talbert (chapter 6 in this volume).

12. This move to consolidate operations and instructional support was piloted first in the Children First Networks. Based on this experience, the DOE expects that the change will help ensure a speedy resolution to operational issues by staff familiar with each school in the network.

13. Most recently, the DOE has announced yet another restructuring in the support and oversight system for schools. Due to concerns about the ability of the SSOs to provide the support and accountability needed to ensure high performance in their member schools, the DOE recently dissolved the SSO structure and replaced it with six clusters. Each cluster will be composed of a set of networks, and each network will consist of approximately twenty-five schools. Each cluster will be led by a cluster lead within the DOE.

14. Jennifer A. O'Day, "Complexity, Accountability, and School Improvement," *Harvard Educational Review* 72, no. 3 (2002): 293-329.

15. Susan A. Mohram and Edward E. Lawler III, "Motivation for School Reforms," in *Rewards and Reform: Creating Educational Incentives that Work*, eds. Susan H. Fuhrman and Jennifer A. O'Day (San Francisco: Jossey-Bass, 1996); and Brian Rowan, "Standards as Incentives for Instructional Reform," in Fuhrman and O'Day, eds., *Rewards and Reform*.

16. See James P. Spillane, Brian J. Reiser, and Louis M. Gomez, "Policy Implementation and Cognition: The Role of Human, Social, and Distributed Cognition in Framing Policy Implementation," in *Confronting Complexity: Defining the Field of Education Policy Implementation*, ed. Meredith I. Honig, (Albany, NY: The State University of New York Press, 2006).

17. Ibid.

18. For example, see Milbrey W. McLaughlin and Joan E. Talbert, *Building School-based Teacher Learning Communities: Professional Strategies to Improve Student Achievement* (New York: Teachers College Press, 2006).

19. This is not to imply that the central office was monitoring this relationship prior to the Bloomberg/Klein administration—only that such monitoring could be helpful for improvement and for equity, particularly in an empowerment-based system.

20. These concerns were exacerbated by the use of the percentage of students at or above proficiency as the measure of progress, as this indicator is highly sensitive to the placement of the proficiency cutoff. This indicator can either overreport progress (if a large number of students move just above the proficiency cutoff) or underreport progress (if scores of students below the cutoff increase but not sufficiently to move them over the proficiency cutoff). Analysis of scale score trends indicate that achievement gaps have indeed been reduced, though substantial inequities in outcomes among student groups remain.

21. In addition to emphasizing access to common standards, the DOE has launched a series of targeted efforts to address the specific needs of these groups. For students with disabilities, the new division has set the expectation that all schools will make flexible use of instructional placements and organizational supports to best meet all students' needs. For ELLs, the DOE has also committed to holding schools and principals accountable for ELL student outcomes while providing targeted support to schools at the network level. Other initiatives include the hiring of parent coordinators in all schools who communicate with parents in their native languages, providing assessments in native languages, and requiring schools to submit reports on services provided to ELLs. According to a senior DOE administrator, "In a big-picture way, we have never paid as much attention to ELLs in the system as we have under Children First." While such initiatives signal a commitment to improving outcomes for these two under-served groups, the challenge will be to ensure that services are integrated into the work of the other divisions in the DOE and into the networks and schools themselves.

Chapter 6

Research described in this chapter was conducted by Stanford University's Center for Research on the Context of Teaching (CRC) through a grant to New Visions for Public Schools from the Carnegie Corporation of New York. CRC colleagues involved in this study are Milbrey McLaughlin, Lambrina Mileva, Pai-rou Chen, M. Ken Cor, and John Schoener. We are grateful to Liz Gewirtzman and Nell Scharff of the Baruch College School of Public Affairs for opening their SAM program practice to our scrutiny and collaborating with us on making sense of the data. We thank New Visions' Robert Hughes, Ron Chaluisan, and Beverly Donohue for actively supporting our research on inquiry in their PSO schools. We are especially grateful to the teachers and principals in approximately eighty NYC schools who have filled out our surveys and talked with us over the past five years, and to the NYC Department of Education leaders we interviewed for this chapter. Several reviewers' comments on an earlier draft helped to get the story right. Thanks to Robert Hughes, Libi Gil, Louis Gomez, and Shael Polakow-Suransky for their helpful feedback on an earlier draft and special thanks to Irma Zardoya and Liz Gewirtzman for their input on multiple drafts. Opinions expressed here are those of the author and do not necessarily reflect the views of funders or reviewers.

1. Stanford University's Center for Research on the Context of Teaching (CRC) conducted the research under the auspices of New Visions for Public Schools. Schools participating in the research include those involved in an inquiry-focused administrator credentialing program since 2005–2006 and all schools in the New Visions for Public Schools Partnership Support Organization (PSO) since it was established in 2007–2008 (approximately seventy-five schools). For information on the design and results of this evaluation research, see Joan E. Talbert and Nell Scharff, "Leading School Improvement with Data: A Theory of Action to Extend the Sphere of Student Success" (paper presented at the Annual Meeting of the Education Research Association, New York City, 2008); Joan E. Talbert, Lambrina Mileva, Milbrey McLaughlin, John Schoener, M. Ken Cor, Pai-rou Chen, and Wendy Lin, *Leadership Development and School Reform Through the Scaffolded Apprenticeship Model (SAM)* (Stanford, CA: Center for Research on the Context of Teaching, 2009); Joan E. Talbert, Lambrina Mileva, Pai-rou Chen, M. Ken Cor, and Milbrey McLaughlin, *Developing School Capacity for Inquiry-based Improvement: Progress, Challenges, and Resources* (Stanford, CA: Center for Research on the Context of Teaching, 2010).

2. Our prior and concurrent research on district system initiatives to promote inquiry-based school reform includes a five-year study (2001–2006) of the Bay Area School Reform Collaborative (BASRC) district reform initiative and ongoing study of Sanger USD in the California Central Valley (2008–). For a distillation of findings from prior research, see Milbrey W. McLaughlin and Joan E. Talbert, *Building School-based Teacher Learning Communities: Professional Strategies to Improve Student Achievement* (New York: Teachers College Press, 2006).

3. The SAM certification program was launched by Liz Gewirtzman of Baruch School of Public Affairs (SPA) in partnership with Ron Chaluisan and Robert Hughes of New Visions for Public Schools. Others involved in the SAM planning process during 2004-05 included Shael Polakow-Suransky, former NYC principal and chief academic officer as of January 2011. He worked with Jim Liebman, Eric Nadelstern, and Alisa Berger in bringing the inquiry model into the DOE's Children First Intensive (CFI). SAM's inquiry model was developed during the pilot year and refined through work with fourteen high school teams during SAM II (2006–2008). SAM leaders contributed lessons gleaned from implementing the administrator credentialing program, as well as tools and professional development, to the DOE's evolving inquiry initiative.

4. For elaboration on this principle and illustrations of how it works in practice, see Helen A Scharff, Deirdre A DeAngelis, and Joan E Talbert, "Starting Small for Big School Improvement: Focusing on Small Changes That Meet the Needs of Struggling Students Can Lead to Changes in Schoolwide Practices," *Principal Leadership* 10, no. 8 (2010): 58.

5. For a map of resources currently available to teacher teams see the DOE's website to support Collaborative Inquiry: New York City Department of Education, Children First Intensive WebSite, http://cfi.sharepointsite.net.

6. As part of this restructuring, the DOE created networks of approximately twenty-five schools each within the SSOs, each guided by a network leader. See introduction and O'Day and Bitter (chapter 5 in this volume).

7. See Marian Robinson, Patricia Kannapel, Joan Gujarati, Hakim Williams, Andrea Oettenger, *A Formative Study of the Implementation of the Inquiry Team Process in New York City Public Schools: 2007–2008 Findings* (New York City: Teachers College, Consortium for Policy Research in Education, 2008).

8. During the second year (2008–2009), the DOE asked schools to establish two or more school teams and communicated the two-year goal of involving 90 percent of teachers in inquiry teams.

9. For a practice-based account of what it takes for a principal to create a school culture of collaborative inquiry, see Nancy Mohr and Allen Dichter, *Stages of Team Development: Lessons from the Struggles of Site-Based Management*, 2001, http://www.nsrfharmony.org/auth_mohr_dichter_stages.pdf. For evidence of a peer facilitator's role in developing a team culture of collective efficacy, see Ronald Gallimore, Bradley A. Ermeling, William M. Saunders, and Claude Goldenburg, "Moving the Learning of Teaching Closer to Practice: Teacher Education Implications of School-based Inquiry Teams," *Elementary School Journal* 109, no. 5 (2009): 537–553.

10. Questions of validity of our research on New Visions PSO schools for documenting NYC's inquiry initiative need to be addressed. First, we do not use these data to estimate the distribution of NYC schools on inquiry implementation or its outcomes. Second, we examined QR ratings for all NYC schools identified by their SSO to assess how well our data from New Visions PSO schools capture the range of school experiences in implementing the inquiry model. New Visions PSO overall school ratings fell in the middle of the distribution (graphic summary available on request). Thus there is no reason to question the reliability of statistical estimates based on our data or the use of case study data from New Visions PSO schools to investigate teachers' experiences in implementing the model.

11. For further analysis of the challenge of developing collaborative practice in high schools, see Milbrey W. McLaughlin and Joan E. Talbert, "Building Professional Learning Communities in High Schools: Challenges and Promising Practices," in *Professional Learning Communities: Divergence, Detail, and Difficulties,* ed. Louise Stoll and Karen Seashore Louis (Maidenhead, UK: Open University Press/McGraw-Hill, 2007).

12. This survey scale combines teacher responses to two items measured on 5-point Likert scales: we use a variety of assessment strategies to measure student progress, and we use assessment data to evaluate our curriculum and instructional practices. The scale's alpha coefficient is .82.

13. A forthcoming monograph documents the developmental trajectories and facilitator moves that support these cultural changes through inquiry: Nell Scharff and Joan E. Talbert, *What It Takes to Develop Evidence-based Practice in Schools: A Developmental Perspective,* in process.

14. Coefficients are .32 (p = .5) and –.47 (p = .1), respectively. School N for the analysis is 38. Results of both student outcome analyses are reported in more detail in Talbert et al., *Leadership Development and School Reform through the Scaffolded Apprenticeship Model (SAM).*

15. The "principal support of inquiry team" scale (Alpha = .88) combines Likert scale responses to three survey items: Principal: establishes conditions for trust and open communication; actively supports our risk-taking; uses authority to push our learning in the service of target students and targeted learning goals. The "team functioning" scale (Alpha = .90) combines three items: Our inquiry team members: establish clear and unambiguous measures for assessing our success; stay focused on results in the face of distractions and competing priorities; willingly make sacrifices for the good of the team and the achievement of our goals. Principal support predicts 2009 IT scores on the team functioning scale after 2008 scores are controlled (coefficients are .78 (p = .01) and .35 (p = .05), respectively. Translated: an IT's functioning improved most in schools where the principal promoted the work.

16. Joan E. Talbert, "Professional Learning Communities at the Crossroads: How Systems Hinder or Engender Change," in *International Handbook of Educational Change*, vol. 2, ed. Michael Fullan, Andy Hargreaves, and Ann Lieberman (Dordrecht, The Netherlands: Springer, 2010).

Chapter 7

We appreciate helpful comments on an earlier draft from Susan Moore Johnson, Vicki Bernstein, and participants at the New York City Retrospective working conference. We are grateful to the New York City Department of Education and the New York State Education Department for the data employed in this paper. Loeb and Wyckoff also gratefully acknowledge the support of the National Center for the Analysis of Longitudinal Data in Education Research (CALDER). CALDER is supported by IES Grant R305A060018 to the Urban Institute. The views expressed in the paper are solely those of the authors and may not reflect those of the funders. Any errors are attributable to the authors.

Some sections of this chapter are taken from Margaret Goertz and Stephanie Levin, "Strategic Management of Human Capital in New York City," 2008, http://www.smhc-cpre.org/download/36/.

1. *Recruitment efforts:* Donald Boyd, Hamilton Lankford, Susanna Loeb, Jonah Rockoff, and James Wyckoff, "The Narrowing Gap in New York City Teacher Qualifications and Its Implications for Student Achievement in High Poverty Schools," *Journal of Policy Analysis and Management* 27, no. 4 (2008): 793–818. *working conditions:* Susan Moore Johnson, Jill Harrison Berg, and Morgaen L. Donaldson, *Who Stays in Teaching and Why* (Cambridge, MA: The Project on the Next Generation of Teachers, Harvard Graduate School of Education, 2005).

2. Donald Boyd, Pamela Grossman, Hamilton Lankford, Susanna Loeb, and James Wyckoff, "How Changes in Entry Requirements Alter the Teacher Workforce and Affect Student Achievement," *Education Finance and Policy* 1, no. 2 (2006): 176–216.

3. Based on calculations by authors using data from NYCDOE, NYSED, and College Board.

4. Donald Boyd, Hamilton Lankford, Susanna Loeb, and James Wyckoff, "Explaining the Short Careers of High-Achieving Teachers in Schools with Low-Performing Students," *American Economic Review Proceedings* 95, no. 2 (2005): 166–171.

5. Hamilton Lankford, Susanna Loeb, and James Wyckoff, "Teacher Sorting and the Plight of Urban Schools: A Descriptive Analysis," *Educational Evaluation and Policy Analysis* 24, no. 1 (2002): 38–62.

6. *Initial search for schools:* Donald Boyd, Hamilton Lankford, Susanna Loeb, Matthew Ronfeldt, and James Wyckoff, "The Role of Teacher Quality in Retention and Hiring: Using Applications-to-Transfer to Uncover Preferences of Teachers and Schools," *Journal of Policy Analysis and Management* (forthcoming); and Donald Boyd, Hamilton Lankford, Susanna Loeb, and James Wyckoff, "Analyzing the Determinants of the Matching of Public School Teachers to Jobs: Estimating Compensating Differentials in Imperfect Labor Markets," NBER Working Paper 9878 (2006); *job retention:* Boyd et al., "The Role of Teacher Quality in Retention and Hiring"; and Eric A. Hanushek, John F. Kain, and Steven G. Rivkin "Why Public Schools Lose Teachers," *Journal of Human Resources* 39, no. 2 (2004): 326–354.

7. Donald Boyd, Pamela Grossman, Marsha Ing, Hamilton Lankford, Susanna Loeb, and James Wyckoff, "The Influence of School Administrators on Teacher Retention Decisions," *American Education Research Journal* (forthcoming); Donald Boyd, Pamela Grossman, Hamilton Lankford, Susanna Loeb, Jeannie Myung, and James Wyckoff "Mentoring and the Matthew Effect: The Implementation of a District-Wide Mentoring Program and its Impact on Retention" (working paper, 2009); Boyd et al., "Explaining the Short Careers of High-Achieving Teachers in Schools with Low-Performing Students"; Hanushek, Kain, and Rivkin, "Why Public Schools Lose Teachers,"; and Johnson, Berg, and Donaldson, *Who Stays in Teaching and Why.*

8. Sean P. Corcoran, Amy Ellen Schwartz, and Meryle Weinstein, *The New York City Aspiring Principals Program: A School-Level Evaluation* (report from Institute for Education and Social Policy, New York University, 2009), http://steinhardt.nyu.edu/scmsAdmin/uploads/003/852/APP.pdfhttp://steinhardt.nyu.edu/scmsAdmin/uploads/003/852/APP.pdf.

9. The New Teacher Project, "Unintended Consequences" (2005), http://www.tntp.org/files/Unintended-Consequences.pdf.

10. Based on calculations by authors from data provided by NYCDOE.

11. See the Agreement Between the Board of Education of the City School District of the City of New York and the United Federation of Teachers, 2000-2003 Article 18 Transfer and Staffing, 120–122.

12. *Education Week*, January 6, 2005, 86.

13. Elissa Gootman, "A New Effort to Remove Bad Teachers," *New York Times*, November 15, 2007, http://www.nytimes.com/2007/11/15/education/15teacher.html?_r=1http://www.nytimes.com/2007/11/15/education/15teacher.html?_r=1

14. Stephen Brill, "The Rubber Room: The Battle over New York City's Worst Teachers," *New Yorker*, August 31, 2009, http://www.newyorker.com/reporting/2009/08/31/090831fa_fact_brill.

15. Julia Koppich and Connie Showalter, *Strategic Management of Human Capital: A Cross-Case Analysis of Five Districts* (Madison, WI: University of Wisconsin-Madison, Consortium for Policy Research in Education, 2008), http://www.smhc-cpre.org.

16. Most of this increase occurred during the period 2000–2002. Between 2002 and 2008 starting salaries increased by 17 percent. After adjusting for inflation this translates to a real increase in salary of less than 0.5 percent.

17. For a complete list of the eligibility requirements see http://schools.nyc.gov/NR/rdonlyres/9720279E-BD06-464A-88F3-ADF67CABB29E/0/LeadTeacherPosting20102011A.pdf.

18. Matthew G. Springer and Marcus A. Winters, "New York City's School-Wide Bonus Pay Program: Early Evidence from a Randomized Trial" (working paper, National Center on Performance Incentives, Vanderbilt University, 2009), http://www.performanceincentives.org/data/files/news/PapersNews/Springer__Winters_200902.pdf.

19. Donald Boyd et al., "The Narrowing Gap in New York City Teacher Qualifications."

20. Charles Clotfelter, Elizabeth Glennie, Helen Ladd, and Jacob Vigdor, "Would Higher Salaries Keep Teachers in High-Poverty Schools? Evidence from a Policy Intervention in North Carolina," (NBER Working Paper #12285 , 2006); Peter J. Dolton and Wilbert van der Klaaw, "The Turnover of Teachers: A Competing Risks Explanation," *Review of Economics and Statistics*, 81, no. 3 (1999): 543–552; Richard J. Murnane, Judith D. Singer, and John B. Willett, "The Influences of Salaries and 'Opportunity Costs' on Teachers' Career Choices: Evidence from North Carolina," *Harvard Educational Review*, 59, no. 3 (1989): 325–346; Todd R. Stinebrickner, "A Dynamic Model of Teacher Labor Supply," *Journal of Labor Economics*, 19, no. 1 (2001): 196–230; Todd R. Stinebrickner, "Compensation Policies and Teacher Decisions," *International Economic Review*, 42, no. 3 (2001): 751–779.

21. Donald Boyd, Pamela Grossman, Karen Hammerness, Hamilton Lankford, Susanna Loeb, Matthew Ronfeldt, and James Wyckoff, "Recruiting Effective Math Teachers: How Do Math Immersion Teachers Compare? Evidence from New York City" (NBER Working Paper w16017, 2009).

22. Even more dramatic differences exist on other measures of qualifications, such as undergraduate college ranking and the percentage who failed the Liberal Arts and Sciences Test (general teacher certification exam) on their first attempt. See Boyd et al., "The Narrowing Gap in New York City Teacher Qualifications."

23. Boyd et al., "Recruiting Effective Math Teachers"; Boyd et al., "Analyzing the Determinants of the Matching of Public School Teachers to Jobs"; and Thomas J. Kane, Jonah E. Rockoff, and Douglas O. Staiger, "What Does Certification Tell Us About Teacher Effectiveness? Evidence from New York City" *Economics of Education Review* 27 (2008): 615–631.

24. For details see Boyd et al., "How Changes in Entry Requirements Alter the Teacher Workforce and Affect Student Achievement"; and Boyd et al., "Recruiting Effective Math Teachers."

25. Boyd et al., "Recruiting Effective Math Teachers."

26. Boyd et al., "The Narrowing Gap in New York City Teacher Qualifications."

27. Ibid.

28. Ibid.

29. Jonah E. Rockoff, Brian A. Jacob, Thomas J. Kane, and Douglas O. Staiger, "Can You Recognize an Effective Teacher When You Recruit One?" (NBER Working Paper 14485, 2008).

30. This section is based on conversations with Vicki Bernstein, executive director of teacher recruitment and quality, NYCDOE.

31. Jason A. Grissom, "But Do They Stay? Addressing Issues of Teacher Retention through Alternative Certification," in *Alternative Routes to Teaching: Mapping the New Landscape of Teacher Education*, eds. Pamela

Grossman and Susanna Loeb (Cambridge, MA: Harvard Education Press, 2008); Richard M. Ingersoll, "Teacher Turnover and Teacher Shortages: An Organizational Analysis," *American Education Research Journal* 38, no. 3 (2001): 499–534; Boyd et al., "The Influence of School Administrators on Teacher Retention Decisions."

32. Boyd et al., "The Influence of School Administrators on Teacher Retention Decisions.

33. New York City Department of Education, *Children First* (2009), http://schools.nyc.gov/NR/rdonlyres/51C61E8F-1AE9-4D37-8881-4D688D4F843A/0/cf_corenarrative.pdf.

34. Ibid.

35. See http://www.nycleadershipacademy.org/overview/overview.

36. See http://www.nycleadershipacademy.org/aspiringprincipals/app_overview.

37. Corcoran, Schwartz, and Weinstein, *The New York City Aspiring Principals Program*.

38. "Mayor Michael R. Bloomberg and Chancellor Joel I. Klein Announce New Mentoring Program for Incoming Teachers," press release, Office of the Mayor, August 23, 2004.

39. Boyd et al., "Mentoring and the Matthew Effect."

40. New Teacher Center, "Understanding New York City's Groundbreaking Induction Initiative" (policy paper, Santa Cruz, CA: New Teacher Center at the University of California Santa Cruz, 2006).

41. Jonah Rockoff, "Does Mentoring Reduce Turnover and Improve Skills of New Employees? Evidence from Teachers in New York City," working paper (2008).

42. Boyd et al., "Mentoring and the Matthew Effect."

43. Agreement Between the Board of Education of the City School District of the City of New York and the United Federation of Teachers, 2003–07 Article 18 Transfer and Staffing; and Timothy Daly, David Keeling, Rachel Grainger, and Adele Grundies, *Mutual Benefits: New York City's Shift to Mutual Consent in Teacher Hiring* (New York: The New Teacher Project, 2008), www.tntp.org/publications/Mutual_Benefits.html.

44. Daly et al., *Mutual Benefits*.

45. Barbara Martinez, "More Teachers to Lose Positions—but Not Pay" *Wall Street Journal*, July 1, 2010, http://online.wsj.com/article/SB10001424052748704334604575339142634105522.html.

46. Daly et al., *Mutual Benefits*; and United Federation of Teachers, *Case Study in Partisanship. A Critique of The New Teacher Project Report* Mutual Benefits: New York City's Shift to Mutual Consent in Teacher Hiring (2008), www.uft.org/news/atrs_tntpl.pdf.

47. Boyd et al., "The Narrowing Gap in New York City Teacher Qualifications."

48. Daly et al., *Mutual Benefits*.

49. Boyd et al., "The Role of Teacher Quality in Retention and Hiring," and Brian A. Jacob and Lars Lefgren, "Can Principals Identify Effective Teachers? Evidence on Subjective Performance Evaluation in Education," *Journal of Labor Economics* 26, no. 1 (2008): 101–136.

50. See New York City School Survey results presentation at http://schools.nyc.gov/NR/rdonlyres/63C6B2F2-A659-4EF9-AB3B-A5BBCDF19850/64127/NYCSchoolSurvey2009ResultsPresentation.pdf.

51. New York City Department of Education, *Children First*.

52. New York State Education Department, "New York State Education Department Proposes Race to the Top Legislative Reforms with Support of New York State United Teachers and the United Federation of Teachers," press release, 2010, http://www.oms.nysed.gov/press/RTTT_NYSUTMay11.html.

53. Donald Boyd, Pamela Grossman, Hamilton Lankford, Susanna Loeb, and James Wyckoff, "Teacher Preparation and Student Achievement," *Educational Evaluation and Policy Analysis* 31, no.4 (2009): 416–440; and Matthew Ronfeldt, "Where Should Student Teachers Learn to Teach?" (working paper, Institute for Research on Education Policy and Practice, Stanford University, 2010), http://irepp.stanford.edu/publications/working_papers/.

Chapter 8

1. National Commission on Excellence in Education, *A Nation at Risk: The Imperative for Educational Reform* (Washington, DC: U.S. Government Printing Office, 1983).

2. In spring 2010, eleven members of the DOE staff were interviewed, all of whom were formerly or currently active in the high school reform efforts. In addition, six high school principals, one union leader, and two members of partner organizations, all with experience before and during the Bloomberg/Klein years, contributed retrospective comments. The quotations in this chapter are from these interviews. The DOE also provided data on the portfolio, on high school performance measures, and a list of closed and closing schools.

3. *A Nation at Risk*, 9, 4, and 18.

4. Brian Rowan, Eric Camburn, and Carol Barnes, "Benefiting from Comprehensive School Reform: A Review of Research on CSR Implementation," in *Putting the Pieces Together: Lessons from Comprehensive School Reform Research*, ed. Christopher T. Cross (Washington, DC: National Clearinghouse, 2004).

5. Leslie S. Siskin, "Achievement and Attainment: The Comprehensive High School and the Problem of Reform," in *Crucial Issues in California Education*, eds. Bruce Fuller et al. (Berkeley, CA: PACE, 2006).

6. Leslie S. Siskin, "When an Irresistible Force Meets an Immovable Object: Core Lessons About High Schools and Accountability," in *The New Accountability: High Schools and High-Stakes Testing*, eds. Martin Carnoy, Richard Elmore, and Leslie S. Siskin (New York: Routledge, 2003): 181.

7. NYC Coalition for Educational Justice, "Looming Crisis or Historic Opportunity? Meeting the Challenge of the Regents Graduation Standards" (New York: NYC Coalition for Educational Justice, 2009).

8. Siskin, "Achievement and Attainment."

9. *Time*, April 9, 2006.

10. Melissa Roderick, "Closing the Aspirations-Achievement Gap: Implications for High School Reform" (New York: MDRC, 2006).

11. http://nces.ed.gov/.

12. Siskin, "When an Irresistible Force Meets an Immovable Object"; Floyd M. Hammack, ed., *The Comprehensive High School Today* (New York: Teachers College Press, 2004); Joseph P. McDonald, Emily Klein, and Meg Riordan, *Going to Scale with New School Designs: Reinventing High Schools* (New York: Teachers College Press, 2009); Milbrey McLaughlin and Joan Talbert, *Professional Communities and the Work of High School Teaching* (Chicago: University of Chicago Press, 2001).

13. Arne Duncan, interview by CNN "U.S. Schools Chief: We're in an Educational Emergency" May 20, 2010, http://articles.cnn.com/2010-05-20/us/arne.duncan. qanda_1_four-day-school-weeks-trade-school-education-arne-duncan?_s=PM:US.

14. Christopher Swanson, "U.S. Graduation Rate Continues Decline," *Education Week*, June 2, 2010, http://www.edweek.org/ew/articles/2010/06/10/34swanson.h29.html.

15. http://listenup.org/project.php?project=education.

16. Joseph P. McDonald and Leslie S. Siskin, "Autonomy and Accountability in New York City School Reform" (paper presented at the Annual Conference of the American Educational Research Association, San Diego, CA, 2009).

17. Dan Barry, "Raze School System, Giuliani Says." *New York Times*, April 23, 1999.

18. McDonald and Siskin, "Autonomy and Accountability in New York City School Reform."

19. Seymour Fliegel, "Creative Non-compliance" in *Choice and Control in American Education*, eds. John F. Witte, William Clune, and Robert La Follette (New York: Routledge, 1990), 199–216.

20. Seymour Fliegel and James MacGuire, *Miracle in East Harlem: The Fight for Choice in Public Education* (New York: Times Books, 1993).

21. Deborah Meier, *The Power of Their Ideas: Lessons from a Small School in Harlem* (New York: Beacon Press, 2002).

22. Linda Darling-Hammond, Jacqueline Ancess, and Susanna W. Ort, "Reinventing High School: Outcomes of the Coalition Campus Schools Projects," *American Educational Research Journal* 39, no. 3 (2002): 639–673.

23. Institute for Education and Social Policy, "Final Report of the Evaluation of the New York Networks for School Renewal, 1996–2001 (New York: IESP, 2001).

24. http://www.newvisions.org/node/313/10/1/49.

25. Michelle Cahill, "Schools and Community Partnerships: Reforming Schools, Revitalizing Communities" (Chicago: Cross City Campaign for Urban School Reform, 1996); Janice M. Hirota, Robert L. Hughes and Ronald Chaluisan, "Partnering for Success: The Creation of Urban Schools that Work Better," *Voices in Urban Education* (2008): 36–48.

26. Janet C. Quint, Janell K. Smith, Rebecca Unterman, and Alma E. Moedano, *New York City's Changing High School Landscape: High Schools and their Characteristics, 2002–2008* (MDRC, New York, 2010); see also Eileen M. Foley, Allan Klinge, and Elizabeth R. Reisner, *Evaluation of New Century High Schools: Profile of an Initiative to Create and Sustain Small, Successful High Schools* (Washington, DC: Policy Studies Associates, Inc., 2007, revised 2008).

27. Office of the Mayor, press release, July 29, 2002, http://www.nyc.gov/portal/site/nycgov/menu-item.b270a4a1d51bb3017bce0ed101c789a0/index.jsp?pageID=nyc_blue_room&catID=1194&doc_name=http%3A%2F%2Fwww.nyc.gov%2Fhtml%2Fom%2Fhtml%2F2002b%2Fpr201-02.html&cc=unused1978&rc=1194&ndi=1.

28. New York City Department of Education, "Children First: A Bold, Common-Sense Plan to Create Great Schools for all Children" (New York: New York City Department of Education, 2008).

29. Quint et al., *New York City's Changing High School Landscape*; see also Clara Hemphill and Kim Nauer, *The New Marketplace: How Small-School Reforms and School Choice Have Reshaped New York City's High School* (New York: New School Center for New York City Affairs, 2009).

30. Marian Robinson et al., "A Formative Study of the Implementation of the Inquiry Team Process in New York City Public Schools: 2007–08" (Consortium for Policy Research in Education, New York, 2008).

31. Siskin, "When an Irresistible Force Meets an Immovable Object": 175–194; McLaughlin and Talbert, *Professional Communities and the Work of High School Teaching.*

32. Joel Klein, testimony to the New York City Council Committee on Education on the Next Phase of the Children First Reforms, January 25, 2007.

33. Elissa Gootman and Robert Gebeloff, "Principals Younger and Freer, but Raise Doubts in the Schools," *New York Times*, May 26, 2009.

34. Hemphill and Nauer, "The New Marketplace."

35. Ibid.

36. Susan Moore Johnson, *Finders and Keepers: Helping New Teachers Survive and Thrive in Our Schools* (Cambridge, MA: Project on Next Generation of Teachers, 2004).

37. Hirota, Hughes, and Chaluisan, "Partnering for Success."

38. Constancia Warren, "Creating Portfolios of Schools," *Education Week*, June 22, 2005, http://www.edweek.org/ew/articles/2005/06/22/41warren.h24.html?querystring=Constancia percent20Warren; see also Paul T. Hill et al., "Portfolio School Districts for Big Cities: An Interim Report" (Seattle: Center on Reinventing Public Education, 2009).

39. Warren, "Creating Portfolios of Schools."

40. Quint et al, *New York City's Changing High School Landscape*; Hemphill and Nauer, "*The New Marketplace.*"

41. http://schools.nyc.gov/community/planning/changes/replace.htm.

42. Ibid.

43. Quint et al., *New York City's Changing High School Landscape.*

44. Kemple, this volume; Howard Bloom, Saskia L. Thompson, and Rebecca Unterman, "Transforming the High School Experience: How New York City's Small Schools Are Boosting Student Achievement and Graduation Rates" (New York: MDRC, 2010).

45. In March 2010, plans for fourteen new high school closings were halted when the UFT, the NAACP, and parent groups filed a lawsuit protesting the absence of meaningful community input in the process. See also Ann Kjelberg and Leonie Haimson, eds., *NYC Schools Under Bloomberg/Klein: What Parents, Teachers, and Policymakers Need to Know* (New York: ClassSizeMatters, 2009).

46. Arthur Goldstein and Leslie O'Grady, "Overcrowded, Oversized, and Overlooked," *Queens Chronicle*, October 15, 2009, http://gothamschools.org/2009/11/02/overcrowded-oversized-and-overlooked; Hemphill and Nauer, "The New Marketplace"; David Bloomfield, "High School Reform: The Downside of Scaling Up," *Politics of Education Association Bulletin* 30, no. 1 (Fall 2005): 6–9; see also Julia Gwynne and Marisa de la Torre, "When Schools Close: Effects on Displaced Students in Chicago Public Schools" (Chicago: Consortium on Chicago School Research, 2009); Erik W. Robelen, "Small Schools' Ripple Effects Debated: As NYC and Chicago Close Failing High Schools, District Officials Encounter Criticism," *Education Week*, May 3, 2006.

47. See Corcoran and Levin, this volume; Quint et al., *New York City's Changing High School Landscape.*

48. Hemphill and Nauer, *The New Marketplace,* 66.

49. Sharon Gewirtz, Stephen Ball, and Richard Bowe, *Markets, Choice and Equity in Education* (Buckingham: Open University Press, 1995).

50. Aaron Pallas and Carolyn Riehl, "The Demand for High School Programs in New York City" (New York City: Research Partnership for New York City Schools, 2007), 9.

51. Bloom, L. Thompson, and Unterman, "Transforming the High School Experience."

52. Parthenon Group, *Pathways to Graduation: Data-driven Strategies for Differentiated Graduation Rate Improvements* (Boston: Parthenon Group, 2008), 4.

53. New York City Department of Education, "Multiple Pathways Research and Development: Summary Findings and Strategic Solutions for Overage, Under-credited Youth," http://schools.nyc.gov/NR/rdonlyres/B5EC6D1C-F884-4610-8F0F-A14D63420115/0/FindingsofOMPG.pdf.

54. McLaughlin and Talbert, *Professional Communities and the Work of High School Teaching*; Bill and Melinda Gates Foundation, "High-Performing School Districts: Combining Pressure, Support, Alignment and Choice," http://www.gatesfoundation.org/education/transforminghighschools/districts.

55. Marian Robinson et al., "A Formative Study of the Implementation of the Inquiry Team Process in New York City Public Schools: 2007–08" (New York: Consortium for Policy Research in Education, 2008).

56. Martin Carnoy, Richard Elmore, Leslie S. Siskin, *The New Accountability: High Schools and High Stakes Testing* (New York: Routledge, 2003).

57. Torie Gorges, Ann House, Aasha Joshi, Barbara Means, Karen Mitchell, Linda Shmear, Becky Smerdon, and Jamie Shkolnik, "Contrasting Paths to School Reform: Results of a Five-Year Evaluation of the Bill and Melinda Gates Foundation's National High Schools Initiative," *Teachers College Record* 110, no. 9 (2008): 1986–2039; Leslie S. Siskin, "Is the School the Unit of Change? Internal and External Contexts of Restructuring," in *The Struggle for Authenticity: Teacher Development in a Context of Educational Change*, eds. Peter Grimmett and J. Neufeld (New York: Teachers College Press, 1994), 121–140.

Chapter 9

The authors would like to thank Tom Gold and Dominique West of the NYC Department of Education for their invaluable help in acquiring data necessary to complete this project. Office of Student Enrollment staff—and in particular Maurice Frumkin, Diana Levengood, and Elizabeth Sciabarra—answered many of our questions and corrected factual errors. Shaun Fratus of the New York State Department of Education provided data on New York State private and charter schools. Sarah Butler Jessen, Carolyn Sattin-Bajaj, Amy Ellen Schwartz, and Jennifer Jennings provided helpful comments, and Brooks Bowden provided substantial assistance in researching the history of school choice in NYC. Kate Levine and Annie Tan lent additional research assistance. All remaining errors are solely our own.

1. Others include Staten Island Technical High School, Queens High School for the Sciences at York College, High School for Mathematics, Science, and Engineering at the City College, High School of American Studies at Lehman College, and The Brooklyn Latin School.

2. Madeleine E. Lopez, "New York, Puerto Ricans, and the Dilemmas of Integration," in *From Grassroots to the Supreme Court: Brown v. Board of Education and American Democracy*, ed. P. Lau (Durham, NC: Duke University Press, 2004); and Jerald E. Podair, *The Strike That Changed New York: Blacks, Whites, and the Ocean Hill-Brownsville Crisis* (New Haven, CT: Yale University Press, 2002).

3. According to Diane Ravitch, of the 12,000 students eligible to transfer under the Free Choice Transfer Policy, only 393 applied for such transfer: Diane Ravitch, *The Great School Wars: A History of the NYC Public Schools* (Baltimore, MD: John Hopkins Press, 1974); see also University of the State of New York, Commissioner's Advisory Committee on Human Relations and Community Tensions, *Desegregating the Public Schools in NYC: A Report Prepared for the Board of Education of the City of New York* (New York: Teachers College, Columbia University, 1964).

4. Raymond J. Domanico, "Model for Choice: A Report on Manhattan's District 4" (Education Policy Paper No. 1, Manhattan Institute, New York, 1989); Seymour Fliegel and James MacGuire, *Miracle in East Harlem: The Fight for Choice in Public Education* (New York: Times Books, 1993); and Mark Schneider, Paul Teske, and Melissa Marschall, *Choosing Schools: Consumer Choice and the Quality of American Schools* (Princeton, NJ: Princeton University Press, 2000).

5. Robert L. Crain, Amy L. Heebner, Yiu-Pong Si, Will J. Jordan, and D. R. Kiener, *The Effectiveness of New York City's Career Magnet Schools: An Evaluation of Ninth Grade Performance Using an Experimental Design* (Berkeley, CA: National Center for Research in Vocational Education, 2009).

6. Ibid.

7. Crain et al., *The Effectiveness of New York City's Career Magnet Schools*; and Richard D. Gampert and Randal Blank, *Educational Options High Schools Admission Policy Study* (report from the New York City Board of Education, Office of Research, Evaluation, and Assessment, 1988).

8. Josh Barbanel, "Is School Choice a Real Choice? New York Citywide Plan Faces Bureaucracy and Shortage," *New York Times*, July 11, 1993; and Peter Cookson and Sonali Shroff, *School Choice and Urban Reform*, Urban Diversity Series, no. 110 (Washington, DC: ERIC Clearinghouse on Urban Education, 1997).

9. Peter Cookson and Sonali Shroff, *School Choice and Urban Reform* (Washington, DC: ERIC Clearinghouse on Urban Education, Urban Diversity Series, No. 110, 1997); and Aaron M. Pallas and Carolyn J. Riehl, "The Demand for High School Programs in New York City" (paper presented at the Inaugural Conference of the Research Alliance for NYC Schools, New York, 2007).

10. Josh Barbanel, "Is School Choice a Real Choice? New York Citywide Plan Faces Bureaucracy and Shortage," *New York Times*, July 11, 1993; and Peter Cookson and Sonali Shroff, *School Choice and Urban Reform* (Washington, DC: ERIC Clearinghouse on Urban Education, Urban Diversity Series, No. 110, 1997).

11. Leanna Stiefel, Robert Berne, Patrice Iatarola, and Norm Fruchter, "High School Size: Effects on Budgets and Performance in New York City," *Educational Evaluation and Policy Analysis* 22 (2000): 27–29.

12. Janet C. Quint, Janell K. Smith, Rebecca Unterman, and Alma E. Moedano, *New York City's Changing High School Landscape: High Schools and their Characteristics 2002-2008* (New York: MDRC, 2010).

13. New York State Department of Education, Directory of Public and Non-Public Schools and Administrators, 2009–10, http://www.nysed.gov/admin/bedsdata.html.

14. Paul Peterson and William G. Howell, "Efficiency, Bias, and Classification Schemes: A Response to Alan B. Krueger and Pei Zhu," *American Behavioral Scientist* 47, no. 5 (2004): 699–717.

15. It should be noted that the dominant ethnic group in the study was Hispanics, and Hispanic voucher recipients showed no academic gains relative to Hispanic nonrecipients; also see Alan B. Krueger and Pei Zhu, "Another Look at the New York City School Voucher Experiment," *American Behavioral Scientist*, 47 (2004): 658–698.

16. This subsection relies heavily on personal interviews with the Office of Student Enrollment.

17. Jess Wislosi, "City Streamlines Pre-K Application," *New York Daily News*, March 24, 2008.

18. Jennifer Medina, "At Some New York Schools, Wait Lists Grow Longer," *The New York Times*, March 23, 2010, http://www.nytimes.com/2010/03/24/nyregion/24waiting.html.

19. Sharon Otterman, "City Seeking New Test for Gifted Admissions," *New York Times*, July 21, 2010, http://www.nytimes.com/2010/06/22/nyregion/22gifted.html.

20. David Herszenhorn, "Mixed Signals Over Fate of Gifted-and-Talented Programs," *New York Times*, December 10, 2003, http://www.nytimes.com/2003/12/10/nyregion/mixed-signals-over-fate-of-gifted-and-talented-programs.html.

21. Elissa Gootman and Robert Gebeloff, "Fewer Children Entering Gifted Programs," *New York Times*, October 29, 2008, http://www.nytimes.com/2008/10/30/nyregion/30gifted.html.

22. Otterman, "City Seeking New Test for Gifted Admissions."

23. Ibid.

24. Regulation of the Chancellor, Number A-101, June 29, 2009, http://docs.nycenet.edu/docushare/dsweb/Get/Document-11/A-101%20Final.pdf.

25. Authors' communication with Sandy Ferguson, Executive Director for Middle School Enrollment, June 4, 2010.

26. Quint, *New York City's Changing High School Landscape.*

27. Our description of the high school choice process relies on Atila Abdulkadiroglu, Parag A. Pathak, and Alvin E. Roth, "The New York City High School Match," *The American Economic Review* 95 (2005): 364; Clara Hemphill and Kim Nauer, "The New Marketplace: How Small-School Reforms and School Choice Have Reshaped New York City's High Schools" (New York: The Center for New York City Affairs at The New School, 2009); and Aaron M. Pallas and Carolyn J. Riehl, "The Demand for High School Programs in New York City" (paper presented at the Inaugural Conference of the Research Alliance for NYC Schools, New York, 2007).

28. Schools founded after the publication of the *Directory* are profiled in a second publication, the *Directory of the New High Schools*, released in February.

29. Examples include SchoolSourceNYC, Insideschools.org, and the searchable online DOE directory, http://www.nyc.gov/schools/ChoicesEnrollment/High/Directory/Search/.

30. In 2008–2009, roughly 72 percent of schools had one core program.

31. Appeals are possible for students who can substantiate a significant hardship related to their match, typically for safety, medical, or travel reasons. In 2008, about 3,700 students (of about 90,000) appealed their match (Hemphill and Nauer, *The New Marketplace*).

32. Steven M. Glazerman, "School Quality and Social Stratification: The Determinants and Consequences of Parental School Choice" (paper presented at the annual meeting of the American Educational Research Association, San Diego, CA, 1998), http://eric.ed.gov/ERICWebPortal/detail?accno=ED425520; and Justine S. Hastings, Thomas J. Kane, and Douglas O. Staiger, "Heterogeneous Preferences and the Efficacy of Public School Choice" (unpublished paper, Yale University, 2009), http://aida.econ.yale.edu/~jh529/papers/HKS_Combined_200806.pdf

33. In the interest of space, these regression results are not presented, but are available from the authors upon request.

34. Sarah Butler Jessen, "A Year in the Labyrinth: A Case Study of Parents and Schools Navigating Mandatory Public High School Choice in New York City" (unpublished doctoral dissertation, Steinhardt School of Culture, Education, and Human Development, NYU, 2010); and Carolyn Sattin-Bajaj, "The Burden of Choice: Latin American Immigrant and African-American Families' Experiences with School Choice in Comparative Perspective (unpublished doctoral dissertation, Steinhardt School of Culture, Education, and Human Development, NYU, 2010).

35. Ibid.

36. In the interest of space, these regression results are not presented, but are available from the authors upon request.

37. Performance on the SHSAT is the sole criteria for admission to eight of the nine specialized high schools. Fiorello H. LaGuardia High School of Music & Art and Performing Arts requires an audition and/or portfolio, as well as a review of academic and attendance records.

38. CREDO, *Multiple Choice: Charter School Performance in 16 States* (Palo Alto. CA: Center for Research on Educational Outcomes, 2009); and Ron Zimmer, Brian Gill, Kevin Booker, Stephane Lavertu, Tim Sass, and John Witte, *Charter Schools in Eight States* (Santa Monica, CA: Rand Corporation, 2009).

39. CREDO, *Multiple Choice.*

40. CREDO, *Charter School Performance in New York City* (Palo Alto. CA: Center for Research on Education Outcomes, 2010).

41. Caroline M. Hoxby and Sonali Murarka, "Charter Schools in New York City: Who Enrolls and How They Affect Their Students' Achievement" (working paper no. 14852, National Bureau of Economic Research, 2009).

42. Sean F. Reardon, *Review of "How New York City's Charter Schools Affect Achievement"* (Boulder, CO, and Tempe, AZ: Education and the Public Interest Center & Education Policy Research Unit, 2009), http://epicpolicy.org/thinktank/review-How-New-York-City-Charter.

43. Will Dobbie and Roland G. Fryer, Jr., "Are High Quality Schools Enough to Close the Achievement Gap? Evidence from a Social Experiment in Harlem" (working paper no. 15473, National Bureau of Economic Research, 2009).

Chapter 10

Research described in this paper was conducted at the Achievement Gap Initiative (AGI) at Harvard University, based at the Graduate School of Education and the Malcolm Wiener Center for Social Policy at the John F. Kennedy School of Government. Robert Hanna and Charlotte Krontiris at the AGI provided excellent research assistance both substantive and editorial. Additional thanks go to Louis Gomez and Jennifer O'Day for their editing of the chapter and to colleague Tyrone Mowatt for very helpful comments on earlier drafts. Robert Ramsdell of Cambridge Education in Westwood, Massachusetts, has managed the Tripod Project for the past several years, including the survey work in New York City. Without his efforts, there would be no New York City Tripod data to analyze. His collaboration is greatly appreciated. Finally, the author would like to thank all of the students, teachers and administrators at the school and system level in New York City who made it possible to conduct both the DOE and Tripod Project surveys on which this paper is based.

1. On the difficulty of improving high schools, see for example, Larry Cuban, *How Teachers Taught: Constancy and Change in American Classrooms, 1890–1980* (New York: Longman, 1984); Paula M. Evans, "A Principal's Dilemmas: Theory and Reality of School Redesign," *Phi Delta Kappan* 84 no. 6 (1984): 424–437; Charles M. Payne, *So Much Reform, So Little Change: The Persistence of Failure in Urban Schools* (Cambridge, MA: Harvard Education Press, 2008); and Ronald F. Ferguson, Robert Hanna, Sandra Hackman, and Ann Ballantine, *How High Schools Become Exemplary* fifth annual Research-to-Practice Conference Report of the Achievement Gap Initiative at Harvard University, Cambridge, MA, 2010), available at www.agi.harvard.edu. For insightful readings on resistance and other impediments to change see, for example, Richard Elmore, *School Reform from the Inside Out: Policy, Practice and Performance* (Cambridge, MA: Harvard Education Press, 2007); Ronald A. Heifetz and Martin Linsky, *Leadership on the Line: Staying Alive through the Dangers of Leading* (Boston: Harvard Business School Press, 2002); and Robert Kegan and Lisa L. Lahey, *Immunity to Change: How to Overcome It and Unlock Potential in Yourself and Your Organization* (Boston: Harvard Business Press, 2009). Also see other chapters of this volume.

2. The data are available on the system's public-use website. We use the 2008 instead of the 2009 or 2010 surveys in order to match the timing of the Tripod Project surveys that the chapter also discusses.

3. Data for seven exam schools were also available, but these schools are excluded because their students are clearly unrepresentative—they are selected into their schools based on high achievement, and nearly all of them graduate with Regents diplomas.

4. Each of the five indices formed under these headings has a Cronbach's alpha rating over .90, measured using the school-level averages. The groupings were formed specifically for this analysis, based on the face-value similarity of particular items and a confirmatory factor analysis.

5. This statement pertains to regression coefficients on the indicator variable for the 2,000–4,500 student size class, in multiple regressions that included controls for the student and teacher characteristics listed in the text. For the school-size indicator variables, the smallest school size category was the omitted base category relative to which the others were estimated.

6. Our statistical analysis indicates that the 8.7 percentage point difference on line 8 of table 10-3 is not statistically distinguishable from zero.

7. Howard S. Bloom, Saskia L. Thompson, and Rebecca Unterman, *Transforming the High School Experience: How New York City's New Small Schools Are Boosting Student Achievement and Graduation Rates* (New York: MDRC, 2010), http://www.mdrc.org/publications/560/overview.html. The authors write: "Serving approximately 100 students per grade in grades 9 through 12 and open to students at all levels of academic achievement, the SSCs in this study were created to serve the district's most disadvantaged and historically underserved students." The MDRC researchers took advantage of the lottery system that DOE uses to assign students to schools when their top-choice schools are oversubscribed. Some students were randomly assigned to SSCs while others were randomly assigned to other schools. For students in this situation, only chance determined whether they ended up in an SSC. That randomness in school assignment is what makes the MDRC study a good test of causal impacts.

8. Prior to graduation, students assigned to SSCs earned more credits in each of the first three years of high school, keeping them on track for graduation in the fourth year.

9. Of course, unlike the MDRC study, the present analysis is based on non-experimental data. In other words, there was no lottery to average away unmeasured differences between students attending smaller and larger schools. Thus it is conceivable that the school-to-school differences in student perceptions reported above reflect not teaching-quality differences, but differences in the dispositions of the types of students who selected themselves into the different types of schools. While conceivable, we do not think this is likely. Instead, we argue below that there really are large differences in what students experience in school and that the differences affect student engagement and learning.

10. The difference was that 39.5 percent of the SSC group received Regents diplomas after four years, while 34.6 percent of the comparison group did. The difference of 4.9 percentage points had a p value of 0.074, thus failing to reach the 0.05 level of significance.

11. The Tripod Project was founded by this author in 2001 in cooperation with educators in Shaker Heights, Ohio. It expanded initially through the Minority Student Achievement Network (MSAN). It is currently operated by Cambridge Education, which is based in the United Kingdom and has U.S. offices in Westwood, Massachusetts. Cambridge Education delivers a variety of school improvement services in forty-five countries.

12. Recall that the analysis above classified schools into five size classes. It turns out that all but one of the nine Tripod schools fall into two size classes:between 500 and 1,000 students and 2,000 and 4,500 students. One school has a reported enrollment of only 425 students, and we group it here with the 500–1,000 student category.

13. One Tripod-surveyed school was missing from the DOE data and therefore is not represented on table 10-4.

14. To understand what percentiles mean with regard to schools, imagine one hundred schools, each with a different rating on a particular teaching-quality measure, such as Stimulation and Relevance. Imagine rank ordering all one hundred of these schools from the lowest to the highest rating on Stimulation and Relevance. The tenth school from the bottom of the rank ordering would be at the tenth percentile position. In other words, 10 percent of the schools would rate no better than that school does on the Stimulation and Relevance index. At the other end of the ranking, there would be a school for which only 10 percent of the others were equal or better than it. This classroom would be at the ninetieth-percentile position. Even if the number of classrooms is different from one hundred, the classroom at the tenth-percentile position is, by definition, the one for which 10 percent of the classrooms rate no better than it does. The classroom at the ninetieth-percentile position is the one at which only 10 percent of the others are equal or better. The classroom at the fiftieth-percentile position is in the middle; half are better and half are worse.

15. One may notice that the values at the fiftieth percentile on table 10-6 are consistently lower than values at the fiftieth percentile on table 10-5, signaling that students agree less with the Tripod statements than with the DOE statements. However, we think this is an artifact of differences between Tripod and DOE in the

way that the response options were framed. On the Tripod survey, respondents are counted as agreeing with a statement when they respond either "totally true" or "mostly true," instead of only "somewhat," "hardly at all" or "totally untrue." The DOE survey uses only four choices, forcing respondents to either agree or disagree. Some respondents who selected either agreement or disagreement on the DOE scale would probably have selected a middle option had there been one. This would probably have reduced the percentage that agreed with any given item, making the fiftieth percentile values in table 10-5 (but not the spreads between the tenth and ninetieth values) more similar to those in table 10-6.

16. This is a different school from the one represented in figure 10-4.

17. Consider the distribution of the Give-Up Index across all teacher respondents in the Tripod sample. One third of the teachers at this particular school were in the top quartile of the Give-Up distribution.

18. All of the correlations have magnitudes in the neighborhood of minus 0.30, which is a noteworthy correlation in social science research.

19. Actually, the "disagree" category here combines "slightly disagree" and "strongly disagree" response options from the survey.

20. There are 166 teachers in the data for Column B.

21. The correlation between the five-level responses to the "I have several ways of explaining" item and the "learning and using new strategies" item is 0.28 with a significance level of 0.0002.

22. Specifically, they represent relatively small percentages of their schools' staffs. And just as they were more cooperative than their peers in choosing to complete the Tripod survey, they may be more cooperative than their peers in choosing to visit one another's classrooms and discuss student work.

23. Ronald F. Ferguson, Robert Hanna, Sandra Hackman, and Ann Ballantine, *How High Schools Become Exemplary,* fifth annual Research-to-Practice Conference Report of the Achievement Gap Initiative at Harvard University (2010), available at www.agi.harvard.edu.

Chapter 11

The author is especially grateful to Jessica Lent who assisted with the analysis and prepared all of the tables and figures and reviewed multiple drafts of the paper. Janet Brand played a central role in constructing the dataset for this paper. Jennifer O'Day, Jennifer Bell-Ellwanger, and Hans Bos provided helpful comments on earlier drafts.

1. New York City Department of Education, *NYC 2010 Mathematics and English Language Arts Citywide Test Results Grades 3–8,* 2010, http://schools.nyc.gov/accountability/Reports/Data/TestResults/2010_MATH_ELA_NYC_FULL%20DECK.pdf.

2. New York City Department of Education, *NYC Graduation Rates Class of 2009 (2005 Cohort),* March 2010, http://schools.nyc.gov/Accountability/Reports/Data/Graduation/GRAD_RATES_2009_HIGH-LIGHTS.pdf; New York City Department of Education, *School Accountability Tools – Progress Report,* 2010, http://schools.nyc.gov/Accountability/tools/report/default.htm.

3. Statewide data on test scores for subgroups of students defined by English language learner (ELL) status, race and ethnicity, and immigrant status prior to 2002 are not publicly available and thus, cannot be analyzed with the methodology used in this paper. A supplement to this paper will provide information on test score trends for these subgroups using an alternative, less rigorous methodology.

4. This statistical methodology has been used widely in education research and evaluation. See Howard S. Bloom, *Estimating Program Impacts on Student Achievement Using "Short" Interrupted Time Series,* MDRC Working Papers on Research Methodology (New York: MDRC, 1999), http://www.mdrc.org/publications/82/full.pdf; and William R. Shadish, Thomas D. Cook, and Donald T. Campbell, *Experimental and Quasi-experimental Designs for Generalized Causal Inference* (Boston: Houghton-Mifflin, 2002).

As in this paper, comparative interrupted time series analyses have been applied primarily to study:

(a) *Broad systemic policies and interventions such as the federal No Child Left Behind Act of 2002:* See Thomas Dee and Brian Jacob, *The Impact of No Child Left Behind on Student Achievement,* NBER Working Paper 15531 (Cambridge, MA: National Bureau of Economic Research, 2009), http://www.nber.org/papers/w15531.pdf; and Manyee Wong, Thomas D. Cook, and Peter M. Steiner, *No Child Left Behind: An Interim Evaluation of Its Effects on Learning Using Two Interrupted Time Series, Each with Its Own Non-equivalent Comparison Series* (IPR Working Paper WP-09-11, Institute for Policy Research, Northwestern University, 2010), http://www.northwestern.edu/ipr/publications/papers/2009/wp0911-pdf).

(b) *Accountability systems:* See Brian A. Jacob, "Accountability, Incentives and Behavior: The Impact of High-Stakes Testing in the Chicago Public Schools," *Journal of Public Economics* 89 no. 5–6 (2005): 761–796, doi:10.1016/j.jpubeco.2004.08.004.

(c) *Comprehensive school reforms such as Accelerated Schools:* See Howard S. Bloom, *Measuring the Impacts of Whole-School Reforms: Methodological Lessons from an Evaluation of Accelerated Schools* (New York: MDRC, 2001), http://www.mdrc.org/publications/76/full.pdf.

(d) *Talent Development High Schools:* See James J. Kemple, Corinne M. Herlihy, and Thomas J. Smith, *Making Progress toward Graduation: Evidence from the Talent Development High School Model,* 2005, http://www.mdrc.org/publications/408/full.pdf.

5. For the purposes of the analysis presented in this chapter, effects of Children First reforms are assessed beginning with the 2002–2003 school year.

6. National Center for Education Statistics, *Common Core of Data (CCD),* 2010, http://nces.ed.gov/ccd/.

7. Statewide test scores from grades 3, 5, 6, and 7 were not available prior to 2002. As a result, they could not be included in this analysis. Also, scale scores are not available for 2005. New York State Education Department, *The New York State School Report Card* (1998–2009), 2010, http://www.emsc.nysed.gov/irts/reportcard.

8. Note that the New York State Board of Regents made dramatic changes in the state testing standards in the 2009–2010 school year. Most notably, it raised the score that students need to reach in order to be classified as meeting the state's proficiency standards (level 3 or level 4). This change is discussed later in the paper.

9. Research Alliance for New York City Schools, *Analysis of Trends in Scaled Scores* (working title), (forthcoming, to be posted on http://steinhardt.nyu.edu/research_alliance).

10. The sample of schools used for these analyses represents 81 percent of all schools that conducted testing of fourth- or eighth-grade students at any time during the period from 1999 through 2010.

11. In controlling for these factors, it is important that the comparison districts and schools be as similar as possible to New York City in their test score trends prior to 2003. The primary findings in this paper are based on analyses that focus on test score trends for New York State's Big Four school districts. As shown in table 11-1, these four districts exhibited quite similar test scores prior to 2003. As urban school districts with high percentages of students with similar characteristics, these districts also experienced many of the same challenges and opportunities presented by national and state education policy initiatives and secular trends.

12. See Schwartz and Stiefel (chapter 3 in this volume).

13. For a general review of research in this area, see Larry V. Hedges, Richard D. Laine, and Rob Greenwald, "Does Money Matter? A Meta-Analysis of Studies of the Effects of Differential School Inputs on Student Outcomes," *Educational Researcher* 23, no. 3 (1994): 5–14.

14. Research Alliance for New York City Schools, *Research Agenda,* 2010, http://steinhardt.nyu.edu/research_alliance/agenda.

15. Analyses were conducted to test the sensitivity of the 2009–2010 findings to a continuous specification. Although the pattern of findings is very similar to that preented here, the steep increases in test scores through 2008–2009 inflates the performance levels that were estimated for 2009–2010. Treating 2009–2010 as a discrete and independent break in the test score trend provides a more accurate indication of changes in Children First effects after the change in state proficiency standards.

16. New York City Department of Education, *NYC 2010 mathematics and English language arts citywide test results grades 3–8.*

17. The figure and discussion focus on proficiency rates in an effort to be consistent with the analysis of proficiency rates from New York State assessments. The pattern of results comparing NYC and New York State NAEP scale scores are similar to those using proficiency rates.

18. The comparisons presented here also do not include controls for demographic differences between NYC and the rest of New York State. These data are not available for NAEP schools.

19. Calculations provided to the author by the U.S. Department of Education, Institute of Education Sciences, National Center for Education Statistics, National Assessment of Educational Progress, through the New York City Department of Education.

20. Test score data for 2010 were not yet available for these subgroups of students at the time this paper was being written. Also, NYSED does not provide test score results for subgroups of students defined by race/ethnicity, socioeconomic status, or English language learning status prior to 2002. Thus, it was not possible to assess Children First effects on test scores for these subgroups using the comparative interrupted time series method.

21. The sample size of schools with lowest poverty rates (N = 7) was too small to generate a reliable estimated counterfactual.

22. Note that students who transferred to private schools or to public schools outside of NYC are classified as discharged from the system and are not included in calculations of graduation rates for the purposes of these analyses. Supplemental analyses using graduation rates that do include students who were discharged pro-

duce results that are very similar to those presented here. Students who transfer to alternative high schools or credit recovery programs and students who drop out of high school altogether are included in calculations of graduation rates for the analysis presented in this paper.

23. It should be noted that both test scores and graduation rates are likely to be associated with other student characteristics such as race and ethnicity, English language learning status, special education status, and family income. Thus, one should not conclude that simply increasing test scores would result in a direct and proportional increase in the likelihood of graduating from high school. Further analysis can provide better evidence about the causal relationship between test scores and graduation rates and, more importantly, about strategies that minimize the negative influences that some of these other characteristics may have on educational attainment.

24. Anthony S. Bryk, Penny B. Seabring, Elaine Allensworth, and Stuart Luppescu, *Organizing Schools for Improvement: Lessons from Chicago* (Chicago: University of Chicago, 2010).

25. Howard S. Bloom, Saskia L. Thompson, and Rebecca Unterman, *Transforming the High School Experience: How New York City's New Small Schools are Boosting Student Achievement an Graduation Rates* (New York: MDRC, 2010).

26. Sean P. Corcoran, *Can Teachers be Evaluated by Their Students' Test Scores? Should They Be?* (Providence, RI: Annenberg Institute for School Reform, 2010); Jennifer S. McCombs, Sheila N. Kirby, and Louis T. Mariano, eds., *Ending Social Promotion Without Leaving Children Behind: The Case of New York City* (Santa Monica, CA: Rand Corporation, 2009).

27. Elaine Allensworth and John Q. Easton, *The On-Track Indicator as a Predictor of High School Graduation* (Chicago: University of Chicago, 2005).

Acknowledgments

Many people contributed to the efforts that produced this book over the past two years. First, we wish to thank all of the New York City stakeholders from schools, support organizations, community and advocacy groups, institutions of higher education, the United Federation of Teachers, and the New York City Department of Education (DOE) who participated in interviews with the authors and provided documentation about Children First, its implementation and impact. Without their insights and contributions, the analyses presented in this volume would not have been possible. Thanks also to those who contributed reflections for our concluding chapter, allowing us to incorporate and present diverse perspectives on key themes emerging from these analyses. We also wish to acknowledge the DOE administrators and staff, particularly Jennifer Bell-Ellwanger, Executive Director, Research and Policy Support, for providing data, arranging interviews, and reviewing the papers for accuracy. Many researchers and practitioners provided feedback on earlier drafts. In particular, we want to acknowledge those who participated in a two-day review session in June 2010: Andres Alonso, Hans Bos, Michele Cahill, Margaret Goertz, Robert Hughes, Susan Moore Johnson, Robert Schwartz, Clarence Stone, and Claire Sylvan. Their insights and suggestions helped to shape and improve the analyses presented here. Thanks also to the Bill & Melinda Gates Foundation, the Carnegie Corporation of New York, the Michael & Susan Dell Foundation, and Robertson Foundation for initiating this effort and for their support and feedback throughout the project. We are grateful to the members of the NYC Education Reform Retrospective Review Panel for their expertise and help in designing the project and choosing topics and authors, and for their feedback on the authors' contributions. We also wish to thank Harvard Education Press (HEP) for publishing this collection and acknowledge the guidance and insights of Caroline Chauncey from HEP as we prepared the volume for publication. Finally, we extend our appreciation to the staff of the NYC Education Reform Retrospective at the American Institutes for Research, including Victoria Rankin-Marks, Suzanne Claussen, Michelle Nayfack, and Philip Esra, for their valuable contributions to this volume and the project as a whole. While all of these individuals contributed insights and ideas to inform the research presented in this book, the authors of the individual chapters bear sole responsibility for the analyses and interpretations.

Jennifer A. O'Day
Catherine S. Bitter
Louis M. Gomez

New York City Education Reform
Retrospective Review Panel Members

Jennifer O'Day, American Institutes for Research (Chair)
Stacey Childress, Harvard Business School*
Libia Gil, American Institutes for Research
Louis Gomez, University of Pittsburgh
Beverly Hall, Atlanta Public Schools*
Susanna Loeb, Stanford University
Charles Payne, University of Chicago
Wendy Puriefoy, Public Education Network
Joan Talbert, Stanford University

Funders

Bill & Melinda Gates Foundation
Carnegie Corporation of New York
Michael & Susan Dell Foundation
Robertson Foundation

*These members recused themselves from the panel in midcourse when potential conflicts of interest emerged due to changes in their respective positions.

About the Editors

Catherine S. Bitter is a senior research analyst at the American Institutes for Research. Her work has focused on district-level reform and accountability policy. She has led a study of the literacy instructional practices associated with the reform efforts in San Diego City Schools, and has served as a senior researcher supporting the California Collaborative on District Reform.

Louis M. Gomez, Helen Faison Professor of Urban Education at the University of Pittsburgh, is also a senior partner at the Carnegie Foundation for the Advancement of Teaching. Professor Gomez works to improve the day-to-day work of teaching and learning and organizational activity. Most recently, he has turned his attention to problem-solving research and development, R&D organized around high-leverage problems embedded in the day-to-day work of teaching and learning and the institutions in which these activities occur.

Jennifer A. O'Day is a managing research scientist at the American Institutes for Research and director of the New York City Education Reform Retrospective project. Her main areas of research include accountability and capacity building strategies in standards-based reform, effects of district and state policy on classroom instructional practice, and equity. She currently chairs the California Collaborative on District Reform, which joins researchers, school district leaders, and state policy makers in ongoing evidenced-based dialogue and joint activity to improve instruction and student learning for all students in California's urban school systems.

About the Contributors

Stacey Childress was a senior lecturer at Harvard Business School (HBS) while working on the chapter for the NYC Education Reform Retrospective. During her time at HBS she studied, wrote, and taught about education entrepreneurship and urban district reform. She is currently deputy director of innovation for the College Ready program at the Bill & Melinda Gates Foundation.

Sean P. Corcoran is an assistant professor of educational economics at New York University's Steinhardt School of Culture, Education, and Human Development. His research focuses on the economics of school funding, the political economy of school choice, and the labor market for elementary and secondary school teachers.

Ronald F. Ferguson has taught since 1983 at Harvard University, where he is a senior lecturer in education and public policy with a joint appointment between the Graduate School of Education and the Kennedy School of Government. An economist by training, he is the creator of the Tripod Project for School Improvement and the faculty co-chair and director of the Achievement Gap Initiative (AGI) at Harvard University. His most recent report from the AGI, coauthored with others, is *How High Schools Become Exemplary* (2010). His most recent book is *Toward Excellence with Equity: An Emerging Vision for Closing the Achievement Gap* (Harvard Education Press, 2007).

Margaret E. Goertz is a professor of education policy and a senior researcher at the Consortium for Policy Research in Education in the Graduate School of Education at the University of Pennsylvania. Dr. Goertz has thirty-five years of experience conducting and leading national and state-level studies on state education finance and accountability policies, state and federal programs for special needs students, the implementation of Title I and NCLB, and school reform and teacher policies. She recently completed a study of human capital management strategies in the New York City school system and in three states.

Eva Gold is a founder and senior research fellow at Research for Action, a Philadelphia-based nonprofit research and evaluation firm. She has served as primary investigator for numerous studies examining the dynamics between schools and communities, with a special interest in the role of community and youth organizing in school reform. She has also published on the topics of privatization of public education, civic capacity in a privatizing school district, and on the transition to high school and systemic barriers to improvement of ninth grade in Philadelphia.

Jeffrey R. Henig is a professor of political science and education at Teachers College, and professor of political science at Columbia University. His book *Spin Cycle: How Research is Used in Policy Debates: The Case of Charter Schools* (Russell Sage Foundation/Century Foundation) won the 2010 American Educational Research Association Outstanding Book award. He is coeditor and contributor to *Between Public and Private: Politics, Governance, and the New Portfolio Models for Urban School Reform* (Harvard Education Press, 2010).

Monica Higgins is a professor of education at Harvard's Graduate School of Education (HGSE), where her research and teaching focus on the areas of leadership development and organizational change. Prior to joining HGSE, she spent eleven years as a member of the faculty at Harvard Business School in the organizational behavior unit. Professor Higgins has also taught in leadership programs for The Broad Foundation and for New Leaders for New Schools.

Paul T. Hill is director of the Center on Reinventing Public Education and John and Marguerite Corbally Professor of Public Affairs at the University of Washington. A political scientist, he seeks answers to the question, "How can we develop forms of public oversight that promote, rather than interfere with, effective schools?"

Ann Ishimaru is a doctoral student at the Harvard Graduate School of Education. Her research focuses on the role and strategies of leadership in enabling schools and communities to collaborate on improving education, particularly for low-income students of color. Her dissertation, a mixed-methods study, examines the joint school reform efforts of district leaders and low-income immigrant parents in a Latino-based community organizing group.

James J. Kemple serves as the executive director of the Research Alliance for New York City Schools and research professor at the Steinhardt School of Culture, Education, and Human Development at New York University. He specializes in the design and management of rigorous evaluations of education reforms and policy initiatives.

Henry M. Levin is the William Heard Kilpatrick Professor of Economics and Education at Teachers College, Columbia University, and the David Jacks Professor of Higher Education and Economics, Emeritus, at Stanford University. He is a specialist in the economics of education. He is the coeditor of *Between Public and Private: Politics Governance and the New Portfolio Models for Urban School Reform* (Harvard Education Press, 2010).

Susanna Loeb is a professor of education at Stanford University, director of the Center for Education Policy Analysis, and a codirector of Policy Analysis for California Education. She is the president of the Association for Education Finance and Policy, an editor of *Education Evaluation and Policy Analysis*, a senior fellow at the Stanford Institute for Economic Research, and a faculty research fellow at the National Bureau of Economic Research. Her research focuses on recruitment, support, and retention of effective teachers and school leaders.

Marion Orr is the director of the A. Alfred Taubman Center for Public Policy and the Frederick Lippitt Professor of Public Policy and Political Science at Brown University. His books include *Public Engagement for Public Education*; *Black Social Capital: The Politics of School Reform in Baltimore*; *The Color of School Reform: Race, Politics, and the Challenge of Urban Education*; *Transforming the City: Community Organizing and the Challenge of Political Change*; and *Democracy and the City: Clarence Stone and the Politics of Inequality*.

Amy Ellen Schwartz is the director of the Institute for Education and Social Policy and professor of public policy, education, and economics at the Steinhardt and Wagner Schools at New York University. Professor Schwartz's research interests lie in education policy and finance, and urban policy more generally. She has served as a consultant to a variety of public and nonprofit organizations, including the Federal Reserve Bank of New York and the Campaign for Fiscal Equity. She is past president of the American Education Finance Association.

Megan Silander is a PhD candidate in education policy at Teachers College, Columbia University. Her dissertation research examines school closure and reconstitution in New York City.

Elaine Simon is the codirector of the Urban Studies Program and Adjunct Associate Professor of Education at the University of Pennsylvania. She is a senior research consultant with Research for Action (RFA). Her research focuses on equity in urban education reform and the intersection of schools and community. Among the projects she has worked on at RFA are studies of curriculum and school governance reform, community organizing and civic engagement in public education, and the role of intermediary organizations in school improvement.

Leslie Santee Siskin is a research professor at New York University's Steinhardt School of Culture, Education, and Human Development, affiliated with the department of Administration, Leadership and Technology and the Institute for Education and Social Policy. She is a specialist in the sociology of organizations whose work on high schools includes *Realms of Knowledge* (Falmer), *The Subjects in Question* (TC Press), and *The New Accountability: High Schools and High Stakes Testing* (Routledge).

Leanna Stiefel is professor of economics and education policy at the Wagner and Steinhardt Schools, associate director of the Institute for Education and Social Policy (IESP), and director of the Education and Social Policy Master's Program, all at New York University. Her current research includes studies of school financing, evaluations of the effectiveness and costs of small high schools and STEM high schools, the characteristics of at-risk college students, and the effects of student mobility on student and peer performance.

Sola Takahashi is a doctoral student at the Harvard Graduate School of Education. She is interested in the intersection of teachers' work and urban school reform. Her dissertation examines the impact of teachers' data-driven decision-making practices on their efficacy beliefs in schools that serve predominantly low-income and racial minority students.

Joan E. Talbert is senior research scholar and codirector of the Center for Research on the Context of Teaching in Stanford University's School of Education. Her research focuses on teacher professional communities, school reform, and district capacity-building initiatives. Recent publications include *Building School-Based Teacher Learning Communities: Professional Strategies to Improve Student Achievement* (with M. W. McLaughlin, Teachers College Press, 2006).

Jim Wyckoff is a professor in the Curry School of Education and director of the Center for Education Policy and Workforce Competitiveness at the University of Virginia. His research explores a variety of issues in teacher labor markets, and much of this work has been focused on an empirical understanding of the preparation, recruitment, and retention of teachers in New York City. This research has received support from a number of foundations, the National Science Foundation and the U.S. Department of Education.

Index